W9-ABB-943

MARKETING STRATEGY:

THE CHALLENGE OF THE EXTERNAL ENVIRONMENT

THE CHALLENGE OF THE EXTERNAL ENVIRONMENT

The Open University Course Team

David Mercer (OUBS), Course Team Chair and Social Block Chair

Valerie Page (OUBS), Course Manager, Production

Glenna White (OUBS), Course Manager, Production

Mo Vernon (OUBS), Course Manager, Rewrite

Pam Cook (OUBS), Course Secretary, Rewrite

Gloria Rippin (OUBS), Course Secretary

Cherry Martin (OUBS), Course Secretary, Production

Sue Treacy (OUBS) Course Secretary, Rewrite

Edith Thorne (OUBS), Economics Block Chair

Harold Carter (OUBS), Politics Block Chair

Rod Barratt (Faculty of Technology), Technology Block Co-Chair

Norman Fox (OUBS), Technology Block Co-Chair

Tony Stapleton (OUBS), Author, Rewrite

Gordon Burt (IET), Author

Richard Maidment (Faculty of Social Sciences), Author

Gordon Dyer (Cambridge Regional Office), Critical Reader

Ray Nelson (Manchester Regional Office), Critical Reader

Susan Mudambi (OUBS), Critical Reader

Margaret Greenwood (OUBS), Maintenance Course Team Chair

Tony Kaye (IET), CoSy

Robin Mason (IET), CoSy

External Contributors

Tony Cox (Aston University), External Examiner, Rewrite

Leyland Pitt (Henley Management College), External Examiner

Michael Beesley (London Business School), External Assessor

Linda Hesselman (Unilever), Author

Philip Holroyd (Bradford Business School), Author

Denis Loveridge (Pilkingtons), Author

Peter Nolan (University of Leeds), Author

Garel Rhys (Cardiff University), Author

John Struthers (Paisley College), Author

Alan Warde (Lancaster University), Author

Ian Pearson (BT), Critical Reader

Jim Attridge (ICI), Critical Reader

Mike Fiszer (Consultant), Critical Reader

Graham Galer (Shell), Critical Reader

David Skyrme (DEC), Critical Reader

Bob Tyrell (Henley Centre for Forecasting), Critical Reader

Production

Tina Cogdell, Print Buying Co-ordinator

Philip Jones, Editor

Roy Lawrance, Graphic Artist

Nancy Marten, Editor

Susan Tilley, Project Control

Doreen Tucker, Compositor

Betty Turner, Print Buying Controller

Nazlin Vohra, Graphic Designer

BBC

Roger Penfound, Producer

Hugh Phillips, Producer

Francis Sealey, Producer

Tricia Bray, Production Assistant

Christine Jackson, Production Assistant

This book is part of the Open University Business School MBA course B885 *The Challenge of the External Environment*. Details of this and other Open University courses can be obtained from the Course Reservations and Sales Centre, PO Box 724, The Open University, Milton Keynes MK7 6ZS.

SAGE Publications
London • Thousand Oaks • New Delhi

in association with

The Open University
BUSINESS SCHOOL

MARKETING STRATEGY:

THE CHALLENGE OF THE EXTERNAL ENVIRONMENT

David Mercer

The Open University, Walton Hall, Milton Keynes MK7 6AA

SAGE Publications Ltd
6 Bonhill Street
London EC2A 4PU

SAGE Publications Inc.
2455 Teller Road
Thousand Oaks
California 91320

SAGE Publications India Pvt Ltd
32, M-Block Market
Greater Kailash - I
New Delhi 110 048

British Library Cataloguing in Publication data

A catalogue record of this book is available from The British Library.

ISBN 0 7619 5875 4 (cased)

ISBN 0 7619 5876 2 (pbk)

Library of Congress catalog card number 97-062267

Edited, designed and typeset by The Open University

Printed in the United Kingdom by Scotprint Ltd, Musselburgh, Scotland

1.1

17304B/b885b1i1.1

CONTENTS

FOREWORD AND WELCOME

This book aims to help you understand and contribute to the long-term future of your organisation. It is also designed to equip you with some of the most important skills needed by members of any board: those skills used to 'manage' the external environment in general and ensure the long-term survival of the organisation in particular.

WHY SHOULD YOU WORRY ABOUT THE WIDER ENVIRONMENT?

Or, to put it another way, why should you devote any of your scarce time and resources to long-range planning? The answer will vary from organisation to organisation.

Some, indeed, may claim that they are forced to focus exclusively on short-term problems – because, without a successful resolution of these, there will be no longer term! However, research undertaken by John Stopford and others from the London Business School[1] tends to indicate that at least some of the organisations which manage to rejuvenate themselves after encountering serious difficulties do so precisely because they focus on longer-term issues.

Other organisations may appear to be operating in such a stable environment that they believe there is little to be gained from monitoring it. They can face the greatest problems of all when unexpected change is finally forced upon them. A whole group of such organisations – think of the British motor-cycle industry overwhelmed by Japanese competition – can be destroyed almost overnight if they fail to recognise in time that their environment is no longer stable.

The reality is that all organisations that survive over the longer term must be constantly aware of their external environment, and be organised in such a way that they can respond to changes in it. This book, therefore, addresses those defensive requirements. Long-range planning, however, goes beyond the basic needs of survival to contribute proactively to improving your organisation's long-term position. In the context of the impact of the external environment we refer to this as long-range marketing – a term we will return to throughout the book.

Objectives

Our main objective is to give you a range of management tools which you will be able to use in your day-to-day work. These tools have four main purposes:

---

[1] Paper presented to the conference on 'Corporate Strategy and Industrial Organisation' at the London Business School, 12 December 1988.

1   Understanding – we will be introducing a number of general theories, including theories from all of the Social Sciences, in order to provide a clearer framework within which the rest of the material may be placed and understood.

2   Analysis – the first practical stage in planning processes is usually an analysis of what needs to be done. Accordingly, the first part of the book offers techniques of scanning, to detect critical changes in the environment, and then of analysis of the changes detected and the impact these may have on the organisation, before using these – combined in scenarios – as the basis for developing robust strategies.

3   Management – we offer a set of (robust) approaches to strategy and some tools to help you to manage the changes needed, so that the long-term position of the organisation may be protected or even enhanced.

In order to use any tools effectively you first need to have some practice in handling them. The approach in this book, therefore, is far from being merely didactic, expecting you simply to absorb information. Instead in most chapters you will find Audits and Activities, guiding you in applying the techniques described to your own organisation. In many cases the exercises suggested will have their value enhanced if you can get colleagues to participate: they will benefit your colleagues as well as you! This text is used in (and was originally written for) the highly successful MBA programme of the Open University Business School (OUBS) and, as you will see, builds on the OUBS's own pioneering research into long-range planning techniques.

THE PERSPECTIVE

The view you should adopt throughout this book is that of the chief executive officer (CEO) or equivalent, or at least of a staff member who is advising him or her on organisation-wide issues in general and the external environment in particular.

This may not be your current job, but the aim of an MBA programme is to equip you to take on such a role. In any case, in many organisations long-range planning processes, including long-range marketing, are diffused through a number of levels of management (albeit often by default rather than by any true intent to delegate this function!). Even in the more sophisticated organisations, the 1970s approach – whereby long-range planning was typically the prerogative of a very specialised team of central planners – has since been displaced by a move to distribute it across all the senior managers. The lessons of the 1970s tended to show that central planning departments produced plans which, no matter how good they may have been, were ineffectively implemented.

The main commitment of this book, therefore, is to train managers throughout the organisation to contribute to the overall planning process, and the ability to employ a board-level perspective is essential to this. It should also ensure that implementation of the resulting plans is that much more effective.

ACKNOWLEDGEMENTS

Grateful acknowledgement is made to the following sources for permission to reproduce material in this book:

Cover

Cover image supplied by Telegraph Colour Library.

Articles

Article 1.1: Reprinted from *Long Range Planning*, 22(2), Makridakis, S., 'Management in the 21st Century', pp. 37–53, Copyright 1989, with kind permission from Elsevier Science Ltd, The Boulevard, Langford Lane, Kidlington, OX5 1GB, UK; *Articles 1.2 and 1.4:* Morgan, G. 1988, *Riding the Cutting Edge of Change*, Copyright © 1988 by Jossey-Bass Inc., Publishers; *Article 1.3:* Reprinted by permission of *Harvard Business Review*. 'Megamarketing', by Kotler, P., Issue March/April 1986, Copyright © 1986, by the President and Fellows of Harvard College; all rights reserved; *Article 3.1:* Mercer, D. 1997, 'Researching the future', from 'Determining aggregated expectations of future outcomes', *Technological Forecasting and Social Change*, 55, M I T Press, © 1997 Massachusetts Institute of Technology; *Article 4.1:* Makridakis, S. 1988, 'Metaforecasting – ways of improving forecasting accuracy and usefulness', Institut European d'Administration des Affaires, copyright © 1988 INSEAD, Fontainebleau, France. All rights reserved; *Article 5.1:* Janis, I. L. 1971, 'Groupthink', *Psychology Today*, November 1971, pp. 43–45 and 74–77, Sussex Publishers Inc.; *Article 6.1:* Godet, M. 1982, 'From forecasting to "la prospective" – a new way of looking at futures', *Journal of Forecasting*, 1, pp. 293–301, John Wiley and Sons Ltd. Reproduced by permission from John Wiley and Sons Ltd; *Article 6.2:* Reprinted by permission of *Harvard Business Review*. 'Scenarios: shooting the rapids', by Wack, P., Issue November/December 1985, Copyright © 1985, by the President and Fellows of Harvard College; all rights reserved; *Article 8.1:* Reprinted from *Long Range Planning*, 25 (4), Kahane, A., 'Scenarios for energy: Sustainable world vs. global mercantilism', Copyright 1992, with kind permission from Elsevier Science Ltd, The Boulevard, Langford Lane, Kidlington, OX5 1GB, UK; *Article 9.1:* Mercer, D. 1997, 'Robust strategies in a day', *Management Decision*, 35 (3), pp. 219–223, M. C. B. University Press Ltd; *Article 10.1:* Reprinted from *Long Range Planning*, 17 (3), Taylor, B., 'Strategic planning – which style do you need?', pp. 51–62, Copyright 1984, with kind permission from Elsevier Science Ltd, The Boulevard, Langford Lane, Kidlington, OX5 1GB, UK.

Table

Table 2.1: Reprinted from *Long Range Planning*, **16 (3)**, Diffenbach, J., 'Corporate environmental analysis in large US corporations', p. 111, Copyright 1983, with kind permission from Elsevier Science Ltd, The Boulevard, Langford Lane, Kidlington, OX5 1GB, UK.

Figures

Figure 2.1: Kotler, P. 1988, *Marketing Management*, p. 49, Prentice-Hall; *Figure 2.2:* Johnson, G. and Scholes, K. 1988, *Exploring Corporate Strategy*, Second edition, p. 54, Prentice-Hall; *Figure 2.3:* Wind, Y. 1982, *Product Policy: Concepts, Methods and Strategy*, p. 199, Addison Wesley Longman; *Figure 2.4:* Fahey, L. and Narayanan, V. K. 1986, *Macroenvironmental Analysis for Strategic Management*, p. 208, West Publishing; *Figures 5.1 and 5.3:* Makridakis, S. and Wheelwright, S. C. 1989, *Forecasting Methods for Management*, Fifth edition, p. 321, John Wiley and Sons Ltd. By permission of John Wiley and Sons Limited; *Figures 5.2 and 5.4:* Hull, J., Mapes, J. and Wheeler, B. 1976, *Model Building Techniques for Management*, p. 142, Saxon House; *Figure 5.5:* Lilien, G. L. and Kotler, P. 1983, *Marketing Decision Making*, p.13, Harper and Row.

PART 1

LONG-RANGE MARKETING: ANALYSIS AND FORECASTING

1 INTRODUCTORY OVERVIEW

AIMS AND OBJECTIVES

This part starts with an introductory chapter that describes the powerful forces that can be at work in an organisation's environment, and examines a number of alternative theoretical perspectives on these forces.

The overall aim of the book is to show how organisations can plan to survive and build on these external pressures, through successful long-range planning. We begin this process by looking at what is involved in both short-term and (in more detail) long-range forecasting. Once produced, such forecasts can form the basis for alternative scenarios of the future environment: we look at how to construct scenarios, and at how they can be used. After working through this part you should not only understand the elements of forecasting and scenario-building, but also be able to apply them in your own organisation.

By the end of this chapter you should be aware of:
- the importance of understanding the impact of external factors on your organisation
- the importance of looking to the longer term, in order to analyse the full effects of these factors
- the scale of the changes which may result from this impact.

Much of the practical work in this book will focus on your own organisation and the industry within which it operates. This will allow you to try out the various theories and techniques. A subsidiary benefit may be that, by the end of it, you will be able to help your organisation steer a better informed course into the future.

This work will revolve around a series of Audits: exercises which enable you to apply and test what you have learned in the context of your own organisation. The onus is on you to choose the medium on which you are going to store the data they generate. The simplest approach is to use an exercise book with a separate page (or more) given over to each Audit, but the choice is yours. The only requirement is that you collect and organise the various items of information needed (most of which will be in verbal, rather than numeric, form).

Audit 1.1 _____

Briefly chart your own organisation's history – or at least some of the critical changes which have taken place over recent years. You may be able to take as the starting point similar material you have gathered for previous courses.

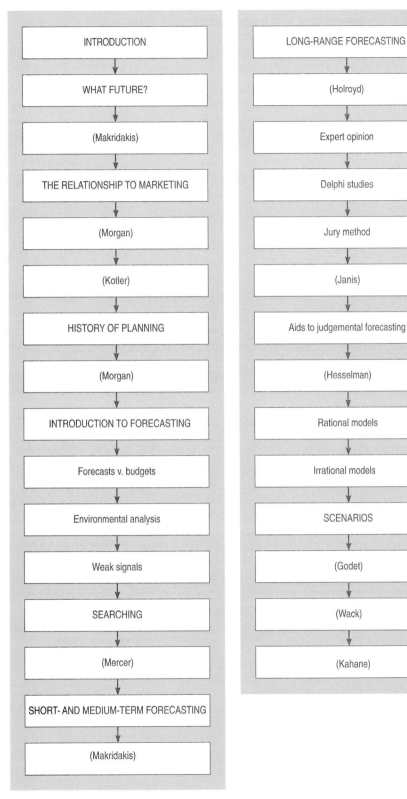

Map of Part 1

If possible, in order to give the longest possible perspective to these developments, this history should compare, say, the key years around 1970, 1980 and 1990 – as well as the current position. It may be valuable, though, if you choose the specific years in terms of the crises or major changes which affected your own organisation. The intention is not to provide a lesson in history, but to help you obtain a feel for the scale of the changes – and the rate at which they have occurred – within your organisation.

Some possible benchmarks may help you get these timescales into perspective:

1970 – the year the Conservative government of Edward Heath came to power, displacing that of Harold Wilson, to face – in 1973 – the oil crisis which led to the uncertainty of that and later decades.

1980 – the first full year of the Thatcher administration, which had replaced the Labour Callaghan government, when the UK economy was hit by the start of a major recession and rapidly escalating unemployment.

1990 – when Margaret Thatcher resigned as prime minister and the UK once more ran into significant economic problems. It was also the year when much of Eastern Europe emerged from the stranglehold that the (Soviet led) communist parties had maintained since World War II.

For each of these dates, provide a very brief, thumb-nail sketch of your organisation (no more than 150 words each, about half a side of A4 paper). This sketch should aim to encapsulate what were seen to be the most important aspects of the organisation at that time. It may (or equally may not!) include such items as:

- size
- growth rate
- customer/client set(s)
- style of management
- structure
- product/service range(s)
- [profitability]
- [markets]
- operational focus [marketing led, finance dominated, etc.]
- culture/philosophy.

Note: the items in square brackets may not be relevant to non-profit organisations.

The most important part of the exercise is using this information to isolate the major changes which occurred over each of these decades.

What were these major changes?

Was there any pattern to them?

How did your organisation react to them?

Did it anticipate them?

Although the changes you have identified are likely to be internal ones (since they are the ones which will have been most visible), were they caused by internal forces, or were they due to external factors? Which factors?

Were they imposed by changes in the external environment within which the organisation was operating?

Note: we recognise you are unlikely to have access to the detailed historical information necessary to definitively examine your organisation's history. You should spend just sufficient time on this Audit to obtain a broad picture of where your organisation has been. We want you to appreciate just how much change has happened: most managers are too involved in the problems of the present to find time to set that present in an historical context. But a long-term perspective is essential to successful strategic planning.

If your organisation is typical of the majority, you will probably find that most of the longer-term changes originated from factors largely outside its control – factors which many organisations tend to dismiss as irrelevant to their short-term operations!

1.1 WHAT FUTURE LIES AHEAD?

We will first look at how some experts describe the field. We will use their own papers to illustrate the diversity of views which exists. In terms of the number of pages, this section is quite long: but its intent is simply to provide you with a context for the rest of the book – indeed, perhaps, just the flavour of this topic. As such, all three papers should be read *quickly*, indeed skimmed, since you will not need to remember the details.

To first give an idea of what may be in store for managers over the next few years, as well as some of the thinking which lies behind the more theoretical versions of long-range planning, we will start with Makridakis's paper, 'Management in the twenty-first century'. As the intention is only to give you a feel for leading-edge work on theory, you can afford to read this material very *quickly*, just skimming it. You should, though, read it *critically*, as you should all that you will be presented with in this book.

Some questions you should consider in relation to this paper are:
- His assumptions – along with many others trying to predict the future, he attempts to draw out some of the drivers which are changing society (or at least business management) over the decades. What are his underlying assumptions, and are they inevitable? Indeed, is it certain that there are any such predictable progressions? Might there be underlying trends which are not yet obvious to us?
- His perspective – Makridakis is one of the world's leading experts on forecasting by *extrapolation* from previous *trends*. In terms of his perspective, though, does the fact that his previous academic work has been largely concerned with extrapolative forecasting colour the picture he paints? Would he have painted a different picture if he had started by

trying to see what the ideal future might be, and how this could be achieved? Has he, in any case, subconsciously projected the ideal future which he would like to see?

- The information revolution – his analysis of the Industrial Revolution is exhaustive but concise. It is much easier to see the trends after the event, and they become even clearer decades – and centuries – later! On the other hand, his comments on the information revolution are, understandably, much more sketchy.

  Is he, and are we, too close to this new revolution to be able to discern the most important trends? It is probably very reasonable to project that employment will move away from the manufacturing sector; indeed that process is now well under way and has been for several decades. The more difficult question, perhaps, is where will it move to. In the Industrial Revolution it was easy to see the move away from agriculture: the vast slums growing up around the new industrial cities made that only too clear. How many observers at the time, though, would have been able to predict accurately the shape of modern (Western) industry or the society and culture it has created?

- Products and production methods – Makridakis makes the assumption that 'several/many firms will be producing the same goods using the same technology' – thus implying a trend to uniformity of product. In fact, in all but a few markets the variety of products on offer has been increasing. One technological forecast even suggests, as a possible outcome, that in many fields customers will be able to demand that the product is individually customised (tailored to their unique requirements). Makridakis himself hints at this possibility later in his paper. The difference between the two extreme views, of uniformity versus variety, does pose major questions over the long-term future of production technologies.

  In particular, a move to variety seriously challenges his assumptions that 'economies of scale will become the single most important factor in gaining competitive advantage in manufacturing' and 'the trend towards larger firms will continue in the twenty-first century, resulting in super-giant manufacturing organisations'! Thus, in the sector most of all subject to economies of scale, Toyota (the world's most efficient car producer) builds assembly lines which produce just 200,000 cars per year. With a mix of four or more models being assembled on each line, this means that model runs can be less than 50,000 units per year – while still gaining the highest economies of scale. It must be noted, though, that engine plants may need over 650,000 units per year – and press-shops well in excess of one million units – to maximise their economies of scale. The choice between these alternatives, larger or smaller, has significant implications for the future organisation of industry.

- Service firms – conversely, Makridakis appears to assume tacitly that service firms can and will be relatively small. Is this a valid assumption? At least some of the most successful service organisations – for example, McDonalds in fast food, Citicorp in banking, Tesco in retailing, the BBC in entertainment – are among the largest of all. Indeed, the world's largest organisation, at least according to some reports – the Indian State Railways

– is clearly a service provider! Are they perhaps employing different economies of scale, those of marketing and finance, for example, or of organisational structure (with McDonalds using franchising on a very large scale)? What does this do to the picture of the future?

- The manager of the future – this section is perhaps the most speculative of all, but probably the one of most direct interest to you. The only question we would ask is, 'What do you yourself think?'

In asking these questions we do not want to question the quality of Makridakis's contribution, let alone his integrity. In fact we, believe that his is one of the most important, intellectually stimulating as well as consistently developed papers written in recent years, and that is precisely why we have included it. The message we would ask you to accept, and the principle we would like you to apply to the rest of the book, is that you can and should challenge even the most basic assumptions behind any views presented to you, even when they come from such an eminent source as Makridakis. Only when you have accepted this principle of challenge will you be able to thread your way through the complexities of planning for the future.

Now read Article 1.1, 'Management in the twenty-first century' by Spyros Makridakis,[1] taking into account the questions above.

Article 1.1 SPYROS MAKRIDAKIS: 'MANAGEMENT IN THE TWENTY-FIRST CENTURY'

Consider that you were a businessman 500 years ago. Your market was local. Most of what you sold was produced regionally and it was practically the same as that sold by your father and grandfather. Shipping took a long time and communications outside your own town were tardy. In your world change was extremely slow and you did not have to worry about forecasting the future environment or what you sold.

Today we live in a global village. Products can be shipped world-wide in a matter of days. Communications are instant. The life-cycle of products is short and competition is high since there are few barriers to entry. Our world witnesses an incredible amount of change by all historical standards, even those of 50 years ago. The fast pace of change has created what Toffler (1970) calls a 'future shock' for those unable to adapt to such change.

This chapter is intended for business executives. It describes major, forthcoming changes in the business environment, businesses themselves, as well as the managers who would be required to run them. Understanding and acting on such changes has become imperative today. First, the fast-changing world does not allow us to wait for a change to come, evaluate its impact, and then react. Instead, executives have to anticipate forthcoming changes, get prepared before they arrive and proact. Second, managers have a social responsibility (Drucker, 1987) as governments are less involved (e.g. through privatisations) with directing a nation towards desired goals. For these reasons a clear idea of the future and what it holds is becoming a necessity, so that the future environment can be moulded into desired directions and business firms become capable of adapting as smoothly as possible to the changes that are bound to arrive. Thus, questions such as those listed in the next paragraph become of critical importance.

What will business firms look like in the twenty-first century? What type of managers will be needed to operate them? Will the trend towards

---

[1] Extracted by permission of Pergamon Press Plc from *Long Range Planning*, vol. 22, no. 2, 1989: 37–53.

larger firms continue? How will the information (computer) revolution affect the organisational structure and mode of operation of the business firms of the next century? Where will the new opportunities be found? What are the dangers lying ahead? What type of strategies will be needed to survive and prosper in the twenty-first century? These are important questions. Can they be answered, however, with any degree of confidence?

Many people have become wary of any form of forecasting, in particular concerning long-term predictions. They view forecasting as nothing more than crystal-balling with little, or no, scientific or rational basis. Such a view has been reinforced by prominent errors in forecasting events that did not materialise (e.g. the forthcoming widespread use of nuclear energy) *as well as* failures in predicting events of far-reaching consequences (e.g. the appearance and impact of computers and the Information Revolution) that have already occurred. It is, therefore, important to persuade the reader that the approach used in this chapter (what I call metaforecasting) has nothing to do with crystal-balling. Instead it is based on rational principles that allow us to arrive at predictions about the future which are scientifically sound.

LONG-TERM PATTERNS IN HUMAN HISTORY

Table 1 lists the major innovations or breakthroughs since the dawn of civilisation. A study of such innovations/breakthroughs reveals that the following conclusions are of importance for long-term forecasting:

1   The manual work performed by human beings has been supplemented (e.g. through the use of tools to better perform certain tasks), substituted (e.g. using tractors in land cultivation), or amplified (e.g. employing levers or cranes to lift heavy weights) by a variety of means.
2   Mental work has been also supplemented, substituted, or amplified by a variety of means, although this occurred much later than is the case with corresponding manual tasks.

3   There are clusters of innovations/ breakthroughs that occur concurrently or within a relatively short time-span.
4   The rate of innovations/breakthroughs has increased considerably during the last 200 years. The reason for this increased rate is the invention of machines that use mechanical energy, to supplement, substitute or amplify manual work. This has given rise to what is now known as the Industrial Revolution.
5   The late 1940s marked the beginning of another revolution, the information or computer revolution. This has also supplemented, substituted or amplified work, but this time, mental, and not manual labour. The Information Revolution has, so far, produced similar results to those of the Industrial Revolution, and has further accelerated the rate of technological change.
6   There are considerable spin-offs of the Industrial and Information Revolutions to all areas of our personal and family lives, as well as to entertainment, transportation and medicine.
7   The importance of technology has increased over time. Consider for instance, the role of technology in the discovery of America by Christopher Columbus vs. its role in the Neil Armstrong moon landing. Furthermore, even in areas such as medicine, or in the harnessing of nature's resources or capabilities, innovations and/or breakthroughs depend to a greater extent on technology now than ever before.

THE BUSINESS FIRM OF THE TWENTY-FIRST CENTURY

Manufacturing firms appeared and prospered during the Industrial Revolution. Their *raison d'être* was to master human and capital resources and use them to apply the machine technology required to produce large quantities of goods. They could, therefore, enjoy large economies of scale, although once these reached a certain size, increased complexity and settled-in bureaucracy minimised the benefits to be gained from them, or even resulted in diseconomies.

Table 1 Major innovations/breakthroughs that changed established trends in human history and/or prevailing attitudes

Epoch	Approximate time (years from 1988)	Innovation/Breakthrough	Consequence/Reason
		I TECHNOLOGY	
A	1,750,000	Primitive tools	• Extending human capabilities
B	100,000	Making and using gear for hunting	
	40,000	Making and using weapons	
D	5500	The wheel	• Reducing and/or making manual work easier
	4,000	Bronze and other metals	
	3,500	Boats and sailboats	
	800	The clock, compass and other measurement instruments	
E	600	Gunpowder	• Facilitating and/or making mental work easier
	500	The printed book	
	350	Mechanical calculators	
F	210	Engines	• Improving comfort and/or speed of transportation
	180	Railroads	
	150	Electricity	
	130	Image and sound reproduction	
G	90	Telecommunications	• Increasing speed and/or availability of telecommunications
	85	Airplanes	
	70	Automobiles and roads	
	60	Mass-produced chemical products	
	45	Nuclear weapons	
	40	Computers	• Improving quality of arts and entertainment
	35	Mass-produced home appliances	
H	35	The transistor	
	30	Extensive use of fertilizers	
	30	Artificial satellites	• Improving material quality of life
	25	Lasers	
	20	Microtechnology (microchips, biochemistry and genetic engineering)	
	20	The moon landing	

Continued on next page ...

13

Epoch	Approximate time (years from 1988)	Innovation/Breakthrough	Consequence/Reason
		II EXPLOITING NATURE'S RESOURCES/CAPABILITIES	
A	400,000	Hunting	• Decreasing dependence on the environment
	300,000	Harnessing of fire	
	150,000	Shelter	
C	20,000	Permanent settlements	• Exploiting nature's capabilities
	20,000	Domestication of animals	
	15,000	Agriculture	
	10,000	Using animals for transportation and labour	
D	3500	Irrigation systems	• Using nature's resources
	3000	Harnessing wind power	
	2000	Using horses for transportation and labour	
E	800	Using the energy of falling water	
F	180	Using coal and oil for energy	• Adapting to changes in the environment
H	45	Nuclear energy	
		III SOCIAL AND INTELLECTUAL HUMAN ACHIEVEMENTS	
A	1,500,000	Social organization to care for children	• Better mastery of environment
	500,000	Language	
	400,000	Immigration	
C	20,000	Religion	• Need for socialization
	7000	First cities	
	5500	Alphabet	
D	5000	Abacus	• Need for knowledge
	3500	Money for transactions	
	3000	Number system	
	2500	Arts, philosophy, sciences	
	2500	Democracy	• Drive towards equality

Epoch	Approximate time (years from 1988)	Innovation/Breakthrough	Consequence/Reason
E	500	Scientific experimentation	• Desire for achievement
	500	The discovery of the new worlds	
	475	*The Prince* by Machiavelli is written	
	400	Large-scale commerce	
	300	Scientific astronomy	
	300	Mathematical reasoning	
F	210	Discovery of oxygen (beginning of chemistry)	• Appreciation of arts
	200	French and American revolutions	
	150	Babbage's failed computer	
G	150	Political ideologies (communism, capitalism)	
	120	Foundations of genetics	
	100	Financial, banking, and insurance institutions	
	80	The theory of relativity	• Desire to reduce future uncertainty
	50	The concept of the computer is demonstrated mathematically	
		IV MEDICINE	
D	2500	The doctor as a healer	• Curing disease
E	500	Therapy based on sound medical reasoning	
H	300	Drugs with real medical value	• Prolonging life expectancy
	90	X-ray	• Providing better diagnostics
	55	Antibiotics	
	30	Oral contraceptives	• Preventing unwanted pregnancies
	20	Tissues and organ transplants	
	10	The CT (CAT or body) scan	

A = The emergence of human domination; B = The first hand-made tools to extend human capabilities; C = The beginning of human civilization; D = The foundation of modern civilization; E = The foundations of modern science and society; F = The start of the Industrial Revolution; G = The Industrial Revolution; H = Spin-offs of the Industrial Revolution, the start of the Information Revolution.

As the Industrial Revolution progressed, technology became more complicated. Specialised forms, to build the machines and tools needed by the manufacturing companies, appeared, making technology available to anyone who could afford to pay for it. The competitive advantages of using better machines specially built for a single manufacturer disappeared. As a matter of fact, new entrants were often at an advantage because their machinery was more modern than that of their established competitors. Competitive advantages (in addition to economies of scale) in production were, therefore, restricted to using the most modern technology bought from the specialised engineering firms producing and selling such technology. Attention was then shifted to marketing the goods produced and to introducing new or better products.

Manufacturing technology proliferated in many areas, including transportation, weapons, agriculture, housing, domestic comforts and home entertainment. In addition, a host of service industries appeared (e.g. banking, insurance, travel, entertainment) to satisfy the needs of the growing (both in size and numbers) business firms and those of the affluent consumers whose income exceeded their requirements for necessities and durable goods. In addition to the manufacture of goods, chemical production was a growing area during the Industrial Revolution. A wide variety of chemicals were discovered and used to improve agricultural production (e.g. fertilisers), replace raw materials (e.g. synthetic rubber and fibres), to produce consumer or industrial goods, and come up with new medicines. The trend towards plentiful and inexpensive goods covering all consumer needs was established.

The strong parallels between the Industrial and Information Revolutions can be used to predict the type of firm that will exist in the twenty-first century. The manufacturing firm of the twenty-first century will be in a position similar to that of the agricultural firm of today. This means that the percentage of people employed in manufacturing will drop substantially (the percentage of people employed in agriculture amounted to about 70% of the population before the Industrial Revolution, while it is less than 2% in the United States today) to a percentage similar to that of agriculture today. Similarly, manufactured products will be in plentiful supply and competition among the firms producing them will be as fierce as it is among agricultural firms today. Competitive advantages among the various manufacturers will be few, as the same high-level technology will be available to all. Differences in the quality of products will be slight or non-existent, as several/many firms will be producing the same goods using the same technologies. Furthermore, since material needs are finite, they will eventually be satisfied. This would result in a slowdown of the growth in demand, bringing over-capacity similar to that existing today in agricultural production.

Economies of scale will become the single most important factor in gaining competitive advantages in manufacturing. This is particularly true for information products because, once developed, they can be reproduced and shipped at almost zero cost. Thus, the larger the production the smaller the unit cost and the faster the recovery of the developmental, sunk costs. Firms would, therefore, be motivated to produce as much as possible, to license or sell their production technology, to achieve the maximum number of distribution channels and, in general, to reach production and distribution levels which are as high as possible. Thus, the trend towards larger firms will continue in the twenty-first century, resulting in some super-giant manufacturing organisations.

Where are the limits to growth? Will increased complexity and reduced efficiency slow down the benefits gained from economies of scale? Similarly, will the reduced motivation of employees working for super-giant companies put the brakes on size? If the organisation of firms does not change considerably from that of today, there is no doubt that a plateau in growth will be reached. However, decentralised, semi-autonomous firms and/or new forms of organisations (e.g. manufacturing/distribution organisations similar to the fast-food chains of McDonald's or Burger King, manufacturing/dealer symbiosis where the dealer is a part-owner of the firm) are likely to emerge. Furthermore, better telecommunications, fewer people working in manufacturing firms, and improvements in computerised management systems are likely to extend the limits of growth in size before diseconomies of scale result.

At present, the largest organisation is the Catholic Church, whose structure and management has not fundamentally changed for almost twenty centuries. There is no compelling reason why, if needed, business firms using creative forms of organisation and new tools cannot and will not achieve or surpass the size of the Catholic Church. Unless, of course, their size is restricted by governments, or other international bodies.

The above discussion does not imply that the only type of manufacturing firms in the twenty-first century will be giant and super-giant ones. Obviously, peripheral firms supplying or serving the giants will also exist. In addition, specialised manufacturers geared towards specific markets will also operate alongside the super-giants. However, the dominant firms of the twenty-first century will inevitably be giant multinational corporations capable of fully exploiting economies of scale in research, manufacturing and marketing.

Together with economies of scale, competitive advantages will be gained by developing/introducing new products (mostly by combining hardware and software technologies) and/or creating new needs. Thus, identifying new markets, creating new wants, and introducing new fads and fashions will become imperative if one is to avoid product saturation and to achieve competitive advantages. In turn, these activities would require huge R & D budgets, and/or enormous advertising/marketing expenditures, further fuelling the need for super-giant firms capable of mastering the required resources and willing to take the risks necessary to develop and commercialise new products/ideas.

Biochemistry and genetic engineering will play roles that are similar or more crucial than those played by chemistry and genetics during the Industrial Revolution. Their growth and importance will increase as the biochemical and genetic engineering technologies are being linked to computers, lasers and computer-driven production. Improved or new products for both consumer and industrial uses will appear, and new, improved industrial processes will emerge. As with manufacturing firms, R & D costs for biochemistry and genetic engineering will be enormous, necessitating the creation of large firms capable of harnessing economies of scale. As the synergy among biochemical/genetic engineering

firms, information technology companies, and the traditional manufacturing corporations becomes more critical, joint firms covering all three areas will eventually emerge. The integrating factor of such firms will be research and development, marketing/distribution capabilities, as well as the capital and human resources required to conceive, develop, manufacture and distribute/market the new products/processes.

The Industrial Revolution has increased the personal disposable income of a large segment of the population. At the same time it has created a class of rich and super-rich whose expectations and needs differ from those of the 'average' consumer. Product positioning to reach the high-income segment has been a successful practice of firms that distinguish themselves and/or their products from those which are mass-produced. The Information Revolution will further increase spending income and create even more rich and super-rich. Marketing skills in segmentation and positioning one's product will, therefore, become critical ingredients in the battle to satisfy the needs of the affluent. The size of the firms in this category could range from the very small, geared to a particular segment, to the super-giants that apply a mixture of high-tech and individualised production to create and/or satisfy the needs of specific segments. Thus, a form of mass-produced, customised products aimed at specific segments (this is possible using computer-driven manufacturing systems) could become possible.

The service sector will grow substantially more than manufacturing, in particular once the Information Revolution has reached a plateau similar to that the Industrial Revolution has entered into today. The growth in services will increase employment and will compensate for decreases in manufacturing workers. Overall employment will, eventually, stagnate or decrease, necessitating fewer hours of daily work, fewer workdays per week, or considerably longer yearly vacations.

Changes in the service sector will be substantial and are also more difficult to predict. New forms of service and new types of service firms will probably emerge. Furthermore, service and marketing practices will most likely change in the twenty-first century. Service industries, as well as the types of service they offer, will be greatly affected by the Information Revolution, as service differentiation and customer loyalty is usually weak in this sector. Small changes in the conception of the service being offered or its perceived utility, or of the by-products of such services, can drastically affect sales and market shares. Service firms will, therefore, have to be constantly re-thinking their business, innovating and/or keeping up with their competitors. The marketing of services will, thus, become the crucial factor determining successful service firms. Furthermore, since barriers to entry would be weak, competition will be keen, necessitating that service firms be flexible and that they constantly monitor the environment for changes that might affect them.

The size of service firms need not be large. Family operations and small firms can operate alongside super-giant multinationals. Economies of scale, although important for advertising purposes, are not critical for providing specialised services which might even be thought to be of greater value if individualised and customised. For instance, high-quality restaurants, small high-priced hotels, first-rate universities, high-power research centres and similar services cannot be mass-produced or mass-marketed. Their value lies in their uniqueness and the limit to the number of customers they can serve. Thus, segmentation and positioning will leave room for small service firms (in particular as there will be a lot of wealthy people willing to spend their money on individualised services if these can identify and appropriately serve the right segment).

Although specific developments are difficult to predict, general trends point towards significant growth in entertainment, education and re-education, travelling, vacationing, medical care, marketing and research/consulting. These can be considered to be the emerging growth services of the twenty-first century that will compensate for decreases in manufacturing and stagnation in other service sectors.

THE MANAGER OF THE TWENTY-FIRST CENTURY

The architects of the Industrial Revolution were engineers. Using their ingenuity, they transformed manual skills (which took many years of apprenticeship and numerous years of practice to acquire) into a machine design that could replicate them and, in so doing, produce similar goods at a fraction of the cost, and at a higher speed. Moreover, their ability to produce such machines economically and repair them when they did not work properly, enabled entrepreneurs to use machines for production purposes.

Initially, a single engineer was capable of mastering the technology required and both creating and repairing the new machines, or variations of existing ones. As technology became more complex, however, specialised engineers (mechanical, civil, chemical, electrical, etc.) were needed. As engineering expertise cannot be instantly acquired, schools specialising in teaching engineering knowledge and skills became essential. As the Industrial Revolution progressed, so did the demand for engineers who were paid high salaries and were often promoted to managerial positions and the top jobs within the firm. This privileged role, high salaries, and the heavy demand for engineers, however, reached a plateau in the 1960s when the focus shifted to MBA education and business graduates. Today, there are still many well-paid engineers, although they are diminishing in number, but their pay is usually less than that earned by MBAs, and their tasks are fundamentally different from those performed by engineers before the peak of the Industrial Revolution.

In machine engineering, for instance, the major task of today's engineers is to develop (design, construct and test) new machines and production processes, or to improve the efficiency of existing ones. Their task is aided by standardised parts which can be purchased from specialised firms that design, construct and produce such parts. Engineers are not obliged, therefore, to start from scratch. Their designs are based on readily available 'building boxes'. Moreover, a few engineers today are involved in machine repair. First, machines do not break down as often as before, but should they, it suffices to identify the problem and change the defective part (an important principle in designing machines today is that they can be easily repaired by substituting the part(s) that frequently cause problems). In other cases, it might even be more economical to replace the inoperative machine by a new one. Engineers, however, are not needed in either case. The repair side of the engineering job has been simplified and standardised in such a way that it can now be delegated to maintenance personnel, who can do the job using appropriate tools and procedures that were also developed by engineers. The end result is a new type of engineer, whose task is to perform creative work, or to solve new, important problems. All other functions that were previously part of engineering jobs have been delegated. In my opinion, the job of managers has followed, and will continue to follow, stages similar to those of engineers.

First there was a single manager, usually the owner, who managed the entire firm. Then came specialised functional managers (finance, production, marketing managers) whose job, in addition to dealing with people, was mostly to perform repetitive tasks required for the day-to-day operation of the business. Today we are at the point in the Information Revolution when many repetitive managerial tasks could be standardised and performed by the computer, or be simplified and made part of an expert system. Computer programs and expert systems would, in turn, permit the delegation of all repetitive managerial tasks to clerical personnel who could perform them aided by the appropriate software program. This raises the question of who the new manager will be and what qualities will be required to manage the firm of the twenty-first century.

The large majority of manual tasks have or will be substituted, supplemented, or amplified by combinations of hardware and/or software technologies. Even a highly skilled task performed by a brain surgeon will be greatly supplemented and amplified by computers, electronic microscopes, TV scans, computer-guided lasers, and a host of other technologies (Makridakis, 1987). The neurosurgeon would be required to be a first-class technician. The judgement of such a neurosurgeon would be restricted to interpreting the information provided and intervening should problems arise. Moreover, experience would become less important, or even disadvantageous, as new doctors, right out of school, would be better masters of the new, fast-changing technology. In the final analysis the only tasks that cannot be substituted by computers and expert systems will be new, important problem-solving situations as well as functions/tasks that require creative thought processes.

Dealing with people will always remain a critical management task. However, its nature will also change. First, there will not be so many people to manage (in particular in manufacturing firms). Second, people will no longer perform routine boring tasks; this will increase motivation and decrease the amount of supervision required. Third, employees will perform well-defined tasks facilitating the evaluation of their performance. Fourth, a great deal of work will be creative (conceiving new products/services, research, strategy, advertising, etc.) requiring new types of imaginative manager capable of maximising the output of such creative people.

Thus, in addition to his or her own creativity, a critical management skill in the twenty-first century will be the capacity to supervise the creativity of others, since creative thinking would be one of the few remaining factors that could not be supplemented, or substituted by computers and which, if properly used, could bring competitive advantages.

Top managers, and their qualities, are more difficult to predict. In my opinion, they will be rare and paradoxical: creative and practical, visionary and pragmatic, flexible and persistent, easygoing and demanding, risk-taking and conservative, in addition to being excellent politicians, superb deal-makers, as well as visible and effective public statesmen. And, once found, they will be paid extremely well.

Can people with creative potential be identified? Can creativity be taught? A present, advertising agencies and R & D departments are some of the few places directly concerned with the management of creativity. But no firm conclusions regarding creativity can be reached. Although creativity can be encouraged, it is not easy to identify creative people beforehand. Moreover, although some organisations (e.g. Bell Laboratories, 3M) seem to have produced more creative output than others it does not seem that rules encouraging organisational creativity can be found and applied across the board. Finally, it does not seem that special education or background increases creativity. On the other hand, we are still in the early stages. Once the importance of creativity becomes clear, resources and talent will concentrate their efforts on finding new 'creative' solutions. In my opinion, this is the new challenge of management education if business schools are not to become obsolete.

CONCLUSIONS

In this chapter, I have predicted the type of business firms and managers most likely to exist in the twenty-first century. In making my predictions, I have attempted to avoid the mistakes made by forecasters of the past, when making long-term predictions. By analysing established patterns in human history (see Table 1), a trend showing that technology has been playing an increasingly important role became obvious. Furthermore, such a trend does not seem likely to change, but, instead, it will probably accelerate through the influence of the Information Revolution. The critical assumption of the predictions made in this chapter has been that there is an analogy between the Industrial and Information Revolutions. If the reader does not accept this assumption, he or she should not accept my predictions. Another important assumption is that, at present, we are at the same time-period on the time-scale as the Industrial Revolution was in the mid-1930s. This assumption is not as critical, since the reader can decide on another time-period. Such a modification will only affect the rate of change expected to result from the Information Revolution in the coming years. Finally, the reader might not agree with some of my reasoning. This is not critical either as different viewpoints and alternative conclusions about the future are inevitable. My objective has been based on an endeavour to provide a consistent rationale showing major trends rather than on the belief that I can predict specific events or the exact time of their appearance. The reader may accept only part of my reasoning and modify the forecasts provided accordingly.

It is necessary to understand and accept that *all* forecasts about the future are uncertain and must always be considered as such. On the other hand, uncertainty must not become an excuse to avoid making decisions and taking actions to prepare oneself to better face up to the future. Such decisions are necessary in order to reduce the impact of future surprises. To this end, major trends must be identified and predictions based on such trends made.

Forecasting presents a paradox. To be accurate, forecasts must be general in terms of the event(s) being predicted and vague in terms of the time the event(s) could occur. However, to be useful, forecasts must be specific and precise. This paradox can only be resolved on a case-to-case basis through individual (or company-wise) thinking. The job of a forecaster is to present a wide range of alternatives which can neither be specific nor precise, in order to avoid inaccuracies. Individuals and companies must consequently evaluate these forecasts and translate them to specific predictions and then decide how they might affect their future existence. In so doing, they must inevitably take certain risks. A list of general and vague (in terms of time) predictions are presented in Table 2. Individuals and companies need to evaluate them to determine which will affect them and how, and what actions and strategies are needed to succeed.

Another mistake forecasters often make is to underestimate the rate and degree of technological change. Table 3 develops further the watch/aeroplane analogy. Although the implications might sound like science fiction, they might not be too far from future reality. Business executives should, therefore, consider the consequences involved and the type of decisions and actions they will need to take at present, in the face of what Toffler (1970) calls the future shock.

Finally, the question is often asked, 'What will happen after the Information Revolution?' The answer is 'Not much'. People perform manual and/or mental tasks. Once such tasks have been replaced to the maximum by machines and/or computers, there will be nothing left. The next stage will come when computers can imitate and/or surpass the highest of the human intellectual abilities, that is problem-solving, learning and creativity. However, such computers are not likely to appear soon. When and if they do, it will be interesting to see if the prediction that, at that time, humans will be to computers what pets are today to humans, will actualise. In the meantime, humans will continue to hold a huge competitive advantage over computers by the fact that they are superb problem-solvers, they can learn, if given adequate feedback, and that they can be creative. These talents, which must be cultivated as far as possible, will become the critical skills of the twenty-first century.

Table 2 Possible future innovations/breakthroughs that would probably change established trends and/or prevailing attitudes

Estimate in years from now widespread applications

Low	Likely	High	Innovation/Breakthrough	Consequence/Reason
			I HARDWARE-BASED TECHNOLOGY	
5	10	20	Mass global telecommunications (message/data, sound, image)	• Continued substitution of unskilled and semi-skilled labour by machines
5	15	35	Super automation (in office and factory)	• Large shifts in employment patterns
5	20	40	Applications of superconductivity	
10	20	40	Mass use of lasers	• Fewer hours of work
15	25	35	Mass use of lightweight super-strength materials (ceramic, plastic, synthetic metals)	• Cheaper and more plentiful products
20	40	150	Super miniaturization	
30	50	150	Super efficient engines	• Faster transportation and speedier and less costly telecommunications
30	60	200	Hypersonic transport (air, train, other)	
			II SOFTWARE-BASED TECHNOLOGY	
5	15	35	Super automation (in office and factory)	• Heavy substitution of office and/or service personnel by 'computer'-based technology
5	15	50	Widely used expert systems	
20	50	100	General purpose robots	
25	50	150	Intelligent products (cars, home appliances, etc.)	
25	100	400	Real artificial intelligence	• Large shifts in employment patterns
50	200	600	Intelligent computers	• 'Automation' of homes and offices
75	400	800	Intelligent robots	
100	600	1000	Super smart specific-purpose robots	
500	5000	20,000	Computers and robots that can imitate or surpass human intelligence, and/or creativity	• Large changes in the way professional work is done

Continued on next page ...

Estimate in years from now widespread applications

Low	Likely	High	Innovation/Breakthrough	Consequence/Reason
			III BIOCHEMICAL AND RELATED TECHNOLOGIES	
5	15	30	Improved agricultural production	• New and improved products
10	20	50	Eradicating pollution	
10	25	60	Improved production from animals	
10	30	70	Mass-produced biochemical compounds	• Cheaper and more plentiful products
25	40	80	Widely used biochemical processes	
15	30	100	New bio and/or genetically engineered products	• Clean air and water
30	50	200	Altering gene structure	
50	300	800	New, powerful energy sources	• New and vast sources of energy
20	1000	5000	New forms of life	
			IV EXPANDING HUMAN PRESENCE	
15	40	80	Full-scale space stations	
20	50	150	Marine life	• Opening new frontiers to expand human presence
30	200	400	Colonizing the moon	
100	400	1000	Colonizing planets of our solar system	
10	500	Never	Communicating with extraterrestrials	
1000	5000	100,000	Colonizing planets beyond our solar system	
			V MEDICINE	
10	30	50	Preventative medicine	• Towards eradicating disease
15	40	60	General purpose drugs	
15	40	60	General purpose vaccines	
15	25	50	Expert systems for medical diagnosis	• Substantially prolonging life expectancy
30	50	100	Mass-produced artificial organs	
40	60	120	Preventive organ transplants	• Improving diagnostics
60	100	400	Cures and preventions before birth	
150	300	2000	Growing limbs naturally	• Replacing the doctor with expert systems

Estimate in years from now widespread applications

Low	Likely	High	Innovation/Breakthrough	Consequence/Reason
			VI HOME LIFE, LEISURE TIME, EDUCATION	
33	6	10	Super-powerful, affordable home computers	• Reducing and facilitating work at home
3	6	10	Electronic post, on-line messages, ordering of goods, reservations, transfer of money and similar transactions through home computers	• Improving quality and expanding entertainment coverage at home
4	8	15	Super-high fidelity sound and image systems	
5	10	20	The fully integrated home communication centre (sound, image, telephone and computers)	• Performing a host of tasks by home computer
5	10	20	Telecopying (buying or renting) and storing music, videos, films, books, newspapers, magazines in home computers	
5	10	25	Vacation supermarkets	• Super-automated homes
5	15	25	Super automation at home	
10	20	30	The home entertainment centre (receiving programmed and live events from around the world in large colour stereophonic TV-type sets)	
10	20	30	Home appliances programmed by computers	• New forms of education and research
15	25	35	Lifelike computer games and realistic simulations	
15	25	40	Specialized research universities	
15	30	50	Specially tailored computer education	
15	30	60	Flexible workplace in widespread use	
30	50	100	Robots as home servants	

Table 3   Making watches 200 years ago and aeroplanes 50 years from now

	Fabricating a watch 200 years ago	Implications	Making a mass-produced watch today
Method	The 250, or so, parts needed to make a watch were made separately using the crude hand-tools that existed at that time	Imagine a watchmaker (or any other person) 200 years ago. Could he, in his wildest dreams, have conceived that a watch could be produced in 10 minutes, or that digital watches showing time in hundredths of seconds, the day of the week, the year, including multiple alarms, calculators and a place for storing telephone numbers and appointments could exist? Could the watchmaker have imagined his skills becoming obsolete?	Digital watches are made automatically using specially designed microchips. Analogue watches are assembled semi-automatically using ready-made parts produced automatically elsewhere.
Time to complete task	About 1 month.	The month has become minutes. A time reduction of between 1200 and 12,000 times.	Less than 1 minute for digital. About 10 minutes for analogue.
Cost in current (1988) US dollars	The equivalent of today's wages (of workers at a similar level of skill) for a master watchmaker, an assistant, and three apprentices, plus equipment, overheads, etc. Estimated cost of about $10,000.	A cost reduction by between 2000 and 10,000 times.	Less than $1 for digital. About $5 for analogue.

	Constructing a jumbo jet today	Implications	Making a mass-produced aeroplane 50 years from now
Method	The various pre-made parts are assembled together by skilled workers and the body is built using an assembly line approach.	Imagine a technology that could produce a small passenger aeroplane in less than 1 hour, at a cost of about $10,000 (based on conservative estimates). Consider the implications: will there be air-traffic jams similar to those on today's highways? Will people live in the Caribbean and work in Atlanta? Will people spend their weekends skiing in the Alps (in the winter) or the Andes (in the summer)? Will houses have two aeroplane-garages? What about vehicles (combining helicopter design with that of an aeroplane) that can take off and land on roofs, or in backyards? Even if the estimates are off by a factor of 10, the basic analogy and trends hold. Alternatively, consider the predictions which will be made, not 50, but 100 or 150 years from now.	Giant machines, guided by computers and robots, construct a conventional aeroplane. A new type of aeroplane (using a completely brand-new technology) is made by a single machine. Less than 2 minutes for aeroplanes using the new technology.
Time to complete task	About 2 months.		About 20 minutes for aeroplanes using the old technology. Less than $7000 for aeroplanes using the new technology.
Cost in current (1988) US dollars	About $75,000,000.		About $40,000 for aeroplanes using the old technology.

REFERENCES

Drucker, P. F. (1987) 'Social innovation – management's new dimension', *Long Range Planning*, 20 (6): 29–34.

Makridakis, S. (1987) 'The emeging long term: appraising new technologies and their implications for management', in S. Makridakis and S. Wheelright (eds), *The Handbook of Forecasting*, 2nd edn, New York: John Wiley.

Toffler, A. (1970) *Future Shock*, Geneva: Orbit Publishing.

Audit 1.2 _____

If Makridakis's predictions are correct, which (if any) will have a significant impact on your own organisation? How? What do you think the organisation should plan to do to counter, or build upon, their effect?

The objective of this book is to give you the skills to answer questions such as those: so we would be naive if we expected you to provide fully worked answers so early in the book. Nevertheless, try to see what your answers might be, based upon your current level of understanding and expertise. With luck, they may give you some insight into just how important questions of this type can be!

Now return to the changes in your own organisation which you detected between the various decades in Audit 1.1. Try to analyse them to see if they can be grouped into meaningful categories (as Makridakis attempted to do with the whole of business management!). Were they driven by, for instance:

- economic events?
- political factors?
- social values?
- technological change?
- competitive pressures?

1.2 RELATIONSHIP TO MARKETING

To obtain a different perspective, now read Gareth Morgan's description below of the 'outside-in' viewpoint in his paper 'Managing from the "outside in"'.[2]

---

[2] Reprinted from G. Morgan, *Riding the Cutting Edge of Change*, San Francisco: Jossey-Bass, 1988.

Article 1.2 GARETH MORGAN: 'MANAGING FROM THE "OUTSIDE IN"'

A proactive relationship with one's environment implies that it is important to keep close contact with that environment. But there is a vast difference in doing this from the 'inside out' as opposed to the 'outside in'.

Many organisations are preoccupied with 'inside out' management. They approach, understand, and act in relation to their environment in terms that make sense from *internal* divisions and perspectives, or in terms of what powerful members want to do. As a result, they often end up acting in fragmented and inappropriate ways.

Some organisations, on the other hand, try to build from the 'outside in', in the sense that they try and 'embrace' the environment holistically, and shape internal structures and processes with this wider picture in mind. They use the views and needs of customers and other key stake-holders as a mirror through which they can see and understand their own strengths and weaknesses. And they use these insights to re-shape their activities and relations with the environment. This 'outside in' approach to management provides the focus of an important managerial competence that can be developed in various ways. Executive discussions identified three specific ways of promoting the approach, summarised here under the following headings:

1 Sustaining a transformative market orientation;
2 Choosing appropriate frontiers for development; and
3 Understanding oneself through the eyes of key stakeholders, especially one's competitors.

SUSTAINING A TRANSFORMATIVE MARKET ORIENTATION

When managers talk about sustaining a market orientation it usually means 'doing good market research', 'listening to customers', and 'trying to find rewarding niches'.

But in the view of some executives, there is another interpretation that embraces the above, but goes far beyond. It involves realising that it is possible to use a focus on potential transformations in one's organisation. This approach requires that we change the definition of market away from the idea that it represents a collection of buyers in the here and now, towards the idea that it represents a *domain* of operation which may change in dramatic ways and, in the process, turn an organisation on a new course.

The significance of this orientation is illustrated in the following example, raised in a group discussion addressing this issue:

I'm the director of a small printing company, and we print a lot of bank cheques. Well, what is technology going to do? Is there going to be a market for bank cheques? You and I, who use cheques, can't tell. (To find out) we have to go to the technology guys and say 'ten years down the road, how are people going to be making payments? Are they going to be using little pieces of paper, ... using plastic debit cards, or what? And if (the latter) is the defining market, how do we handle that? Will (the market for printed cheques) disappear completely, or is there going to be a sort of residual that is going to be there?' ... (The approach) has got to be market-driven, but it sure doesn't depend on the immediate purchaser of the product to tell you what the market is going to be like. He doesn't depend on the immediate purchaser of the product to tell you what the market is going to be like. He doesn't know. It's the technology boys in town (that know).

The printing firm is faced with a dilemma as to how to stay in business: by securing a niche that will keep it in the paper-printing trade, or by moving in new directions that will involve new technologies, and perhaps move it outside the printing trade as traditionally conceived.

The dilemma is shared by many other firms in a wide variety of fields. For example, many firms in the financial services industry are having to re-think their products and identity, as traditionally separate services such as banking, consumer credit, real estate, and insurance become integrated under the umbrella of 'one stop' financial centres. These services are now being built from a customer standpoint, rather than from an internal production or supplier standpoint, the premise on which the separate services have been developed. The general trend is widespread. For example, many consumer goods manufacturers are now moving to a customer- rather than production-oriented view of their products – e.g. integrated stereo, TV and other audio-visual systems, rather than separate televisions, radios, record players, telephones, and computers. The trend will challenge and change the identity, and in many cases, the very existence of firms operating in these various industries.

The transformative forces that a market-oriented firm needs to monitor are wide-ranging, and involve a sensitivity for the changing needs of one's existing customers, an awareness of emerging technological possibilities, the activities of competitors and potential competitors, the emergence of the internationalised global economy, and other broad contextual trends. As one executive expressed it:

The degree of complexity you've got to exhibit is increasingly complex. You've got to be sensitive to so many damn things ... having your antennae twitching in all these directions at once, and still be able to make sense of it, and to be able to say 'Okay, this is what I do now. But I'm positioning myself now so that I will be ready for the things that I think are going to happen in five or ten years' time, and I will be able to stand up to things that appear over the horizon that I have never even thought about.' It's a very, very demanding position for senior executives.

CHOOSING APPROPRIATE FRONTIERS FOR DEVELOPMENT

An 'outside in' perspective requires managers to distance themselves from current operations, and to ask very fundamental questions about the basic identity of their organisation. For as one executive put it:

If we see ourselves (as being) defined by the tasks we are performing right now, we might turn out to be less able to see what else we might be doing. Our product influences our description of ourselves ....

What business are we really in? Are we a product? Or, are we a technology? Are we a distribution system? Are we just a 'market niche'? As is well known, questions such as these can do much to help an organisation focus on appropriate frontiers for development. For example, as the executive quoted above went on to suggest:

Typically, integrated oil companies are providers of oil products to the consumer ... (But) you see the most shrewd ones becoming (more) like traders of products ... They have changed their emphasis (towards) that of a trading company .... There are other industries that are (moving in the same direction).... For example, there are organisations that are shifting out of manufacturing ... into the business of providing products to consumers (e.g. by putting their label on products produced by others). That is their job. And that restructures the nature of (their business).

Executives discussing this issue of frontier development made much of the need to develop competences that will encourage the kind of questioning reflected in the following examples:

Are we a printing firm producing bank cheques, or a firm meeting the evolving requirements relating to the documentation of financial transactions? Are we in the paper-printing trade? Or are we a firm that will seek to operate with a variety of technologies?

Are we an insurance company, or in the financial services industry? Are we going to specialise in selling a range of separate financial packages, or in selling investment services concerned with financial planning, etc.?

Are we in the motorcycle business or in the distribution of leisure products?

Are we an integrated oil company moving resources from the ground to an end consumer, or are we a commodity trading company?

Are we in mining or refining?

Are we a producer of electronic hardware, or in the information management business?

Are we manufacturers; should we be distributors who subcontract the manufacturing?

We're in metal-stamping; should we be in plastics?

We're a software firm; as more and more programming is built onto silicon chips should we become a trouble-shooting firm that specialises in making computer systems work in practice?

These executives also emphasised the importance of being very clear about the kind of distinctive advantages that one's organisation is going to pursue, for example, in terms of:

- an emphasis on innovation;
- an emphasis on product differentiation;
- an emphasis on marketing and promotional skills;
- an emphasis on 'service' and continuing customer relations;
- an emphasis on low-cost production;
- an emphasis on distribution;
- an emphasis on the possibility of developing collaborative relations with other actors.

Executives' opinions varied with regard to which of these frontiers of development were of greatest importance, since it was recognised that conditions vary from one sector of the economy to another. For example, some executives perceived the importance of developing continuing capacities for R & D and innovation as being of key significance, while others stressed the importance of focusing on 'adding-value', service to customers, an edge in low-cost quality production, the ability 'to time entry', e.g. into new markets, and in the use of new technologies. The following quotations illustrate the range of opinion:

I believe that the success of my organisation (in the packaged goods industry) has a lot more to do with our laboratory engineering people than it has to do with the fifty or sixty million dollars we spend on advertising.... The marketing efforts (of different organisations) neutralise each other .... You have to have it, but the market is more sensitive to innovations in your product.

In my industry (electronics) you have to have good marketing, and you have to have a fast production line, because you need to get the product out of the door before the competitors can.

In my industry (electronics/communications) there is a recognition that you won't be able to differentiate yourself in the market-place significantly through product advantage or technological advantages. These are very short term. They last a matter of months, and then the

competition is there.... (So you have to) focus on differentiating in the market place through response to customer needs or customer satisfaction.

A focus on adding value at every stage (in software development) would set us out alone (when compared with our competitors).

If you're a low-cost producer you can always serve your customer. If you're high-cost you have less room to manoeuvre. Quality is not enough. For example, successful quality producers like IBM force the price down and the competition out .... If you can make money in bad times, you'll be OK in the good. In inflationary times you can pass on your sins of omission; in deflationary times you can't – it's too competitive.

We are under attack (by new companies entering the automotive parts market) so we are trying to go with distribution strength. My management team knows that we have got to become more market-driven; we have got to control more distribution; we have to expand our product range, to make us more important to our customers .... If we can get the distribution in place we will be able to hold off the competition.

As noted above, it is unwise to make generalisations on which of these frontiers are most important. It all depends on the evolving character of the situation with which one is dealing, e.g. in terms of the structure of competition with which one is faced, the length of product life-cycles, and so on. The important point is that managers should approach the positioning process in a systematic and critical way, choosing appropriate frontiers for development that will keep them in close touch with the demands of the changing environments with which they have to deal.

UNDERSTANDING ONESELF THROUGH THE EYES OF KEY STAKEHOLDERS, ESPECIALLY ONE'S COMPETITORS

An 'outside in' approach to management can also be fostered by focusing on key stakeholders in the environment. For example, an organisation can learn much about itself by asking senior executives to define the main corporate competitors. The choice of a competitor implies a choice about the frontiers within which an organisation sees itself conducting business.

Who are our competitors now?

How are they competing with us?

What does this tell us about the critical frontiers within which we are conducting business?

How can we change these frontiers to be more effective?

If we change, who will our new competitors be?

How can we be effective in relation to these new competitors?

Where will our competition be coming from in five years' time? In ten years' time? In twenty years' time?

What does this tell us about the future frontiers on which we will have to do business?

What new competencies will we need to develop?

What transitions will we have to make?

This line of questioning can be enormously constructive. For it encourages an 'outside in' approach to the identification and choice of frontiers for development, especially when an organisation recognises that its main competition may be coming from outside its immediate business domain. As one executive put it:

When the competition seems to be coming from outside rather than from inside your industry, you need a new understanding of the business you're in.

The point has relevance for many industries and organisations: for courier firms and the Post Office, confronting competition in the form of national and international electronic mail; for schools, universities and business schools facing increasing competition from 'market-oriented' educational programmes launched in the corporate sector; for Western manufacturing firms that must confront the reality of competition in the Third World; for copper producers facing the challenge of fibre optics and plastic pipes; for unions facing the problem that they cannot unionise robots and microprocessors; and so on.

When one thinks about one's competition in such broad terms, it is difficult to avoid re-thinking the nature of one's business and the strategies being pursued. Further, when the standpoint of potential competitors is used to identify the specific strengths and weaknesses of one's existing organisation, many detailed operational insights of relevance to the here and now emerge.

For example, one of the executives involved in this project described how the planning process in his organisation is energised by producing 'competitor plans'. Regular task-forces are established with the mandate of adopting the perspective of a primary competitor, and of producing a plan that will give that competitor an advantage over the parent firm. This view from the outside, free from the constraints of how the parent is doing business at present, and free from the internal politics of decision-making that may lead people to favour one strategy over another, provides the basis for a critical evaluation of the parent's position, and what it should do to take account of the strengths and weaknesses of the competitor plan. The approach allows the organisation to see and challenge itself in an open and constructive way through a process that is only bounded by the imagination and ingenuity of the task-force producing the competitor plan. There is great potential for making this kind of critical review from the outside a part of an organisation's ongoing management process.

Despite its unusual terminology, you should recognise that this outside-in perspective is at the heart of most marketing theory, if not of marketing practice! After all, understanding the consumer's viewpoint, which is by definition from the outside, is the definitive skill of marketing as opposed to selling; this applies to all organisations (including non-profit-making ones as much as commercial ones).

Gareth Morgan goes rather further than most marketers, however, for he talks about 'identifying early warnings of the need for potential transformations in one's organisation'. This leads to his conclusion that 'the transformative forces that a market-oriented firm needs to monitor are wide-ranging, and involve a sensitivity for the changing needs of one's existing customers and awareness of emerging technological possibilities'. His view of the environment is much broader than most, and in many ways matches that of this book.

Audit 1.3

Does your organisation maintain such a 'transformative market orientation'? That is, in simpler terms, does it accept the marketing viewpoint to such an extent that it sometimes is willing to, and actually does, significantly transform its approach to the outside world?

What are its frontiers for development? What distinctive advantages is it going to pursue?

Who are your competitors? Who will they be in five years' time? What does this tell you about where you are going?

1.3 MEGAMARKETING

The marketing perspective is also the starting point for one of the most effective attempts to focus attention on the wider environment: 'Megamarketing', a paper by one of the most influential marketing academics, Philip Kotler.

Now, once again *quickly,* read 'Megamarketing'[3] below, and compare Kotler's approach with that of Gareth Morgan.

Article 1.3 PHILIP KOTLER: 'MEGAMARKETING'

Megamarketing impinges on the responsibilities of some non-marketing executives and argues that marketers should feel comfortable using power to accomplish their purposes.

Successful marketing is increasingly becoming a political exercise, as two recent episodes – one international and the other domestic – illustrate:

- Pepsi-Cola outwitted its arch rival Coca-Cola, by striking a deal to gain entry into India's huge consumer market of 730 million people. Coca-Cola had dominated the Indian soft drink market until it abruptly withdrew from India in 1978 in protest over Indian government policies. Coca-Cola, along with Seven-Up, tried to re-enter, but hard work and effective political marketing gave Pepsi the prize.

[3] Reprinted from *Harvard Business Review*, March–April 1986, pp. 117–24. Copyright © 1986 by the President and Fellows of Harvard College.

Pepsi worked with an Indian group to form a joint venture with terms designed to win government approval over the opposition of both domestic soft drink companies and anti-MNC legislators. Pepsi offered to help India export its agro-based products in a volume that would more than cover the cost of importing soft drink concentrate. Furthermore, Pepsi promised to focus considerable selling effort on rural areas as well as major urban markets. Pepsi also offered to bring new food-processing, packaging, and water treatment technology to India. Clearly, Pepsi-Cola orchestrated a set of benefits that would win over various interest groups in India.

- Citicorp, the US banking giant, had been trying for years to start full-service banking in Maryland. It had only credit card and small service operations in the state. Under Maryland law, out-of-state banks could provide only certain services and were barred from advertising, setting up branches, and other types of marketing efforts.

In March 1985, Citicorp offered to build a major credit card centre in Maryland that would create 1000 white-collar jobs and further offered the state $1 million in cash for the property where it would locate. By imaginatively designing a proposal to benefit Maryland, Citicorp will become the first out-of-state bank to provide full banking services there.

These two instances demonstrate the growing need for companies that want to operate in certain markets to master the art of supplying benefits to parties other than target consumers. This need extends beyond the requirements to serve and satisfy normal intermediaries like agents, distributors, and dealers. I am talking about third parties – governments, labour unions, and other interest groups – that, singly or collectively, can block profitable entry into a market. These groups act as gatekeepers, and they are growing in importance.

Markets characterised by high entry barriers can be called *blocked* or *protected* markets. In addition to the four Ps of marketing strategy – product, price, place and promotion – executives must add two more – power and public relations. I call such strategic thinking *megamarketing*.

Marketing is the task of arranging need-satisfying and profitable offers to target buyers. Sometimes, however, it is necessary to create additional incentives and pressures at the right times and in the right amounts for non-customers. Megamarketing thus takes an enlarged view of the skills and resources needed to enter and operate in certain markets. In addition to preparing attractive offers for customers, megamarketers may use inducements and sanctions to gain the desired responses from gatekeepers. I define megamarketing as the strategically co-ordinated application of economic, psychological, political, and public relations skills to gain the co-operation of a number of parties in order to enter and/or operate a given market. Megamarketing challenges are found in both domestic and international situations.

This chapter describes marketing situations that call for megamarketing strategies and shows how companies can organise their power and public relations resources to achieve entry and operating success in blocked markets.

STRATEGIES FOR ENTRY

As they mature, markets acquire a fixed set of suppliers, competitors, distributors, and customers. These players develop a vested interest in preserving the market's closed system and seek to protect it against intruders. They are often supported by government regulatory agencies, labour unions, banks, and other institutions. They may erect visible and invisible barriers to entry: taxes, tariffs, quotas, and compliance requirements.

Examples of such closed markets abound. A long-standing complaint against Japan concerns the visible and invisible barriers that protect many of its markets. Besides facing high tariffs, foreign companies encounter difficulty in signing up good Japanese distributors and dealers, even when the non-Japanese companies offer superior products and better margins. Motorola, for example, fought for years to sell its telecommunications equipment in Japan. It succeeded only by influencing Washington to apply pressure on Japan and by redesigning its equipment to comply with Japan's tough and sometimes arbitrary standards.

Other countries as well are erecting barriers to the free entry of foreign competitors to protect their manufacturers, suppliers, distributors, and dealers. France, for example, has adopted a number of official and unofficial measures to limit the number of Japanese cars and consumer electronics products entering its market. France for a time routed Japanese video-cassette recorders into Poitiers, a medium-sized inland town, for record-keeping and inspection purposes; only two inspectors were assigned to handle the mounting volume of Japanese goods. The goods sat in customs for so long that Japan's market share and profits were severely restricted.

The British and French developers of the Concorde airplane encountered obstacles in their efforts to obtain landing rights to serve a number of cities; most prominent among the opposition were entrenched airlines and protesters against noise. The Concorde group, which needed to sell sixty-four planes to break even, sold only sixteen; the result was the costliest new product failure in history.

Of course, companies that have trouble breaking into new markets are not always victims of blocked markets. The problem may be inferior products, overpricing, financing difficulties, unwillingness to pay taxes or tariffs that other companies pay, or protection of the market by a legitimate patent. By blocked markets, I mean markets in which the established participants or approvers have made it difficult for companies with similar or even better marketing offers to enter or operate. The barriers may include discriminatory legal requirements, political favouritism, cartel agreements, social or cultural biases, unfriendly distribution channels, and refusals to co-operate. These create the challenge that megamarketing has to overcome.

How can companies break into blocked markets? There is usually an easy way and a hard way. The easy way is to offer many concessions, thus making it almost unprofitable to enter the market. Japan recently won a coveted contract in Turkey to build a 3576-foot suspension bridge spanning the Bosphorus Strait. Its bid was so low that both the competitors and the Turks were startled; the rivals were left grumbling about unfair competition. Complained the manager of

Cleveland Bridge & Engineering, 'It would be cheaper [for Japan] to go to the Turks and say, "We'll give you the bridge".'

The hard way is to formulate a strategy for entry, a task calling for skills never acquired by most marketers through normal training and experience. Marketers are trained primarily in the use of the four Ps: product, price, place, and promotion. They know how to create a cost-effective marketing mix that appeals to customers and end-users. But customers and end-users are not always the main problem. When a huge gate blocks the company's path into the market, it needs to blast the gate open or at least find the key so that its goods can be offered to potential customers.

To further complicate matters, not one but several gates must be opened for the company to reach its goal of selling in the blocked market. The company must identify each gatekeeper and convert it by applying influence or power.

Moreover, the strategic marketing effort does not end with successful entry into the protected market. The company must know how to stay in as well as break in. Indian government regulations forced Coca-Cola and IBM to leave the country after many years of operating there. Today, IBM in France is doing its best to withstand French protectionist sentiment; its programme includes political and public opinion strategies.

MEGAMARKETING SKILLS

The following two examples help illustrate megamarketing problems and the skills needed to cope successfully.

Freshtaste and the Japanese market

Freshtaste, a US manufacturer of milk-sterilising equipment, wants to introduce its equipment into Japan but has encountered numerous problems (Cateora and Hess, 1979). Sterilised milk is a recent innovation that offers two main advantages over fresh milk: it can be stored at room temperature for up to three months and has twice the refrigerated shelf-life of ordinary milk after the package is opened. Freshtaste has developed superior equipment for sterilising milk that avoids the unpleasant side effects of sterilisation – a cooked and slightly burnt taste and a filminess that lingers in the mouth after the milk is swallowed.

In searching for new markets for its equipment, the company sees Japan as a good candidate. Japan has a large population, a low but growing rate of per capita milk consumption, and a limited availability of fresh milk. As Freshtaste sets out to sell its equipment to large Japanese dairies, it encounters the following obstacles:

1   It has to develop an advertising campaign to change Japanese milk consumption habits and convince Japanese consumers of the advantages of buying and drinking sterilised milk.

2   The Consumers' Union of Japan opposes the product because of concerns about sterilised milk's safety.

3   Dairy farmers located near large cities oppose the distribution of sterilised milk. They fear competition from faraway dairies, since sterilised milk has a long inventory life and can be shipped long distances.

4   Several large retailers say they will not carry sterilised milk because of interest-group pressure. Milk speciality stores, which thrive on home deliveries, also oppose the introduction of sterilised milk.

5   The Health and Welfare Ministry and the Ministry of Agriculture and Forestry have indicated they will wait and gauge consumer acceptance of sterilised milk before taking action to approve or disapprove general distribution.

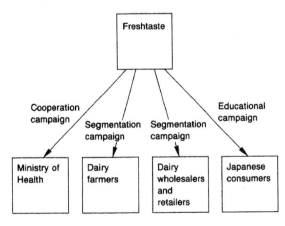

FIGURE 1   Freshtaste's megamarketing challenge

Freshtaste must thus undertake campaigns tailored to each barrier, as shown in Figure 1. It must seek co-operation from the Ministry of Health; attract support from favourable segments of dairy farmers, wholesalers, and retailers; and educate Japanese consumers. The company faces a formidable megamarketing problem calling for adroit political and public relations skills as well as normal commercial ones. It must be sure that the Japanese market is large enough, and the probability of successful entry high enough, to justify the cost and time involved in trying to enter this market.

Japanese consumer electronics in India

Japanese companies have coped with blocked markets in ingenious ways. India, for example, banned the import of luxury consumer electronics products in a drive to conserve its foreign hard currency and protect its fledgling home consumer electronics industry. Yet Japanese companies like Sony, Panasonic and Toshiba have taken steps to pry open the Indian market, however slightly, to its brands of televisions, video-cassette recorders, and stereos (Rajan Varadarajan, 1984).

Although many Japanese consumer electronics products are not officially available in India, several Japanese companies advertise their products in Indian newspapers and magazines in order to build preference for them should they become available at a later date. In the meantime, this advertising influences the selection of Japanese products by Indian tourists in Sri Lanka, Singapore, and other free markets as well as by Indian workers labouring in other countries. Furthermore, some Japanese products enter the Indian market unofficially and are immediately purchased by consumers.

In addition, the Japanese government supports Japanese companies by lobbying the Indian government for a relaxation of the ban or for its transformation into quotas or normal tariffs. In return, Japan offers to buy more Indian goods and services.

Thus, although the Japanese businesses cannot export certain products to India, they have pursued megamarketing actions on several fronts to gain access to this vast and fertile market.

MEGAMARKETING VS. MARKETING

Although companies face a growing number of blocked markets, they are rarely organised to develop or execute megamarketing strategies. By comparing megamarketing with marketing, Table 1 suggests why. The comparison means reviewing elementary aspects of marketing effectively.

Marketing objectives

In normal marketing situations, a market already exists for a given product category. Consumers understand that category and simply choose among a set of brands and suppliers. A company entering the market will define a target need or customer group, design the appropriate product, set up distribution, and est. blish a marketing communications programme On the other hand, megamarketers face the problem of first gaining market access. If the product is quite new, they must also be skilled in creating or altering demand. This requires more skill and time than simply meeting existing demand.

Parties involved

Marketers routinely deal with several parties: customers, suppliers, distributors, advertising agencies, market research firms, and others. Megamarketing situations involve even more parties: legislators, government agencies, political parties, public-interest groups, unions, and churches, among others. Each party has an interest in the company's activity and must be sold on supporting, or at least not blocking, the company. Megamarketing is thus a greater multiparty marketing problem than marketing.

Marketing tools

Megamarketing involves the normal tools of marketing (the four Ps) plus two others: power and public relations.

Power

The megamarketer must often win the support of influential industry officials, legislators, and government bureaucrats to enter and operate in the target market. A pharmaceutical company, for

Table 1	Marketing and megamarketing contrasted	
	Marketing	**Megamarketing**
Marketing objective	To satisfy consumer demand	To gain market access in order to satisfy consumer demand or to create or alter consumer demand
Parties involved	Consumers, distributors, dealers, suppliers, marketing firms, banks	Normal parties plus legislators, government agencies, labour unions, reform groups, general public
Marketing tools	Market research, product development, pricing, distribution planning, promotion	Normal tools plus the use of power and public relations
Type of inducement	Positive and official inducements	Positive inducements (official and unofficial) and negative inducements (threats)
Time frame	Short	Much longer
Investment cost	Low	Much higher
Personnel involved	Marketers	Marketers plus company officers, lawyers, public relations and public affairs staff

example, that is trying to introduce a new birth control pill into a country will have to obtain the approval of the country's ministry of health. Thus the megamarketer needs political skills and political strategy.

The company must identify the people with the power to open the gate. It must determine the right mix of incentives to offer. Under what circumstances will the gatekeepers acquiesce? Is legislator X primarily seeking fame, fortune, or power? How can the company induce this legislator to co-operate? In some countries, the answer may be with a cash payoff (a hidden P). Elsewhere, a payoff in entertainment, travel, or campaign contributions may work. Essentially, the megamarketer must have sophisticated lobbying and negotiating skills in order to achieve the desired response from the other party without giving away the house.

Public relations

Whereas power is a push strategy, public relations is a pull strategy. Public opinion takes longer to cultivate, but when energised, it can help pull the company into the market.

Indeed, power alone may not get a company into a market or keep it there. In the late 1960s, for example, Japanese chemical companies received permission to open chemical factories in Korea by exploiting Korea's desperate need to expand its heavy industry. They played the power game with the Korean government by offering technological assistance, new jobs, and side payments to government officials. In the early 1970s, however, the Korean media accused Japanese factories of exposing young female workers to toxic chemicals; most of them became infertile. The Japanese companies tried to pay government officials to quiet the media but they could not silence public opinion. They should have paid more attention to establishing responsible production methods and cultivating the public's goodwill.

Before entering a market, companies must understand the community's beliefs, attitudes, and values. After entering, they need to play the role of good citizen by contributing to public causes, sponsoring civic and cultural events, and working

effectively with the media. Olivetti, for example, has won a good name in many markets by making large contributions to worthwhile causes in host countries. It has shown skill in the strategic management of its corporate public image.

Type of inducement

Marketers are trained primarily in the art of using positive inducements to persuade other parties to co-operate. They believe in the voluntary exchange principle: each party should offer sufficient benefits to the other to motivate voluntary exchanges.

Megamarketers, however, often find that conventional inducements are insufficient. The other party either wants more than is reasonable or refuses to accept any positive inducement at all. Thus the company may have to add unofficial payments to speed the approval process. Or it may threaten to withdraw support or mobilise opposition to the other party. The relationships of auto manufacturers with their franchised dealers and of drugstore chains with some pharmaceutical manufacturers demonstrate how companies use raw power from time to time to gain their ends (Ridgeway, 1957; Palamountain, 1955).

Although companies occasionally use negative as well as positive inducements, most experts believe that positive inducements are better in the long run (Skinner, 1971). Negative inducements are ethically questionable and may produce resentment that can backfire on the marketer.

Time frame

Most product introductions take only a few years. Megamarketing challenges, on the other hand, usually require much more time. Numerous gates have to be opened and, if the product is new to the public, much work has to be done to educate the target market.

Investment cost

Because the effort must be sustained over a long period and may entail side payments to secure the co-operation of various parties, megamarketing involves higher costs as well as more time.

Personnel involved

Marketing problems are normally handled by a product manager, who draws on the services of advertising specialists, market researchers, and other professionals. Megamarketing problems require additional skilled personnel, both inside and outside the company: top managers, lawyers, public relations and public affairs professionals. Megamarketing planning and implementation teams are large and require much co-ordination. For example, when KLM, the Dutch airline, sought landing rights in Taiwan, the company's president participated, its international department exploited its contacts with Taiwan officials, its public relations department put out favourable news stories and arranged news conferences, and its lawyers participated in the negotiations to make sure the contracts were sound.

Although new skills are required to enter blocked markets, marketing professionals need not be specially trained in the additional skills. Rather, they need to broaden their view of what it takes to enter these markets and to co-ordinate various specialists to achieve the desired goals.

MARKETERS AS POLITICAL STRATEGISTS

Few marketers are trained in the art of politics and are thus unaccustomed to using power to achieve favourable transactions. Most marketers think that value, not power, wins in the marketplace.

The growth of protected markets, however, requires marketers to incorporate the notion of power into their strategies. Marketing is increasingly becoming the art of managing power. What do they need to know about power? They need to know that power is the ability of one party (A) to get another party (B) to do what it might not otherwise have done. It is A's ability to increase the probability of B's taking an action. A can draw on at least five bases of power to influence B (French and Raven, 1959).

Rewards

A offers to reward B for engaging in the desired behaviour. The reward might be recognition, entertainment, gifts, or payments. Marketers are expert in the use of rewards.

Coercion

A threatens to harm B in the absence of compliant behaviour. A may threaten physical, social, or financial harm. Marketers have been loath to use coercive power because of its doubtful ethical status, because it does not square with the marketing concept, and because it can create hostility that can backfire on the marketer.

Expertise or information

A offers B special expertise, such as technical assistance or access to special information, in exchange for B's compliance.

Legitimacy

A is seen to have a legitimate right to make certain requests of B. An example would be the Japanese premier asking Nippon Electric Company to put Motorola on its approved supplier list.

Prestige

A has prestige in B's mind and draws on this to request B's compliance. An example would be Chrysler president Lee Iacocca requesting a meeting with officials in a foreign country to present arguments for opening a Chrysler plant in that country.

Power is key to megamarketers. Companies that find themselves blocked from a market must undertake a three-step process for creating an entry strategy: mapping the power structure, forging a grand strategy and developing a tactical implementation plan.

Mapping the power structure

Executives must first understand how power is distributed in the particular target community (city, state, nation). Political scientists identify three types of power structure (Mitchell and Lowry, 1973). The first type is a pyramidal power structure in which power is invested in a ruling elite, which may be an individual, a family, a company, an industry, or a clique. The elite carries out its wishes through a layer of lieutenants, who in turn manage a layer of doers. The marketing strategist who wants to operate in such a community can get in only if the ruling elite approves or is neutral.

The second type is a factional power structure in which two or more factions (power blocs, pressure groups, special-interest groups) compete for power in the community. Political parties are an example. The competing parties represent different constituencies – labour, business, ethnic minorities, or farmers. Here the company's strategists must decide with which factions they want to work. In allying with certain factions, the company usually loses the goodwill of others.

The third type is a coalition power structure in which influential parties from various power blocs form temporary coalitions. When power is in the hands of a coalition, however temporarily, the company has to work through the coalition to secure its objectives. Or the company can form a countercoalition to support its cause.

Identifying the power structure as pyramidal, fictional, or coalition is only the first step of the analysis. Executives next have to assess the relative power of various parties. A's power over B is directly related to B's dependence on A. B's dependence on A is directly proportional to B's chance of achieving the goals without A. In other words, A has power over B to the extent that A can directly affect B's goal attainment and B has few alternatives (Emerson, 1962).

FORGING A GRAND STRATEGY

In planning entry into a blocked market, the company must identify opponents, allies, and neutral groups. Its aim is to overcome the opposition, and it can choose from three broad strategies:

1   Neutralise opponents by offering to compensate them for any losses. The theory of welfare economics holds that a proposed action will generally be supported if everyone benefits or if those who benefit can satisfactorily compensate those who are hurt. Compensation costs should be included as part of the total cost when determining whether it pays to go forward with the project.

2   Organise allies into a coalition. The company's potential supporters may be scattered in the community, and their individual power is less than their potential collective power. Thus the company can further its cause by creating a coalition of allies.

3   Turn neutral groups into allies. Most groups in a community will be unaffected by the company's entry and thus indifferent. The company can use influence and rewards to convert these groups into supporters.

A growing number of companies are forming strategic alliances – licensing arrangements, joint ventures, management contracts, and consortia – to overcome blocked markets. Examples of strategic partnering in the automobile industry include General Motors-Toyota, Ford-Mazda, and Renault-AMC. In other industries, we have such examples as Honeywell-Ericsson in communications, Sharp-Olivetti in office automation equipment, and Philips-Siemens in voice-synthesis technology (Conrads, 1983). Intercompany networking offers a superior means for securing entry and operating clout in otherwise blocked markets.

Still another approach is to harness the power of one's government to aid in opening another country's market. This calls for effective 'at home' lobbying of the sort Motorola did in getting the US government to pressure Japan into opening its telecommunications market. Similarly, American computer companies lobbied in Washington to get President Reagan to threaten banning various Brazilian exports to the United States if Brazil did not rescind its bill banning the sale of foreign-made computers in Brazil.

Developing a tactical implementation plan

Once a company has chosen a broad strategy, it must create an implementation plan that spells out who does what, when, where, and how. Activities can be sequenced in two broad ways: in linear or multilinear fashion (Figure 2). Adopting a linear approach, Freshtaste (described earlier) can try first to win the approval of Japan's Minister of Health to market its product because, without that approval, the company cannot succeed. If it gets the approval, Freshtaste might then try to convince one or more large retailers to carry sterilised milk. Again, if it cannot accomplish this, it will withdraw. In this way, Freshtaste accumulates successive commitments before entering the market.

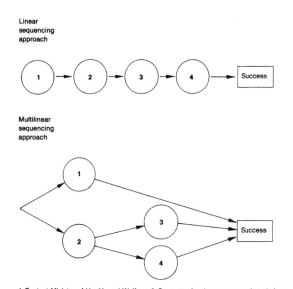

Linear sequencing approach

Multilinear sequencing approach

1 Contact Minister of Health and Welfare; 2 Contact a few large supermarket chains; 3 Contact some key dairies; 4 Run an educational campaign for consumers.

FIGURE 2   Two ways to implement a tactical plan

Multilinear sequencing will shorten the time required for accomplishing the project. Freshtaste executives could contact the minister and the supermarket chains simultaneously. If some supermarket chains sign up, Freshtaste can then contact some dairies and start a consumer education campaign. If, however, some crucial commitment is not forthcoming, Freshtaste will withdraw. This approach may lose more money but settle the issues earlier.

IMPLICATIONS OF MEGAMARKETING

Megamarketing broadens the thinking of marketers in three ways:

1   Enlarging the multiparty marketing concept. Marketers spend much time analysing how to create preference and satisfaction in target buyers. Because other parties – governments, labour unions, banks, reform groups – can block the path to the target buyers, marketers must also study the obstacles these parties create and develop strategies for attracting their support or at least neutralising their opposition.

2   Blurring the distinction between environmental and controllable variables. Marketers have traditionally defined the environment as those outside forces that cannot be controlled by the business. But megamarketing argues that some environmental forces can be changed through lobbying, legal action, negotiation, issue advertising, public relations, and strategic partnering (Zeithaml and Zeithaml, 1984).

3   Broadening the understanding of how markets work. Most market thinkers assume that demand creates its own supply. Ideally, companies discover a market need and rush to satisfy that need. But real markets are often blocked, and the best marketer does not always win. We have seen that foreign competitors with offers comparable or superior to those of local companies cannot always enter the market. The result is a lower level of consumer satisfaction and producer innovation than would otherwise result.

Some may oppose the enlarged view of marketing proposed here. After all, megamarketing impinges on the responsibilities of some non-marketing executives and argues that marketers should feel comfortable using power to accomplish their purposes. Marketers normally deal with other parties in the most courteous manner; many will suffer image shock in adopting the megamarketing approach. Yet this innocence has led companies to fail in both international and home markets where transactions are marked by tough bargaining, side payments, and various complexities. Megamarketing offers executives an approach to dealing with rising international and domestic competition for large-scale and long-term sales.

Note

The author would like to thank Professor Nikhilesh Dholakia of the University of Rhode Island, Professor David Ford of the University of Bath, England, Clive Porter of Marketing Science International of Australia, and Professor Hans Thorelli of Indiana University for their helpful comments.

REFERENCES

Cateora, Philip R. and Hess, John M. (1979) *International Marketing*. Homewood, IL: Richard D. Irwin. p. 234.

Conrads, Robert J. (1983) 'Strategic partnering: a new formula to crack new markets in the 80s', *Electronic Business Management*, March: 23.

Emerson, Richard M. (1962) 'Power-dependence relations', *American Sociological Review*, February: 31.

French, John R. P., Jr and Raven, Bertram (1959) 'The bases of social power', in Dorwin Cartwright (ed.), *Studies in Social Power*. Ann Arbor, MI: Institute for Social Research. p. 118.

Mitchell, John B. and Lowry, Sheldon G. (1973) *Power Structure, Community Leadership and Social Action*. Columbus: Ohio State University Co-operative Extension Service.

Palamountain, Joseph C. (1955) *The Politics of Distribution*. Cambridge, MA: Harvard University Press.

Rajan Varadarajan, P. (1984) 'A strategy for penetrating Third World markets with high entry barriers: an exposition of the Japanese approach'. Unpublished paper, Texas A&M University.

Ridgway, Valentine F. (1957) 'Administration of manufacturer-dealer systems', *Administrative Science Quarterly*, March: 464.

Skinner, B. F. (1971) *Beyond Freedom and Dignity*. New York: Alfred A. Knopf.

Zeithaml, Carl P. and Zeithaml, Valarie A. (1984) 'Environmental management: revising the marketing perspective', *Journal of Marketing*, Spring: 47.

Kotler's suggestion that traditional marketing theory be extended by adding two further Ps is ingenious. He emphasises the significant differences in terms of resources (both money and people) to be invested in this extension, as well as the longer timescales. All of which, he proposes, lead to a 'grand strategy' owing as much to political theory as to conventional marketing. Once again, this is an important contribution to the theory in this field. But, once more, you need to examine critically its applicability in comparison with Morgan's and Makridakis's work.

Audit 1.4

Are any of Kotler's techniques used by your own organisation?

Rewards?

Coercion?

Expertise or information?

Legitimacy?

Prestige?

If no, is this because their use was unnecessary, or because they were not known about, or because their use was covert – and not widely advertised? How, therefore, does your organisation deal with these matters?

If (in the admittedly unlikely event!) yes, how and why were they used?

Are there any situations where you think they might have been suitable for use by your organisation, or would be in the future?

1.4 HISTORY OF LONG-RANGE PLANNING

Planning for the future has had a long history. The East India Company may not have promised to win the whole of the Indian subcontinent as a result of its efforts (though it ultimately did just that), but it certainly did understand it was making a very long-term investment in return for the potential of substantial gains. On the other hand, it sought, as do many modern corporations faced with similar risks, a degree of state support!

Formalised long-range business planning, in particular that taught as a discipline in business schools or just reported in business books, has a rather shorter history. The post-1945 boom in business theory led, in the 1950s and 1960s, to a focus on forecasting as a major component of planning. The principle then adopted was that existing trends could be extrapolated into the medium- and long-term future. The techniques were mainly numerical, and largely based on time-series analysis; though regression analysis, for investigating historical trends, eventually also emerged as a much reported technique. The seemingly mathematical accuracy of the techniques was seductive and, in the relatively stable decade of the 1960s, it often appeared that they worked well, even in the longer term.

The 1970s brought an end to this stability, most notably in the repercussions of the ending of the Bretton Woods agreement on currency stability closely followed by the oil shock of 1973. The emphasis moved to the development of alternative forecasts. The attempt then was to see what the possible range of alternative futures might be, so that contingency plans could be laid to handle whatever occurred in practice. It was the decade of the futurologists, led by the group at SRI (Stanford Research Institute) and, in particular, publicised by Herman Kahn (of the Hudson Institute).

The optimism of these futurologists, even if just in their focus on the future, was overtaken by the pessimism of the 1980s. Even during the 1970s the Club of Rome's report (forecasting the problems posed by population growth at the same time as the depletion of natural resources) was already offering a very pessimistic, indeed alarmist alternative. In terms of the more general swing during the 1980s, it may have been significant that in the earlier part of the decade the main proponents of futurology disappeared from the scene: Kahn died and the SRI group was broken up. On the other hand, it was also a period of world-wide recession when business managers' thoughts turned to more urgent matters – such as survival!

The OECD, reporting at the end of the 1980s, described the international scene in terms of:

- increased international interdependence
- growing complexity in international relationships
- growing economic competition between nations
- heightened uncertainty.

The result was that many organisations reverted to planning only for the relatively short term, if at all. The optimism of the futurologists was judged to be out of step with the gloomier mood of the times. Planning horizons, even for some of the more sophisticated organisations, shrank from ten years to five to three. Most concentrated once more on the one-year (budgetary) planning cycle they knew and understood.

In recent years many organisations in the United Kingdom have put an increasing stress on short-term management and, it is argued, have been reinforced in this approach by the short-term concerns of financial markets. Competitive strategy – which preoccupied many organisations during the 1980s (even including, by analogy at least, those in the public and non-profit sectors!) – often focused on the short-term reactions necessary to improve competitive advantage. This emphasis on competitive rivalry has sometimes obscured the importance of the major external structural factors shaping industry attractiveness described in Michael Porter's excellent book,[4] and of longer-term changes in the structures of industries which can systematically disfavour some participants while helping others. By the end of the 1980s, even IBM, for long one of the leaders in long-range planning, was reported as having pulled back the horizons used in its routine planning from the more than five years it had employed in the 1970s to one year or less.

There are practical limits to the resources which can be devoted to long-range planning. It can be a time-consuming process, absorbing large resources of money and people, which many organisations do not have (or are unwilling to make available). In too many organisations, however, it is also constrained by ignorance or indifference. One aim of this book is to redress the balance. With very few exceptions, both long-term and short-term planning are needed for successful corporate management.

Proactive management

As the experiences of the 1970s and 1980s showed, unpredictable changes can be very disorienting. Once again, Gareth Morgan describes the implications particularly well in 'Developing proactive mindsets', another part of chapter 3, 'Proactive management', in *Riding the Cutting Edge of Change.*

Morgan concentrates – positively – on the opportunities offered by what he describes as the fractures in the environment. These major changes, usually discontinuities rather than trends, will largely determine the long-term future of the organisation. He stresses the need to handle these opportunities as positively as possible: 'opportunity seeking', 'turning negatives into positives', 'being a leader rather than a follower', 'driving in forward mode'.

---

[4] Michael E. Porter, *Competitive Strategy* (The Free Press, 1980).

Now read 'Developing proactive mindsets' below, which is taken from the same book by Gareth Morgan.[5]

Article 1.4 GARETH MORGAN: 'DEVELOPING PROACTIVE MINDSETS'

DEVELOPING PROACTIVE MINDSETS

To what extent are our organisations still operating in a catch-up mode, down-sizing and down-scaling in response to yesterday's challenge, without really coming up with tomorrow's response? ... Many organisations are talking tomorrow, but operating in catch-up mode ... How do we separate catch-up from leap-ahead, and jump on the latter?

As the above quotation suggests, many organisations are approaching the future while locked in the past. They are busy trying to adapt to changes that have already happened, overlooking the fact that by the time appropriate adjustments have been made, the future will have moved on. To ride the cutting-edge of change one must do more than react. One must anticipate possible change and position oneself to deal with opportunities and challenges in a proactive rather than reactive way.

Executives involved in discussing this issue recognised that while the situation can vary from one sector of the economy to another, this ability to be proactive will become an increasingly important competence. Four aspects of this proactive orientation attracted particular attention during the course of discussion:

1 'looking ahead' and 'driving in forward mode';
2 adopting an opportunity-seeking attitude;
3 turning negatives into positives; and
4 being a leader rather than a follower.

Driving in 'forward mode'

The ability to get out of a 'react-mode' so that one is 'in the driving seat', shaping rather than being shaped by change, was seen as being particularly important. As one chief executive expressed the problem:

We need to keep looking ahead ... We need to drive in forward mode, to get out of react mode. We need to look at the future on a regular basis ... In my organisation we've been in a react mode for years – not wanting to face the realities out there ... CEOs in particular need an ability to take off the blinkers, to look ahead, to step outside, and to be consistently monitoring what's coming down the pipe; they need an ability to anticipate.

Operationally this means that organisations must be able to 'tune into the future' by developing and using 'intelligence' and information-gathering functions, keeping abreast of emerging trends in a way that will allow one to take appropriate initiatives. In particular, senior executives need to adopt a 'change can come from anywhere' philosophy, and to understand the context in which they are operating as broadly and deeply as possible.

How can I zero in on the 'discontinuities', 'break points', 'sheers', 'rival scenarios' or 'fracture-lines' (different executives characterise the discontinuities in different ways) that are going to change the shape and future of my organisation and my industry?

How can I begin to understand these forces in a way that will allow my organisation to take advantage of the changes and dislocations that are likely to arise?

These are the kind of questions that can help keep an understanding of one's context actionable and focused. By attempting to identify the critical fractures or break-points shaping one's environment, managers have a means of identifying those 'seven or eight issues' that are crucial for the future of their organisation. The very attempt to identify these issues can itself make an enormous contribution to an

---

[5] Reprinted from G. Morgan, *Riding the Cutting Edge of Change*, San Francisco, Jossey-Bass, 1988.

organisation's understanding of its environment. And systematic efforts to unfold their consequences can do much to create a future-oriented view that is able to take account of a wide range of possible outcomes. So often, organisations are in search of 'one budget' and 'one plan' rather than being sensitive to the idea that any one of several scenarios are equally possible. By using some form of fracture analysis to explore the future in a focused yet relatively open way, one can bring the implications of these possible futures into the present, and consider their likely impacts. All this helps an organisation understand its existing strengths and weaknesses much more clearly, and identifies the directions in which it can move.

An 'opportunity-seeking' attitude

We need to invent more opportunities and to enlarge our horizons ... Increasingly we need people who can perceive opportunities, and not just come up with new ideas. It's a kind of entrepreneurship, but the work is much abused ... With a proactive mindset you identify opportunities in a very active way. You don't just gather information on what's there: you create!... Everyone from the CEO down needs to find ways of enlarging opportunities ... If we don't, then our competitors are going to put us out of business ... We are facing broad challenges, and we need to search for opportunities on a macro basis. ... We will need to develop this skill in the future. In the past we've been mainly concerned with optimising the use of scarce resources, never much more. Now we have to go beyond (this kind of) stewardship. In the new environment we have to invent demand (for products and services), and new skills and attitudes are necessary.

Astute managers are responsible for creation ... they look for fracture points ... they recognise that opportunity comes with change, and that change creates the opportunity to do the right things .... There must be a way of sensitising people to break-points, and of showing them how to handle them.

This ability to develop and seize opportunities was emphasised in many aspects of executive discussion. It was prominent in discussions suggesting that organisations should actively search their environments for potential fracture points to identify new entrepreneurial initiatives. And it was prominent in discussions on problem-solving. For example, it was suggested that even the blackest clouds could be made to have silver linings, and that an optimistic 'there must be a way of dealing with this' attitude is crucial for developing a proactive approach.

The process of opportunity-seeking leads one to emphasise one's creative potential in shaping relationships with the environment. It recognises that success or failure is not something that just 'happens' to an organisation, but is something which is the product of the way an organisation chooses to deal with the threats with which it is faced, and the opportunities which it can make. The proactive approach is best fuelled when members of an organisation always approach problems and issues with a view to enlarging their set of opportunities. The approach fine-tunes an organisation's ability to deal with change. And, as one chief executive put it, it can actually lead one to create change as a means of developing a competitive advantage:

If there is a highly stable market area in my industry, then I will take a close look and try to find a way of creating some change. We create change to keep at the front edge.

The opportunity-seeking attitude is crucial for establishing a leading-edge position, whether for organisations moving from innovation to innovation, or for those that wish to sustain a well-established niche by developing operational competencies that are better than those of anyone else. Opportunity-seeking keeps an organisation above and vibrant – enthused rather than overwhelmed by the challenge of change. And, as noted by many of the executives involved in this project, it is a quality that needs to be widely spread throughout an organisation.

Turning negatives into positives

In discussing this opportunity-seeking attitude, much was made of the need to use the negative aspects of situations as reference points for creating new opportunities. A number of chief executives expressed this sentiment in the following terms:

> You have to turn the negatives into positives.

> Competitive forces force *me* to become more competitive.

> Sometimes, from those dark holes, you tend to look and say, well 'What's available?', and you start to produce.

> By identifying all the negatives out there you can identify really nice profitable opportunities. But you have got to list them; you have to identify them and look around. It is now part of our (corporate) culture that we really get those negatives on the table. We call them major factors, but they always tend to be negative. We identify them, and ask 'How are we going to drive a strategy around them?'

The approach is well illustrated in the philosophy of an organisation that has extensive relations with government and other public organisations, and has to deal with a tangle of regulations and interest groups in securing contracts. Rather than fight against the regulations, opinions and differing viewpoints, managers see these influences as a series of constraints which must be tackled in a creative way. Their approach is to identify all the negative factors relating to the project as early as they possibly can, for example, the factors that are likely to add to costs, or create delays, and then forge a creative design that will either eliminate the basic concerns and problems, or meet them in a direct and satisfactory manner. The potential problems result in special features that help to sell the project and make it a success.

Being a 'leader rather than a follower'

> You have to be ready to move very quickly ... If you can get to the point where you are ahead, and everybody else reacts to you, and keep that rolling, you will be very successful and get a lot of benefits.

> In our business the difference between ourselves and one of our competitors (which is going to move from a $70 million profit to a $10 million loss in just two years) is the difference between who was first and who was second. The difference, the biggest variable, and our research shows it, was innovation ... We were first in terms of an across-the-board set of changes.

> Being number one. Whether it is in implementing a production process or recognising a trend, that is where the action is these days – recognising things ahead of other people; being aware of what is coming down. We can get hung-up sometimes on words and phrases out of books and studies and all the rest of it, but the facts are: if there is something out there that is going to happen, you had better recognise it, and you had better be doing the things now which will help you through that situation.

These quotations speak for themselves and reinforce a point made above: it is usually much better to be leading initiatives rather than responding to those of others. The essence of the proactive mindset rests in this kind of positive, energetic approach to the management of internal and external relations. Building on the idea that in a changing world one usually has to change or be changed, it favours action rather than reaction. Sometimes this will mean 'going with the flow' of anticipated events, and at other times it will mean trying to alter the nature and direction of the flow, especially through action with others. Proactive management may lead to various kinds of joint action in relation to shared concerns, that can transform the environment in very significant ways.

[...]

DEVELOPING POSITIONING AND RE-POSITIONING SKILLS

> Perhaps the most important investment an organisation can make is to ensure that it has the capacity to adjust to the fractures and other changes occurring in its environment.

> If the jolts are coming with increasing rapidity, and greater impact, then ... you've got to have a response capacity built in.

The kind of proactive, 'outside in' management described in previous sections demands much in terms of an organisation's 'response capacities', and general ability to rise to the opportunities and challenges of a changing environment. Executives involved in this project were pretty well unanimous on the importance of developing such capacities, for all too often, it is in the implementation phase that potentially great projects begin to flounder.

But there are a number of specific points relating to problems often encountered in the positioning and re-positioning process that will demand special attention in the development of future competencies. They will be discussed here under four headings:

1   Risk-taking, 'sticking to the knitting', and the 'bottom line';
2   The problem of 'packaging': incrementalism versus grand designs;
3   Balancing creativity and discipline; and
4   The importance of timing.

Risk-taking, 'sticking to the knitting', and the 'bottom line'

The positioning process raises a major paradox for many organisations, because there is often a tension between trying to achieve significant shifts in direction, and maintaining healthy financial performance in the here and now. Major new projects can call for long- or short-term investments that may put an enormous strain on the financial viability of an organisation, fuelling a financial conservatism that can often block or get in the way of desirable change. The problems of handling this tension, and of finding creative ways of launching new investments, point towards important new managerial competencies in the financial sphere.

In addition, there are important social and cultural aspects to this tension, for the risk-taking and changes involved in any significant re-positioning can often run against widely held corporate values. For example, the very act of seeking to reposition an organisation may itself open an executive to criticism. As one executive expressed it:

> The process (of re-positioning) contradicts a very strong value that has been found to be very, very responsible behaviour in business ... stick to your knitting and do what you do best.

And, as another put it:

> You are more easily punished for the risk that goes wrong than the risk that you didn't take, or the mistakes you didn't make.

The point is that in terms of corporate values, there may be important pressures favouring conservative actions rather than those with an above-average degree of risk. The development of appropriate response capacities in an organisation thus requires that close attention be devoted to these aspects of corporate culture.

Attention also needs to be paid to the problem of reconciling the demands for effective operation in the 'here and now' with the transitions and demands required for effective re-positioning. The problem can create much division in the organisation, for as one executive put it:

> As I see it, you have to build a schizophrenic organisation, one aspect of which ... deals with the here and now: ... since to make a profit this year, we've got to ship the goods out of the door, and we've got to satisfy the customers today ... and another aspect of which builds for the long-term future, by building a structure that is competitive with the main business. I mean, its purpose eventually – I know we don't articulate it this way – but its purpose is to put the here and now aspect out of business. And over a period of time it will do that. Now, that creates a tension in that organisation that we don't know how to manage.

Here again there is an important area for the development of managerial competence. Whether we are talking about the 'schizophrenic' potential described above, or the problems of overcoming technical or departmental divisions, effective re-positioning demands an ability to rally the energies of employees so that they help rather than block the required changes.

The problem of 'packaging': incrementalism versus grand designs

Many of the problems discussed above can be partly resolved in the way change is introduced and handled. For example, there are many ways of minimising risk and exposure by moving in an incremental way. Some of the key issues were expressed by one executive in the following terms:

> In the management of organisations we tend to think in terms of packages. We need an ability to take opportunities and structure them into packages of incremental decisions, to avoid putting oneself totally at risk. We have to expand our horizons to take new opportunities without endangering everything. The approach needed is not a total systems engineering approach (where everything is laid out from beginning to end), but one which is much more incremental. It's more than experimenting, and real skills are needed ... (Perhaps) we can develop clear ideas about packaging.

When the strategists and systems designers get involved many blocks arise, because they can't see the end point. For example, (in a large corporation) it is often possible to get one's foot in the water by seeing whether an experiment can succeed: spending $10 million to see whether you want to spend $500 million. But many corporate thinkers say 'What's the point, unless you can move to the $500 million straight away?' They are only interested in the big projects. But by spending $5 or $10 million in a number of places you may be able to get to the one that will require $500 million.

The idea that incremental, experiment-oriented approaches to change can provide an effective way of approaching the re-positioning process occurred in many guises throughout executive discussions. To adopt this kind of incrementalism does not mean that an organisation commits itself to aimless trial and error. For the experimental approach can be implemented within the context of a clear sense of corporate mission, and of what the organisation is ultimately trying to do. Indeed, one of the most important skills required of top executives is that of being able to translate an overall sense of

direction into 'actionable packages', thus making a vision a reality. This important leadership skill is crucial in developing the general capacities required for effective re-positioning.

Balancing creativity and discipline

The re-positioning process requires a creative, opportunity-seeking approach. But it also requires great discipline. For opportunities, once found, must usually be followed and explored in a systematic way. The 'schizophrenic' properties evident in the tensions created between present and future discussed above, are also found in the tensions between creativity and discipline. For many creative people who thrive on the challenge, excitement and openness of the idea-generating process, often shun the rigour required to make their ideas a success. It is thus important to strike some balance and integration here. For some organisations it will be found, to use the words of one chief executive:

> In cycles of searching for opportunities followed by working through their effects ... periods in entrepreneurial mode, followed by consolidation, then breaking again into a more entrepreneurial view.

In other organisations, especially where innovation and change are the main driving force, creativity and discipline have to be integrated in an ongoing way. In both cases, important managerial skills are required to ensure that creativity and discipline are sustained on a continuous basis, and ride in tandem.

The importance of timing

Finally, there is the issue of making the right move at the right time. For example, as two executives expressed the problem:

> With product life-cycles as short as eighteen months, and products sometimes taking years to develop, a product can be obsolete before it gets to market. Timing is crucial.

> You go through a technological change (e.g. fast production lines to minimise cost). Then, a couple of years later you are going in reverse (e.g. slower lines with smarter machines that can make greater adjustments to accommodate changing product designs, and hence consumer preferences) ... This is

one of the great problems in manufacturing and other fields. You say: 'Hey, there is a direction', and you go with it, and you invest for a three or four year return, and then the market-place does a turnabout on you, and you have got a problem. You are sitting there with obsolete or unused equipment. I think this area, for managers, is a very critical one. I am faced with precisely this issue right now. Do I go a particular route or another one? I have got a ten million dollar proposal in front of me. And I am looking at it and saying, 'I don't know'.

An organisation can read the environment in an appropriate way, and make all the right decisions. But if the timing is incorrect, or the 'windows of opportunity' are different from those anticipated, the best laid plans can flounder. There are no obvious recipes for improving managerial judgements on these difficult issues. But they will undoubtedly play an important part in the competences of managers in the years ahead, and the general effectiveness of the kind of proactive management discussed in this chapter.

Audit 1.5

Does your organisation scan the environment to detect the fractures or discontinuities that Gareth Morgan describes?

How does it react when it finds them, or they eventually find it?

Is it proactive?

Is it opportunity seeking?

Does it turn negatives into positives?

Is it a leader or a follower?

In our original research for the OUBS course of which this book forms part, we found that most of our students had a strong understanding of how long-range planning might impact upon their organisations. At the same time, however, we found that almost all of these managers were confused as to exactly what was involved in long-range planning. Where, for example, they had a clear idea of what was meant by marketing (and what range of theories and techniques this discipline encompassed), they had no similar intellectual map of long-range planning. The dozen or so members of the original OUBS course team took nearly a year of hard fought discussion to come to the conclusions that formed the simple map upon which the course – from which this book originates – is based, and even then there had to be a degree of arbitrariness about some of the elements included or discarded. The extensively rewritten version of the course – including this book – incorporates a further five years of experience; but even so, we are only slowly coming to a full understanding of the subject.

2 FORECASTING

As has already been explained, the main benefit deriving from any observation of the external environment lies not in recording what it is now or even what it has been, but in predicting what it is likely to be in the future, so that strategic plans can allow for this. The key skills which this book seeks to develop are those exercised in looking at the future: in particular, the skill of forecasting. The outcome of forecasting must always be action now. Forecasts are not just for information; they are to be acted upon, even if the action consists of a decision simply to continue the existing programme of activities.

This part of the book looks at techniques of long-range forecasting. Unlike their short-term equivalents, these techniques are *qualitative* rather than quantitative, since they have to allow for a considerable degree of uncertainty. The precise degree ranges from the relative certainties of some aspects of technological forecasting through to the broad alternative futures described by scenarios. Scenarios (which we explain in Chapter 6) are of particular interest since, in addition to their main value as aids in forecasting the future, they are especially useful for synthesising (in effect amalgamating) many of the other approaches.

2.1 TERMINOLOGY

First, we need to avoid the confusion which often surrounds the terms used in discussing long-range planning. There are many different definitions for each of them; indeed some definitions of the same term are mutually exclusive! One clear view is offered by Philip Kotler[1] (see Figure 2.1).

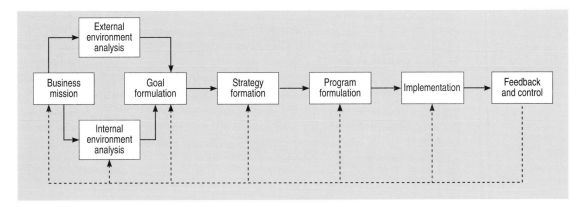

FIGURE 2.1 The business strategic planning process (source: Philip Kotler, *Marketing Management* (Prentice Hall, 1988), p.49)

[1] Philip Kotler, *Marketing Management* (6th edn, Prentice-Hall, 1988).

Kotler describes the function of the *mission statement*, the start of the now *traditional* approaches to corporate planning, thus:

> A well-worked-out mission statement provides company personnel with a shared sense of opportunity, direction, significance, and achievement. The company mission statement acts as an 'invisible hand' that guides geographically scattered employees to work independently and yet collectively toward realising the organisation's goals.

Goals he describes even more succinctly:

> ...indicates what the business unit wants to achieve in the planning period.

Goals and objectives often have the same meaning. Kotler stresses that as far as possible they should be quantitative and realistic.

Strategy is about how the goals are to be achieved:

> Goals tell where a business wants to go; strategy answers how it plans to get there. Every business must tailor a strategy for achieving its goals. The strategy must then be refined into specific programmes that are implemented efficiently and corrected if they are failing to achieve the objectives.

This quotation from Kotler also illustrates what is involved in the implementation of programmes or tactics, which in turn lead to short-term plans with a number of targets being set.

These terms can helpfully be thought of by reference to a single factor: time. The mission is the description of the main, permanent values which ultimately motivate the organisation. Goals or objectives specify where the organisation wants to be in the future (typically in three to five years' time, depending upon its planning horizons). Strategy is the broad course of action planned to enable the organisation to achieve its goals. Tactics are the specific programmes of activities needed to implement the strategy in the shorter term (typically within the annual budgetary cycle).

Of course, organisations differ. Three years may be beyond the furthest time horizon for the fashion trade or pop records. Five years may be too short for those involved in energy provision or aircraft manufacture. But in our experience, reference to such timescales does clarify what is seen to be strategic and what is tactical. Even the use of three to five years as the horizon can cause confusion, for some managers still try to fit this into the tactical framework. In this book, therefore, we deliberately regard the long-term context as being beyond the ten-year horizon; ideally beyond fifteen years. Indeed, the robust strategies which we will investigate in the last part of the book look to decades-long timescales, in contrast with the shorter timescales addressed by corporate strategies.

2.2 TYPES OF UNCERTAINTY

In looking to the future we are dealing with uncertainty. Indeed, the processes described in this book largely aim to identify these uncertainties and manage their impact on the organisation. In this context, there are (using the terminology of Kees van der Heijden[2]) three main types of uncertainty:

1 *Risks* – where historical evidence of similar events allows us to estimate the probabilities of future outcomes.
2 *Structural uncertainties* – where the event is unique enough not to offer evidence of such probabilities.
3 *Unknowables* – where we cannot even imagine the event.

We are well used to handling 'ordinary' risks. Managers regularly come into contact with such risks and, indeed, this is one aspect of entrepreneurial activity managers are supposed to even relish.

Where no probable pattern of outcomes can be derived from previous experience the decisions involved become much more a matter of judgement; and this is the area where scenario planning – described in more detail in Chapter 7 – can make a major contribution.

Unknowables are, by definition, unknown, so we can do nothing about them in advance; except develop our ability to react rapidly to them.

2.3 PLANNING FOR SURVIVAL

We saw earlier that organisations will differ in what they regard as 'long-term', and said we would adopt longer rather than shorter timescales. In this part of the book we start our search – in the form of global scenarios which review developments across the whole of the globe – at 30 years ahead! Within the global framework which emerges from this initial review, we then look more closely at scenarios covering fifteen or more years ahead. This is also the timescale we adopt when looking at the future of the organisation itself within the industry.

It should, therefore, be obvious that we are looking to achieve rather more than conventional planning sets out to do. In particular, where most conventional planning extrapolates from existing *trends*, we are attempting to detect the major *discontinuities* (or fractures, in Gareth Morgan's terminology), which may derail these trends. The greatest long-term threat faced by organisations, and by whole industries, comes from unexpected discontinuities which undermine the way that they do business.

One example of this has been the coal industry, especially in the United Kingdom. Barely two decades ago miners were the 'aristocrats' of manual labour, working in an industry – one of the fundamentals in any economy – which seemed to have a very prosperous future. The trends were there for all to see: steadily growing use of electrical power, which had to be produced by

[2] Kees Van Der Heijden, *Scenarios: The Art of Strategic Conversation* (Wiley, 1997).

large coal-burning power stations, which depended upon deep pits nearby for their supplies. In fact, as we all now know, the outcome was very different. The reasons for this are complex, but a number of unexpected discontinuities contributed to this:

1   Economics – the introduction of bulk carriers, a development in the technology of sea-borne transport, meant that coal could be delivered cheaply from vast open-cast mines on the other side of the world. Indeed, despite the distances involved, it could be delivered to the power stations at prices considerably below that of the coal expensively hewn from the deep pits nearby.

2   Society – the emergence of a powerful environmental lobby, opposed to the pollution (especially acid rain) caused by coal-burning stations, changed the ground rules. Much of the foreign coal had a low sulphur content, so that it required less treatment of the emissions, while local coal needed significant investment in 'scrubbers'. Worse still, the newly available supplies of natural gas did not need any such treatment.

3   Technology – a new generation of gas-powered generators were not just more efficient and less polluting, but required a capital investment which was only a fraction of their coal-fired competitors.

4   Politics – all of this was, at the end of the day, overshadowed, in the United Kingdom at least, by political developments. At one extreme, the onset of privatisation created regional electricity companies which wanted to control their own supplies – even at a cost – and the lower investment in gas-powered stations met this need. At the other extreme, the Conservative government wanted to contain the power of the trade unions; and the miners – with leaders who powerfully symbolised all that was seen to be wrong with the previous political balance – were naive enough to allow themselves to be used in the destruction of the coal industry as a major weapon in the government's campaign.

Caught in the middle of these discontinuities, the coal industry changed from being a major part of the economy, employing hundreds of thousands of manual workers, to a few privatised pits, with a few thousand workers.

This is just one example – albeit a very dramatic one – of a major industry disappearing into oblivion, in a mere decade or so, as a result of fractures which nobody foresaw. It demonstrates the reason for long-range planning; that of ensuring survival. This objective is widely recognised by individual managers. Indeed, our research indicates that the survival of humanity is the main driver underlying the widespread interest in 'protection of the environment'.

There are, of course, some organisations which need to plan decades ahead as part of their 'business as usual'. Shell, for instance, needs to plan its 'upstream' investments, in refineries and especially in new oil fields, a decade ahead; as do others across the range of chemical industries and utilities. Equally, IBM needs to plan the plants which will produce its new mainframes, as do the chip manufacturers their own equivalents; and BT needs to plot the shape of its infra-structure in the decades to come. It is not surprising, therefore, that organisations such as these are recognised as the leaders in long-range planning. Some of the very sophisticated techniques which we use when we are working with these are described later in the book.

2.4 FORECASTING, BUDGETING AND ORGANISATIONAL DYNAMICS

In the shorter term, there is often confusion between *budgeting* and *forecasting*. They are sometimes used interchangeably, but should be distinguished as shown below.

Forecasting is the activity of predicting what will happen in the future (usually expressed, in the short and medium term, in terms of statistics – and especially the organisation's own key figures). The important element, which we have not spelled out before, is that it is based upon certain general assumptions (typically that all other things are equal, without any special action being taken on the part of the organisation making the forecast). These assumptions may or (usually) may not be explicit.

Budgeting expresses what the organisation believes is specifically achievable and intends will be achieved, by its planned actions. The budget is a target which the organisation sets for itself, so that the budget becomes management's commitment to action.

In theory, if not in practice, the unbiased forecast (albeit usually based upon hidden assumptions) should be an input into the subsequent budget, which is then a measure of where the organisation intends to go – and indeed is targeted to go! Many so-called forecasts prepared by organisations should, therefore, more correctly be called budgets.

This represents not just a dispute about terminology, but a major problem of confused attitudes. The forecast is the basis for planning, and has to be as accurate and unbiased as possible. The budget is directly linked to implementation and to accountability by management: it has to be practical and achievable. The requirements of the two are, therefore, very different; to confuse them weakens both processes. As soon as the organisation introduces a bias resulting from this budgeting element the subsequent forecasts become less independent – the relationships between the elements more complex, the assumptions more clouded, and the figures less easily understood by the participants.

A further problem with the organisational dynamics of forecasting is the adaptation of forecasts to changed circumstances in the external environment. It is often assumed that forecasts are immutable: the annual forecast is to be renewed in 12 months' time, and not a moment earlier; the five-year plan will only be replaced in five years' time. It is felt an admission of failure if such forecasts have to be changed. This is understandable where these so-called forecasts are actually targets to which the organisation is committed.

But clearly true forecasts (as opposed to budgets or targets) should be amended as and when the environment changes. The best managed organisations probably have a quarterly review of their annual forecast (and associated budgets), so that forecasts for the remaining quarters can be based on the latest information. The most sophisticated indulge in rolling forecasts whereby at each quarter a full year ahead is forecast – in other words a new fourth quarter is added to the plan. This takes much of the drama out of the annual planning cycle, and means that there is not a period in the year when the forecast may only cover a matter of days. This can happen, and often does, if the new annual forecast is only agreed in December, to cover January onwards!

Even five-year forecasts may need to change quite dramatically each time they are reviewed, in this case typically on an annual basis. Over the preceding year it is more than likely that the external environment, as well as the organisation's own internal environment, will have changed significantly – and in ways that were not predicted. The overall economy will have changed direction, competitors will have changed strategies, consumers will have changed their tastes. The new five-year plan has to take all this into account.

IBM, which has one of the most sophisticated forecasting processes of any organisation, finds that it can forecast accurately for just 13 months ahead, based on the 13-month leading indicators (one of the most important to IBM in the UK is the CBI survey of business confidence). Accordingly, IBM's five-year forecasts can change significantly from year to year, as it takes into account these changes in its environment.

The position may be different in the case of long-range planning, since it may look decades ahead. The effort involved in such a process may mean that such forecasts are repeated less frequently; typically every three to four years, rather than three to four times a year. This is acceptable when the time horizon is two decades or more – since any interim changes are unlikely to have direct impact on the shorter-term budgets – though any major changes detected should, even so, prompt an immediate review.

Audit 2.1

Take your organisation's main forecasts (in particular those covering a year or more ahead). Which are true forecasts and which are budgets (or targets)? Are any attempts at forecasts biased by the inclusion of planning assumptions and objectives? What does this say about the information content of these forecasts?

How then do you forecast the future? The starting point is usually the past.

2.5 SCOPE OF RESEARCH

The basis for investigating the future must be an understanding of the present. The first requirement, therefore, is that you have the best possible picture of the overall environment as it currently exists, together with the changes which have affected it in recent years and longer-term trends which can be seen over past decades. This is now usually described as market intelligence.

The research needed for long-range planning is, in most important respects, identical with that conventionally undertaken as part of the marketing research process. In view of its much wider coverage, there will probably be a greater emphasis on desk research. Indeed, the costs of survey-based long-term research are likely to be so high that it will almost certainly remain the province of a very few large organisations – in particular, consultancies which are able to spread the costs across a large number of clients. Thus, the very sophisticated research which is the basis for our own analyses is probably only affordable by very large organisations. Its cost may run well into six figures, beyond the means of most organisations.

The research needed for long-range planning will start by looking at the broadest possible external environment. In the remainder of this chapter we shall look at this environmental analysis, before our detailed consideration of forecasting techniques.

2.6 ENVIRONMENTAL ANALYSIS: SCANNING

The first stage in addressing the wider environment is discovering what threats and opportunities it holds for the organisation. The steps in this process are illustrated by Johnson and Scholes,[3] who show a steady progression (and concentration) from information obtained by a general audit of the wider environment to identification of the key strategy needed to deal with the opportunities and threats emerging from analysis of this information: see Figure 2.2. The heart of this process, starting with the audit, has been called *scanning*.

Fahey and Narayanan[4] identify three basic goals for environmental analysis:

First, the analysis should provide an understanding of current and potential changes taking place in the environment....

Second, environmental analysis should provide important intelligence for strategic decision makers....

Third, environmental analysis should facilitate and foster strategic thinking in organisations....

---

[3] Gerry Johnson and Kevan Scholes, *Exploring Corporate Strategy* (2nd edn, Prentice-Hall, 1988).
[4] Liam Fahey, and V.K. Narayanan, *Macroenvironmental Analysis for Strategic Management* (West Publishing, 1986).

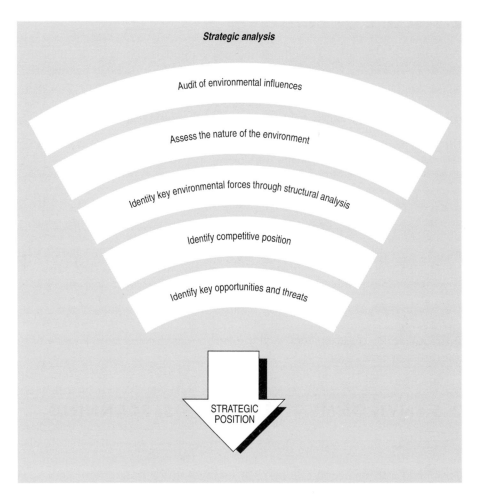

Strategic analysis

Audit of environmental influences

Assess the nature of the environment

Identify key environmental forces through structural analysis

Identify competitive position

Identify key opportunities and threats

STRATEGIC POSITION

FIGURE 2.2   Steps in environmental analysis (source: Gerry Johnson and Kevan Scholes, *Exploring Corporate Strategy* (2nd edn, Prentice-Hall, 1988), p. 54)

Thus, scanning is a very wide-ranging activity. It is also a very practical one. In its broadest sense it encompasses all those activities which the organisation uses, formally and informally, to keep abreast of changes in the wider environment which will affect its future. Scanning can embrace all the factual material to be seen on television or read in the newspapers and periodicals! It may also include the employment of specialist press-cutting services. Here the simplest advice must be to maintain maximum exposure to the widest range of media – certainly not relying on just one newspaper (even the *Wall Street Journal* or *Financial Times*), which will almost inevitably be biased in one way or another.

Francis Joseph Aguilar[5] distinguishes four modes of scanning:

Undirected viewing is defined as general exposure to information where the viewer has no specific purpose in mind with the possible exception of exploration. This mode is characterised by the viewer's general unawareness as to what issues might be raised. The sources of information are many and varied, the amounts are relatively great, and the screening is generally coarse...alerting the businessman to the fact that something has changed....

Conditioned viewing is defined as directed exposure, not involving active search, to a more or less clearly identified area or type of information...the viewer is sensitive to the particular kinds of data and is ready to assess their significance....

Informal search is defined as a relatively limited and unstructured effort to obtain specific information for a specific purpose...the information is actively sought.

Formal search refers to a deliberate effort...to seek specific information....

He goes on to add an important warning:

Scanning is costly; information is boundless. In practice an organisation can attend to only a small fraction of the information that keeps pouring in upon it from its environment. The rules of scanning must be framed with reference to the economics of this activity, and costs must be weighed against benefits.

Of these processes, undirected viewing potentially represents the greatest expenditure of resource, but it also offers the most important benefits in terms of long-term survival. Fahey and Narayanan,[6] for instance, highlight its importance:

In the current and retrospective sense, scanning identifies surprises or strategic issues requiring action on the part of an organisation....Scanning frequently unearths actual or imminent environmental change because it explicitly focuses on areas that the organisation may have previously neglected, or it challenges the organisation to rethink areas to which it had paid attention.

Unfortunately, as they also report, undirected viewing is also the most difficult process to control.

Scanning is the most ill-structured and ambiguous environmental analysis activity. The potentially relevant data are essentially unlimited. The data are inherently scattered, vague, and imprecise, and data sources are many and varied. Moreover, a common feature of scanning is that early signals show up in unexpected places. Thus, the purview of the search must be broad, but no guidelines exist as to where the search should be focused. In short, the noise level in scanning is likely to be high.

Even on a limited scale, therefore, these resource demands imply the necessity for a team approach (such as that needed to produce 'robust strategies', which is described in the last part of this book).

---

[5] Francis Joseph Aguilar, *Scanning the Business Environment* (Macmillan, 1967).
[6] Fahey and Narayanan, *Macroenvironmental Analysis.*

One of the most interesting suggestions for handling undirected viewing came from an organisation which asked all its employees (shop-floor workers as well as managers) to clip any news item they felt might be relevant to the future of the organisation. All of these clippings, from the most sensational tabloid newspapers to the serious press, were then scanned by the environmental analysis group. When a pattern emerged of a phenomenon being reported across a number of such sources, it was tracked in more detail. This seems to offer a particularly comprehensive approach to such coverage; and it is not too different to the more formal approaches we ourselves use. It may be beyond the culture of most organisations, but it could be adapted to work across a smaller group (say, those in the marketing or corporate strategy department).

At the OUBS we have tried to involve a wider range of participants in our work; mainly by using computer conferences. Over a period of more than two years we ran these conferences, covering dozens of subjects with literally hundreds of contributors from almost as many organisations. We were fortunate that, in addition to our students, we were also able to involve – in our Millennium Project (now the 'Futures Observatory') – members of the Strategic Planning Society and of the Demos think-tank; resources which are not available to most organisations. It is possible, though, to use a similar process internally, bringing in managers and staff from around your own organisation. Shell, for example, runs computer conferences, as part of its three year long-range planning cycle, which involve hundreds of its managers around the world.

John Naisbitt[7] extends the scope of the analysis: 'The most reliable way to anticipate the future is by understanding.' He also puts the process of scanning the media into a more academic, historical context:

> We learn about this society through a method called 'content analysis', which has its roots in World War II. During that war intelligence experts sought to find a method for obtaining the kinds of information on enemy nations that public opinion polls would have normally provided. Under the leadership of Paul Lazarfel and Harold Lasswell...it was decided we would do an analysis of the content of the German newspapers.... Although this method of monitoring public behaviour and events continues to be the choice of the intelligence community – the United States annually spends millions of dollars doing newspaper content analysis in various parts of the world – it has rarely been employed commercially.

He adds that the greatest strength of such academic analysis comes about because

> For economic reasons the amount of space devoted to news in a newspaper does not change significantly over time. So, when something new is introduced something else or a combination of things must be omitted. The news-reporting process is a forced choice in a closed system. In this forced-choice situation, societies add new preoccupations and forget old ones. In keeping

---

[7] John Naisbitt, *Megatrends: Ten New Directions Transforming Our Lives* (McDonald & Co., 1982).

track of the ones that are added and the ones that are given up, we are in a sense measuring the changing share of the market that competing societal concerns demand.

He is probably correct in assuming that this degree of sophistication is employed nowhere outside of the intelligence services, though some commercial consultancies claim to use similar approaches, but a more practical level of scanning might include the use of regular opinion surveys (most probably shared omnibus surveys). Taking regular reports from consultancies which specialise in this field, such as the Henley Centre for Forecasting, is another approach. If you belong to an active industry association, then this too might provide good support; Esso UK, for instance, believes that its industry association is its most important source of external input.

This continuous scanning may be supplemented by conducting ad hoc research as deemed necessary, or by commissioning consultancies – such as Stanford Research Institute (SRI) – to conduct such studies on your behalf. This material can offer important insights into specific developments. The danger of relying on such ad hoc work, though, is that the most important developments may be overlooked since the brief does not cover them!

2.7 PROCESS OF ENVIRONMENTAL ANALYSIS

Yoram Wind[8] spells out the stages which were deemed necessary, in the heyday of large-size planning in the 1970s, for the whole process from environmental analysis through forecasting to the final development of strategies (see Figure 2.3). Phase I covers the analysis described in this section of the book. Phase II looks for the interdependencies among these environmental forces using the technique of cross-impact analysis. The overall picture is integrated, in Phase III, by the production of a set of related scenarios, and again this process is described later in this book. The probability of each scenario occurring, and its impact on the organisation, is the subject of the analysis in Phase IV so that the levels of risk can be estimated and the priorities set accordingly. Phases V and VI are part of the planning process. As you will see in later chapters, we now recommend much simpler techniques.

Continuous scanning, probably mainly derived from the mass media, is thus one of the most important externally oriented activities undertaken by any organisation. John Diffenbach,[9] however, found (from a 1977 survey of 66 firms, from the Fortune 500 that replied to his questionnaire) the users of environmental analysis, at least in these larger corporations, saw their activities in terms of the more formal processes which relate to the later stages of analysis (albeit based on expert opinion), rather than the more difficult (but correspondingly more rewarding) earlier stages of true scanning (see Table 2.1).

[8] Yoram Wind, *Product Policy: Concepts, Methods, and Strategy* (Addison-Wesley, 1982).
[9] John Diffenbach, 'Corporate environmental analysis in large US corporations', *Long Range Planning*, vol 16, no. 3, 1983.

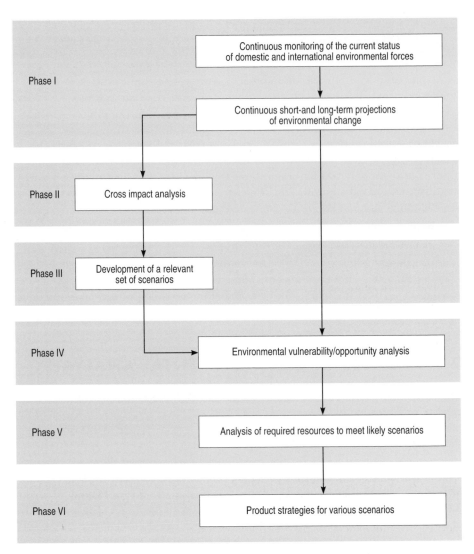

FIGURE 2.3   Utilisation of environmental analysis and forecasting (source: Yoram Wind, *Product Policy: Concepts, Methods and Strategy* (Addison-Wesley, 1982), p. 199)

Table 2.1 Use of environmental analysis techniques by large industrial corporations	
Technique	**Percentage of companies reporting use of techniques***
Expert opinion	86
Trend extrapolation	83
Alternate scenarios	68
Single scenarios	55
Simulation models	55
Brainstorming	45
Causal models	32
Delphi projections	29
Cross-impact analysis	27
Input-output analysis	26
Exponential forecasting	21
Signal monitoring	12
Relevance trees	6
Morphological analysis	5

*Percentages are based on the responses of the 66 firms that reported having environmental analysis activities.
Source: John Diffenbach, 'Corporate environmental analysis in large US corporations', *Long Range Planning*, vol. 16, no. 3, 1983, p. 111.

The range of processes involved is illustrated in Figure 2.4. This is complex, but it does give a feel for the wide range of techniques which can be applied. We would now suggest that the simplest techniques are probably the best – not least because those using them understand them!

Resource constraints may pose barriers to sophisticated techniques in smaller organisations, but perhaps the most important ingredient is attitude, particularly on the part of the management most directly involved. Douglas Brownlie[10] suggests:

> Management attitudes have a vital role to play in creating an organisational climate that enables the firm, not only to operate what should in effect be an open window of perception on the past, present and prospective business scene, but also to act upon the insight it provides.

[10] Douglas Brownlie, 'Environmental analysis', in Michael J. Baker (ed.), *The Marketing Book* (Heinemann, 1987).

	Social			Political			
	Demographics	Life-styles	Social values	Political milieu	Regulatory	Economic	Technological
Data-gathering methods							
Type of sources	Primarily quantitative; Secondary sources	Quantitative and qualitative; Secondary and primary	Inferential/qualitative; Primary and secondary	Real-time personal; Qualitative	Historical/real-time; Primary and secondary; Qualitative	Historical/real-time; Secondary; Quantitative	Mostly primary/qualitative; Secondary sources for later stages
Techniques	Market research techniques	Focus groups; In-depth interviews; Panels	In-depth interviews; Panels; Content analysis	Content analysis of speeches; Lobbying; Opinion leaders	Content analysis of legislation; Regulatory opinions; Expert opinion	Outputs of models	Expert panels; Interviews with experts
Forecasting methods							
Techniques	Simulation; Logistic equation models; Transition matrices; Geographic mobility models	Life-style profiling; Probability-diffusion matrices	Analytical; Value profile; Social pressures, priority analysis	Event history analysis; Political risk analysis; Networks	Network analysis	World and industrial dynamics; Econometric models; Input-output analysis; Simulation models; Trend extrapolation; Time-series analysis	Historical analysis; Probability-diffusion matrices; Morphological methods; Delphi; Relevance trees; Logistic curves
Characteristic	Generally robust	Variable in robustness	Very reliable	Weak in robustness	Moderately robust	Robust in terms of direction of change	Variable/inventive
Integrative forecasting methods	Scenarios, delphi, cross impact matrices						

Sociopolitical forecasting

FIGURE 2.4 Environmental analysis techniques (source: Liam Fahey and V.K. Narayanan, *Macroenvironmental Analysis for Strategic Management* (West Publishing, 1986), p. 208)

On the other hand, he too has difficulty in specifying exactly what are the relevant techniques:

> Writers in the field of strategic management have added little to the basic notion, implicit to the marketing concept, that an alertness and sensitivity to the external business environment is an essential ingredient of success and longevity.

A study by Engledow and Lenz[11] suggested that a similar range of principles was necessary for success:

1. Make a Long Term Commitment

2. Continually Evaluate Objectives

3. Demand Linkages to Present Strategies and Operations

4. Fit the Style and Culture of Your Organisation

5. Design Flexible, Versatile Systems

As we have seen, environmental analysis can be undertaken at a range of levels – many of them quite suited to the practical needs of less well-resourced organisations. Possibly the simplest, and best, advice is to cultivate a deep, on-going curiosity about the external world coupled with an ability to recognise which signals, from the mass of data which every new day brings, are relevant – and important – to the future of the organisation. This philosophy should ideally be shared by others in your organisation for, as a survey by Aguilar[12] showed, 23% of the information about the external environment came from subordinates (while superiors and meetings provided only 9%!). It is not surprising, therefore, that he suggests

> ...much, if not most, of the burden of developing, performing, and controlling scanning activities must be entrusted to subordinate executives.

He does, though, add the rider that

> Somewhere along the line, critical information should get the seal of approval by someone in whom the top executives have confidence.

This last point is especially important. Ideally the scanning should be undertaken by the CEO personally since this is most likely to guarantee the necessary response. Where, more likely, scanning is delegated to others, they must have the full support of the CEO (together with his or her personal involvement in the overall process).

The ultimate incentive to invest the necessary time and resources in these activities is a realisation of how important they may be to preserving the long-term future of the organisation.

---

[11] Jack L. Engledow and R.T. Lenz, 'Whatever happened to environmental analysis?', *Long Range Planning*, vol. 18, no. 2, 1985.
[12] Aguilar, *Scanning the Business Environment*.

2.8 DETECTING WEAK SIGNALS

It is arguable that many organisations have difficulty recognising the strong signals that face them. There has, however, been a considerable amount of academic discussion about weak signals. These are small pieces of information that signal important changes which are as yet unrecognised, since their main impact has yet to come.

The discussion, largely by academics, has concentrated upon retrospective analysis. Thus, the signals that Japanese manufacturers were coming to dominate certain industries (the motorbike industry, for instance) were, once you look for the related weak signals, apparently obvious; yet they were totally overlooked by the existing suppliers in these markets. This is an important message to convey to those conservative organisations which have long since settled into a comfortable rut and may not be able to read the danger signals.

The problem is that while it is easy to see these patterns with the benefit of hindsight, it proves very difficult indeed to detect them in advance. This severely limits the practical implementation of any formal scanning processes. Since those signals are by definition weak, there is no obvious evidence of their special importance, and hence they are not easy to spot. Worse still, they are buried amidst large amounts of similar data which act as 'noise', drowning out these faint signals. The only generally recommended solution is that the reader should be an informed observer – who knows rather better than most (because he or she is an expert in the industry, for instance) which of these weak signals is most important. Even so, the task is a very difficult one.

Joseph Martino[13] suggests that the key is to look for patterns – a sequence of signals – but two errors can follow. The first, and most likely, is to miss the signals altogether. The second, at the opposite extreme, is to find a pattern which is not really there:

> The human mind has an amazing facility for finding patterns in what is really nothing but random noise.

Martino suggests that, in the field of business, the movements of key experts or management (or changes in management structure) in competitors may offer a useful, early insight into competitive developments at least.

Igor Ansoff[14] states that

> Perhaps the most important step is to convert senior managers, who must manage the system, to acceptance of the weak signals approach.... Detection of weak signals requires sensitivity, as well as expertise, on the part of the observers. This means that the detection net must be cast wide, and numerous people involved in addition to the corporate staff charged with managing issues.

---

[13] Joseph Martino, *Technological Forecasting for Decisionmaking* (American Elsevier Publishing Company, 1972).

[14] H. Igor Ansoff, *Implanting Strategic Management* (Prentice Hall, 1984).

Martino,[15] on the other hand, suggests that one way of tracking weak signals is to set thresholds (for instance, that a senior politician has to become involved with an issue or that a journal considers it worth an editorial comment), above which signals are then tracked. It has to be recognised, however, that setting any such thresholds requires considerable expertise.

In general, then, the best approach is to undertake the sort of environmental analysis or scanning described in the last section. Whether the result is described as an identification of weak signals or not does not matter! The important point is that advance warnings are received in time. Perhaps the most important rule – but one all too often neglected in practice – is that the suspected weak signals (on their way to becoming strong signals) are then tracked!

Audit 2.2

What scanning does your organisation systematically undertake? If (as is likely) the answer is 'none', why not? What scanning does it informally undertake? What is it missing? What has it missed in the past?

What weak signals can you detect in your current environment – in terms of factors which will significantly affect your organisation? What should be done about these?

Audit 2.3

At this stage you should start building a clippings file, which will be used as a resource throughout the rest of the book. Into this file you should put articles and news items, clipped from the press and journals (or reports which come into your possession), relating to factors in the external environment which you feel may become important to your organisation's future. This is, in effect, the process that would be undertaken by a specialist press cuttings service employed by your organisation.

This process should, of course, be built upon the lessons, particularly those of scanning, you have learned in the preceding sections. Needless to say, it will depend upon your own, and your organisation's, unique requirements. Even so, there are a number of basic steps:
1   Coverage – this material will probably be identified during the course of your normal reading. It is important, therefore, that your reading is as extensive as possible.
    It is often recommended that environmental analysts read a range of daily papers. This would, however, impose an undue burden on our readers and students. Instead we suggest that they take two quality Sunday papers, from either end of the political spectrum. Thus if you already take The Sunday Times or Sunday Telegraph, take The Observer or Independent on Sunday and vice versa. This is, however, only a suggestion. It is not

[15] Martino, *Technological Forecasting for Decisionmaking.*

essential for satisfactory understanding of the rest of this book, though you may find the extra material and the alternative viewpoints both interesting and informative.

Similarly, you may wish to consider taking a weekly periodical. *The Economist* is the one that most obviously springs to mind. Indeed, despite its title and its age (it was founded a century and a half ago), this journal offers the most comprehensive coverage of all.

2   Clipping – the maximum number of items should be clipped, even if there are doubts about their relevance. At this stage, if in doubt clip. If the material comes from sources which cannot be clipped, for instance material circulated to you, then photocopy it.

3   Selection – after a suitable period of time (typically two or three weeks), when a bundle of clippings has built up, go through them and more rigorously select the ones which are likely to be relevant. The need here is to keep the clippings file down to a manageable size. But remember that the least promising topics often turn out to be the most important. That is why there is time for reflection: to allow a better perspective to develop and possibly for other occurrences of the same topic to reinforce the original "weak signal".

4   Organisation – to be useful, the clippings need to be filed in a logical order. The exact order will be decided by your specific requirements, but a useful approach is to give each topic encountered a simple, easily remembered title, and then to organise them alphabetically (held together by large paper clips, say). One of the widely available expanding filing wallets (a concertina file) might offer a practical device for this.

5   Analysis – as should be clear from the earlier sections, there is no generally guaranteed form of analysis available; it is all down to an understanding of the organisation's environment – and to not a little intuition.

Even so, the best approach is probably to review all the material regularly (albeit skimming it very briefly) every two weeks or so – when you file in the new additions. At the same time you can further edit the existing clippings, to scrap those which are then seen to be less relevant. Keeping the quantities down to a manageable size is a key to success.

If you begin to suspect that a topic is in danger of becoming critical to the organisation's future, remove it to become part of your (rather smaller) monitoring system.

3 MARKETING RESEARCH

3.1 OVERVIEW OF MARKETING RESEARCH

Using Aguilar's terminology, the sort of scanning we have been describing so far equates to 'viewing'; both 'undirected' and 'conditioned'. The next step is typically a move to the 'search' elements – 'informal' and especially 'formal' – which more closely relate to conventional *marketing research*. You may be familiar with this topic, but Figure 3.1 provides a brief guide to the eight stages typically followed in marketing research.

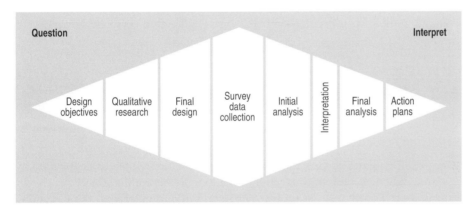

FIGURE 3.1   The research diamond

In this representation of the marketing research process, the horizontal dimension broadly indicates the passing of time as the project progresses, and the vertical one the number of people involved at each stage.

Hidden Time – the main message which emerges from the horizontal progression is that the more obvious elements where you might expect time to be taken, especially those involved in the seemingly complex and lengthy process of data collection, typically represent only a minor part of the overall process. If the research is to be fully productive then the periods at the beginning when it is designed, and at the end when it is used as the basis for action plans, must be allowed to progress at their own pace. Rushed research is too often wasted research. Sometimes you do need answers very fast, but you must then recognise that, in such a situation, the questions had better be very simple.

The Bulge in the Middle – it is in the middle of the diamond where the main manpower resources are eaten up (and the major costs incurred). But this is usually a matter of relatively menial legwork. Getting the first, design stage right can often reduce this bulge to a more manageable size. Thus, time spent earlier, on design, can often save money – and not infrequently time as well – since the later stages are better planned.

The Cutting Edges – the diagram is well named the 'Research Diamond' since its most important features (albeit the least well recognised) are the cutting edges at the beginning and end. The most important input to research is the design objectives. If you have only a fuzzy idea what you want out of it at the beginning, you will get a fuzzy set of results at the end.

But the more important cutting edge is that at the end: the *action* which is generated as a result. Indeed, the focus on that action must begin with the objectives. If no actions depend on the research you must question why it is being done. You must act on what you eventually find. The Japanese often seem less sophisticated in the research they carry out, but they always do something with the results. What is more, they usually do something significant. Western marketers are all too prone to look at the many pages of results they receive, find them quite interesting and then file them; before continuing their business activities once again, untainted by what they have just read!

3.2 DESK RESEARCH: INTERNAL DATA

We will start by briefly reviewing the desk research which is often undertaken before the objectives of survey research are decided.

Even when you are looking into the far future, the first elements of this desk research may well be found in the information already held within your organisation. Fortunately, in recent years – and in particular with the widening availability of computerised databases – the whole process of collecting and distributing internally held management information has become systematised. If the basic data is suitably organised, on a computer database, it may even be possible to access it from your desk, and the abstracted data can then be processed to suit a variety of perspectives. This means that ad hoc reports or enquiries on almost any subject may be easily prepared.

More information is not necessarily a boon, however, if there is so much that it cannot be used effectively. There are a number of ways of taming a potential torrent of data: the simplest – for numeric data – is the ABC Analysis, which means that reports are sorted with the most 'important' elements (customers or products or whatever is the subject of the report) at the beginning. This may, for example, be in terms of volume (or value) of sales. Customers are ranked in order of their sales off-take, with the highest volume (and hence most 'important') customers at the top of the list and the many low volume customers at the bottom (since it matters less if they are not taken into account in decisions).

Data expressed in words rather than figures may seem to make the job easier; for many managers are more at ease with words than numbers. But, because this verbal data seems so approachable, there is an unfortunate tendency to accept it at face value. Your critical faculties are suspended, particularly if the message reinforces your own prejudices. In addition, such 'data' is often difficult to analyse; writers of reports tend to use the same words to mean different things, and the importance they attach to events more often reflects their own enthusiasm rather than any objective measure.

The increasing use of 'electronic mail' is already having a dramatic effect on the availability of such information. Using this, it is almost as easy to send a memo to a hundred recipients as to one. Indeed if, as is the case with most such systems, 'standard' distribution lists are available, it is even easier. In this way, the data now becomes available to everyone immediately and it may be distributed to ten times as many managers, providing them with data they previously might have missed and yet needed for their work. More likely, but equally important, it provides them with a better perspective of what is happening throughout the organisation. Most important of all, it avoids the 'filters' which would previously have consigned important data to the waste-basket.

3.3 DESK RESEARCH: EXTERNAL DATA

We now move on to look at external data – that is, data which does not come from within the organisation. It has been published (in its widest sense), and is often referred to as secondary data (because it has been generated in response to someone else's questions).

Some useful sources of such data are:
- Libraries
- Directories
- National and local agencies
- Databases
- Trade associations
- Exhibitions and conferences
- News media.

The widest ranging source of published data (on everything from details of ancient civilisations through to the latest stock market prices) is usually a library, typically a public library. Many libraries have a wide selection of non-fiction books which will provide background reading on most subjects, and should not be ignored as a source of data. The reference libraries which are usually part of the central library will hold even more. More important, though, is that these libraries have access to national libraries. As a result, if you can find sufficient information to specify the book (usually Author, Title, Publisher and Date of Publication – though often just the Author and Title may suffice) it can usually be retrieved from this source.

On the other hand, much of the published data is located in journals, often specialist periodicals, and the best source may then be one of the more specialised libraries, such as those run by trade associations; though, increasingly, journals are also being made available on the Internet.

The most important directories will also be available in your central library; but, again, the more specialised ones may only be found in those of trade associations. National and local government departments and agencies are often major providers of data, especially to support specific initiatives – but they may still be useful for other purposes.

A rapidly growing amount of information is being made available (mainly by commercial information providers, but also by government bodies) on computerised databases; and, again, much of this is now becoming available on the Internet – often with free access – on your desktop (personal) computer. This data covers almost every subject, with vast quantities of information on technical subjects, such as patents, as well as environmental information.

Membership of trade associations can be a valuable source of 'informal' data acquired during conversations at meetings and similar contacts. There is usually a fee for membership; but this is frequently very good value, in terms of what may be learned.

Indeed, face-to-face contact may be the most important source of external data: through trade associations, at exhibitions and conferences (perhaps the most fruitful source) and, of course, by members of the sales force in business-as-usual sales calls.

We have already seen how important the news media are for scanning the wider environment, but they are also the most significant source of external data for all managers (especially morning newspapers and television news and current affairs programmes). The amount of information these provide is probably vastly greater than that received from any other source.

3.4 MARKETING RESEARCH: KEY PRINCIPLES

After considerable effort in undertaking such 'desk research', at the OUBS we followed much the same approach as is traditionally adopted by market researchers in conducting our own most recent work on the long-term future. This is explained below in Article 3.1, by the author of this book, which reminds you of the key principles which apply to marketing research in general, whilst introducing you to the rather more specialised use we make of them. Where necessary, however, we expand upon the original paper, to cover the techniques in some more detail. These expansions are highlighted by italics.

The key elements are repeated in more directly usable form later in the book; *so*, at this stage, you need only *skim* the article to set the *context* for the later material.

Now quickly read Article 3.1, 'Researching the future' by David Mercer.[1]

Article 3.1 DAVID MERCER: 'RESEARCHING THE FUTURE'

INTRODUCTION

This article describes a viable set of techniques which allows managers in larger organisations to make meaningful measurements of relevant global trends, even in an otherwise uncertain macro-environment, and hence offers a possibility of intervention. The techniques were developed as part of the Open University's (OU) 'Millennium Project', working with more than a thousand large organisations and government departments. The 'Millennium Project', overall, attempts to improve the accuracy of long-range forecasting using new research techniques [1, 2, 3] derived from a combination of scenario-planning and focus-groups.

BACKGROUND

The origin of this *sophisticated* package of techniques for larger organisations (including governments) lies, paradoxically, in our work in developing simpler techniques for smaller organisations. Thus, much of the formal work on 'mapping' the long-term future has now become so complex that in recent years it has been effectively restricted to the specialist staff groups in larger think-tanks, and a very few multinationals; using, for example, Delphi techniques [4] or cross-impact matrices [5]. Even then, the results they have obtained (from experts) have often been challenged as being too inaccurate for the purpose of serious long-range planning [6], and have usually been unsuitable for tracking changes in their macro-environment. In any case, in the context of this earlier aspect of our development work, such techniques were not practical for smaller organisations or departments within larger ones. The work most widely reported in the media, on the other hand, has been that of individual futurists, usually reporting their own subjective viewpoints. Perhaps most (politically) influential work in this context has been that of the Tofflers [7].

None of these approaches provided the practical support for the long-range planning undertaken by most (smaller) organisations. Accordingly, as part of our development of the teaching material involved in the MBA, we were forced to develop new techniques – such as 'simpler scenarios' [1, 2] – as integral elements of the strategic planning process.

[You will find a paper describing this aspect of our work – 'Robust strategies in a day' – in Chapter 9.]

As part of this overall development work, we have found an increasing need to develop more specific research techniques for identifying the key forces for change emerging in the external environment; techniques which are – accordingly – of interest to the larger organisations. As one result, we have been attempting to develop new, formal research techniques which may be used for this purpose [3]. This paper reports our progress to date – with some new techniques which appear to successfully produce both qualitative and quantitative results in terms of identifying macro-environmental (global) trends.

The initial stages of research

The (global) research described in this paper is the latest stage of a programme aimed at improving our understanding of long-term global trends. It has so far lasted more than half a decade. The previous stages [after the desk research which we have already discussed] have been, in chronological order:

1 Depth Interviews – the first element – intended to sketch out how knowledge of the wider environment, over the longer term, was incorporated into strategy – comprised depth interviews with 50 senior executives from multinationals and government departments.

[1] Published in *Technological Forecasting and Social Change*, 55, 1997, under the title 'Determining aggregated expectations of future outcomes'.

This form of research is commonly used as the basis, sometimes the only basis, for published work on the future. We took it as our starting point.

Depth interviews are free-form, one-on-one, face-to-face interviews with individuals. Lasting perhaps an hour or so, they require the use of an expert interviewer. They are most typically used in industrial marketing research where the overall 'population' (those individuals who are the sales targets, say) are low in number but crucial in terms of individual importance.

In the specific context of scenario planning, Northeast Consulting (Boston, USA)[2] start their process with 25 face-to-face interviews with senior managers and stakeholders – each lasting 60–90 minutes; based upon an interview guide and 'questionnaire' developed in advance. British Airways,[3] undertaking their own scenario forecasting, started with 40 one-hour-long structured interviews with BA management. They also interviewed selected outsiders, such as key academics, who could make important contributions. The Centre for Defence Analysis (DERA),[4] interviewed 100 key people in the wider community, as the first part of its Insight programme, and the results from this were then transcribed into a computer database of around 1,000 statements.

2   Computer Conferences – based on the views of these executives, a series of computer conferences – under the general umbrella of the 'Millennium Project – were run; in which 400 managers, members of The Strategic Planning Society and Demos as well as OUBS students, debated both the techniques involved in long-range planning and especially the management issues which were going to be important over the longer term. Although the scale of this research was much larger [8], it was still exploratory in nature; though it did indicate some interesting deviations from accepted 'facts', which stimulated further research.[5]

This is still an unusual approach, one which has rarely been used for such research – not least because such computer conferencing is a relatively recent development in terms of its widespread use.

3   Industry Scenarios – to obtain a better picture of these issues, 200 OUBS students each completed detailed scenarios of the future of their own industry. These were then content analysed as the basis for statistical analysis. This was originally intended to represent our major research effort; offering definitive sector predictions: which could then be aggregated into a global view. In reality [based on our original approach], the resulting 'industry view' proved to be limited – with 'short-termism' dominating the picture, and considerable emphasis on regulatory considerations. This picture, of organisations in effect sub-contracting their long-term future to government, was interesting in its own right [10] but it did not offer the global perspective we were seeking [9].

These various pieces of research were intended to provide results in their own right. On the other hand, as is often the case in on-going *programmes* of research, their main benefit – not least in terms of demonstrating their shortcomings as global tools – proved to be as input to our progressive development of research techniques for investigating longer-term global futures. This paper reports the techniques we now use to successfully address these.

Global futures and the aggregated expectations hypothesis

Although the specific techniques involved 'emerged' from previous stages, the key underlying assumptions behind the latest stages of the research are derived from the hypothesis of 'Aggregated Expectations'. Crucially, in the context of this paper, the most important

---

[2] James Herman, How to Run Workshops, Strategic Planning Conference, 14 May 1997.

[3] Kathy Moyer, Structuring Scenarios, Strategic Planning Conference, 14 May 1997.

[4] Andrew Sleigh, A Case Study, Strategic Planning Conference, 14 May 1997.

[5] For instance, one debate, contributed to by managers from a number of multinationals, provided the surprising insight that these organisations do not recognise common interests with other multinationals in general, but only with those in their own (or closely related) industries!

implication of this theory is to be seen in its emphasis on observation and measurement of these expectations.

'Thus, the starting point must be an understanding of what the population's existing expectations are; and, hence, what will happen if no intervention occurs. Without knowing where you are, and in what direction you are currently going, it is impossible to steer a course to the destination you want.'

[This hypothesis emerged from the various workshops we held with our students. In academic research, such as this was, it is usually necessary to develop such an hypothesis which can then be tested by subsequent research.]

QUALITATIVE RESEARCH

Simpler scenarios

One key research element, reported here as the final stage of our qualitative research on global futures, was the framework derived from the techniques we have developed for simpler scenario forecasting.

*[This part of the work is explained more directly – and in more detail – later in this book, so you only need to skim the material **very** quickly at this stage, to obtain a flavour of how the process is used in practice.]*

This originated with the work of Shell Oil [11 ,12, 13], and indeed the initial stages of our own development work were conducted in conjunction with management from that organisation. In the context of our 'simpler scenarios', as initially developed for use by smaller organisations [1, 2], this process comprises five main steps – all to be followed sequentially by the managers wishing to investigate the future of their organisations:

1 Decide The Drivers For Change
2 Bring Drivers Together Into A Viable Framework
3 Produce Initial (Seven To Nine) Mini-Scenarios
4 Reduce To Two To Three Scenarios
5 Write The Scenarios.

In the new form of qualitative global research, specifically reported here, only the first two steps are undertaken exclusively by our participants and the last two are undertaken exclusively by ourselves. In the case of step 3 there is an overlap. Following this framework:

Step 1 – Decide the Drivers for Change

The first, crucial stage of our usual (simpler) scenario forecasting process is to examine the results of the prior environmental analysis – such as that described by Aguilar [14] – to determine which are the most important factors that will decide the nature of the future environment within which the organisation operates. In the case of the global work described here, however, there is no prior analysis, since all the members of the groups come fresh to the work. On the other hand, they all will have been exposed to a wide range of analytical inputs from the media; and this has proved, in our tests, to be quite sufficient for them to productively engage in the debate – and for them to produce meaningful results.

In any case, perhaps the most difficult aspect of any scenario planning is freeing the participants from the preconceptions they take into the process with them. Due to the disparate backgrounds of the members of our global futures groups, we have found that this is not a problem. Equally, the requirement that they look 30 years into the future creates few objections – and poses no significant problems in practice.

The specific technique we have developed for implementing the first stage of scenario forecasting, in general, is based upon:

Self-documenting focus-groups

Once more, the simple technique we use for the first stage of our scenario work is one we have previously developed for general usage by all our focus groups, not just those which are involved in our (global) scenario work. It is based on the now almost universal availability of Post-it™ Notes and is a very simple technique; since it requires only a conference room with a bare wall and copious supplies of 3M Post-it™ Notes.

The result is a very powerful form of creative interaction within the group, which is applicable to a wide range of situations (but is especially powerful in the context of these global scenario groups). In view of the short time available for such groups to work together, just one or two hours, it also offers a very obvious context for those who are coming to the process for the first time. Since the workings are largely self-evident, participants very quickly come to understand exactly what is involved.

Focus Groups in General

This example represents a particularly sophisticated form of 'focus group'. Such groups – which form the backbone of qualitative marketing research – do not use Post-it™ Notes and are more generally led by an interviewer ('group leader' or 'moderator'), who has to be skilled in the technique and often is a trained psychologist. He or she carefully leads the discussion, ensuring that all the group members are able to put forward their views. Even so, the interviewer's role is essentially a passive one, where his or her prime concern is to foster group interaction (and to avoid any one individual dominating the group).

The essence of such group discussions is that the participants can develop their own ideas in an unstructured fashion; interacting with, and stimulating, others. Indeed it is based upon the somewhat surprising observation, derived from clinical psychology, that individuals who share a problem are more willing to talk about it amid the security of others sharing the same problem. As a result it can be very powerful in revealing hidden attitudes.

Rather than being captured (self-documented) by the postings to the wall, as we did, the whole session is traditionally captured on a tape recorder for later analysis in depth. This approach thus allows insights which may be hidden from the pre-conceived questions posed in questionnaire surveys. In particular it allows your customers' own language to emerge, so that the subsequent survey questions can be phrased in ways which are meaningful to them.

It is an excellent method for generating hypotheses when little is known, and is thus a particularly productive approach to piloting the first stage of larger research projects. It is, though, increasingly being used as a cheaper and faster alternative for those organisations which cannot afford the full-scale research – and, in line with the move to low-cost research, even for those which can. This is arguably better than nothing, but if such use is planned you should beware of attributing too much

significance to it. The sample sizes are usually far too small to allow any statistical conclusions to be drawn.

Repertory grids

Another, especially powerful method of starting the process of unearthing the customer's deeper motivations is Repertory Grids. By removing interviewer (and questionnaire-designer) bias, whilst allowing the respondent free rein to his or her own ideas (and indeed 'forcing' this process), this questionnaire-based technique can give you a very clear picture of what really motivates respondents. It is, though, a very sophisticated and expensive process.

The precise aim of this technique, often called Kelly Grids after the name of the inventor, is to discover what are the key dimensions of the respondents' attitudes towards the matter in hand (usually a product or brand – typically as part of a positioning exercise). Thus, in an individual interview, each respondent is presented with a list of items. These items (around 15–20 being the recommended number) are normally presented in simple word form, for example the names of products or brands, or statements about them. Three of the items ('triads' – in the jargon) chosen at random from the list are presented to the respondent at a time. The respondent is asked to choose the two most alike. He or she is then asked to say why these two are similar, and are different to the third. The remaining items on the list are then sorted equally between these two extremes. The process is repeated with three further stimuli, again selected at random, and the respondent is asked to give another way in which the selected pair are the same, and different to the third. The whole process continues until the respondent cannot find a further new reason for the similarity/difference (which typically occurs after ten or so triads, depending upon the complexity of the subject being studied).

A number of such interviews (from 10–50) are conducted and the output analysed – usually these days by computer – to see which factors can be identified. This stage of the process (as well as the interview itself) requires considerable skill – if the information is to have any worth. The output, though, is a set of dimensions by which the customers themselves would describe the situation (usually something like a product/brand position).

Its great virtue is that it forces the market researcher subsequently, in the quantitative survey research which is the second stage to all these pilot investigations, to research dimensions which are meaningful to the consumer rather than to the supplier.

It has to be admitted, though, that using Repertory Grids is relatively expensive (at least in terms of pilot research) and, possibly as a result, they are rarely used in practice. This is a pity, since they offer one of the most valuable starting points for sound marketing research.

Bringing the factors together

As the initial flow of ideas slows down, participants [using the 'self-documenting focus group' approach] can easily be introduced to the next stage, with rather more ease than in a traditional focus group [15], though many of the groups may well move on of their own volition. The key fact is that the facilitator can progress the group through the stages of the research especially easily; and without undue intervention – again requiring less skill. In addition, as the record of the previous discussions is retained – on the wall – the participants rarely need to be reminded of where they have been.

One aspect which is much more difficult to achieve with conventional focus groups, is to ask the participants to develop the relationships between the various factors – something which may be particularly important, say, for work leading to factor analysis or (as in our futures research) to establishing the dimensions to be explored in subsequent quantitative work. Thus, in the case of our scenario groups, they were asked to try and arrange the drivers, which had emerged from the first stage, into groups which seemed to make sense to them, where the final aim of this stage was to lead into the creation of the six to eight larger groupings; 'mini-scenarios'.

Needless to say, the highly visual nature of the patterns produced by the various arrangements of the Post-it™ Notes is especially effective in stimulating investigation into the relationships between them.

SIMPLER SCENARIOS CONTINUED

Reverting to the framework which specifically relates to global scenarios, and applying the techniques of self-documenting focus groups:

Step 2 – Bring drivers together into a viable framework

At this stage, therefore, our participants are asked to try and arrange the global drivers, which emerge from the first stage, into groups which seem to make sense to them. This is usually the most (conceptually) difficult step. It is where managers' 'intuition' – their ability to make sense of complex patterns of 'soft' data which more rigorous analysis would be unable to handle – plays an important role. In practice, there are initially many such small groups of drivers created; but these are then gradually refined down to a smaller number.

This is the stage which is completed by all of the groups – and is the main basis for our subsequent analysis.

Step 3 – Produce initial (seven to nine) mini-scenarios

Indeed, the outcome, in the case of our 'simpler scenarios', is usually between seven and nine logical groupings of drivers. In practice, due to the scope of the research (covering all aspects of society) our global groups tend to produce rather more clusters; typically around 10–12 in number.

This stage is also completed by all of the groups, but is only used as a check on the main work which is undertaken by ourselves.

Self-documentation

A final, major advantage of the new, self-documenting focus groups' approach is that the main 'documentation' of the results is progressively accumulated as a natural part of the process – in the form of the Post-it™ Notes adhering to the wall – by the participants themselves. It is they who decide, in this way, what they want to say; and this requires no interpretation to be useful [16]. The process may be tape-recorded, or a video made, but the prime record is the notes on the wall – which may then be most easily photographed to form a permanent record. Following the same line of argument, the analysis, at least at the first-level focus group work, has already been started by the participants – in terms of their own clusters and patterns – reducing the need for content analysis [17]. In the case of global scenarios, however, it should be noted that this is only a 'cross-check' on the central analysis – which starts again with the individual drivers for change.

Step 4 – Reduce to two to three scenarios

In our scenario planning theory for smaller organisations, the main action, undertaken by all the participants as the next stage, is to reduce the seven to nine mini-scenarios/groupings detected at the previous stage to just two or three larger scenarios [18]. We have found, however, that the time limitations prevent our global scenario groups from fully completing the later stages of the process in the one session available; which typically cannot last longer than two hours. Thus, in the earlier (global) groups, the rearrangement of the drivers to produce fully-fledged scenarios was incomplete; though, even so, the results were enlightening and useful in suggesting what the final scenarios might have been. In the later groups we achieved the same effect by specifically asking the groups to derive 'scenario titles' separate from the drivers – though clearly influenced by the work they had done on them – and this has now become our standard (global scenarios) approach.

In this 'global' research, therefore, the transformation into the final scenarios (and even the production of the overall 'mini-scenarios') is now undertaken by ourselves rather than the participants. The prime input to this process is all the drivers identified – for instance, by the 17 research groups (covering some 140 organisations) in the original research. Once more using the standard (Post-it™ Notes) scenario forecasting technique we have developed [1], all these drivers (from all the groups involved) are progressively clustered – by central staff – into aggregated 'mini-scenarios' regardless of how they have originally been clustered by the groups. This overall clustering is, however, then compared

(cross-checked) with the separate work of the groups – to ensure that it is still meaningful in broad terms. This has generally proved to be the case. It is our experience that there is, in any event, some considerable convergence between the results of most of the groups.

These combined mini-scenarios are then transformed into the final scenarios. In view of the very broad scope of the investigation, covering the whole of society, it has proved necessary to utilise four scenarios – rather than the two we would normally recommend for our more traditional work with smaller organisations. These are again compared with those suggested by the groups, and once more we found that there were no major disagreements between them in our original research.

Testing

In the normal scenario forecasting process, having grouped the factors into two scenarios, the next step is to examine them for consistency. In our global work, in general, this is supplemented – as mentioned above – by the comparison with the groups' own scenarios. In the case of the original research, however, this test also took the form of a comparison with the published work of a wide range of other futurists. Here too there was a surprising degree of agreement. Though the nature of future developments is often seen to be a controversial issue, one result from the research was therefore that, at least amongst those studying the long-term future, there seems to be a degree of unanimity; a workable consensus. Indeed, one major aspect of our results turned out to be a surprising degree of convergence between the outcomes reported by almost all the various groups – ranging from uninformed generalists to informed futurists – in contradiction to the uncertainty generally reported by the media. It is this convergence, indeed, which we believe goes a long way to underwriting the viability of the techniques.

Confidence levels

So far, most of the technique(s) described have been assumed to be those applying to just one group of eight participants. It should have been obvious, however, that in the last two steps we aggregate the drivers produced by a number of such groups. The requirement for significant numbers of participants, even – unusually – at this qualitative stage of the overall research, is generated by the need to ensure that all the significant drivers (the dimensions to be quantified in subsequent stages) have been identified. As there may be more than a hundred such drivers, if the research is genuinely to be 'global', it may be necessary to run five or more groups, so that multiple occurrences of each of these significant drivers may be observed. Otherwise, researchers cannot be confident that the single occurrences (emerging from a smaller number of groups) may not just represent one individual's idiosyncrasies. The problem may be resolved at the quantitative stage, but it will waste respondent's time and – worse – annoy them, by the questionnaire's apparent triviality, to such an extent that this distorts the results.

Above all, though, the more participants recruited to the process the more confident the researchers, and the 'customers' for their work, will feel that all the significant drivers have been identified.

Detecting 'wild cards'

One group of events which have traditionally caused problems for long-range forecasters [19] are those 'wild cards' which surprise everyone. According to strict theory, these 'wild cards' must be unpredictable (or at least of low predictability) as well as of high impact; and, hence, these might cause problems even for those using the techniques described here.

There is, though, one important sub-category of wild cards, those involving slow hidden processes, which are present over long periods but suddenly emerge (as 'creeping catastrophes'[20]). This category – which accounts for a large proportion of wild cards overall – may be detected by the technique(s) described here, as long as sufficient numbers of participants are involved. Essentially, researchers should look for two or more occurrences which surprise them. They need two such occurrences because it is almost certain that otherwise they will reject the issue as unbelievable!

Clearly, the more participants the greater the chance of two such occurrences emerging. Indeed, it is unlikely that they will emerge from less than ten or twenty groups (comparable with the number we, ourselves, completed). As a result, this is an approach more suited to larger organisations, with their larger budgets.

As these wild card issues are – almost by definition – unbelievable for most respondents, it is that much more difficult to incorporate these in the quantification stage. On the other hand, once they have been identified, these 'creeping catastrophes' typically become *certain* factors; not needing further research.

Structural factors

One specific, remaining limitation of the techniques described is a failure to highlight structural changes occurring in the macro-environment. This is partly because the techniques typically tend to be most effective in aggregating large numbers of 'small' expectations. But it is mainly because Western managers are 'culturally blind' to many of the structural changes which occur across society as a whole; one group of Third World participants who had a Marxist background, for instance, did detect such structural factors.

The result is that the central staff, aggregating the drivers into the final scenarios, must themselves detect where the issues reported are symptoms of underlying structures. In practice this proves less problematic than might be expected; where the academic researchers, involved in our work to date, are motivated to find such structural trends.

Once more, it is difficult to quantify these, but – again – these structural changes (once detected) also typically prove to be certain.

Step 5 – Write the scenarios

Conventionally the resulting scenarios are then 'written up' in the form most suitable for the target audience; and, indeed, a summary of our initial work was published conventionally [21]; and summaries of the future developments are already scheduled for publication in the same way. In the case of the original material, due to the very wide scope of the investigations, the final 'report' ran to more than 80,000 words. Accordingly, the publication of the more detailed material has been on the Internet 'World Wide Web' (WWW). All of the original – qualitative – results, together with details of the research techniques, are therefore described in the various parts of the database available, free of charge, through the index on:

http://oubs.open.ac.uk/future.html

A 7,000 word summary is also available at this address.

Quantitative research

The output from such qualitative focus group research is often used to determine the questions for subsequent quantitative research [15]. In particular, it is used to determine the dimensions to be investigated in market segmentation and product positioning [22]. As the requirement for quantifying our futures research was very similar, we chose this approach – in preference to Repertory (Kelly) Grids [23] – because of the large number of dimensions involved. Thus, the results of this qualitative research have been used to identify the 162 dimensions, the most likely factors (drivers) for change, to be explored in the subsequent quantitative research.

Using rather more traditional marketing research techniques, in an initial mail-survey conducted with 300 OUBS students, each of the 162 factors (questions) is now presented in terms of two semantic differentials [24]. The first of these asks for a date (from AD 2000 to 2050) when this factor will become a reality; or, if thought less likely, the percentage chance (10–50% or $<10\%$ chance). The second asks for rating of its importance to the manager's organisation (on a scale from 1, unimportant, to 7, very important). Although the result may look like an early stage of a conventional Delphi study [4], and might even be used as such, the dimensions are already derived from the wider population rather than being in the process of being sought from expert opinion.

Despite the complexity of the questionnaire, 160 responses (53%) were received from the initial survey – in line with our normal response rate – and this performance was repeated in the follow-up survey a year later. Less than ten per cent of these were completed incorrectly. In addition to simple tabulation, these detailed results will be factor/cluster analysed, to establish the relationships between them.

Survey research

The most widely used formal marketing research is, or at least should be, survey research such as this. Typically, this may be designed to find out, descriptively, what are the participants' habits, attitudes, wants etc. It is simply based on asking the participant, the respondent, a number of questions; in our case covering the 162 dimensions. As the key to survey research, the questions must be very carefully and skilfully developed. In the first instance they must be comprehensive. Secondly, they will need to be in a language the respondent understands, so that the answers will be clear and unambiguous. Finally, they should not be leading questions, drawing out the answer expected by the researcher (or the client). The questions must be neutral, to encourage the respondent to reply truthfully.

Questionnaires

The next stage of the research traditionally occurs when the army of interviewers descends on the unsuspecting public. There are, however, a number of possible methods of contacting respondents. Mail is the cheapest solution and large overall samples can be used, allowing investigation of small markets groups – especially in industrial markets – still within acceptable statistical levels; this was indeed our own choice. But, in some respects, it may be the least satisfactory one. The questions which can be asked are necessarily simpler and the questionnaire shorter. Ours was in fact long, but each 'question' was only a variation on a standard question. It must also be particularly well designed – to keep the respondent interested and motivated to reply – in our case we relied, mainly, on the high level of motivation of OU students. More fundamentally, the response rates may be so low that their statistical validity may be questioned; since it is arguable that the majority, the non-respondents, might behave differently to those who have responded. It is worth noting, however, that response rates in fact may not be significantly worse than those for the typical face-to-face interview. The only difference is that in the latter case the 'non-responses' are not known (or at least are not recorded). Some – very carefully managed – mail surveys may, therefore, offer a viable alternative to face-to-face approaches.

Alternatively, the interviewer might use a telephone to contact respondents. It is a very fast survey technique; so that results can be available in a matter of hours, and hence it is often now used for those opinion polls where time is of the essence. It is also relatively cheap (and, hence, often affordable even in industrial markets). On the other hand, the interview can only last a short time and the types of question are limited. Even so, it is probably under-used as a technique, since it is relatively cheap and quite flexible in use.

Interviews

Personal interviewing is the traditional (face to face) approach to marketing research, and it still is the most versatile. The interviewer is in full control of the interview, and can take account of the body language as well as the words. It is the most expensive, however, and is dependent on the reliability of the interviewer; and on his or her skill in the case of some of the more sophisticated techniques. This means that the quality of the supervision provided by the field research agency is critical; which may be a problem where so many organisations now place the emphasis on cost-cutting.

Samples

The basic principle of sampling (derived from statistical theory) is that you can obtain a representative picture of a whole 'population' (the term used by theorists to describe the total group of people, or objects, being investigated) by looking at a small 'sample'. The number is usually, in this context, only a few hundred – but correctly handled it may still give an accurate picture of an overall population of millions. This applies to testing grain sold by the farmer just as much as it does, here, to market research. It is, needless to say, a very cost-effective way of obtaining information.

As quality does, though, depend very directly upon the quality of the interviewer, and in particular on the quality of supervision, it is the approach most likely to suffer from the shaving of quality to achieve cost savings. At the worst level, badly controlled, it may all too easily degenerate into 'convenience sampling'; which is a polite phrase for interviewing whoever comes easiest to hand – and is not a genuine form of sampling by any standard!

There are some nice statistical calculations which will show you how many interviews you will need to conduct. As a very rough guide, though, if you want to achieve an accuracy of around two or three per cent, which is satisfactory for most occasions, you will probably need a sample of between 500 and 1,000 respondents. Sample sizes as low as 300–400 are often found to be acceptable. The point to notice is that you rarely need more than 1,000 and, much more important, you can equally rarely expect to get accurate results with fewer than 200 respondents.

CONCLUSIONS

The overall project involved the development of two new sets of research techniques. The first of these, 'simpler scenarios' [1, 2], allows this approach to be used as a framework for more general research. The second, 'self-documenting focus groups' (reported here in full for the first time), enables a large number of dimensions to be generated, as input to the subsequent quantitative research which uses well-tried techniques (based on semantic differentials). As initially evidenced by the observed convergence of results, the combination allows the expectations of a large population to be investigated – and, thus, future outcomes to be more accurately predicted.

REVISED RESEARCH TECHNIQUES

Following the publication of this paper, and the start of the latest stages of our research, we now believe that four stages of research/analysis should be employed when researching the far future (once again based upon our Aggregated Expectations Hypothesis):

Stage 1 – Initial qualitative research

This remains the most important stage of the overall project, and uses the two new sets of qualitative research techniques described earlier. This enables a large number of dimensions, key factors or drivers for change, to be generated; as input to the second, quantitative research.

Stage 2 – Quantification of the current research position

As described in the previous sections, this uses the same postal questionnaires based on well-tried techniques (semantic differentials) to establish, for each of 100+ events (dimensions), its importance, its probability of occurring, and the most likely date it will occur. It quantifies the current position held by individuals – influenced by the culture (the environment) in which they are immersed – and this provides the starting point for future plans. The key element, as shown by our pilot work, is that this represents a relatively conservative figure; which is useful, in itself, as the most accurate measure of the starting point, but does not necessarily indicate the potential developments.

Stage 3 – Exploration of future possibilities

As a result, and unusually in such research, the next step – the first in the new set of techniques – is to return to the 'qualitative' work to determine how it might be possible to influence the current position of the participants. The first aspect of this extended process is to determine 'whether' desired changes might be possible. The second is estimation of the 'effort' required to achieve such changes. The rationale for using the 'qualitative' approach is that this is undertaken in groups; and, as members of the groups interact, these provide a dependable indication of how positions may be shifted. The only caveat is that the work should be undertaken on such a scale, with upwards of ten (eight-person) groups, that the results approach a degree of statistical validity.

Stage 4 – Expert analysis of structural factors

The main limitation, of even the qualitative work, is that the participants tend to be culturally blind to the underlying structures. Accordingly, their final output often focuses upon symptoms rather than the causes. It is, therefore, passed – as the final stage – to expert analysts who use their own expertise (and that of the reports from other experts onto which the output is mapped) to synthesise the material into the most meaningful patterns.

Our own overall qualitative work covered a relatively large number of groups; 17 in total, with 140+ organisations involved.

NOTES

[1] Mercer, D., 'Scenarios made easy', *Long Range Planning* 28(4), 81–86 (1995)

[2] Mercer, D., 'Simpler scenarios', *Management Decision* 33(4), 32–40 (1995)

[3] Mercer, D., 'A new qualitative technique for exploring the future', *Marketing Education Group (MEG)*, Warwick (August, 1996)

[4] Twiss, B. C., *Managing Technological Innovation*, Longman, London, 1980

[5] Kane, J., 'A primer for a new cross impact language – KSIM', *Technological Forecasting and Social Change*, 4 , 129–42 (1972)

[6] Makridakis, Spyros, 'Metaforecasting: ways of improving forecasting accuracy and usefulness', *International Journal of Forecasting*, (4), 467–491 (1988)

[7] Toffler, A. and Toffler H., *Creating a New Civilisation*, Turner Publishing, Atlanta, 1994

[8] Mercer, D., 'Large-scale conferencing for inexpert users', *Proceedings of the 1993 TeleTeaching Conference – Trondheim*, Elsevier, Oxford, 1993

[9] Mercer, D., 'The foreseeable future – "Millennium Project" qualitative results', *OR38 (Operational Research Society Conference)*, (September, 1996)

[10] Acemoglu, D. and Scott, A., 'Consumer confidence and rational expectations: are agent's beliefs consistent with the theory', *The Economic Journal*, 104 (January), 1–19 (1994)

[11] Wack, P., 'Scenarios: uncharted waters ahead', *Harvard Business Review*, 1985 (September–October), 139–150 (1985)

[12] Wack, P., 'Scenarios: "shooting the rapids"', *Harvard Business Review*, 1985 (November–December), 139–150 (1985)

[13] Schwartz, P., *The Art of the Long View*, Doubleday, London, 1991

[14] Aguilar, F. J., *Scanning the Business Environment*, Macmillan, London, 1967

[15] Wells, W. D., 'Group interviewing', in *Handbook of Marketing Research*. Robert Ferber, ed., McGraw-Hill, London, 1974

[16] Krueger, R. A., *Focus Groups: A Practical Guide for Applied Research*, Sage, London, 1988

[17] Holsti, O. R., *Content Analysis for the Social Sciences and Humanities*, Addison-Wesley, Wokingham, England, 1969

[18] Kahane, A., 'Scenarios for energy: Sustainable World vs. Global Mercantilism', *Long Range Planning*, 25(4), 38–46 (1992)

[19] Rockfellow, J. D., 'Wild cards: preparing for the "Big One"', *The Futurist*, 1994 (January–February), 14–19 (1994)

[20] Steinmuller, K., 'The future as wild card, 5'. *Internationale Sommerkademie des Sekretariats für Zukunftsforschung – Gelsenkirchen* (September, 1996)

[21] Mercer, D., 'The foreseeable future', *Management Decision*, 34(3), 55–61 (1996)

[22] Johnson, R. M., 'Market segmentation: a strategic management tool', *Journal of Marketing Research*, 8 (February), 13–18 (1971)

[23] Sampson, P., 'Qualitative research and motivation research', in *Consumer Market Research Handbook*, 3rd. ed., R. Worcester and J. Downham, eds, McGraw-Hill, Maidenhead, England, 1986

[24] Osgood, E. C., Succi, G. J. and Tannenbaum, P. H., *The Measurement of Meaning*, Urbana, New York, 1957

3.5 MONITORING

The discussion has concentrated so far upon the most difficult aspects of intelligence gathering, that of scanning and searching to detect the unexpected. Once the unexpected has been detected and has thus become the expected (in other words, a strong signal), the process moves into a different – easier – phase: monitoring subsequent developments in the field.

At this stage, key aspects of the phenomenon (usually, where possible, numeric features – such as sales volumes, penetration, opinion shifts, etc.) are scheduled for regular monitoring. This process can be almost routine, even to the extent that it can be run on an exception basis (only, for example, being reported to senior management when certain trigger levels are exceeded). Thus, for instance, Shell International scans the environment in general for all kinds of weak signals, but specifically monitors the consumption and supply of oil in considerable detail (because these are clearly the vital indicators for its business).

4 SHORT- AND MEDIUM-TERM FORECASTING

After undertaking appropriate research and environmental analysis, the next stage is to use your data to predict what will happen in the future – that is, to produce the forecast. The most traditional form, in business terms, is the numeric forecast associated with the annual budgetary procedures. You will no doubt have received a more than adequate grounding in such techniques, including time-series analysis, in earlier studies.

The main thing to be noted about relatively short-term forecasts is their unreliability. The evidence is that their accuracy is quite limited; unfortunately, many managers using them believe their accuracy is much higher than it actually is or ever could be! However, if the organisation is not to degenerate into anarchy, it must believe in and commit itself to the budget/target figures.

In Article 4.1 we will look at Makridakis's caveats about forecasting. He emphasises the limitations of short- and medium-term forecasting – which are the most common forms of forecast. A sound appreciation of these limitations is necessary for a grasp of the book as a whole. You should study his paper carefully so that you appreciate the concepts being discussed (though not the detail), and especially understand the major limitations on the use of such forecasts. *You do not, however, need to understand the statistical techniques described!*

The first part of the paper concentrates on the statistical limitations to forecasting, something which is intuitively felt by many managers (though not understood by them). The extent of inaccuracies and the number of different types of error may surprise many managers.

The key point of Makridakis's section on common mistakes is his emphasis that the test of any forecasting method is not how well it fits past data but how well it will predict future data. It is unfortunately a feature of business, along with many of the social sciences, that new techniques are invariably tested and justified on historical data. In the natural sciences, on the other hand, tests (which are much easier to make since the variables are usually under the control of the experimenter) are almost invariably undertaken in terms of the technique's ability to predict new events.[1] Unfortunately, this approach is a luxury not normally available to managers, and the complex uncertainties usually involved make business events much less predictable. Accordingly, forecasts in the business field are often heavily influenced by value-based judgements, and too many professional forecasters are busy selling products which achieve far less accuracy than is claimed for them.

In his final section on 'developing and using appropriate models', Spyros Makridakis once more makes his plea that forecasting techniques should be kept as simple as possible, since this means that managers are more likely to

---

[1] Karl R. Popper, *The Logic of Scientific Discovery* (Hutchinson, 1959).

make use of the forecast. What he does not say, but is equally important, is that models which are easily understood are those in which the limitations are most obvious to the user – and deviations more immediately evident.

His eventual recommendation is not that you should ignore forecasting (and hence long-range planning), but that you should understand the uncertainty involved. Uncertainty (where the probabilities are unknown, as opposed to risk, where they can be calculated) is a key feature to be taken into account in any long-range planning.

Now *quickly* read Article 4.1 below by Spyros Makridakis.[2] This is a very sophisticated critique of forecasting techniques – sometimes in considerable detail – and your task is to appreciate the general thrusts of his argument, without drowning in the detail!

Article 4.1 SPYROS MAKRIDAKIS:[3] 'METAFORECASTING – WAYS OF IMPROVING FORECASTING ACCURACY AND USEFULNESS'

ABSTRACT

Forecasting has a long history. An understanding of such history coupled with the study of the empirical evidence can provide invaluable information for improving the accuracy and usefulness of predictions. Statistical forecasting methods suffer from their inability to predict temporary or permanent changes in established patterns and/or relationships, while people oscillate between ignoring and overreacting to such changes. Moreover, statistical methods do not fully utilise the historical information that data contains, while subjective forecasters are selective, biased, and inconsistent in the way they use such information. Also, whereas statistical methods are objective, people are influenced by personal and political considerations, wishful thinking, and what may be undue optimism or pessimism. Finally, both judgmental and statistical methods usually underestimate future uncertainty. This paper deals with these issues and their influence on forecasting. It discusses how forecasting accuracy can be improved by understanding and correcting the problems inherent in statistical methods and the past mistakes of judgmental forecasters. Furthermore, it looks at the complementarity of judgemental and statistical forecasting and the need to wed the two, and considers their relative advantages/drawbacks along with the benefits of accurate forecasts and the uncertainty and errors.

INTRODUCTION

Forecasting is an indispensable activity in planning, strategy, and all other forms of future-oriented decision making, at both the individual and organisational levels. At the personal level it ranges from such trivial decisions as the time to get up in the morning so as not to arrive late for work to such important decisions as where to invest one's savings. Business decisions to build new factories, phase out or introduce new products, or invest in new technologies and a myriad of other undertakings depend upon accurate forecasts. Similarly governments determine monetary and fiscal matters, research funding, educational priorities, and industrial policies, basing these and similar decisions upon projections of future economic, technological, demographic, and competitive conditions. It thus becomes important to be able to forecast as

[2] Published by INSEAD, 77305 Fontainebleau Cedex, France, 1988.

[3] I would like to thank Chris Chatfield, Claude Faucheux, Robert Fildes, Ira Horowitz, Rob Weitz, and Robert Winkler for helpful comments on earlier drafts of this paper.

accurately as possible and to recognise the best way of utilising such forecasts to make more intelligent decisions.

The past few decades have witnessed some major developments in the field of forecasting. However, we have now reached a point which allows us to go beyond available forecasting methods and practices by changing our approach and way of thinking about forecasting. This is what I call metaforecasting. It requires an understanding of the problems of statistical methods and the mistakes made by judgemental forecasters so that new, imaginative, and realistic solutions can be found.

The paper is organised as follows: first, the perceptions and reality of forecasting are presented, with an emphasis on empirical evidence and the experience that has been accumulated through forecasting applications. Second, the extent of future predictability, and the factors that affect forecasting accuracy, are discussed. Third, the sources of forecasting errors and future uncertainty are outlined. A distinction is made between random forecasting errors, and those that result from temporary or permanent changes in established patterns and/or relationships. Fourth, common judgemental mistakes made while producing and utilising forecasts are examined, their implications considered, and ways of avoiding similar mistakes in the future are proposed. Finally, ways for improving forecasting accuracy, both statistically and judgementally, as well as for bettering the process of making and utilising the forecasts are proposed.

THE PERCEPTIONS AND REALITY OF FORECASTING

In 1965, Paul Fama of the University of Chicago published an influential paper in which he proved that predicting stock market changes (i.e. increases or decreases from "today's" level), either as a whole or for any individual stocks, could not be done any better than using "today's" price as a forecast. This implies that investors in the stock market cannot profit from individual forecasts of stock prices, without inside information (an illegal activity). Fama proved scientifically what others before him had discussed, and what has been

observed since the early 1920s. In actual comparisons, stock market experts and professional managers do not outperform such market averages as Standard and Poor's 500 stocks. Indeed, the 1986 performance of institutional money managers climbed in value by only 16.9% while the S & P 500 rose 18.7%, beating out more than 67% of the managed funds surveyed (Wallace, 1987). Similarly, in 1987 all equity funds increased 3.3% while the S & P 500 climbed 5.2%. Moreover, the same statistics/figures for the 1983–87 period are 12.5% and 16.4% for mutual funds and the S & P 500 respectively (Laiderman, 1988).

Even today, the great majority of investors (both individuals and institutions) still prefer a stock analyst or a professional manager to take care of their money. Although by luck some analysts or managers might do better than a market average for a certain period of time, all evidence suggests that *consistent* above-average performance is virtually impossible. This means that a random portfolio of stocks will perform on average as well as one that is selected by an expert. However, few people feel comfortable with a random selection when investing their life savings.

The example of the stock market is not unique. Future markets, exchange rates, interest rates, and numerous other variables cannot be predicted any more accurately than by taking the most recent value available as the best forecast for the future. A major activity within the field of forecasting has been the evaluation of hundreds of thousands of forecasts made in the past to determine their accuracy. The truth about forecasting that has emerged from this evidence is not what the great majority of people would like to believe. Although some events can be predicted with a high degree of accuracy, others are less predictable, or completely unpredictable. Individuals, business managers, and government administrators, as users of forecasts, need to know specifically what *can and cannot* be predicted, since there are important consequences if the future turns out to be different from that for which plans have been made. Most people, however, experience a strong psychological need to know the future. This is partly due to fear of the unknown and the anxiety accompanying such fear, and partly due to the realisation that if the future could be predicted threats could be avoided and opportunities exploited. Thus, people feel more secure by believing that someone can forecast the future for them. Such beliefs, however, are illusory and run contrary to strong empirical evidence.

THE PREDICTABILITY OF THE FUTURE

Although certain animals (bees and ants, for example) do possess some concept of the future, humans are unique in their ability to comprehend and plan for a wide range of future events. Humans can predict the future by observing regularities in certain phenomena (the daily sunrise or the seasons of the year) or causal relationships (cultivating seeds and growing crops or intercourse and pregnancy). A *prerequisite* of any form of forecasting, whether judgmental or quantitative, is that a pattern or relationship exists concerning some event of interest. If it does exist, the pattern/relationship has to be correctly identified and projected in order to be able to forecast. When patterns/relationships do not exist, forecasting is not possible although judgemental assessments based on similar past events can be made. Scientific progress has considerably improved our ability to predict future events, albeit unevenly across various areas. In the frictionless natural/physical domain, forecasting accuracy is perfect for all practical purposes. In other areas, notably in the economic/business fields, predictability ranges from excellent to nil.

In the frictionless physical/natural domain, not only are patterns exact and relationships precise but, for practical purposes, they do not change over time. This, however, is not the case in the economic or business fields, where patterns and relationships are intermixed with random noise and can change (sometimes considerably) over time. Two major aspects that cause patterns and/ or relationships to change are the capriciousness of human behaviour (e.g. shifts in attitudes brought on by fashions or differences among individuals) and people's ability to influence future events with their actions (the forecasts themselves can become selffulfilling and/or self-defeating prophecies that change established patterns/relationships).

Exhibit 1 summarises the factors that influence predictability and the characteristics of patterns/ relationships as a function of the events involved and the forecasting horizon. The longer the forecasting horizon, the greater the chance of a change in patterns or relationships, because people's behaviour or attitudes can change, there is more time to use the forecasts to change the future in order to achieve desired benefits, or because of some fundamental changes in the environment, e.g., technology. Furthermore, exhibit 1 describes some general factors that systematically influence predictability. These factors are briefly described below:

1   *Number of items*: The larger the number of items involved (all other things being equal), the more accurate the forecasts. Because of the statistical law of large numbers, the size of forecasting errors (and therefore accuracy) decreases as the number of items being forecast increases and vice versa. Thus, we can more accurately predict the number of telephone calls arriving at a switching station during a five-minute interval than the number of Apple computers sold on a certain day.

2   *Homogeneity of data*: The more homogeneous the data (all other things being equal), the more accurate the forecasts and vice versa. Thus, data referring to a single region can predict seasonality more accurately than data covering many regions of varying weather patterns. Similarly, sales of consumer goods only could be predicted more accurately than sales covering both consumers and industrial customers.

3   *Elasticity of demand*: The more inelastic the demand (all other things being equal), the more accurate the forecasts. Thus, the demand for necessities can be forecast with a higher degree of accuracy than that for non-necessities and demand for non-durable goods with a higher degree of accuracy than for durables. Related to the elasticity of demand is the influence of business cycles. Such cycles impact least on inelastic demand and most on elastic demand. People must eat and acquire necessities which are given priority over other purchases in case of income reductions, as during recessions.

4   *Competition*: The greater the competition (all other things being equal), the more difficult it is to forecast since by their actions competitors can use the forecasts to change the course of future events, thus invalidating the forecasts.

SOURCES OF FORECASTING ERRORS AND FUTURE UNCERTAINTY

In frictionless physical/natural sciences, the identification and verification of patterns/relationships is exact and objective. For all practical purposes, precision instruments reduce measurement errors to zero, and laboratory or controlled experimentation allows keeping all factors constant except the one being tested. Moreover, feedback is unambiguous. In the economic and business domains, however, measurement errors abound, laboratory-type experimentation is not possible, and feedback is infrequent and often not clear. Furthermore, because of the complexity of economic/business situations, the inconsistency of human behaviour, the varying time lags between action and outcome, and several other factors, forecasting errors much larger than those observed in natural/physical sciences are a fact of life. The size and persistence of such errors depend upon the following factors.

Erroneous Identification of Patterns/Relationships: an illusory pattern or relationship identified when none exists. This is possible both in judgemental and statistical forecasting. In their quest to master and control the environment people often see illusory correlation, while statistical models based on a small number of observations (as, for instance, with new products) can 'identify' a pattern that is not maintained over a longer period. Similarly, a relationship between two variables might be spurious, existing only because a third factor causes both variables to move in the same direction. Alternatively, patterns or relationships that exist might be wrongly identified or ignored, either because sufficient information/data is not available or because reality is too complex to be understood and/or modelled with a limited number of variables (see Einhom and Hogarth, 1987). Illusory or inappropriate identification can cause serious and persistent

forecasting errors, since the future could turn out to be very different from that which had been postulated by an erroneous pattern or relationships.

Inexact patterns and/or imprecise relationships: in the social sciences, patterns are not exact and relationships are not precise, for the reasons discussed above. Although an average *pattern* or relationship can be identified, fluctuations around such an average exist in almost all cases. The purpose of statistical modelling is to identify patterns/relationships in such a way as to make past fluctuations around the average as small and random as possible. Whether or not this is a good strategy is questionable (see below), but, even assuming it is appropriate, we cannot guarantee that future errors will be random or symmetric or that they will not exceed a certain magnitude.

Changing patterns/relationships: in the social sciences, patterns and/or relationships are constantly changing over time in a way which, in the great majority of cases, is not predictable. Changes in patterns and/or relationships can cause large and persistent errors the magnitude of which cannot be known in advance. The size of such errors would depend upon the magnitude and duration of the change.

Uncertainty caused by forecasting errors

Forecasting errors are inevitable in a wide variety of situations. For planning and strategy purposes it is important to assess the size of such errors in order to minimise their negative consequences (e.g. having no products to sell or accumulating large inventories). If it is *assumed* that the pattern/relationship (a) has been correctly identified *and* (b) would not change unpredictably during the forecasts, the errors around the average pattern or relationship can be found and their variance computed. In statistical models, once the variance is known and if it is *assumed* that the errors are (c) random, (d) normally distributed, and (e) constant, it is possible to assess the magnitude of future errors and, therefore, the uncertainty in forecasting.

The standard procedure used in statistics is to construct a symmetric interval around the most likely forecast of the identified pattern or relationship that would include the actual future value, say, 95% of the time. The range of this

Exhibit 1   Extent/ability to forecast and factors involved

Events/situations that can be forecasted for all practical purposes with a perfect degree of accuracy	Forecasting horizon	Events/situations that can be forecasted with a high degree of accuracy	Events/situations that can be forecasted with a medium degree of accuracy	Events/situations that can be forecasted with a low degree of accuracy	Highly inaccurate forecasting of events/situations	Unable to forecast more accurately than utilising the most recent actual values to do so	Unable to forecast more accurately than statistical (actuary) averages	Unable to forecast at all
Frictionless Natural/ Physical events/ phenomena (e.g. the exact arrival of Halley's comet or its nearest distance to the earth; the exact time of sunrise a day, month or year from today; the result of putting two atoms of hydrogen and one of oxygen together).	Short (up to 3 months)	Large numbers of items (products, customers, services)	(a)		Small numbers of items	Events determined by the collective actions of many individuals/ organisations (attempting to maximise their benefits) when information is disseminated efficiently (e.g., the stock and futures markets, exchange rates, prices of almost all raw materials and most finished products).	Unusual and/or infrequent events (e.g., a fire destroying one's home or a factory; a major car accident; the accidental death of a young, healthy person; an extremely severe snowstorm).	Unexpected or inconceivable events (e.g., the growth and importance of computers for someone before 1950; the oil crisis for a decision maker in the 1960s; the fall of the Shah of Iran for a political analyst before 1970).
		Highly aggregate quantities	(b)		Single items			
			(a) and (b)					
	Medium (3 months to 2 years)	Forecasting horizon close to 3 months		(c)	Forecasting horizon close to 2 years			
		Inelastic demand		(d)	Elastic demand			
		No competition		(e)	Strong competition			
	Long (2 years or more)	Forecasting horizon close to 2 years	(a), (b), (c), (d) and (e)		Forecasting horizon of many years			
		Low degree of technological change			High degree of technological change			
		Strong barriers to entry			No barriers to entry			

Characteristics of pattern/ relationships
- Patterns or relationships do not change over time.
- Events cannot be influenced by human actions.
- Patterns are exact.
- Relations are precise.

Characteristics of patterns/relationships
Patterns/relationships vary widely (ranging from those listed in the column on the left side to those listed in the three columns on the right) depending upon the factors specified above.

Characteristics of patterns/ relationships
- Patterns and relationships change over time.
- Events can be influenced by human actions.
- Patterns are not exact.
- Relationships are not precise.

Characteristics of patterns/ relationships
- Aggregate patterns (involving large numbers of cases/ people) exist. The larger the number involved, the more precise the pattern and vice versa.
- Patterns might change over time but usually do so slowly. Relationships are weak or non-existent.

Characteristics of patterns/ relationships
- Patterns and/ or relationships do not exist or they cannot be identified given today's knowledge.

confidence interval denotes the *normal* uncertainty associated with the forecast if assumptions (a), (b), (c), (d), *and* (e) hold true. In such a case, forecasting errors are random. Furthermore, since it is assumed that they are and will remain constant and normally distributed, their size can be estimated for the great majority of cases (e.g. 95% of the time). Alternatively, it can be said that the actual value being forecast would be within the confidence interval postulated by the model 95% of the time. This postulated range defines the normal uncertainty (covering 95% of the cases) to be the equivalent to the 95% confidence interval. But what about the remaining 5%?

On average, 5% of the time some actual values would be outside the 95% confidence interval postulated by the forecasting model. This involves additional uncertainty which inevitably exists but cannot be routinely incorporated into planning. It is generally too expensive to be constantly prepared to face large forecasting errors that would appear about one time out of twenty. Dealing with this *unusual* uncertainty would depend to a great extent upon the costs of ending up with extremely large overestimates or underestimates of the actual values (in the emergency room of a hospital, for instance, the cost of running out of a certain type of blood is much higher than having too much stock). The costs of over- or underestimating the future are not, in other words, symmetric. Although often ignored, the 5% representing unusual errors must also be taken into consideration by forecasters and dealt with, using a formalised approach such as a Bayesian framework.

When assumptions (a), (b), (c), (d) and (e) do *not* hold, forecasting errors are not necessarily *random or symmetric*. Furthermore, assessing their magnitude is not always possible since they can persist for several/many periods. Although invalidation of any of the five assumptions mentioned above can cause nonrandom and non-symmetric errors, it is assumption (b) – constancy of patterns/relationships – that is the most critical. As has been mentioned, in real life few patterns or relationships involving economic or business situations stay constant over time. Furthermore, although the validity of assumptions (a), (c), (d), and (e) can be checked, it is *not* usually possible to do so with assumption (b). The beginning,

duration, and importance of changes in patterns or relationships, even if known to have occurred in the past, cannot usually be predicted. Furthermore, unexpected changes that occur for the first time can also take place.

The process of estimating forecasting errors and future uncertainty judgementally does not provide more accurate or precise answers than those of statistical models. One might expect experts to be able to assess forecasting errors and uncertainty in an accurate fashion. This, however, is rarely the case. Furthermore, the process used to make judgemental estimates of uncertainty is not well understood (Lawrence and Makridakis, 1988). People have difficulty in assessing forecasting errors realistically and dealing with their consequences. Forecasting errors and future uncertainty are topics they feel threatened by and do not usually approach in an objective and rational manner.

The following is a list of major sources of change (both of a temporary and permanent nature) in established patterns and/or relationships and therefore of serious forecasting errors.

Special events: A fire, a major breakdown in machinery, an extremely cold winter or hot summer, and other similar environmental events, over which one has little or no control, can occur, bringing changes in established patterns.

Special actions: Special actions of the organisation (such as an advertising or promotional campaign, the announcement of or an actual price increase, or similar actions of competitors) can influence future events and modify established patterns of relationships. Some of these special actions (and their effects) can be known, while some others (in particular, those of competitors) cannot be predicted.

Cycles: General and business-related variables are often influenced by economic cycles, the average duration of which is about 4.5 years and possibly also by long-term cyclical waves the duration of which can be as long as 50–60 years. Although cycles are repetitive, their duration and depth can vary considerably in a way that cannot be predicted except on the average. Cycles do, therefore, cause temporary drifts in established patterns and/or relationships and become a major source of errors and uncertainty in forecasting.

Fashions: Fashions and other fads can modify established patterns in a substantial way. By definition the effect of fashions/fads is temporary and can become a source of huge errors in forecasting. For example, the exponential growing demand for C.B. radios or video games became negative in a period of a few months, causing huge errors in forecasting and the bankruptcy of many companies which had predicted and planned for a continuation of the exponential growth.

Technological and environmental change: Technological innovations, coupled with considerations about health and quality of life, can bring about fundamental changes in established attitudes and consumption patterns. Such technological innovation, coupled with governmental actions (e.g. deregulation), increased specialisation, and changes in international trade, can lead to basic changes in established patterns and/or relationships. In addition, political parties with various economic philosophies, consumer sentiments, fashions, the international political climate, and the international competitive structure can change over time in an unpredictable way, causing drifts in long-established trends or long-held relationships.

Exhibit 2 summarises the various types of forecasting errors and distinguishes three types of uncertainty (expected, unexpected, and inconceivable); and it classifies changes in patterns or relationships as temporary and permanent. Planning and strategy have to deal with all three types of uncertainty. The benefits and costs involved in being prepared to face each type of forecasting error versus the dangers associated with not being prepared to deal with such errors need to be taken into consideration (see below).

COMMON MISTAKES IN MAKING AND USING FORECASTS

Forecasting users are often discontented with large errors, as well as with the failure to foresee changes in the economy or in specific events. Their complaints are well founded and are supported by many evaluations of past forecasts and their degree of accuracy. Ascher (1978), for instance, found errors ranging from a few to several hundred percentage points when he evaluated GNP, population, transportation, and energy forecasts. Moreover, he concluded that it was impossible to know beforehand the most accurate method or forecaster. Furthermore, each forecast was based on several assumptions the evaluation of which by a potential user was as time-consuming as making new forecasts. Ahlers and Lakonishok (1983), Armstrong (1985), Hogarth and Makridakis (1981), Makridakis *et al.* (1982), Zamowitz (1984), and Makridakis (1986) have reached similar conclusions after evaluating large numbers of forecasts made in the past. Does this evidence mean that forecasting is useless and should be abandoned as an activity or field? The answer is a definite no.

Abandoning formal forecasting would mean that predictions about the future would be made in an intuitive or judgemental fashion, since forecasts are required, in one form or another, for planning, strategy, and future-oriented decision making. Empirical evidence (Armstrong (1985), Dawes (1986), Goldberg (1970), Hogarth and Makridakis (1981), Makridakis (1986)) shows, in an unambiguous manner, that the accuracy of intuitive, judgemental approaches is *not* any better than that of statistical models in the great majority of cases. In addition, judgemental forecasts are much more expensive than equivalent statistical ones. Thus, we *cannot* shy away and abandon formal forecasting because of problems, since the alternative is even worse. Ways of improving the accuracy of formal forecasting must be found. As a beginning, a clear understanding of existing problems and mistakes made in the past is needed.

Judgemental mistakes

People can be easily persuaded that someone (person or method) can forecast for them accurately. Although this might be possible in the domain of the natural/physical sciences, it is rarely or never the case in people's personal lives or the business/economic fields. Forecasting errors can result from many sources (see exhibit 2) and cannot be eliminated by more sophisticated models or more gifted forecasters. Believing that uncertainty can be eradicated through forecasting is therefore dangerous and has no empirical backing. Worse, it results in bad surprises.

Exhibit 2 Forecasting errors and types of future uncertainty				
Causes of forecasting errors	Types of future uncertainty			
	Expected		Unexpected	Inconceivable
	Normal	Unusual		
Random fluctuations	95% of the errors around the average pattern or relationship	The remaining 5% of errors. That is, large errors that would occur, on average about one time out of twenty.	A not-too-serious car accident.	
Changes in patterns/ relationships Temporary	Special events (e.g., a colder than average winter) & special actions (e.g., a promotional campaign, a new product introduced by a competitor, etc.)	An "average" recession not too different from previous ones. A fire.	A serious recession of the 1974/75 type. The energy crisis (for planning and strategies considered at the end of the 1970s).	The 1973/79 energy crisis (for planning and strategies being considered in the 1960s).
Permanent	Gradual changes in consumer attitudes and buying trends caused by technological innovation and concerns about health and quality of life.	Big changes in attitudes and buying trends caused by new technologies or governmental intervention (e.g. the deregulation of the airline industry at the end of the 1970s).	A collapse of the international financial system. The Industrial Revolution (for people living at the beginning of the 18th century).	A large meteorite hits and destroys life on earth. A major nuclear accident or war destroying life on earth (to someone living before 1930).

Claims about forecasting accuracy and usefulness need to be checked against reality. Concretely, forecasting users must ask for specific evidence of how accurately the person/method did in correctly *predicting changes* in the relevant event(s), as in many cases it is trivial to predict the continuation of a prevailing condition. Furthermore, it is not enough to be told how well a model fits past data, or how accurately the forecasts have been over a *limited* range of time in the past. In addition, it is important to know how well the forecasts have done in accurately predicting not only the event of interest but also its complement (e.g. if someone always predicts a recession for the coming year, he or she would inevitably predict all recessions perfectly, but this does not mean much since he or she would be wrong in predicting the non-recession years). Unless these facts can be established, it is dangerous to believe naively in claims of superior forecasting accuracy or the alleged benefits from such forecasts.

Judgemental forecasts are greatly influenced by wishful thinking and political considerations. Furthermore, judgemental biases are common in forecasting (see Hogarth and Makridakis, 1981; Moriarty and Adams 1984; Schnaars, 1984). Intuitive or judgemental forecasts can lead to large and systematic errors caused by biases in the way information about the future is recalled and processed. Exhibit 3 lists the *most* critical biases affecting forecasting and briefly outlines ways of reducing their negative consequences. Since no empirical work has been done to identify the most important judgemental biases relating to forecasting, those listed in exhibit 3 are based on my own experience with judgemental forecasts made mostly in business organisations.

Exhibit 4 shows an example of a judgemental bias, recency. Recency effects have, for example, greatly influenced oil price forecasts during the last 20 years, while basic economic considerations, substitution effects, and supply-and-demand factors have been ignored. The costs of such a bias in terms of actual expenditures have been enormous (see exhibit 4 for some examples). For instance, G.M., assuming that oil prices were going to continue to increase, has spent more than $60 billion since 1975 to come up with new, small, gas-efficient cars. It seems that, for the most part, this $60 billion was wasted (Hampton and Norman, 1987), primarily because the forecast that the price of oil would keep increasing turned out to be wrong. Mexico and several other oil-producing countries almost went bankrupt in the early 1980s by basing their development budget on oil prices of $40 a barrel.

STATISTICAL MODELS: PROBLEMS/ MISCONCEPTIONS

Statistical models assume constancy of patterns and/or relationships or predictability in the way that changes will occur. This is a critical assumption which is not made clear to those studying or using forecasting. The assumption, although correct in the frictionless natural/physical sciences, is not realistic for the business/economic fields. Once constancy or predictability has been assumed, a model is *fitted to past data*. In methods originating in the field of statistics, choosing an appropriate model is guided by two

criteria. First, the errors ought to be random; and second, the sum of the square errors for *one step-ahead forecasts* ought to be as small as possible. It must be realised, however, that both of these criteria apply to past data, when constancy or predictability of changes has been assumed. There is therefore no guarantee that future errors will be random, symmetric, or within the range postulated by the variance of past errors, since future patterns/relationships can be different than those assumed by the statistical model.

Minimizing the one-step-ahead errors of a model fitted to historical data cannot ensure that future errors will be minimal since constancy and/or predictability of patterns and/or relationships cannot be ensured. The rank correlations between model fitting and forecasting for eight methods and eighteen forecasting horizons for the series in the M-Competition, for instance, are small to start with and become zero after the fourth horizon (Makridakis, 1986).

Exhibit 5 shows a series (MNM61) of the M-Competition and the forecasts of eight methods used in this competition. All methods (except single exponential) assumed that the uptrend in the data would continue and forecast appropriately. Single exponential smoothing assumed a 'no change' approach and extrapolated a horizontal trend. Since the trend changed (see exhibit 5, to the right of 'Present', *all* methods except single exponential smoothing made enormous errors in forecasting. The reason that single exponential smoothing did better is not that it knew that a change in pattern would take place but because it always forecasts horizontally. Not much could have been done statistically with the data of exhibit 5 to have predicted the sudden change in trend. In such a case, only judgemental knowledge could have been used to predict the change in the data pattern.

Exhibit 6 shows a more interesting situation. The series involved (QND37) has increased substantially for five periods, then in the last two has started declining. In such a case the forecasts of the same eight methods behave very differently. Some methods (Box–Jenkins, Parzen) completely ignored the decline in the last two periods, assuming it to be random, and extrapolated a continuation of the latest uptrend. Bayesian forecasting, however, decided that the latest

Exhibit 3	Common biases in judgemental forecasting and proposed ways of reducing their negative impact	
Type of bias	**Description of bias**	**Ways of reducing the negative impact of bias**
Optimism, wishful thinking	People's preferences for future outcomes affect their forecast of such outcomes	• Have the forecasts made by a third, uninterested party • Have more than one person make the forecasts independently
Inconsistency	Inability to apply the same decision criteria in similar situations	• Formalise the decision-making process • Create decision-making rules to be followed
Recency	The importance of the most recent events dominates those in the less recent past, which are downgraded or ignored	• Realise that cycles exist and that not all ups and downs are permanent • Consider the fundamental factors that affect the event of interest
Availability	Ease with which specific events can be recalled from memory	• Present complete information • Present information in a way that points out all sides of the situation to be considered
Anchoring	Predictions are unduly influenced by initial information, which is given more weight when forecasting	• Start with objective forecasts • Ask people to forecast in terms of changes from statistical forecasts and demand the reasons for doing so
Illusory correlations	Belief that patterns exist and/or two variables are causally related when this is not true	• Verify statistical significance of patterns • Model relationships, if possible, in terms of changes
Conservatism	Failure to change (or changing slowly) one's own mind in light of new information/evidence	• Monitor systematic changes and build procedures to take action when systematic changes are identified
Selective perception	Tendency to see problems in terms of one's own background and experience	• Ask people with different backgrounds and experience to prepare the forecasts independently
Regression effects	Persistent increases or decreases might be due to random reasons which, if true, would increase the chance of a change in trend	• Explain that in the case of random errors the chances of a negative error increase when several positive ones have occurred.

downturn was permanent. Thus, it correctly predicted the change in the data pattern and produced forecasts that turned out to be the most accurate. The predictions of Holt's exponential smoothing are somewhere in between those of Box–Jenkins/Parzen and Bayesian forecasting.

Regression ignored both the most recent uptrend and the latest decline, assuming them to be random fluctuations around the long-term trend. Single exponential smoothing has, as always, assumed a 'no change' attitude. In the final analysis, the forecasting accuracy of the various

Exhibit 4	Oil prices and oil forecasts			
Year	Actual oil prices	Reasons for prevailing prices	Forecasts made for future periods and their reasoning	Economic facts ignored in the period 1950–1987
Before 1970	Between 1950 and 1970 oil prices (in current dollars) did *not* change.	Multinational oil companies (mostly the seven sisters, as they were called) had complete control of oil production and therefore supply. It was in their interest to keep oil prices low and so they did.	Prices will continue to be cheap or at least they will grow below inflation and energy supply will be abundant.	The importance of long term economic forces was ignored. This was the case before 1970 when the cartel of oil companies and its ability to maintain low oil prices were not questioned.
				• After 1973 decision makers overreacted to the price increases in oil. They assumed that prices would continue increasingly at high rates or in the best of scenarios 1–2% above inflation.
1971 to 1973	Oil prices were raised from $1.80 in 1970 to $3.30 in 1973.	OPEC became a cohesive cartel (to a great extent as a reaction to the existing cartel of oil companies). Prices were raised to make up for the lost buying power as oil prices had not followed increases in inflation.	Oil prices will increase to follow inflation. Although energy will not be as cheap as before 1970 no major problems were envisioned. OPEC's share of the market in the year 2000 was forecasted as 66.7%.	• The fact that similar producers' cartels have not worked in the past was not taken into account.
				• The importance of basic economic laws (e.g. higher prices increase supply and decrease demand) was not taken into consideration/account in making oil price forecasts.
1974 to 1978	A huge increase brought the price of a barrel of oil to $11.60. It was followed by several smaller increases bringing the price to $13.	The 1973 Arab-Israeli war was used as an excuse to raise prices by 300%. OPEC became a major political force internationally. The trade surplus of oil-producing countries reached many billions of dollars.	Since oil was going to run out soon it was natural that its price was going to go up. Prices of $50 per barrel of oil by 1985 were common. OPEC's share of the oil market in the year 2000 had dropped in the meantime to 55%.	**Typical mistakes made in the period 1950–1987** • Utilities switched from coal to oil in the sixties and back to coal in the seventies.

Continued on next page ...

Year	Actual oil prices	Reasons for prevailing prices	Forecasts made for future periods and their reasoning	Economic facts ignored in the period 1950–1987
1979 to 1981	Another huge increase in 1979 raised the price of a barrel of oil to $30. Several smaller increases bought prices to a record $36 a barrel.	OPEC, by controlling production, kept raising prices. Industrialised nations and third world countries became hostages of OPEC pricing decisions.	Prices will continue rising above inflation. Forecasts of $65 in 1990 and $333 by the year 2000 were common. OPEC's share of the world market in the year 2000 had dropped further to 30%.	• Oil-producing countries (e.g. Mexico) almost went bankrupt by basing their development budget on oil prices of $40 or more.
1982 to 1985	Oil prices started decreasing. By end of 1985 the price of a barrel of oil was $28.	Energy conservation, new oil discoveries, alternative sources of energy, smaller and more efficient cars, and decreased consumption because of higher prices decreased demand for OPEC oil and reduced OPEC's economic and political power.	The tempo of increases in oil prices will slow down but the increases will still be 1–2% above inflation. In the mean time the forecast of OPEC's share in the year 2000 had dropped to 20%.	• Oil-consuming countries (e.g. Japan) negotiated long-term contracts to purchase oil at $30 or $40 a barrel. • R&D projects were initiated for developing new energy sources. These projects were abandoned as oil prices dropped.
1986 to 1987	Prices of oil tumbled. After having dropped to as little as $10 a barrel they finished at $13 a barrel by the end of 1986.	Inability to control production resulted in the actual collapse of OPEC as a cartel capable of controlling production and therefore oil prices. Long-term economic forces brought an equilibrium to the supply and demand of oil.	Oil prices will stay in the $10–15 a barrel range (in constant 1986 prices). No shortages of oil will develop. OPEC's share in the year 2000 will drop to 15%.	• New exploitations of oil fields bought at high costs were abandoned. • High investments made to extract oil from tarsands, shale oil, synthetic oil etc., were abandoned with losses in the billions of dollars.
1987	Oil prices have been fluctuating around $17.	OPEC countries have been observing a production limit and most non-OPEC countries go along. Saudi Arabia is cutting its production when supply exceeds demand.	*Author's forecast:* At present oil is overpriced by $4–8 a barrel (depending upon estimate). Once this has been corrected oil prices will, in the long run, follow inflation. If demand for oil increases more than average, oil prices will increase more than inflation in the short and medium term. When efficient engines and/or new energy sources are discovered oil prices will, in the long run, decrease below inflation.	

methods depended on the fact that the latest downturn continued during the eight quarters the forecasts were tested. This is not always the case, however.

The model fitting, one-step-ahead Mean Square Error (MSE) or the corresponding Mean Absolute Percentage Error (MAPE), of exhibits 5 and 6 give no indication of the impending disaster during forecasting. Furthermore, the confidence intervals constructed are too narrow and miss almost all actual values for most of the methods. The series in exhibit 5 is very different from that in exhibit 6. In the series in exhibit 5 there are no indications of the forthcoming downturn. In exhibit 6, however, there are several indications during the past of temporary drifts from the established pattern. Forecasting in period 24 for periods 25–32 or in period 34 for periods 35–42 would have resulted in high errors similar to those during the forecasts for periods 41 to 48. However, such information was ignored by all forecasting methods which based their predictions on one-step-ahead forecasting errors and the fact that a change in data (uptrend and then a brief decline) took place in the recent past (Makridakis, 1987).

Combined judgemental/statistical misconceptions

Contrary to widespread belief, empirical evidence has shown that predicting cyclical turning points is extremely difficult or impossible, even at macro-economic levels (Makridakis, 1982; Ahlers and Lakonishok, 1983; McNees, 1979; Zarnowitz, 1984). The cycles that characterise many series are of varying duration and depth, and, although statements about 'average' behaviour can be made, individual differences among cycles can be enormous. This makes 'the next' turning point virtually impossible to predict unless it occurs at a level that is close to the average of the past. Moreover, leading indicators do not provide consistent warnings of impending turns sufficiently in advance to be useful for forecasting purposes. Their biggest advantage is to confirm after the fact that a cyclical turn has occurred.

The belief that competitive behaviour can be predicted (e.g. Porter, 1985) is optimistic to a fault. Although in the past competitive actions in certain industries could have been inferred through competitive signalling, this is hardly the case for the great majority of industries or for the future. First, it is difficult even to define what constitutes competition. Second, competitors often give false signals. Third, competitors' behaviour could change drastically during periods of worsening economic conditions when the need for accurate forecasting is the keenest. Fourth, external events (e.g. new technologies, legislation, exchange rates, foreign entrants, etc.) that cannot be predicted in advance can substantially change the competitive structure of a given industry. Thus, the assertion that a model or a person can predict competitive actions is not supported either by empirical evidence or by theoretical reasoning.

Finally, both statistical models and people tend to underestimate uncertainty. In statistical models, the underestimation was the largest for yearly series (28%), the smallest for monthly ones (5%), and in between for quarterly data (25%) (Makridakis and Hibon, 1987). Judgemental forecasters also tend to underestimate uncertainty most of the time. Such underestimation is influenced by the complexity of and familiarity with the task, as well as the involvement of the person making the forecasts (see Fischoff, Slovic and Lichtenstein, 1977; Lawrence and Makridakis, 1988).

Exhibit 7 summarises a great deal of the preceding discussion. It also lists common mistakes made in the past and ways of avoiding them, both classified according to forecasting horizons. In summary, the major mistake in the short term has been to ignore special events and actions and their implications for planning. In the medium term, the major mistake has been to ignore cycles or other turning points and their implications for planning and strategy. In the long term, finally, managers have oscillated between an inability or unwillingness to introduce new technologies on the one hand, and premature investment in new technologies which turn out not to be commercially viable on the other. This has been particularly true when managers are over-dazzled by the alleged technological wonders of new inventions of which they tend to overestimate the importance and applicability. In an extensive study of forecasts made between 1960 and 1980, Schnaars and Berenson (1986) concluded that the majority of long-term new product forecasts failed because of unbridled optimism in overvaluing new technologies.

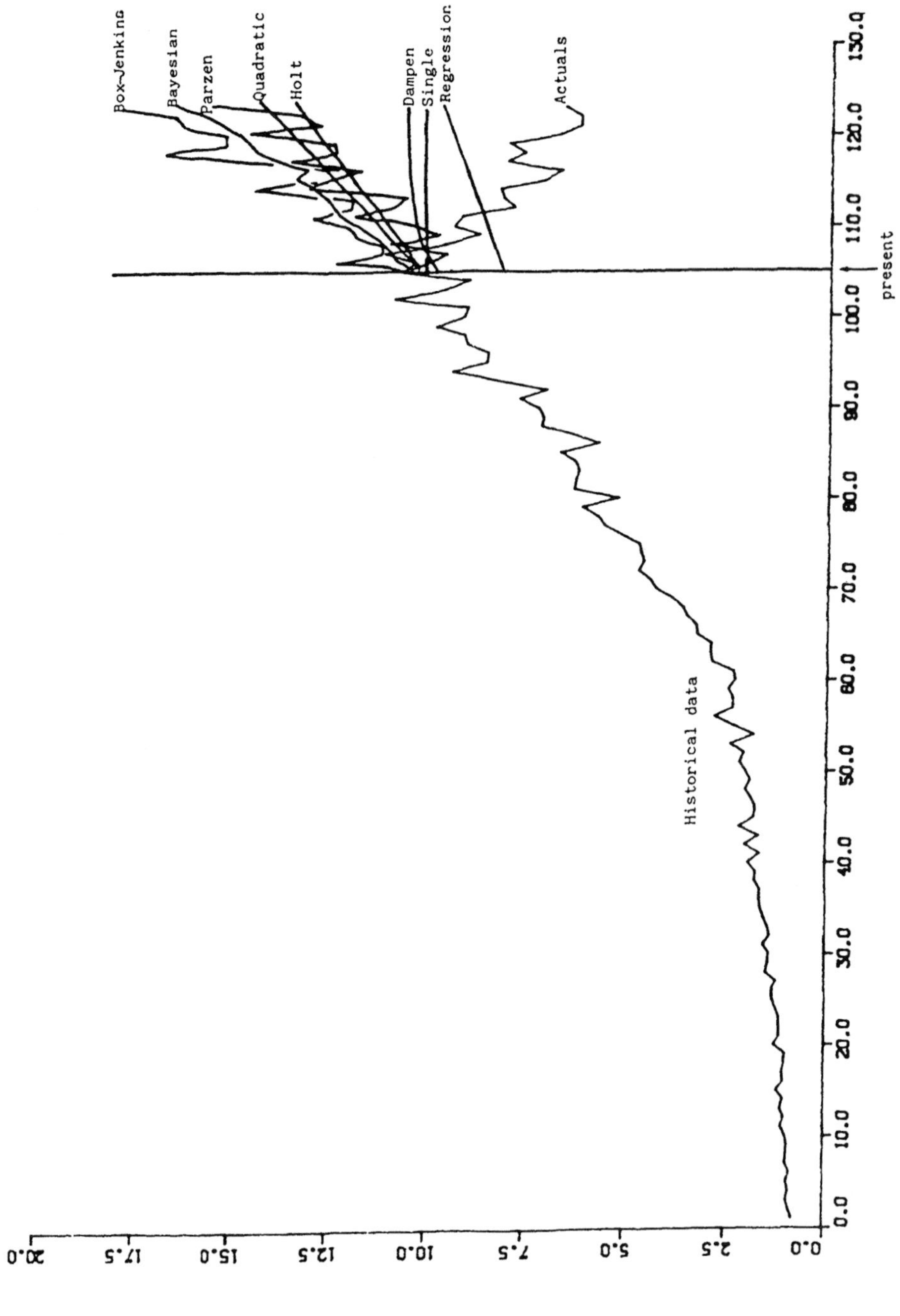

EXHIBIT 5   A monthly series (MNM61) of the M-Competition (with an unexpected pattern change while forecasting) and the forecasts of eight methods

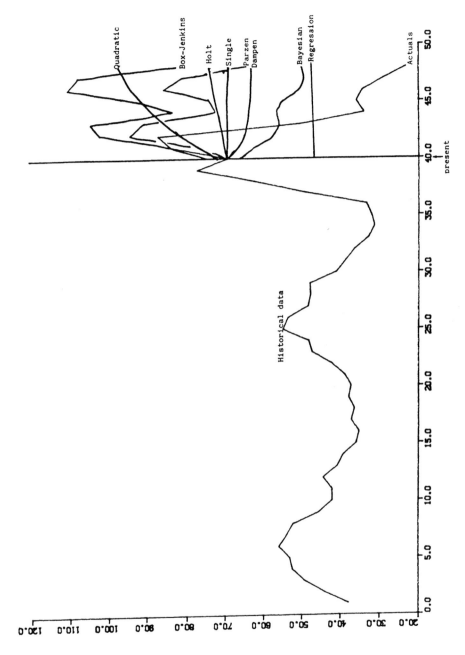

EXHIBIT 6   A quarterly series (QND37) of the M-Competition (with a pattern change just before forecasting) and the forecasts of eight methods

Exhibit 7   Areas/aspects that can and cannot be forecasted and implications involved

Time Horizon of Forecasting	Major areas/aspects that can be forecasted with a reasonable degree of accuracy	Major benefits from accurate forecasting	Major sources of surprise or unexpected forecasting errors	Problems/difficulties caused by surprise or unexpected forecasting errors	Typical mistakes (found through the empirical evaluation of past forecasts) that caused surprises and unexpected errors	Improving the forecasting process and the utilisation of forecasts
Short Term (less than 3 months)	• Seasonality in sales • Promotional and advertising actions • Required level of inventories • Impact of price changes • Cash inflows and outflows • Raw and other material requirements • Workforce, personnel needs	• Improved customer satisfaction • Better production and/or service scheduling • Fewer inventories • More effective advertising/promotion policies • More effective pricing • Policies • More profitable cash management • Better material and personnel management	• Unexpected events (e.g. a fire, a major machine breakdown) • Special events (e.g. a big snowstorm, a strike) • Special competitive actions (e.g. an advertising campaign or a price decrease by a competitor) • Sales of new products	• High inventories • Under-utilised workforce • Lost sales, loss of market share • Liquidity squeeze • Opportunity losses • Decreased profits or losses	• Inconsistency while forecasting • Unreserved optimism • Underestimating effects of uncertainty • Ignoring possible occurrence of unexpected or unusual events • Ignoring influence of special events/actions	• Systematising the forecasting process and making it objective • Keeping track of forecasting errors to determine systematic deviation • Becoming prepared to deal, if necessary, with unusual events • Taking into consideration the possibility of special actions • Recording effects of special events/actions in order to improve forecasting of future similar case

Time Horizon of Forecasting	Major areas/aspects that can be forecasted with a reasonable degree of accuracy	Major benefits from accurate forecasting	Major sources of surprise or unexpected forecasting errors	Problems/difficulties caused by surprise or unexpected forecasting errors	Typical mistakes (found through the empirical evaluation of past forecasts) that caused surprises and unexpected errors	Improving the forecasting process and the utilisation of forecasts
Medium Term (3 months to 2 years)	• Established trends/patterns • Average length of recovery, expansion of business cycle • Average length of recession • Length of a recession • Average number of months between a change in the index of leading indicators and a change in the level of economic activity • Theoretical effects of fiscal/monetary policies on the economy • Estimation of existing relationships	• Better financial management • Improved allocation of resources • Reduced levels of inventories • Improved profits or reduced losses • Better competitive position	• Booms continuing longer than expected • Recessions started sooner than average or unexpected • Business climate and consumer attitudes different than expected • Changes in relationships • Sales of new products	• Underutilisation of personnel • High inventories • Lost sales • Lost market share • Serious financial problems • Opportunity losses • Decreased profits or losses • Decline in long-term competitive position	• Forgetting that booms or recessions do not last forever • Undue optimism and unwillingness to consider undesirable situations • Excessive pessimism during period of bad economic or business conditions • Underestimating uncertainty	• Maintaining adequate liquidity • Understanding and taking into account the fact that economic/business conditions are cyclical • Accepting that recessions cannot be predicted • Creating a recession fund • Building adequate financial flexibility • Diversifying in moncyclical industries • Better monitoring of economic/business conditions

Continued on next page ...

Time Horizon of Forecasting	Major areas/aspects that can be forecasted with a reasonable degree of accuracy	Major benefits from accurate forecasting	Major sources of surprise or unexpected forecasting errors	Problems/difficulties caused by surprise or unexpected forecasting errors	Typical mistakes (found through the empirical evaluation of past forecasts) that caused surprises and unexpected errors	Improving the forecasting process and the utilisation of forecasts
Emerging (2 years to 5 years)	• Established trends • Technological changes and their implications • Changes in attitudes and their implications • Demographic changes and their implications • Economic and political realities • Competitive realities • Financial resources and requirements	• More effective strategy formulation • Capacity to introduce changes in the organisation • Identifying promising areas for capital investments, realising, however, that competitors might have access to similarly accurate forecasts • Identifying promising R&D projects • Improve (or maintain) competitive position	• Underestimating effects of emerging technologies and their implications on society • Unwillingness to consider flattening or negative trends • Unwillingness to accept effects of possible major environmental changes • Assuming that fads will continue	• Inability to introduce change • Inability to harness advantages of new technologies • Inability to deal with major environmental changes • Loss of competitive advantages • Losses from getting involved in fads the demand of which dries up • Opportunity losses	• Ignoring obvious changes • Believing the effects of change to come much later • Conservative • Excessive optimism • Thinking that competitive advantages (and other barriers to entry) are adequate to guard against competition • Underestimating uncertainty • Being overdazzled by technological discoveries and their profit-making potentials	• Financial flexibility • Identification of major emerging technologies and their influence • Effective strategy that accepts and can deal with the uncertainty in long-term forecasting • Considering the effects of environmental change on the fundamentals (customer, markets, products, competition, prices) • Identifying major problems/opportunities in the future

Time Horizon of Forecasting	Major areas/aspects that can be forecasted with a reasonable degree of accuracy	Major benefits from accurate forecasting	Major sources of surprise or unexpected forecasting errors	Problems/difficulties caused by surprise or unexpected forecasting errors	Typical mistakes (found through the empirical evaluation of past forecasts) that caused surprises and unexpected errors	Improving the forecasting process and the utilisation of forecasts
Distant (5 years to 15 years)	• Established trends • Some technological innovations • Some demographic changes • Basic economic, competitive, and financial realities	• Building consensus • Initiation of feasibility studies for promising R&D projects • Establishing strategic directions	• Overestimating applicability of new technologies (e.g. nuclear power, artificial intelligence) • Overemphasising capacity to forecast new technologies and their impact or usefulness	• Losses from unsuccessful projects involving untested technologies	• Automatically accepting economic advantages and ability of new technologies • Believing the time between a discovery and its practical utilisation to be short and easy • Accepting that barriers to entry cartels, oligopolies, and monopolies can protect status quo	• Maintaining financial strength • Dynamic and flexible objectives • Evolving strategy • Considering economic advantage of new technologies (do *not* be dazzled by advocates of technological wonders) • Spreading risks
Far Away (15 years or more)	• Established trends • General tendencies in: – technology – societal attitudes – economic environment – demography – political environment – competition	• General strategic directions	• Inability to forecast major technological innovations and their impact on business/society (e.g. growth and importance of computers)	• Wasting resources to make forecasts whose usefulness is dubious	• Unwillingness to accept that the future can be different from the past • Unwillingness to understand that radically new technologies nobody envisions today are possible in the future	• Better understanding the future and the forces that shape it • Being flexible in order to deal with a radically changing environment • Being willing to accept future uncertainty and take calculated risks

IMPROVING THE MAKING AND UTILISATION OF FORECASTS

The challenge that lies ahead is to eliminate or lessen the disadvantages of statistical and judgemental forecasting while simultaneously exploiting to the maximum the advantages of each.

M-step-ahead actual forecasts

A novel approach to statistical forecasting would be to choose four or five appropriate methods including those that minimize one-step-ahead, model fitting errors. Such methods should be complementary in their ability to accurately predict specific characteristics of the series being forecast. Then, instead of selecting the method that minimizes the one-step-ahead Mean Square Error (MSE) or Mean Absolute Percentage Error (MAPE) of the historical data, the actual forecasting accuracy for m forecasting horizons can be computed. This can be done using a sliding simulation which starts at some early period and proceeds by presuming that the values beyond this period are *not* known.

An appropriate model for each of the methods can be found and m forecasts made at each period of the sliding simulation. The accuracy of such forecasts can be computed since the actual values are known. The same process can be repeated using one more data point to estimate the model and make new m forecasts. This forecasting simulation can be continued until all but one of the data points has been used (see Makridakis, 1987, for details). The sliding simulation permits the following:

1   Realistic accuracy measures (and variances for confidence intervals) based on actual forecasting performance.
2   Accuracy measures based on *m-step-ahead forecasts*, not just one-step-ahead.
3   The sampling variation (standard error) of the accuracy measures on each of the m-step-ahead forecasts.
4   A rationale for combining different methods if it is found out that their accuracies are *not* significant in a statistical way.

5   The use of a preferred method, as long as the statistical evidence does not suggest rejecting the null hypotheses that such a method is the best.
6   A flexible selection process that permits the combination of various selection criteria.
7   The selection of a different method or model for each of the m forecasting horizons if so desired (it is not necessarily true that the method that does best for a one-step-ahead forecasting horizon will also do so for two-, three-, or, m-step-ahead forecasts).
8   An understanding of how the data behaves by knowing the performance of each method in the various accuracy measures and forecasting horizons. Such an understanding lets us know if changes in patterns and/or relationships have occurred in the past.

The two disadvantages are the amount of data and the computing time required to do the simulation. The amount of data can be great and the time long since *several* methods are used and *many* forecasting simulations are made. Nevertheless, as data bases are built and the cost of computing rapidly decreases, the problem posed can be overcome if reasonably simple methods are selected. Furthermore, once the simulation is done its results can be updated recursively.

Although additional research is required, the results I have obtained so far are extremely encouraging. Using single, dampen-trend (Gardner and McKenzie, 1985), and Holt's exponential smoothing, as well as an autoregressive method capturing the long-term trend, I came up with results that beat *all* methods in the M-Competition in a variety of criteria (see Makridakis, 1987). For instance, the best overall MAPE for all forecasting horizons (by simply combining the best three methods for each horizon) is 13.6%. The same MAPE for Parzen's ARARMA models (the best method in the M-Competition) is 15.4%. The improvement of 1.8% is more than the improvement of 1.4% of ARARMA models over single exponential smoothing (the corresponding MAPE of which is equal to 16.8%). I expect that further work on improving the selection criteria and the methods to be included should increase accuracy even more. In my judgement, the simulation approach I suggest here is the only realistic way to select a forecasting method or methods.

Developing and using appropriate models

Some simple rules need to be followed in developing appropriate forecasting models and in their subsequent use. Models should not be 'black boxes.' Forecasting users are less likely to utilise models the forecasts of which they do not understand. Thus, intuitive models should be preferred to non-intuitive ones. In my experience, a major reason for the attractiveness to practitioners of decomposition methods, linear trend extrapolation, and single or Holt's exponential smoothing is their intuitive understanding of the forecasts of these methods. The contrary is true with ARIMA models of which the forecasts are 'black boxes.'

Second, models should be developed in terms of predicting changes. (This is particularly true with regression-type explanatory models). Modeling changes reduces the chances of spurious interpretation of correlations and provides more realistic measures of how well the model can predict the future. When models cannot be expressed in terms of changes (as in time series) a benchmark model is necessary. Such models can be the equivalent of forecasting that 'tomorrow' will be the same as 'today' (that is, a random walk, or what I call the Naïve 1 method), or alternatively that 'tomorrow' will mirror 'today' after seasonality has been introduced (i.e. the Naïve 2 method). More complex models can, then, be compared to these simple benchmarks (Naïve 1 or Naïve 2) to determine not only the extent of improvement but also whether the extra accuracy justifies the extra cost of the more complex model.

Third, explanatory models do *not* necessarily forecast accurately when their $R2$ is high. For example, a model might perfectly explain ups and downs in sales by relating sales to changes in GNP and changes in prices. The forecasting value of this model might be nil because changes in GNP and prices are usually not known in advance. Moreover, suppose the explanatory model postulates that a decrease in price of $1 would increase sales by $25. Would this prediction materialize? The answer in the great majority of cases is no, since it is most likely that competitors would also decrease their prices, thus invalidating the model's forecast which assumes that competitors would do nothing.

The value of explanatory models lies in helping us better understand and measure what causes sales to go up and down. Such an understanding is essential in helping us assess future uncertainty and in taking steps to be prepared to face changes in patterns and/or relationships while forecasting. Although this is where the biggest value of explanatory models lies, such value is not being adequately exploited. Instead, explanatory models are used to forecast with unsatisfactory results, at least at the level of business firms.

Finally, when forecasting is not possible (as, for example, in predicting cyclical changes) the best alternative is to monitor the event(s) of interest as precisely *and* in as timely a manner as possible. Such monitoring would allow us to determine departures from established patterns and/or relationships and give us early warning of persistent errors in forecasting so that appropriate actions can be taken.

Judgemental consideration

By nature people are optimistic. Furthermore, personal and/or political considerations influence forecasting to a great extent. Thus, introducing objectivity must become the first and paramount concern in improving forecasting accuracy. Objectivity can be introduced either by asking a third party to make the forecasts or by having more than one person independently predict the event of interest.

It is often claimed that sales forecasts are purposely inflated in order to motivate the marketing force to reach the level of the optimistic forecasts. Although there might be some benefits from high forecasts, the negative consequences are considerable since these forecasts determine production schedules and result in high inventories. Thus, unless sales forecasts can be separated from the scheduling and/or production planning process, it does not seem beneficial to deliberately inflate future predictions. Another justification marketing people often advance for their undue optimism is that sales margins are so high that it makes no sense not to *always* have adequate inventories at hand. This claim might have had some value in the 1960s, but it becomes less and less valid as competition increases and with it the need to cut costs.

Little work has been done on debiasing judgmental forecasts. My approach to doing so is based on the following three principles (see also exhibits 3 and 4):

Anchoring the forecasts: Start the decision-making process of arriving at final forecasts by presenting a set of objective, statistically-based forecasts. Explain to the decision makers that these are the best possible forecasts when it is assumed that the future will not be very different from the past. Then ask them to use their knowledge of the company, market, and economy to determine how these forecasts should be *modified*. Also ask them to state *reasons* for such modifications. Furthermore, I have discovered that if I ask the executives to write their answers on a piece of paper anonymously it is much easier to avoid having some of them stick to stated opinions when there is no agreement about changing the statistical forecasts.

Presentation of information: Information should be presented in a way that brings out all important aspects of the situation being considered without simultaneously providing unnecessary details. Up-to-date information about the evolution in sales, prices, competition, economy, etc., needs to be presented, preferably in graph form. Such information should use deseasonalised data highlighting established trends as well as pattern changes (recessions or booms, changes in trends, etc.). Often I find it useful not to ask managers to come up with numbers but rather to request that they trace their forecasts on the graph of deseasonalised (or trend-cycle) historical values; I then have such forecasts recorded from there. This is especially useful when *budget* forecasts are made, since the common practice of basing predictions of growth rates on the previous year's level can provide misleading forecasts (see Makridakis, 1986, pp. 24–29).

In addition to specific forecasts, the various types of forecasting errors and future uncertainty need to be considered in meetings where managers finalise forecasts. To do so, previous errors must be presented and cases where substantial mistakes were made given. The argument that managers should not be made aware of the true range of confidence intervals because they will be less willing to believe in the forecasts, is, in my opinion, entirely wrong. Knowing the true uncertainty would allow them to take steps, if necessary, to deal with such uncertainty in a realistic way.

Keeping track of judgemental errors: Unless people are provided with feedback they are unlikely to improve their ability to forecast accurately. I therefore suggest that forecasting users' modifications of statistical forecasts be recorded so that they can understand what went wrong or determine the extent of their improvements over the (statistical) forecasts. In doing so, I emphasise that the purpose is not to blame them if they go wrong, but is instead a way of providing feedback and facilitating learning and future improvements. As a matter of practice, the feedback is provided only to the individual involved and is in no way made public.

STATISTICAL MODELS VERSUS JUDGEMENT

There is little doubt that there are advantages and drawbacks to the ways that both statistical models and people forecast (see exhibit 8). The challenge ahead lies in our ability to use to optimal advantage both statistical models and individual judgement while avoiding their drawbacks. Doing so would involve the following suggestions.

People must decide what method or model to use. Such a choice is *not* value free, as it has a major impact on the forecasts. Adaptive models, for instance, are reactive, overemphasising non-random changes in the recent past. Single exponential smoothing provides conservative forecasts, as it assumes a horizontal extrapolation. In contrast, trend regression ignores pattern changes, emphasising the long-term trend in the data. Similarly, for forecasting purposes there is a big difference if a logarithmic transformation is made, how the data is differenced, or if an auto regressive versus a moving average ARIMA model is selected. The implications of such choices are enormous for forecasting and, if they are not known, need to be verified, using the type of simulation suggested above.

Exhibit 8	Advantages/disadvantages of statistical methods versus judgemental forecasts	
	Statistical methods	**Judgemental forecasts**
Changes in established patterns and/or relationships	Cannot be predicted	Could be predicted but can also be ignored or people can overreact to them
Utilising available information/data	Not all information in past data is used	People are selective, biased and inconsistent
Objectivity	Based on some specific selection criterion/criteria	Depends upon personal and political consideration, and under optimism/pessimism
Uncertainty	Grossly underestimated	Grossly underestimated, mostly on the optimistic side
Cost	Cheap to use	Expensive to use

Since statistical methods cannot predict changes in patterns and/or relationships, nor distinguish if they are temporary or permanent, it becomes necessary for people to do so by selecting appropriate models, and incorporating their own judgements in order to modify the statistical forecasts. Predicting changes in patterns and/or relationships is another human task. Plotting the data, and the sliding simulation suggested above, would allow the identification of changes that have occurred in the past. The major preoccupation of judgemental forecasters is the need to consider when similar changes might occur in the future and/or when brand new ones might take place. Similarly, they must realistically assess the forecasting errors and uncertainty that would be caused by such changes. This is the most critical task of forecasting users, since statistical methods are not suited to predicting changes in patterns and/or relationships.

The forecasting process can be rationalised if people concentrate on predicting the influence on forecasting of changes in established patterns and/or relationships while statistical methods specialise in predicting the continuation of such patterns/relationships. Furthermore, it would be necessary to formalise the forecasting process by adapting a consistent approach in dealing with changes. More than one person should be asked independently to predict forthcoming changes in patterns and/or relationships and their effects on the future. Along the same lines, a committee can be formed to search for major new changes that are forthcoming and consider their possible consequences. Such a search should be guided by identifying important problems (disequilibria) in the economy, critical legislation that might be enacted, new competitive forces, emerging fashions/fads, and new technological innovations.

Finally, the historical data used to develop the statistical model need to be consistent and adjusted judgementally for special events and/or actions. Data should be refined in order to be consistent from beginning to end. Changes in accounting procedures, in definitions of what constitutes a division, product family, product group, etc., must be recorded and their effects estimated. Consequently, past data need to be adjusted so that it is consistent throughout. Furthermore, judgmental adjustments must be made for special events and actions. The influence of a strike or an extremely cold winter that will not repeat itself for another twenty years needs to be removed from the data while forecasting. This needs to be done by estimating judgementally the effect of such an unusual change and adjusting the actual data accordingly. At the same time, the original values need to be kept to warn us of unusual changes and their influence on forecasting errors. Keeping track of special events or actions and their influence can, in addition to eliminating what otherwise would be considered randomness factors by the mode, facilitate the estimation of how similar special events or actions in the future would influence the forecasts.

FORECASTING, PLANNING, AND STRATEGY

Forecasting users often complain that too much uncertainty about the future makes planning and strategy extremely difficult or impossible. Although it is true that uncertainty in forecasting can be enormous, there is not much those who prepare forecasts can do apart from pointing out that it is not realistic to pretend that future uncertainty does not exist or can be eliminated. It is, however, extremely useful to evaluate not only the average forecasting errors, but also the large ones, so that uncertainty can be better understood and the risks involved with future predictions taken into consideration. Decisions can then be made in such a way as to minimise the risks indicated through forecasting, since positive and negative errors while forecasting do not carry the same risks for given organisations. Furthermore, one extremely large error does not usually have the same impact as two errors that add up to the same sum.

Although uncertainty is psychologically difficult to deal with, decision- and policy-makers must heed Russell's advice to learn '*how to live without certainty, and yet without being paralysed by hesitation.*' Ignoring future uncertainty or pretending that it does not exist is not realistic and will inevitably result in unpleasant surprises.

Dealing with future uncertainty in a realistic manner requires considering the trade-offs involved in making different kinds of forecasting errors. In considering, for instance, the possibility of investing in a new technology, there are two types of risk. One alternative is to decide that it is not worth investing in the new technology. In such cases competitors can gain an edge if they introduce the new technology and it is successful. By introducing the new technology, however, one can incur serious losses if it proves to be a flop or if it does not turn out to be commercially viable. Both types of errors can be costly and managers must consider both possibilities.

During the past, both types of mistakes have been made (see Schnaars and Berenson, 1986). Schnaars and Berenson suggested that forecasters must take several simple guidelines into account in evaluating the advantages and dangers of new technologies. Fundamental questions are: Who are the customers? How large is the market? What benefits does the new technology provide compared with existing ones? Are these benefits worth the extra price? Can they break down people's resistance to change and make them buy new products or services? Would the demand for the products or services provided by new technologies continue beyond the initial craze? Would the competition be rough (in particular in high-tech areas)? Such questions can help one to evaluate the possible economic benefits (as opposed to the technical benefits) of the new technologies.

Examples abound of both ignoring new technologies and losing great amounts of money by investing in them. AM International, Inc., for instance, completely ignored the photocopying technology being introduced by Xerox, lost its leading market position, and eventually went bankrupt. Nuclear energy, picture phones, plastic paper, synthetic oil, and many other highly regarded technological innovations did not bring the expected benefits and it might take a long time before they can become a commercial success. Moreover, in high-tech and high-growth markets, competition is extremely keen, causing innumerable bankruptcies and/or low profits even if a forecast about a technological invention turns out to be accurate. Strategists, therefore, need to be concerned with the accuracy and effectiveness of forecasting in a more fundamental way than is the current practice.

The opportunities and risks inherent in new technologies are different for established companies than they are for new ones. It would have been easy for AM International to acquire the new photocopying technology or to diversify to new markets when it was in a leading position and possessed strong financial and competitive advantages (e.g., a large distribution and repairs network). It did not do so, however, because its management ignored the new technology until it was too late. In contrast, Xerox had no choice but to embrace the new technology and market it as forcefully as possible, as it had no other way of replacing AM's leading market position.

Products or services the growth of which is temporary and which depend upon fashions and other fads are even more difficult to deal with than new technologies. Fashions or fads start suddenly and might end even faster. Trying to predict them is thus extremely difficult, which makes the forecasting errors and the resulting uncertainty enormous. Should a company invest in order to exploit a fad? That is a difficult situation that can only be dealt with by considering the risks involved for the specific company and whether or not its management is willing to accept them. However, whatever the final decisions, organisations dealing in fashionable products or services must be flexible and capable of monitoring and reacting to changes in established patterns and/or relationships.

Recessions provide similar dilemmas for management. If a recession is predicted, production (and expenditure) is cut. If the recession materialises the right decision has been made. If the recession does not take place, production might not be sufficient to fill orders and customers might be lost to competitors. If no recession is predicted and one occurs, inventories would be high and profits low or negative. Some companies might not even be able to ride the recession through and might have to cease operations because of cash flow or other financial problems. Managers need to consider the costs of predicting a recession that does not occur as well as the costs when a recession is not forecast and does occur. The costs involved are not symmetric and thus the risks are different in each case and depend to a great extent upon the specific organisation involved, its financial strength, and the values of its management.

Organisations must be prepared to face errors caused by changes in patterns and/or relationships in a general way, since they cannot know when such errors might occur and how large they might be. Flexibility and financial strength are important ingredients in dealing with unlikely or unexpected events and need to be included as an integral part of organisational strategy. Japan and Germany were the two countries least affected by the oil crisis (an unexpected and unforecast event) and the large changes it produced in established patterns and relationships. Although both countries import all their oil, they managed to ride out the crisis well because of their strong financial

positions and their good competitive positions at the international level.

Strategies need to take into account the dangers of being wrong in forecasting, as well as the possibility of unexpected and/or inconceivable events occurring in the future (see exhibit 2). Furthermore, strategists have to come to grips with the degree of risk they would be willing to assume by considering the risks and trade-offs involved in any future-oriented decision. In the final analysis, there is no such thing as a free lunch. In an uncertain environment gains cannot be made without taking risks. The role of forecasting is to point out and help management assess uncertainty and risks, but uncertainty cannot be eliminated. The future can always turn out to be different from the forecast.

The roles of forecasting, planning, and strategy are interrelated. The more accurate the forecasts, all other things being equal, the more effective the planning and the less great the need for a strategy. However, in an uncertain environment where large non-random errors are possible, planning can go wrong and uncertainty is high, thus making the need for an effective strategy imperative. Conventional approaches to strategy advocate identifying and exploiting opportunities in the environment while simultaneously avoiding dangers. They assume accurate forecasting of the opportunities and dangers and also accurate predictions of competitors' actions. Assume, for instance, that an opportunity in the environment is identified and a company invests heavily to exploit it. That does not guarantee profits, even if the opportunity has been predicted correctly, if existing competitors and new entrants have also decided to invest in the same technology. Overcapacity, price wars, and similar events caused by competitive factors can change the opportunity into a disaster. At the same time, consider a danger such as a slowdown or negative growth in a certain market. If the forecasts drive the majority of competitors out of the market, the event can present a golden opportunity to those who have decided to stay (Makridakis and Heau, 1987).

CONCLUSIONS

Forecasting users must learn to become realistic by accepting that uncertainty in any future-oriented prediction can be great. They should understand past mistakes, as well as the illusory quest to eradicate future uncertainty. Furthermore, forecasting users ought to avoid judgemental biases. Preparers of forecasts need to better understand the problems in the forecasting methods currently in use and devise ways of avoiding these problems. In this paper I have argued for an approach that simulates the testing of forecasting models so that a realistic assessment of forecasting errors and a more accurate method selection can be made. Moreover, preparers of forecasts will have to better explain to users the limitations of statistical models and their implications for predicting the future. In addition, a serious effort would be required to formalise the task of forecasting by utilising the best of statistical methods and individual judgements, while avoiding their deficiencies as much as possible. Finally, forecasting users must consider the trade-offs involved in making various types of errors, with the resulting uncertainty, so as to operate at an acceptable level of risk consistent with their corporate philosophy.

References

Ahlers, D. and J. Lakonishok, 1983, A study of economists' consensus forecasts, *Management Science* 29, 1113–1125.

Armstrong, J.C., 1985, *Long-Range Forecasting: From Crystal Ball to Computer*, 2nd ed. (Wiley–Interscience, New York).

Ascher, W., 1978, *Forecasting: An Appraisal for Policy Makers and Planners* (Johns Hopkins University Press, Baltimore. MD)

Berenson, C. and S. Schnaars, 1986, Growth market forecasting revisited, *California Management Review*, Summer.

Dawes, R.M., 1986, Forecasting one's own preferences, *International Journal of Forecasting* 2, 5–14.

Einhorn, H.J. and R.M. Hogarth, 1987, Decision making: Going forward in reverse, *Harvard Business Review*, January–February, 66–70.

Fama, P., 1965, The behaviour of stock market prices, *Journal of Business*, Jan., 34–105.

Fischoff, B., P. Slovic and S. Lichtenstein, 1977, Knowing with certainty: The appropriateness of extreme confidence of extreme confidence, *Journal of Experimental Psychology: Human perception and performance,* 3, no. 4, 552–564.

Gardner, E.S.E. and E. McKenzie, 1985, Forecasting trends in time series, *Management Science* 31, no. 10, 1237–1246.

Goldberg, L.R., 1970, Man versus model of man: A rationale, plus some evidence for a method of improving on clinical inferences, *Psychological Bulletin* 73, no. 6, 422–432.

Hampton, W.J. and J.R. Norman, 1987, General Motors: What went wrong, *Business Week*, March 16, 44–51.

Hogarth, R.M. and S. Makridakis, 1981, Forecasting and planning: An evaluation, *Management Science* 27, no. 2, 115–138.

Laderman, J.F., 1988, The best mutual funds, *Business Week*, Feb. 22, 54–58.

Lawrence, M. and S. Makridakis, 1988, Factors affecting judgmental forecasts and confidence intervals, *Organisational Behaviour and Human Decision Processes*, forthcoming.

McNees, S.K., 1979, Forecasting performance in the 1970s, in: S. Makridakis and S.C. Wheelwright, eds., *TIMS studies in management science*, Vol. 12 (North-Holland, Amsterdam).

Makridakis, S., 1982, Chronology of the last six recessions, *Omega 10*, no. 1, 43–50.

Makridakis, S., 1986, The art and science of forecasting: An assessment and future directions, *International Journal of Forecasting* 2, 15–39.

Makridakis, S., 1987, A new approach to statistical forecasting, *Working Paper 1987/20* (INSEAD, Fontainebleau).

Makridakis, S. and D. Heau, 1987, The evolution of strategic planning and management, in: W.R. King and D.l. Cleland, etc., *Strategic Planning and Management Handbook* (Van Nostrand Reinhold, New York) 1–20.

Makridakis, S. and M. Hibon, 1987, Confidence intervals: An empirical investigation for the series in the M-competition, *International Journal of Forecasting* 3.

Moriarty, M.M. and A.J. Adams, 1984, Management judgement forecasts, composite forecasting models, and conditional efficiency, *Journal of Marketing Research* 21, Aug., 239–250.

Porter, M., 1985, *Competitive Advantages: Creating and Sustaining Superior Performance* (Free Press, New York).

Schnaars, S.P., 1984, Situational factors affecting forecast accuracy, *Journal of Marketing Research* 21, Aug., 290–297.

Wallace, A.C., 1987, 'Mechanical' index funds edge out savvy managers, *New York Times*, Feb. 19.

Zarnowitz, V., 1984, The accuracy of individual and group forecasts from business outlook surveys, *Journal of Forecasting* 3, 11–26.

Audit 4.4

Before we later ask you to undertake exercises which revolve around what *should* be done, let us for the record make a note of what actually *does* happen at present in your own organisation.

What formal forecasting does it undertake?

What technique(s) does it use for making these forecasts?

Does it appreciate the limitations on forecasting accuracy?

What is the size of the errors allowed for?

How does it allow for these errors?

Does it undertake long-range forecasts (say, three years ahead or beyond)?

How does it handle uncertainty?

5 LONG-RANGE FORECASTING

Long-range forecasting is inevitably even less certain than its short-range counterpart. This is reflected in the fact that most of the techniques are qualitative rather than quantitative. Even so, it is important that these views of the future be as accurate and meaningful as possible.

5.1 TECHNOLOGICAL FORECASTING

The most accurate, in appearance at least, is that which can be applied to the progression of successive waves of new technology.

In this vector approach (sometimes referred to as growth curves) the average growth or development rate is calculated. As with many conventional short-term approaches, the 'line of best fit' is used for this calculation. This plots the historical developments and tries to fit (usually visually) a line (normally a straight one) to these points. *Forecasting Methods for Management* by Makridakis and Wheelwright contains a classical example of this sort of long-term forecasting, illustrated in Figure 5.1.

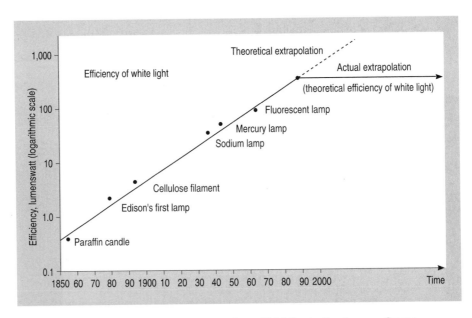

FIGURE 5.1   Curve-fitting approach to forecasting artificial illumination (source: Spyros Makridakis and Steven C. Wheelwright, *Forecasting Methods for Management* (5th edn, John Wiley, 1989), p. 321)

It is as well at this stage, however, to inject a note of caution into our view of these long-term forecasts. To be of major predictive value, the plots of time-series data will usually have to cover the results over several decades. Makridakis and Wheelwright[1] state that 'such data must span a period of more than 100 years' and add the caution that 'the fact that a long-term trend has been identified does not mean it cannot change'.

In practice, most forecasts emerge from an individual. In the small company it may be the owner. In the larger organisation it may be the marketing manager. In the largest of all it may be the brand manager or even the manager of the forecasting department. Sometimes, particularly in the case of the smaller organisations, it may be outside experts, who often publish opinions as to what will happen in the future – which may then be followed slavishly by some readers.

The individual forecast is inevitably a personal judgement. Indeed, no matter how many historical facts are available to support the judgement, the act of forecasting is generally an art rather than a science. Perhaps the most famous attempt to overcome the limitations of individual judgement is the Delphi technique described below by Philip Holroyd.

5.2 DELPHI STUDIES

by Philip Holroyd

The Delphi method of assessing the importance of identified events which may occur in the future was developed in the late 1960s by Olaf Helmer and Ted Gordon of the American RAND Corporation. Its purpose was to overcome the distortions that can emerge when simply acquiring the views of experts. In the original Delphi concept, the participants – the experts – remain anonymous, their identity known only to the Delphi study organiser. During the exercise, the participants respond to a questionnaire that is very precisely defined: specific events are identified and the expert is asked to make a judgement of the probability of the event occurring before certain dates.

Thus, a question may be 'what is the probability of a pill being developed that will extend the average life-span to greater than 100 years in or before the year 2000, 2005, 2010, 2020, 2050, never?'

An expert in medical developments may respond:

Year:	2000	2005	2010	2020	2050	never
Probability:	0.0	0.0	0.1	0.15	0.5	0.0

---

[1] Spyros Makridakis, and Steven C. Wheelwright, *Forecasting Methods for Management* (5th edn, John Wiley, 1989).

However, a second expert may respond:

Year:	2000	2005	2010	2020	2050	never
Probability:	0.0	0.1	0.4	0.5	0.9	0.0

Some disagreement clearly exists between these experts. Now, if this were a discussion between them, then the argument may be won by the most senior expert or the most aggressive expert or the most powerful expert. It is to avoid just this sort of bias that the Delphi method maintains anonymity among its participants.

In order to allow adjustments to occur, however, the results of the first round of responses are statistically analysed and fed back to all participants. Each can then see to what extent their own initial responses were close to or far from the mean. If they desire, they can then decide to modify their first response. Indeed, in some Delphi studies, those participants whose responses are far from the mean are asked to justify their opinion if they wish to maintain it. Then, others may be persuaded to shift their own responses.

In this way, a wide range of opinion is captured in the first set of responses and amended in a second, or even a third, round of questions. It is found that such an approach often leads to a narrowing of the range of responses and that the final statistical analysis of the results can be a good guide to the eventual future outcome.

The actual Delphi study process may be outlined as follows:[2]

1   Area of study defined.
2   Questionnaire prepared.
3   Panel of experts selected by organiser(s).
4   Questionnaire circulated to experts.
5   Replies analysed and statistical overview prepared.
6   Feedback of median and interquartile range of responses. Request experts to reconsider judgements and those lying outside the interquartile range asked to justify opinions.
7   Analysis of round 2 results.
8   Feedback of round 2 replies with reasons supporting any extreme views. Request reconsideration again.
9   Final analysis or further rounds if necessary.

The Delphi method is time consuming and difficult to organise: the delay in receiving replies from the various rounds can be considerable, participants drop out and so on. Also, it was found that the way the questions were put could introduce bias into the responses. In order to avoid this problem, Gordon recommended a follow-up face-to-face session by the organiser(s) with the participants. In this way, shades of opinion can be judged and included in the final analysis. However, this increases the organisational difficulty of the Delphi exercise.

[2] B.C. Twiss, *Managing Technological Innovation* (Longman, 1980).

5.3 DELPHI IN PRACTICE

This technique was very much in vogue during the 1970s. A significant shortcoming is that the assumptions often turn out to be heavily influenced by the prevailing fashions. One of the most interesting aspects of the continuing work being done by the University of Southern California, which has been conducting Delphi Studies every year for a couple of decades, is the light it sheds on the ideas *current* at the time each of the previous forecasts was made (and perhaps rather less on the future!). The other main problem is that almost all experts have tended to be optimistic about timescales. They nearly always expect changes to happen well in advance of when they actually do take place. On the other hand, our colleagues in the American Committee of the United Nations University have used the technique successfully in their global, 'Millennium Project' in which we at the OUBS have participated.

A variation on this technique, which has been used in particular by the US military, is role playing. In this case the experts play the main actors involved – and attempt to deduce how they might react in the equivalent real-life situations. As Scott Armstrong[3] comments:

> From a theoretical viewpoint, role-playing offers advantages over opinions for predicting the outcomes in conflict situations. It facilitates a realistic examination of the interaction among the parties. This is expected not only to improve accuracy, but also to provide a better understanding of the dynamics which, in turn, might lead to the development of new strategies.

This is, though, an expensive approach and accordingly little used.

5.4 JURY METHOD

The so-called jury method is another of the formal ways of attempting to overcome the limitations of individual opinion. In essence, a panel of experts (or corporate executives) is brought together in committee to pool members' individual forecasts. Then, having agreed (or at least discussed) their individual cases, a corporate forecast emerges and is agreed. As the quality of the forecast depends upon the quality of the participants, the jury should comprise the best possible team of relevant experts, from within the organisation and outside it.

Such a jury may dilute the expertise of the best forecasters on it; worse, it may follow the ideas of the most persuasive (or those with the highest status) rather than the most knowledgeable. The ways in which this can happen are discussed in Article 5.1 on 'Groupthink', by Irving L Janis.

Now *quickly* read Article 5.1.[4]

---

[3] J. Scott Armstrong, 'Forecasting methods for conflict situations', in George Wright and Peter Ayrton (eds), *Judgmental Forecasting* (John Wiley, 1987).
[4] Reprinted from *Psychology Today*, November 1971.

Article 5.1 IRVING L. JANIS: 'GROUPTHINK'

'How could we have been so stupid?' President John F. Kennedy asked after he and a close group of advisers had blundered into the Bay of Pigs invasion. For the last two years I have been studying that question, as it applies not only to the Bay of Pigs decision-makers but also to those who led the United States into such other major fiascos as the failure to be prepared for the attack on Pearl Harbour, the Korean War stalemate and the escalation of the Vietnam War.

Stupidity certainly is not the explanation. The men who participated in making the Bay of Pigs decision, for instant, comprised one of the greatest arrays of intellectual talent in the history of American Government – Dean Rusk, Robert McNamara, Douglas Dillon, Robert Kennedy, McGeorge Bundy, Arthur Schlesinger Jr, Allen Dulles and others.

It also seemed to me that explanations were incomplete if they concentrated only on disturbances in the behaviour of each individual within a decision-making body: temporary emotional states of elation, fear, or chronic blind spots arising from a man's social prejudices or idiosyncratic biases.

I preferred to broaden the picture by looking at the fiascos from the standpoint of group dynamics as it has been explored over the past three decades, first by the great social psychologist Kurt Lewin and later in many experimental situations by myself and other behavioural scientists. My conclusion after poring over hundreds of relevant documents – historical reports about formal group meetings and informal conversations among the members – is that groups that committed the fiascos were victims of what I call 'groupthink'.

'GROUPY'

In each case study, I was surprised to discover the extent to which each group displayed the typical phenomena of social conformity that are regularly encountered in studies of group dynamics among ordinary citizens. For example, some of the phenomena appear to be completely in line with findings from social-psychological experiments showing that powerful social pressures are brought to bear by the members of a cohesive group whenever a dissident begins to voice his objections to a group consensus. Other phenomena are reminiscent of the shared illusions observed in encounter groups and friendship cliques when the members simultaneously reach a peak of 'groupy' feelings.

Above all, there are numerous indications pointing to the development of group norms that bolster morale at the expense of critical thinking. One of the most common norms appears to be that of remaining loyal to the group by sticking with the policies to which the group has already committed itself, even when those policies are obviously working out badly and have unintended consequences that disturb the conscience of each member. This is one of the key characteristics of groupthink.

1984

I use the term groupthink as a quick and easy way to refer to the mode of thinking that persons engage in when *concurrence-seeking* becomes so dominant in a cohesive in-group that it tends to override realistic appraisal of alternative courses of action. Groupthink is a term of the same order as the words in the newspeak vocabulary George Orwell used in his dismaying world of *1984*. In that context, groupthink takes on an invidious connotation. Exactly such a connotation is intended, since the term refers to a deterioration in mental efficiency, reality testing and moral judgements as a result of group pressures.

The symptoms of groupthink arise when the members of decision-making groups become motivated to avoid being too harsh in their judgements of their leaders' or their colleagues' ideas. They adopt a soft line of criticism, even in their own thinking. At their meetings, all the members are amicable and seek complete concurrence on every important issue, with no bickering or conflict to spoil the coy, 'we-feeling' atmosphere.

KILL

Paradoxically, soft-headed groups are often hard-hearted when it comes to dealing with outgroups or enemies. They find it relatively easy to resort to dehumanising solutions – they will readily authorise bombing attacks that kill large numbers of civilians in the name of the noble cause of persuading an unfriendly government to negotiate at the peace table. They are unlikely to pursue the more difficult and controversial issues that arise when alternatives to a harsh military solution come up for discussion. Nor are they inclined to raise ethical issues that carry the implication that *this fine group of ours, with its humanitarianism and its high-minded principles, might be capable of adopting a course of action that is inhumane and immoral.*

NORMS

There is evidence from a number of social-psychological studies that as the members of a group feel more accepted by the others, which is a central feature of increased group cohesiveness, they display less overt conformity to group norms. Thus we would expect that the more cohesive a group becomes the less the members will feel constrained to censor what they say out of fear of being socially punished for antagonising the leader or any of their fellow members.

In contrast, the groupthink type of conformity tends to increase as group cohesiveness increases. Groupthink involves non-deliberate suppression of critical thoughts as a result of internalisation of the group's norms, which is quite different from deliberate suppression on the bias of external threats of social punishment. The more cohesive the group, the greater the inner compulsion on the part of each member to avoid creating disunity, which inclines him to believe in the soundness of whatever proposals are promoted by the leader or by a majority of the group's members.

In a cohesive group, the danger is not so much that each individual will fail to reveal his objections to what the others propose but that he will think the proposal is a good one, without attempting to carry out a careful, critical scrutiny of the pros and cons of the alternatives. When groupthink becomes dominant, there also is

considerable suppression of deviant thoughts, but it takes the form of each person's deciding that his misgivings are not relevant and should be set aside, that the benefit of the doubt regarding any lingering uncertainties should be given to the group consensus.

STRESS

I do not mean to imply that all cohesive groups necessarily suffer from groupthink. All ingroups may have a mild tendency toward groupthink, displaying one or another of the symptoms from time to time, but it need not be so dominant as to influence the quality of the group's final decision. Neither do I mean to imply that there is anything necessarily inefficient or harmful about group decisions in general. On the contrary, a group whose members have properly defined roles, with traditions concerning the procedures to follow in pursuing a critical inquiry, probably is capable of making better decisions than any individual group member working alone.

The problem is that the advantages of having decisions made by groups are often lost because of powerful psychological pressures that arise when the members work closely together, share the same set of values and, above all, face a crisis situation that puts everyone under intense stress.

The main principle of groupthink, which I offer in the spirit of Parkinson's Law, is this: *the more amiability and esprit de corps there is among the members of a policy-making in-group, the greater the danger that independent critical thinking will be replaced by groupthink, which is likely to result in irrational and dehumanising actions directed against outgroups.*

SYMPTOMS

In my studies of high-level governmental decision-makers, both civilian and military, I have found eight main symptoms of groupthink.

Invulnerability

Most or all of the members of the in-group share an *illusion* of invulnerability that provides for them some degree of reassurance about obvious dangers and leads them to become overoptimistic and willing to take extraordinary risks. It also causes them to fail to respond to clear warnings of danger.

The Kennedy in-group, which uncritically accepted the Central Intelligence Agency's disastrous Bay of Pigs plan, operated on the false assumption that they could keep secret the fact that the United States was responsible for the invasion of Cuba. Even after news of the plan began to leak out, their belief remained unshaken. They failed even to consider the danger that awaited them: a world-wide revulsion against the US.

A similar attitude appeared among the members of President Lyndon B. Johnson's in-group, the 'Tuesday Cabinet', which kept escalating the Vietnam War despite repeated setbacks and failures. 'There was a belief', Bill Moyers commented after he resigned, 'that if we indicated a willingness to use our power, they [the North Vietnamese] would get the message and back away from an all-out confrontation .... There was a confidence – it was never bragged about, it was just there – that when the chips were really down, the other people would fold'.

A most poignant example of an illusion of invulnerability involves the in-group around Admiral H.E. Kimmel, which failed to prepare for the possibility of a Japanese attack on Pearl Harbour despite repeated warnings. Informed by his intelligence chief that radio contact with Japanese aircraft carriers had been lost, Kimmel joked about it: 'What, you don't know where the carriers are? Do you mean to say that they could be rounding Diamond Head (at Honolulu) and you wouldn't know it?' The carriers were in fact moving full-steam towards Kimmel's command post at the time. Laughing together about a danger signal, which labels it as a purely laughing matter, is a characteristic manifestation of groupthink.

Rationale

As we see, victims of groupthink ignore warnings; they also collectively construct rationalisations in order to discount warnings and other forms of negative feedback that, taken seriously, might lead the group member to reconsider their assumptions each time they recommit themselves to past decisions. Why did the Johnson in-group avoid

reconsidering its escalation policy when time and again the expectations on which they based their decisions turned out to be wrong? James C. Thomson Jr, a historian who spent five years as an observing participant in both the State Department and the White House, tells us that the policy-makers avoided critical discussion of their prior decisions and continually invented new rationalisations so that they could sincerely recommit themselves to defeating the North Vietnamese.

In the fall of 1964, before the bombing of North Vietnam began, some of the policy-makers predicted that six weeks of air strikes would induce the North Vietnamese to seek peace talks. When someone asked, 'What if they don't?' the answer was that another four weeks certainly would do the trick.

Later, after each setback, the in-group agreed that by investing just a bit more effort (by stepping up the bomb tonnage a bit, for instance), their course of action would prove to be right. *The Pentagon Papers* bear out these observations.

In *The Limits of Intervention*, Townsend Hoopes, who was acting Secretary of the Air Force under Johnson, says that Walt W. Rostow in particular showed a remarkable capacity for what has been called 'instant rationalisation'. According to Hoopes, Rostow buttressed the group's optimism about being on the road to victory by culling selected scraps of evidence from news reports or, if necessary, by inventing 'plausible' forecasts that had no basis in evidence at all.

Admiral Kimmel's group rationalised away their warnings, too. Right up to 7 December 1941, they convinced themselves that the Japanese would never dare attempt a full-scale surprise assault against Hawaii because Japan's leaders would realise that it would precipitate an all-out war which the United States would surely win. They made no attempt to look at the situation through the eyes of the Japanese leaders – another manifestation of groupthink.

Morality

Victims of groupthink believe unquestioningly in the inherent morality of their in-group; this belief inclines the members to ignore the ethical or moral consequences of their decisions.

Evidence that this symptom is at work usually is of a negative kind – the things that are left unsaid in group meetings. At least two influential persons had doubts about the morality of the Bay of Pigs adventure. One of them, Arthur Schlesinger Jr, presented his strong objections in a memorandum to President Kennedy and Secretary of State Rusk but suppressed them when he attended meetings of the Kennedy team. The other, Senator J. William Fulbright, was not a member of the group, but the President invited him to express his misgivings in a speech to the policy-makers. However, when Fulbright finished speaking the President moved on to other agenda items without asking for reactions of the group.

David Kraslow and Stuart H. Loory, in *The Secret Search for Peace in Vietnam*, report that during 1966 President Johnson's in-group was concerned primarily with selecting bomb targets in North Vietnam. They based their selections on four factors – the military advantage, the risk to American aircraft and pilots, the danger of forcing other countries into the fighting, and the danger of heavy civilian casualties. At their regular Tuesday luncheons, they weighed these factors the way school teachers grade examination papers, averaging them out. Though evidence on this point is scant, I suspect that the group's realistic adherence to a standardised procedure induced the members to feel morally justified in their destructive way of dealing with Vietnamese people – after all, the danger of heavy civilian casualties from US air strikes was taken into account on their checklists.

Stereotypes

Victims of groupthink hold stereotyped views of the leaders of enemy groups: they are so evil that genuine attempts at negotiating differences with them are unwarranted, or they are too weak or too stupid to deal effectively with whatever attempts the in-group makes to defeat their purposes, no matter how risky the attempts are.

Kennedy's groupthinkers believed that Premier Fidel Castro's air force was so ineffectual that obsolete B-26s could knock it out completely in a surprise attack before the invasion began. They also believed that Castro's army was so weak that a small Cuban-exile brigade could establish a well-protected beach-head at the Bay of Pigs. In addition, they believed that Castro was not smart enough to put down any possible internal uprising in support of the exiles. They were wrong on all three assumptions. Though much of the blame was attributable to faulty intelligence, the point is that none of Kennedy's advisers even questioned the CIA planners about these assumptions.

The Johnson advisers' sloganistic thinking about 'the Communist apparatus' that was 'working all around the world' (as Dean Rusk put it) led them to overlook the powerful nationalistic strivings of the North Vietnamese government and its efforts to ward off Chinese domination. The crudest of all stereotypes used by Johnson's inner circle to justify their policies was the domino theory ('If we don't stop the Reds in South Vietnam, tomorrow they will be in Hawaii and next week they will be in San Francisco,' Johnson once said.) The group so firmly accepted this stereotype that it became almost impossible for any adviser to introduce a more sophisticated viewpoint.

In documents on Pearl Harbour, it is clear to see that the Navy commanders stationed in Hawaii had a naive image of Japan as a midget that would not dare to strike a blow against a powerful giant.

Pressure

Victims of groupthink apply direct pressure to any individual who momentarily expresses doubts about any of the group's shared illusions or who questions the validity of the arguments supporting a policy alternative favoured by the majority. This gambit reinforces the concurrence-seeking norm that loyal members are expected to maintain.

President Kennedy probably was more active than anyone else in raising sceptical questions during the Bay of Pigs meetings, and yet he seems to have encouraged the group's docile, uncritical acceptance of defective arguments in favour of the CIA's plan. At every meeting, he allowed the CIA representatives to dominate the discussion. He permitted them to give their immediate refutations in response to each tentative doubt that one of the others expressed, instead of asking whether anyone shared the doubt or wanted to pursue the implications of the new worrisome issue that had just been raised. And at the most crucial meeting, when he was calling on each member to give his vote for or against the plan, he did not call on

Arthur Schlesinger, the one man there who was known by the President to have serious misgivings.

Historian Thomson informs us that whenever a member of Johnson's in-group began to express doubts, the group used subtle social pressures to 'domesticate' him. To start with, the dissenter was made to feel at home, provided that he lived up to two restrictions: (a) that he did not voice his doubts to outsiders, which would play into the hands of the opposition; and (b) that he kept his criticisms within the bounds of acceptable deviation, which meant not challenging any of the fundamental assumptions that went into the group's prior commitments. One such 'domesticated dissenter' was Bill Moyers. When Moyers arrived at a meeting, Thomson tells us, the President greeted him with, 'Well, here comes Mr Stop-the-Bombing.'

Self-censorship

Victims of groupthink avoid deviating from what appears to be group consensus; they keep silent about their misgivings and even minimise to themselves the importance of their doubts.

As we have seen, Schlesinger was not at all hesitant about presenting his strong objections to the Bay of Pigs plan in a memorandum to the President and the Secretary of State. But he became keenly aware of his tendency to suppress objections at the White House meetings. 'In the months after the Bay of Pigs I bitterly reproached myself for having kept so silent during those crucial discussions in the cabinet room,' Schlesinger writes in *A Thousand Days*. 'I can only explain my failure to do more than raise a few timid questions by reporting that one's impulse to blow the whistle on this nonsense was simply undone by the circumstances of the discussion.'

Unanimity

Victims of groupthink share an *illusion* of unanimity within the group concerning almost all judgements expressed by members who speak in favour of the majority view. This symptom results partly from the preceding one, whose effects are augmented by the false assumption that any individual who remains silent during any part of the discussion is in full accord with what the others are saying.

When a group of persons who respect each other's opinions arrives at a unanimous view, each member is likely to feel that the belief must be true. This reliance on consensual validation within the group tends to replace individual critical thinking and reality testing, unless there are clear-cut disagreements among the members. In contemplating a course of action such as the invasion of Cuba, it is painful for the members to confront disagreements within their group, particularly if it becomes apparent that there are widely divergent views about whether the preferred course of action is too risky to undertake at all. Such disagreements are solely to apprise anxieties about making a serious error. Once the sense of unanimity is shattered, the members no longer can feel complacently confident about the decision they are inclined to make. Each man must then face the annoying realisation that there are troublesome uncertainties and he must diligently seek out the best information he can get in order to decide for himself exactly how serious the risks might be. This is one of the unpleasant consequences of being in a group of hard-headed, critical thinkers.

To avoid such an unpleasant state, the members often become inclined, without quite realising it, to prevent latent disagreements from surfacing when they are about to initiate a risky course of action. The group leader and the members support each other in playing up the areas of convergence in their thinking, at the expense of fully exploring divergencies that might reveal unsettled issues.

'Our meetings took place in a curious atmosphere of assumed consensus,' Schlesinger writes. His additional comments clearly show that, curiously, the consensus was an illusion – an illusion that could be maintained only because the major participants did not reveal their own reasoning or discuss their idiosyncratic assumptions and vague reservations. Evidence from several sources makes it clear that even the three principals – President Kennedy, Rusk and McNamara – had widely differing assumptions about the invasion plan.

Mindguards

Victims of groupthink sometimes appoint themselves as mindguards to protect the leader and fellow members from adverse information that might break the complacency they shared about the effectiveness and morality of past decisions. At a large birthday party for his wife, Attorney General Robert F. Kennedy, who had been constantly informed about the Cuban invasion plan, took Schlesinger aside and asked him why he was opposed. Kennedy listened coldly and said, 'You may be right or you may be wrong, but the President has made his mind up. Don't push it any further. Now is the time for everyone to help him all they can.'

Rusk also functioned as a highly effective mindguard by failing to transmit to the group the strong objections of three 'outsiders' who had learned of the invasion plan – Under-Secretary of State Chester Bowles, USIA Director Edward R. Murrow, and Rusk's intelligence chief, Roger Hilsman. Had Rusk done so, their warnings might have reinforced Schlesinger's memorandum and jolted some of Kennedy's in-group, if not the President himself, into reconsidering the decision.

PRODUCTS

When a group of executives frequently displays most or all of these inter-related symptoms, a detailed study of their deliberations is likely to reveal a number of immediate consequences. These consequences are, in effect, products of poor decision-making practices because they lead to inadequate solutions to the problems under discussion.

First, the group limits its discussions to a few alternative courses of action (often only two) without an initial survey of all the alternatives that might be worthy of consideration.

Second, the group fails to re-examine the course of action initially preferred by the majority after they learn of risks and drawbacks they had not considered originally.

Third, the members spend little or no time discussing whether there are non-obvious gains they may have overlooked or ways of reducing the seemingly prohibitive costs that made rejected alternatives appear undesirable to them.

Fourth, members make little or no attempt to obtain information from experts within their own organisations who might be able to supply more precise estimates of potential losses and gains.

Fifth, members show positive interest in facts and opinions that support their preferred policy; they tend to ignore facts and opinions that do not.

Sixth, members spend little time deliberating about how the chosen policy might be hindered by bureaucratic inertia, sabotaged by political opponents, or temporarily derailed by common accidents. Consequently, they fail to work out contingency plans to cope with foreseeable setbacks that could endanger the overall success of their chosen course.

SUPPORT

The search for an explanation of why groupthink occurs has led me through a quagmire of complicated theoretical issues in the murky area of human motivation. My belief, based on recent social psychological research, is that we can best understand the various symptoms of groupthink as a mutual effort among the group members to maintain self-esteem and emotional equanimity by providing social support to each other, especially at times when they share responsibility for making vital decisions.

Even when no important decision is pending, the typical administrator will begin to doubt the wisdom and morality of his past decisions each time he received information about setbacks, particularly if the information is accompanied by negative feedback from prominent men who originally had been his supporters. It should not be surprising, therefore, to find that individual members strive to develop unanimity and *esprit de corps* that will help bolster each other's morale, to create an optimistic outlook about the success of pending decisions, and to reaffirm the positive value of past policies to which all of them are committed.

PRIDE

Shared illusions of invulnerability, for example, can reduce anxiety about taking risks. Rationalisations help members believe that the risks are really not so bad after all. The assumption of inherent morality helps the members to avoid feelings of shame or guilt.

Negative stereotypes function as stress-reducing devices to enhance a sense of moral righteousness as well as pride in a lofty mission.

The mutual enhancement of self-esteem and morale may have functional value in enabling the members to maintain their capacity to take action, but it has maladaptive consequences in so far as concurrence-seeking tendencies interfere with critical, rational capacities and lead to serious errors of judgement.

While I have limited my study to decision-making bodies in Government, groupthink symptoms appear in business, industry and any other field where small, cohesive groups make the decisions. It is vital, then, for all sorts of people – and especially group leaders – to know what steps they can take to prevent groupthink.

REMEDIES

To counterpoint my case studies of the major fiascos, I have also investigated two highly successful group enterprises, the formulation of the Marshall Plan in the Truman Administration and the handling of the Cuban missile crisis by President Kennedy and his advisers. I have found it instructive to examine the steps Kennedy took to change his group's decision-making processes. These changes ensured that the mistakes made by his Bay of Pigs in-group were not repeated by the missile-crisis in-group, even though the membership of both groups was essentially the same.

The following recommendations for preventing groupthink incorporate many of the good practices I discovered to be characteristic of the Marshall Plan and missile-crisis groups:

1   The leader of a policy-forming group should assign the role of critical evaluation to each member, encouraging the group to give high priority to open airing of objections and doubts. This practice needs to be reinforced by the leader's acceptance of criticism of his own judgements in order to discourage members from soft-peddling their disagreements and from allowing their striving for concurrence to inhibit critical thinking.

2   When the key members of a hierarchy assign a policy-planning mission to any group within their organisation, they should adopt an impartial stance instead of stating preferences and expectations at the beginning. This will encourage open inquiry and impartial probing of a wide range of policy alternatives.

3   The organisation routinely should set up several outside policy-planning and evaluation groups to work on the same policy question, each deliberating under a different leader. This can prevent the insulation of an in-group.

4   At intervals before the group reaches a final consensus, the leader should require each member to discuss the group's deliberations with associates in his own unit of the organisation – assuming that those associates can be trusted to adhere to the same security regulations that govern the policy-makers – and then report back their reactions to the group.

5   The group should invite one or more outside experts to each meeting on a staggered basis and encourage the experts to challenge the views of the core members.

6   At every general meeting of the group, whenever the agenda calls for an evaluation of policy alternates, at least one member should play devil's advocate, functioning as a good lawyer in challenging the testimony of those who advocate the majority position.

7   Whenever the policy issue involves relations with a rival nation or organisation, the group should devote a sizeable block of time, perhaps an entire session, to a survey of all warning signals from the rivals and should write alternative scenarios on the rivals' intentions.

8   When the group is surveying policy alternatives for feasibility and effectiveness, it should from time to time divide into two or more subgroups to meet separately, under different chairmen, and then come back together to hammer out differences.

9   After reaching a preliminary consensus about what seems to be the best policy, the group should hold a 'second-chance' meeting at

which every member expresses as vividly as he can all his residual doubts, and rethinks the entire issue before making a definitive choice.

HOW

These recommendations have their disadvantages. To encourage the open airing of objections, for instance, might lead to prolonged and costly debates when a rapidly growing crisis requires immediate solution. It also could cause rejection, depression and anger. A leader's failure to set a norm might create cleavage between leader and members that could develop into a disruptive power struggle if the leader looks on the emerging consensus as anathema. Setting up outside evaluation groups might increase the risk of security leakage. Still, inventive executives who know their way around the organisational maze probably can figure out how to apply one or another of the prescriptions successfully, without harmful side-effects.

They also could benefit from the advice of outside experts in the administrative and behavioural sciences. Though these experts have much to offer, they have had few chances to work on policy-making machinery within large organisations. As matters now stand, executives innovate only when they need new procedures to avoid repeating serious errors that have deflated their self-images.

In this era of atomic warheads, urban disorganisation and ecocatastrophes, it seems to me that policy-makers should collaborate with behavioural scientists and give top priority to preventing groupthink and its attendant fiascos.

Nevertheless, as in the judicial system, juries do sometimes seem to be able to take commendably sensible decisions, particularly where the members also have to implement their forecasts or act on the assumptions contained in them.

Such approaches are, though, not necessarily as accurate as some of their proponents would suggest. Makridakis and Wheelwright[5] report that

> A counterintuitive result of a number of studies by psychologists is that as the amount of information increases in a judgmental setting, predictive ability does not necessarily improve. Instead, the main effect of the additional information tends to be over-confidence in judgement.

Steven Schnaars[6] followed up a survey, conducted by *Industrial Research* journal in 1969, of research directors who were asked to state what developments would occur in the next ten years ('a manageable time span'). Of the 22 predictions made in 1969, only one proved to be a definite success, another was close to success and two more almost so. But this was less than a 20% hit rate only a decade into the future – the timescale of many long-range plans!

In general, the uncertainty associated with future events is severely underestimated. Schnaars suggests:

---

[5] Makridakis and Wheelwright, *Forecasting Methods for Management*.

[6] P. Steven Schnaars, *Megamistakes: Forecasting and the Myth of Rapid Technological Change* (The Free Press, 1989).

> Be conservative in your estimates of the potential for new products based on innovative technologies. Cut or damp any trend estimates with which you are provided.... Be suspicious. Be especially suspicious of forecasts that are based on accelerating trends in growth.

This is sound advice! A healthy scepticism as to accuracy, and an awareness of the related dangers posed by groupthink, might be seen as the main skills required in making and using practical long-term forecasts.

5.5 AIDS TO MAKING JUDGEMENTS IN FORECASTING

There are also a range of other techniques which are not forecasting techniques in themselves, but which are useful aids for experts when they are making their judgements.

Analogy

One approach, described in some detail by Joseph Martino,[7] is to look for an analogy. This may come from history, or from another field, or from another country. If the analogy matches the parameters involved, it can offer a useful insight into the processes at work. This may be a simple (indeed simplistic) approach, but under the right circumstances it can be a powerful one. Indeed, in one form or another it is probably the most popular technique used by managers.

Synectics

Synectics is defined as the study of processes leading to inventions with the end aim of solving practical problems. Applied to forecasting this technique, practised mainly by R & D departments, also uses analogy. How have other organisations solved similar problems? Are there any scientific analogies or natural analogies? Are there any solutions to similar problems in other countries or other industries? This approach often involves group discussions where the participants are carefully chosen, being deliberately drawn from a wide spectrum of backgrounds and possibly also screened for high creativity ('divergent' or 'lateral' thinking in the terms of De Bono[8]). In practice, if not conducted by experts, this may be a very scientific sounding name for simply looking to see if someone has already solved the problem in another context! In the right hands, however, it can represent a major source of ideas (more details can be found in Gordon[9]).

---

[7] Martino, *Technological Forecasting for Decisionmaking.*

[8] Edward De Bono, *Lateral Thinking* (Ward Lock Education, 1970).

[9] W.J.J. Gordon, *Synectics: The Development of Creative Capacity* (Harper & Row, 1961).

Tree structures

Another aid to qualitative forecasting is the use of tree structures. The main factors affecting the organisation's environment (for example) are plotted and the possible alternatives (or decisions, hence the name 'decision trees', sometimes used when a more formal, statistical/probabilistic framework is applied to this process) are shown at each stage. These branch at each level like a tree. An example is the choices facing an inventor described by Hull *et al.* (see Figure 5.2).

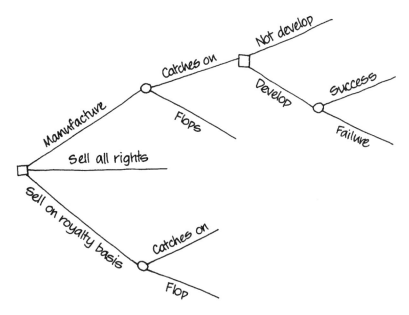

FIGURE 5.2   Decision tree for inventor example (source: John Hull, John Mapes and Brian Wheeler, *Model Building Techniques for Management* (Saxon House, 1976), p. 142)

At the end of this process all of the various possible combinations (or at least all that the forecaster chooses to take into account) will have been documented, including some which might not otherwise have been thought of – and that is the main value of the technique. The obvious problem is in dealing with the sheer number of alternatives that then become apparent. Also the judgements taken are still normative: the forecaster chooses the alternatives. Such normative methods help to structure the problem and ensure completeness, but they tend to impose rigidity on the solutions proposed (particularly where any appended numbers, such as statistical probability, appear to add validity).

A specialised form is the relevance tree, where the approach is used to force a panel of experts to identify technological deficiencies or areas where research is needed, for instance, and to determine priorities or attach relevance ratings – as illustrated by Makridakis and Wheelwright (see Figure 5.3).

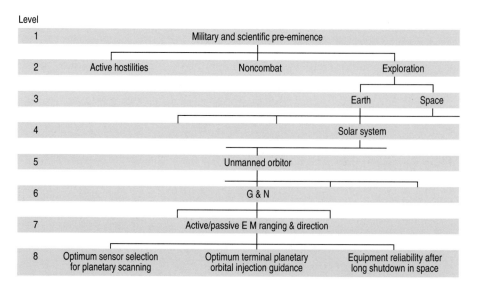

FIGURE 5.3   Sample relevance tree (source: Spyros Makridakis and Steven C. Wheelwright, *Forecasting Methods for Management* (5th edn, John Wiley, 1989), p. 321)

Morphological analysis

This pushes brainstorming approaches to their limits by looking at all the viable combinations of all the contributory elements. It requires working through all possible relationships between all the variables involved. For each of the combinations, of which there may be many, a development path is postulated. Inevitably, most of these will not be viable, but perhaps a few will.

Bayesian decision theory

The most sophisticated application of the tree-structured approaches is to apply probabilities to each of the decisions; Bayes's Theorem offers a simple formula (but one which is still incomprehensible to non-statisticians!) for dealing with conditional probability. The branches at each level are weighted by the probability of their occurring – a probability which is set by the forecaster (or by the group in the Jury or Delphi techniques). The resulting probabilities of all the possible outcomes can then be calculated. This process can be taken even further by calculating the composite pay-offs (the product of the calculated – monetary – value of the outcome multiplied by the probability) for each alternative (see Figure 5.4). With computing power now easily available, these quantified outputs can help give a good measure of the optimum outcomes, as long as, once more, it is recognised that all the input factors are opinions rather than hard facts.

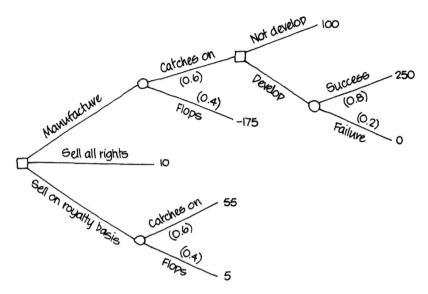

FIGURE 5.4   Decision tree with probabilities and pay-offs for inventor example (source: John Hull, John Mapes and Brian Wheeler, *Model Building Techniques for Management* (Saxon House, 1976), p. 143)

The wise forecaster also tries to understand how the various elements interact. The same pay-off may be achieved by low risks on low return activities or high risks on high returns – and most organisations (following risk averse strategies) would probably favour the former.

Audit 5.1

Looking back over the history of your organisation, has there been a significant switch in the level of technology involved in your products or services (or in that used to produce them)?

Does your organisation undertake any forecasting of the types described in the preceding sections? If so, how?

Does it use Delphi techniques, or any of the others mentioned in the previous section? What success has it had with these?

If not, how does it allow for the problems posed by changes in the external environment, in particular those caused by technological change?

5.6 USE OF MODELS

Throughout this book you will find references to 'models'. In this context a model is anything which claims to describe the relationships between the factors (the variables) involved, or at least a set of assumptions about these relationships which it is believed will explain them.

Schoner and Uhl[10] suggest

> three basic purposes of building a model. One is to predict the future.... Such models are descriptive... they become fixed, in a given prediction.... A second purpose in building a model is explanation of some phenomenon. Explanatory models may also be termed theories. A third purpose in model building is problem-solving.

This last category is the one to which many management models belong, and the one we will encounter most in this book.

Even so, the most popular use of models, consciously or not, is to predict the future. The user of a model, in basing his or her decision upon it (and upon the assumptions inherent in it), is assuming that the outcomes predicted by the model will occur. The importance of understanding the detail of models is to expose all the assumptions, including the hidden ones. If the model is explicit in this way, and its features are debated among those involved, a number of other benefits may accrue:

- Understanding – it may improve understanding of the processes, particularly where it brings together the separate ideas of a number of contributors.
- Communication – indeed, perhaps the most important element of explicit models is that they allow the participants to communicate their ideas (and assumptions) to each other.
- Limitations – making the model explicit can highlight its inadequacies and, in particular, gaps in its coverage.

Lilien and Kotler illustrate three of the most frequently used types of model structure (see Figure 5.5).

In its most mathematically rigorous and perhaps most recognisable form, a model will take the third of the forms shown, when it will usually comprise one or more equations. $Z = X + Y$ is the simplest such model (predicting what will happen to Z when X or Y changes). Mathematical models are obviously formal, but some verbal models can be just as formally recorded. Most models, however, use much less definite words – and are very informal. Indeed, they are not even recognised by those using them as models. In most decision-making the models behind the decisions are hidden, as are the assumptions inherent in them. Those taking the decisions do not even consider that they might re-evaluate these assumptions.

As Lunn, Blamires and Seaman[11] state:

> It cannot be emphasised too strongly that even the most unsympathetic critics of formal models in practice base their management decisions upon implicit models, which may well be totally misleading.

---

[10] Bertram Schoner and Kenneth P. Uhl, *Marketing Research: Information Systems and Decision Making* (John Wiley, 1975).

[11] Tony Lunn, Chris Blamires and David Seaman, 'Market modelling', in Robert Worcester and John Downham (eds), *Consumer Market Research Handbook* (McGraw Hill, 1986).

(a) Verbal model

New product growth often starts slowly, until some people (early triers) become aware of the product. These early triers interact with nontriers to lead to acceleration of sales growth. Finally, as market potential is approached, growth slows down.

(b) Graphical/conceptual model

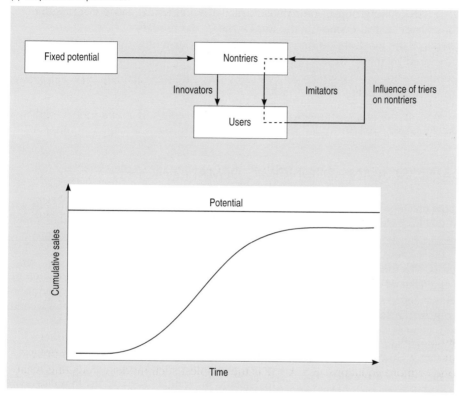

(c) Mathematical model

$$\frac{dx}{dt} = (a + bx)(N - x)$$

where x = number of purchases by t

N = market potential

a, b = constants

FIGURE 5.5   An illustration of three model structures (source: Gary L. Lilien and Philip Kotler, *Marketing Decision Making* (Harper and Row, 1983), p. 13)

They go on to suggest, in the specific context of market modelling, that

> a particularly important function of a modelling exercise is to make explicit the
> implicit assumptions held about market structure by both marketing men and
> researchers, thereby enabling these assumptions to be criticised, tested and
> developed.

This principle also holds true of all the other areas where decision-making is
practised. One group of models is particularly influential, since it forms the
basis for classical economic theory. Of these, the models of demand are
perhaps the most important of all; not least because they underpin the 'market'
favoured by many Western politicians. They are – at least in theory – rational
models; and, as an example of such models in general, we will now explore
them in more detail.

Now *quickly* read Article 5.2 by Linda Hesselman.[12]

Article 5.2 LINDA HESSELMAN: 'ECONOMIC DEMAND MODELS'

Economists analyse how much people choose to buy
in terms of a demand function which specifies the
individual's purchases as a function of the price of
the good, the price of other goods, the individual's
income and other factors. The function is very often
represented in terms of a demand curve: a graph
which plots quantities demanded against the price of
the good. If the other factors including income and
the price of other goods change, this will shift the
demand curve; a new 'shifted' line will need to be
drawn showing the new relationship between the
price of the good and the volume demanded. The
theory is concerned not with how much individuals
want or need of the good as such, but how
much they will choose to purchase, how much they
can afford, given their income and other
expenditures.

Neo-classical economics assumes that every 'good'
(every product or service consumed) holds a
certain 'utility'. This value, which may be seen
differently by each consumer, represents the utility
which that consumer obtains from the good.
Unlike marketing, which generally approaches the
same problem from the direction of models of
consumer (purchasing) behaviour, neo-classical
economics explores this utility in terms of
mathematical analyses of 'utility functions', which
relate utility to the quantity of goods consumed.

Neo-classical demand theory, therefore, begins with
a consumer who has such a utility function. Suppose
there are only two goods. We could write this:

$$U = U(q_1, q_2).$$

In other words, the utility derived is a function of
the quantity consumed, where q_1 is the quantity of
the first good and q_2 is the quantity of the second
good. It is assumed that an increase in the
quantity consumed increases utility, but that as
consumption rises each additional unit gives less
utility. (In mathematical terms, for those who
understand differential calculus, the first derivative
of U with respect to q is positive, the second
derivative negative.) This assumption, 'diminishing
marginal utility', matches the 'law of diminishing
returns' in production, where you get less
additional output for each additional unit of input
you use. The first derivative (again using
mathematical notation) of this function, the extra
utility of the last unit consumed, is called the
marginal utility. The consumer then chooses the
amounts of the two goods to consume subject to a
budget constraint:

$$(p_1 * q_1) + (p_2 * q_2) = Y$$

where Y is the consumer's income and p_1 and p_2
are the prices of the two goods. The equation
simply says that the total amount spent on good 1

[12] Written by Linda Hesselman of Unilever.

plus that spent on good 2 equals the consumer's income (in this very basic example).

To take another example: William spends his pocket money on sweets and comics. What others might think of his tastes is of no interest to William or economists; he knows his utility increases the more sweets he eats and the more comics he reads, though he admits that he does not get quite as much pleasure from the 25th bulls-eye as from the first! His pocket money is fixed, so he has to think how many sweets he is giving up for that extra comic. Being a sensible lad, he will plan his purchases so he gets the same pleasure from the money he spent on the last sweet as from the money spent on the last comic. If he had been getting more pleasure from the sweets, he would have bought more of them instead of the last comic. The fact that the utilities from the last units of expenditure are equal implies that at the quantities that maximise utility, the ratio of the marginal utility from good 1 to the marginal utility from good 2 is equal to the ratio of their prices. The idea is that at an efficient allocation that maximises utility, the marginal benefit given by the last unit consumed is equal to its cost.

From this calculation we can derive a demand curve which gives the amount (q) of each good that will be consumed by the individual as a function (D) of the prices of the goods (p) and the income available (Y).

William works out the relative price of comics as how many sweets he has to give up to buy a comic – the higher the price, the more sweets he has to give up, the fewer comics he will buy. If his pocket money goes up, he will buy more of both.

Figure 1 shows two demand curves for good 1 (where there are only two goods available). They slope down: as the relative price of good 1 falls, more is demanded, and they differ because income is higher in situation B, therefore the demand curve (D_A) is shifted out to position D_B and more is demanded. Extending the principle, the total demand curve for sweets and comics faced by the local corner store comes not just from William's demand, but from the aggregate of similar demand curves generated by all the other children who buy there.

When we describe demand curves, we usually do it in terms of 'elasticities'. Thus, the *price elasticity of demand is the percentage change in the*

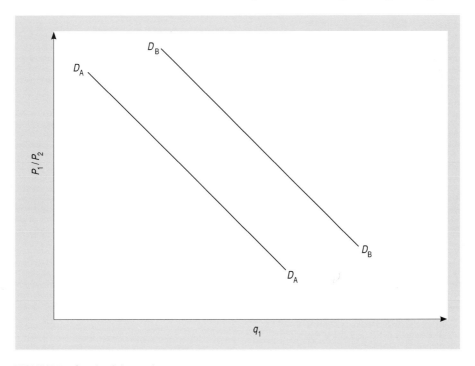

FIGURE 1   Graph of demand curves

quantity demanded in response to a 1% change in price. An elasticity of one means that a 1% increase in price causes a 1% fall in demand. An elasticity of two means that a 1% rise in price causes a 2% fall in demand. Goods with demand elasticities greater than one are said to have elastic demands, and are very sensitive to price. On the other hand, the elasticity may depend on the price *level*: at very low prices the good may have elastic demand and at high prices inelastic demand. If the price elasticity is one, then consumers spend the same amount on the good irrespective of price changes; the change in price is exactly matched by the change in quantity purchased. Those with demand elasticities below one, which are insensitive to price changes, are said to be inelastic.

The elasticity will depend on the market, for instance whether there are close substitutes. The elasticity for all comics might be quite low, but the elasticity for a particular title much higher; if

the price of that title increases while other comics do not, children are likely to decide it is bad value and switch.

Elasticity may be related to factors other than price. Thus, for instance, the income elasticity of demand is the percentage change in quantity consumed that results from a 1% change in income.

The utility maximising model can be generalised to allow for more than two goods; then the demand function for any one good depends on income and the prices of all goods. More specifically, assuming that all other factors remain the same (income is constant, as are all other prices) allows us to identify the main features of the analysis: the traditional demand curve, which relates demand to price. In Figure 2 the curve is shown in its more generally accepted form. It still slopes downwards, but it is no longer shown as a straight line – it is curved to reflect the effects of diminishing marginal utility.

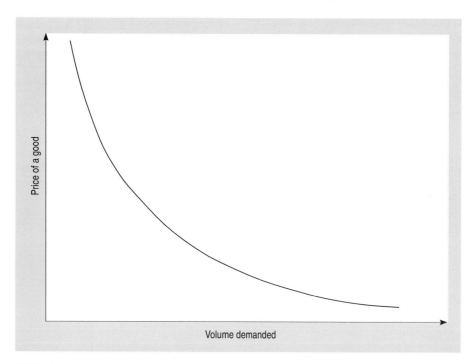

FIGURE 2   Demand curve

As an aside from the main thrust of this discussion, but to complete the picture as it is conventionally represented in many textbooks, we will now also add a line representing supply. In Figure 3 the supply curve is, in simple terms, the reverse of the demand curve. The higher the price, the *more* will be supplied because the higher price makes the market more attractive to the firm. At the point where these two curves cross – the equilibrium point – lies the price at which demand equals supply; in economic jargon, the market 'clears' (put more simply, the quantity demanded exactly equals that offered for supply). This diagram encapsulates what are often referred to as the 'laws of supply and demand'.

Returning to demand alone, other factors can be included in the utility function. For instance, the utility a household gets from buying disposable nappies depends on whether they have a baby in the house. Having a baby shifts the household's demand curve. Intertemporal allocation is important for some goods: your demand today will depend on your past purchases. Some goods are durable while others are addictive. So if you bought a new car yesterday, you are unlikely to

buy another one today, whereas if you bought cigarettes yesterday, you are very likely to buy them today.

This economic framework may appear narrow and abstract, but it is very flexible. Consider a charity that solicits contributions. It needs to forecast contributions in order to plan its support programme. The contributors are the customers. Demand, that is the flow of contributions, will vary with the seasons (peaking at Christmas usually), customers' incomes, advertising, etc. These influences can be modelled to provide a forecast. The model will also help to determine the optimal amount of advertising. Demand (contributions) is also likely to increase if the cost of the product (contributing) is reduced. This can be done by securing tax concessions from the Inland Revenue or organising payroll-giving, perhaps.

Forecasts are made for different purposes by different parts of an organisation. The objectives of the forecasters may not correspond to the objectives of the organisation as a whole: thus there is a danger of forecast bias. In the charitable organisation the project manager (a function like

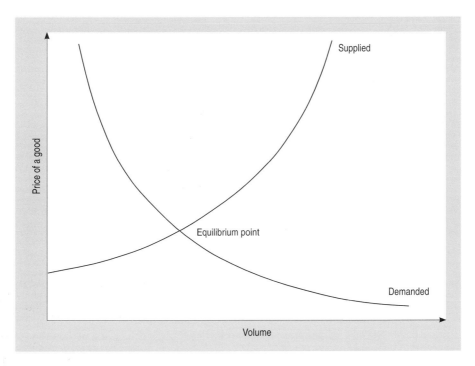

FIGURE 3   Graph of supply and demand

marketing in a commercial firm) concerned with all the unmet needs may be inclined to take an optimistic view of contributions in the coming year. The appeals manager (a function like finance), conscious of the danger of bankrupting the charity and the difficulty of persuading people to give, may be much more cautious about likely contributions. Most senior managers are aware of these organisational biases and adjust the forecasts appropriately.

There is a final issue concerning terminology. Short term, medium term and long term do not refer to chronological time but decision-making time. A foreign exchange dealer regards short term as minute-to-minute and long term as the end of the day when the books are squared. The timescale depends on when and what sort of decisions are made. In macroeconomics short term is quarter to quarter, medium term is a couple of years ahead, and long term is more than five years.

Activity 5.1

Take a recent business decision you have made, preferably a reasonably complex and important one. Did you use any models (theories – formal or informal) in the analysis which preceded the decision (analysis which, perhaps, was designed to predict the outcomes of alternative actions)?

Irrational models

In general there has been less emphasis on models which explore the irrational nature of management processes. This is perhaps understandable where social scientists in general, and management theorists in particular, have been trying to emulate the hard-edged methods of the physical sciences. Thus, they look to Isaac Newton, not to Sigmund Freud, for their example.

Irrational models (as opposed to false models, which are just incorrect) seek to describe (in a useful and usable way) the unpredictability of human processes. Hence the term 'irrational models': what they describe rationally is an irrational process. There are a number of common factors which underpin much of 'irrational' theory. Some of these factors are:

- Boolean (probability based) logic – in the field of 'irrationality', many of the more accurate numerical measurements revolve around probability. The yes/no decisions are rarely evident; instead there typically remains a percentage chance of each decision going one way or the other. Statistical theory is, therefore, a mainstay of 'irrational' planning.

- Catastrophe theory – in many physical and social events, change is not gradual. The switch is unlikely to come smoothly at some balance point, but rather will occur very rapidly after the conditions have been forced some way beyond the point of balance. This lag in response to changed conditions comes about because of the inertia inherent in the processes, which has to be overcome before anything can happen. The mathematics (or at least surface modelling) of catastrophe theory have been used to attempt to generate models of these kinds of events; as has that of 'chaos theory'.

- Atomic processes – a number of theories attempt to describe macro results (the movements of a national economy, say) in terms of the aggregation of many (often millions or even billions) individual, atomic decisions (by the people involved). Our own 'Hypothesis of Aggregated Expectations', which you will encounter later in the book, is one such theory.
- Interaction – unlike in the physical sciences, however, these atomic elements constantly interact in complex and often unpredictable ways. There may be positive feedback which reinforces apparent trends, or there may be negative feedback damping down (and perhaps conservatively frustrating) the emerging trends. This is one reason why, for instance, our own work emphasises the importance of actually measuring the current state of the various parameters; using sophisticated forms of marketing research.

Activity 5.2

Returning to that recent decision we looked at in Activity 5.1, what 'irrational models' do you think may have been involved?

Models as communication devices

A very important aspect of many models (the informal and irrational ones just as much as the formal) is their use for the communication of shared ideas. If an economic model says inflation will fall, and sufficient numbers of people accept its validity, then economic actors may resist the temptation to raise prices and accordingly inflationary pressures reduce! Thus a model with little objective basis may none the less turn out to be a good predictor of future events, provided it is believed by enough people and with sufficient fervour.

The predictive power of models as based on their persuasive ability therefore depends upon just two factors:

- How widely they are accepted. If only a minority accept the validity of a model, then its performance as a predictor will probably be limited. If a majority (no matter how misguided) do, it will be likely to offer strong predictions.
- How strongly they are accepted. If a model is the subject of strong (and general) support, then it will generally succeed in predicting outcomes and will indeed tend to operate as a law.

A major implication of the above is that changes in strongly held models do not occur slowly, but are subject to paradigm shifts.

Activity 5.3

Which are the most important vehicles by which you receive your own models? How important are the media, consultants, textbooks, etc. in forming your ideas?

Models in management

One of the main reasons for including this section on models is to alert you to the hidden models which influence much of management decision-making. Managers usually see themselves as rational beings, yet many of their decisions are constrained by irrational models.

Some models which become 'irrational' in the ways they influence behaviour may result from mis-statements by others of what were – in the hands of their authors – highly rigorous rational models. The Boston Matrix, which we will examine later in the book, was a major contribution to management theory. During its incorporation into the popular management culture, however, many of its features were often distorted beyond recognition. (Worse, these distortions were then sometimes amplified by poorly written or researched management textbooks!) As a result, many poor strategic decisions have been based upon misunderstanding and mis-statements of the Boston Consulting Group's position, and a rational model has been transformed by others into a magical talisman, used to justify the unjustifiable in ways which the model could never have done if applied correctly.

Many more models will, however, simply be hidden. The assumption that the best way of motivating people is by monetary incentives linked to the performance desired is rarely discussed, but it is a very basic (and, in reality, controversial) assumption of one model of behaviour. Equally, the concept that price will be a major determinant of sales represents a (management) cultural model which is difficult to challenge in a market economy.

The important lesson to be learned from this section is an awareness of what hidden assumptions (models) are influencing your decisions. If you can step back and recognise them, your decision-making may become that much less constrained.

The book will present you with a range of models. It is important that you recognise them for what they are, and apply the lessons of this section – not least to employ a degree of healthy positive scepticism!

Activity 5.4 _____

Take the last major set of management decisions you were involved in – a small project, for example. What broad models (of behaviour, for instance) were assumed in taking those decisions?

Did you, and the others involved in those decisions, assume that the participants would make their decisions rationally? If so, was this a reasonable assumption? What would have happened if you had explored the effect of 'irrational' decision-making?

6 SCENARIOS

Activity 6.1

In the preceding sections you have examined a variety of different techniques which may be applied to long-range forecasting. What features do these techniques have in common?

By now you should recognise that these techniques are all based on what must be essentially *judgemental* inputs, even though the related theory sometimes (falsely) claims a degree of scientific accuracy. In one form or another, they are founded on individual 'guesses' about the future. Most of the techniques, therefore, attempt to control the biases that may arise in individual judgements. Some do this by providing structures to force the participants to consider all the possible outcomes. Some do it by employing juries of experts to average out the worst excesses. They all try, with varying degrees of success, to deal with the uncertainty which is a characteristic element of most long-range forecasting.

What you might *not* have noted down is that most of these approaches still aim to deliver *one* forecast of the future. While they avoid the pitfall of simple extrapolation, they still assume that it is desirable, and possible, to predict a single set of outcomes.

6.1 SCENARIOS COMPARED TO OTHER FORECASTING TECHNIQUES

This leads us to the concept of scenario forecasting, which is by far the most sophisticated of such techniques. It can incorporate all the other techniques, while allowing for uncertainty by examining alternatives rather than offering a single prediction.

Now *skim* Article 6.1 by Michel Godet,[1] which was written in 1982, not long after the 1973 'Oil Crisis' which had a dramatic impact on the use of forecasting.

---

[1] Reprinted from *Journal of Forecasting* 1 (1982). Reproduced by permission from John Wiley and Sons Ltd.

Article 6.1 MICHEL GODET: 'FROM FORECASTING TO "LA PROSPECTIVE" – A NEW WAY OF LOOKING AT FUTURES'

CLASSICAL FORECASTING AND ITS ERRORS

The economic history of industrial society has been marked by repeated forecasting errors. What is serious is not so much the existence of errors, as the systematic ignoring of past errors when new forecasts are made.

In 1972, before what came to be known as the energy crisis, forecasts of energy consumption reckoned on the continuance of a declining trend in relative oil prices until 1980–5. The present economic crisis is partly due to the forecasts that cheap energy would continue to be available. The enormity of the errors highlights the ridiculous precision with which the forecasts are presented. In a period of a few years, forecasts of energy prices increased more than fourfold.

The need for an overall view

Most of the forecasting models include a few explanatory variables, most of which can be easily quantified. They do not take into account the development of new relationships and the possible changes in trends. A major failure in forecasting arises from the fact that the economy is regarded as autonomous. Economic forecasting is therefore divorced from social and political forecasting and is itself fragmented into technological, demographic and other forecasts.

On the other hand, there is a strong need to study an entire system in which everything is more and more interdependent and in which the whole, as distinct from the sum of the parts, is reflected in each part. Since the parts are interdependent, reasoning based on the assumption of 'everything else being held constant' cannot explain the evolution of social economic phenomena where everything moves simultaneously. An understanding of the whole is necessary, therefore, to deal with the individual parts of a system, and not the other way round, as is advocated by 'classical' long-term forecasting approaches.

The limits of quantification and models

The impossibility of forecasting the future as a function solely of past data explains the weakness of econometric modelling which does not integrate qualitative and non-quantifiable parameters such as the wishes and behaviour of relevant actors. It should be emphasised that the dangers of false quantification – quantifying involves giving priority to what is quantifiable at the expense of what is not – should not lead to the total rejection of numbers. But we should use them with extreme caution, especially since statistics are flawed by errors. As Morgenstern (1972) emphasises, national income and consumers' purchasing figures include errors of the magnitude of plus or minus 10–15%. Thus input data are incomplete and contain errors; furthermore, the choice of model is not neutral, but conditions the result. The model embodies a theory whose value is limited by the fact that, although there is a single set of data used, there can be a multiplicity of models and interpretations. Model users, on the other hand, believe unduly in the objectivity of their models.

In addition, models are deterministic, but the future depends largely on human actions based on the exercise of free will, which makes them unrealistic. Furthermore, 'classical' forecasting models are not only deterministic, but also assume structural stability, which is another source of forecasting error, since changes are always possible.

Finally, quantitative models tend to reassure. Their mathematics has become more and more sophisticated and, in relying on them, it is easy to forget that the hypothesis and choice of model determine the results achieved. 'The use of mathematics does not in itself solve the problem, even if it allows the problem to be posed more rigorously. For instance, a system of false concepts remains a system of false concepts even when a whole body of theorems is rigorously deduced. The formulation of equations does not in itself confer scientific quality' (Amin, 1971).

The absence of neutrality of information and forecasts

Information about the future, as that of the present or the past, is rarely neutral: usually it services specific interests. How many studies and analyses are lying hidden in drawers because they are politically undesirable; how many pertinent reports are emptied of their substance by careful selection of words; how many realities are ignored because they do not fit preconceived ideas. Information is manipulated simply because it is a major source of power. As Crozier and Friedberg (1977: 107, 181) have pointed out 'information is a rare commodity, and its communication and exchange are not neutral and free processes. To inform someone, to give him information which he does not possess, is to divest oneself, to relinquish those trump cards which could be sold, to make oneself vulnerable in the face of takeover attempts.... Total communication is impossible. To enter into a relationship with another, to seek to open up to him is at the same time to hide and to protect oneself behind fortifications and to oppose him. Briefly any relation with another is strategic and contains a power component, however repressed or sublimated it may be'.

The past and the present are irreversible, unique and certain, but the knowledge we have of them is incomplete; even if the facts of the past are certain, they are only a tiny part of the unknown number of phenomena that make up reality. In consequence, history is only a bet on one of many interpretations (the facts are unique, their interpretations are multiple). It is in this sense that we can say that there are several pasts, or rather several approximations to the same past which one never totally knows.

By the same token, any forecasting requires choices within a system of values, and an ideology, implicit or explicit. Forecasting is, therefore, only valid in so far as this system and ideology is itself acceptable to the reader or the user.

The publication of forecasts themselves influences the future as people inevitably react to forecasts. Thus, a forecast that there will be a scarcity of sugar can become a self-fulfilling prophecy when large numbers of people believe it and rush to buy sugar, thus creating a real scarcity.

TO 'LA PROSPECTIVE' AS AN APPROACH TO DEALING WITH THE FUTURE

The inadequacy of 'classical' forecasting techniques can be explained by their down playing, or outright ignoring, of the role played by creative human actions in determining the future. This creative attitude is recognised by the 'prospective' approach, which reflects awareness of a future that is both deterministic and free, both passively suffered and actively willed.

'Prospective', first used by Berger (1964) has become widespread in expressing this new attitude to the future. The word 'forecasting' remains too strongly shared with its classical meaning of prediction and is used mainly in the sense of quantified calculations.

The future is not written: it has still to be built

To understand the future, one must first start with the past; what we regret about the past is usually the future ahead of us. Thus, the past is a dead future. The only determinism we grant the past consists of the varying degrees of freedom that past actions have left us to act in the present so as to realise some future plan. What happens in the future results from our past actions, while our desire explains present actions. From this viewpoint, there is no determinism except in the sense that a given evolution of the past presents one particular range of possible futures and not another. Man, in so far as he has not committed or mortgaged his future, retains many degrees of freedom from which he can profit. He can, then, promote one or another alternative future(s) depending upon what he regards as more desirable in relation to his own objectives.

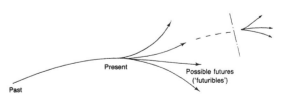

FIGURE 1   A multiple and uncertain future

The future should not be envisaged in a unique and predetermined mode, or as a continuation of the past: the future is multiple and uncertain. The plurality of the future and the degrees of freedom for human action go hand in hand; the future is not written; it remains to be built. This is an advantage since man has control over what might come; on the other hand, the ability of man to influence the future is a major source of uncertainty as far as forecasting is concerned. There are constraints in terms of how much the future can be influenced. Nevertheless, in a world which is unequal and confrontational, the future is the result of the interaction of unequal human forces, shaped by human actions, trends, and constraints. Finally, the future does not belong to everyone in the same way and the same degree; some actors exercise a greater influence than others.

To accept that the future is multiple, and that there is no unique model describing its evolution, is also implicitly to acknowledge that the horizons of 'prospective' are to be viewed in the plural (see Figure 1). Structural changes, resistances, and discontinuities are part of the future. Furthermore, the acceleration of change, coupled with the variety of systems studied, leads to accepting a range of different time-scales. From this point of view, the concepts of short, medium and long term are not important except as a function of the problem being studied. For instance, 'long-term' is when many things may have changed.

THE FUTURE IS THE *RAISON D'ÊTRE* OF THE PRESENT

Societies are most frequently in a state of transition when the old equilibrium of forces has disappeared. But when the old equilibrium is not yet born or stable, it is necessary to look at the future to clarify the present, so that 'the future is the *raison d'être* of the present'. 'Prospective' is an anticipated retrospective.

We are well familiar with the forces of the past, but to explain the present, we must also ask ourselves about the future. To understand more fully today the events that occurred in 1960 or to understand what is happening today, we must place ourselves in 1990 or beyond. With regard to the essentially subjective nature of reflection about the future, it is primarily the idea we form of the future that explains the present. For example, in basing an individual's consumption at a given moment on expected future income (theory of continuous income), Milton Friedman places importance on psychological factors. To say that production in a given year depends on prices in previous years explains nothing in itself. What is important for the entrepreneur is his idea of the price in future years, whether or not it is relative to that of past years. This determines his production and investment plans. The image of the future thus imprints itself on the present.

On that basis, and if several futures are possible, the one which will in fact be produced is born as much from the confrontations of the projections of the various actors as from the continuation of existing trends. The various actors present in a system often have contradictory ideas and preferences about possible futures. The future must be considered as the result of these different forces. In order to identify the most probable results, it is necessary to understand fully the projects and intentions of the actors, their methods of action on one another, coupled with the constraints imposed on them.

The image of the future is not solely speculative; it is, in particular, normative and results as much from actions as from constraints. The purpose of the prospective approach is to prepare the way (both desirable and feasible) for the future. Its aim is to guide our present actions so as to expand the field of the feasible. It should, in particular, lead to the careful consideration of decisions that could irreversibly determine the future, or deprive us of freedom of movement. A prospective decision, therefore, is less concerned with maximising short-term advantage. Its major consideration is to keep as many choices open as possible.

Central to the approach advocated in this chapter is that the future is emerging, but its details are unknown. Despite these unknowns, it is necessary to take decisions today which will commit us in the future. Often our ability to predict future events is limited, and in the lack of precise information, we might find it necessary to gamble. This must be done, however, without mortgaging the future. We need freedom of action. The future is unpredictable, increasingly changing, and uncertain.

A KEY TO UNDERSTANDING CRISES

[2977]In our view, the future is mainly the result of conflicts between unequal actors in a system of variable constraints. The future possibilities are multiple and undetermined – to be an actor implies freedom and, consequently, uncertainty. By looking at desires or wishes as a production force of the future it is possible to understand better why political, economic and social structures break down when constraints increase beyond a certain level. Problems inevitably arise when the gap between reality and aspirations becomes too wide. This is why it is important to deal with these problems by understanding the gap between wishes and aspirations.

Crisis reflects a change in the rules of the game and the functioning (relationships) of a system. This change is desired by certain actors and rejected by others. There is a crisis when, as a result of the changing balance of power, the gap between reality and aspirations becomes too great and requires new rules. The crisis takes place when the change is sufficiently powerful to disturb the former rules of the game, but not powerful enough to impose new rules. As long as the old is dying, but the new is not yet born, the system will be unregulated and in a state of crisis.

The monetary, economic and energy crises which we have experienced since the beginning of the 1970s confirms this analysis. The monetary crisis reflects the relative political and economic decline of the United States as compared with the other Western nations. In the new relationships, the dollar is not sufficiently powerful to play its former role as a regulator, but is still too powerful to be ignored. The crisis will last until another rule is found and accepted by the participants of the monetary game.

The energy crisis is of similar type – the quadrupling of oil prices does not result from a sudden change in the quantities available or required but only from a change in the conditions of the supply, that is to say in the balance of power between producers and consumers.

The old price-fixing rules have disappeared, new rules were established for which we were not prepared and which we refused to accept. There was a gap between the new reality and the former aspirations. Current and future increases in oil prices can only confirm or nullify the authority of the new rules of the game. The physical shortages which are predicted are only the logical consequences of our refusal to clearly see the new reality facing us and take necessary measures (capital investments, exploration, energy-savings).

Crises, on the other hand, develop because we refuse to adapt our behaviour and our structures to the new rules of the game. Crises can be visualised as the difference between existing rules, which we have already learnt, and those which still have to be learnt. It must be accepted that crises will last as long as our period of learning. We cannot expect to end crises other than by changing our behaviour and possibly our lifestyles (for more details, see Godet, 1980).

Comparing 'classical' forecasting and 'la prospective'

Partial viewpoints, quantitative variables, the perception of relationships as static, the explanation of the future by the past, the search for a unique and predetermined future with the help of deterministic models, are embodied in 'classical' forecasting. The result of such attitudes towards forecasting can be huge forecasting errors. Most important however, is that actions and wishes, the things that cannot be expressed by equations, have no place in 'classical' forecasting.

The 'prospective' approach actively participates in the creation of the future. Its characteristics are radically different from those of 'classical' forecasting. Numerous forecasting errors and, in fact, the crisis in forecasting as a whole could be avoided by using the prospective approach. Table 1 shows seven characteristics of the 'prospective' approach and distinguishes them from those of 'classical' forecasting.

The scenario method, widely used in 'prospective', is a powerful tool for constructing alternative futures. It is from these futures that decision-makers can choose the one which best fits their objectives and which can be attained given existing constraints.

Table 1   Characteristics of classical forecasting compared with those of the prospective approach

	Classical forecasting	Prospective approach
Viewpoint	Piecemeal 'Everything else being equal'	Overall approach 'Nothing else being equal'
Variables	Quantitative, objective and known	Qualitative, not necessarily quantitative, subjective, known or hidden
Relationships	Static, fixed structures	Dynamic, evolving structures
Explanation	The past explains the future	The future is the *raison d'être* of the present
Future	Single and certain	Multiple and uncertain
Method	Deterministic and quantitative models (econometric, mathematical)	Intentional analysis Qualitative (structural analysis) and stochastic (cross-impacts) models
Attitude to the future	Passive or adaptive (future *comes* about)	Active and creative (future *brought* about)

THE METHOD OF SCENARIOS AS USED BY 'LA PROSPECTIVE'

'La prospective' accepts that the future is multiple, the outcome of various actors and their actions. The scenarios method, as used in the 'prospective' approach, is concerned with deriving these multiple futures and with exploring the pathways leading to them. Literary scenarios, however, although they may represent a stimulating exercise for the imagination, suffer from a lack of credibility. It is impossible to verify the validity and plausibility of the hypotheses advanced. This is why an alternative way has been developed by the 'prospective' approach whose objectives are:

1   To identify which points should be studied as a matter of priority (key variables), by confronting the variables relating to the phenomenon being studied and the variables describing the environment, using an overall explanatory analysis as exhaustive as possible. Structural analysis makes it possible to take this overall view. In particular, the MICMAC 1 (Cross Impact Matrices-Multiplication Applied to Classification) method, which analyses the direct relationships and feedback effects between variables, makes it easier to understand the dynamics of the system being studied (Godet, 1979).

2   To determine the interrelationships among the key variables, the relative power of the fundamental actors, their strategies, the resources which they have at their disposal, their objectives, and the constraints which they must overcome. This is the specific object of the retrospective and the present situation analysis.

When a scenario has been chosen, some 'classical' forecasting techniques can be used, within the framework defined by the scenario, to translate this scenario into quantitative terms.

The method of scenarios has been applied in many cases during the last few years. It consists of three major phases (see Figure 2):

(a)   The construction of the base, where the problem posed is situated in its broadest environment and where the existing state of the system is studied so as to understand the mechanisms and to identify the development prospects.

(b)   The elaboration of the scenarios, where, using the results of the previous phase, the probabilities of realisation of the various possible final images are obtained, with the use of cross-impact matrix methods (Duperin and Godet, 1975). This makes it possible to select from among the most probable scenarios

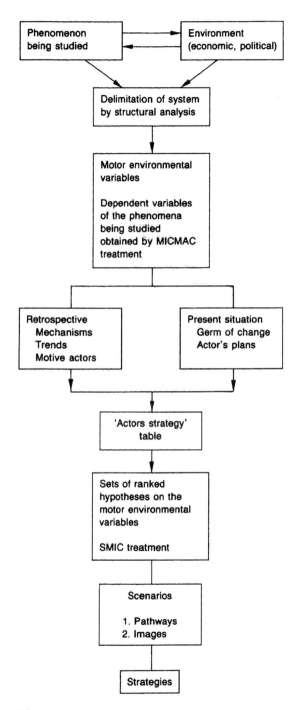

FIGURE 2   The method of scenarios as used by the prospective approach

a reference scenario, which is then supplemented by the study of contrasted scenarios (optimistic and pessimistic scenarios). Each of these qualitative scenarios is translated in quantitative terms through appropriate forecasting techniques.

(c) The selection of the strategic actions to be taken so that the organisation may attain its objectives, taking into account the possibilities of change in the system in which it is involved.

CONCLUSIONS – COMPLEMENTARITY BETWEEN 'LA PROSPECTIVE' AND FORECASTING

To criticise is not to reject. Although quantification at any price may seem dangerous, the numerical results of 'classical' forecasting models (time series econometric) do provide stimulating indicators and valuable reference points for a consideration of the future. We believe that there is a certain complementarity between the 'prospective' and 'classical' forecasting. A forecasting model is valuable only by virtue of its hypotheses (econometric, political, ...) whereas the objective of the 'prospective' approach is to discuss and validate the hypotheses that will make the model consistent and realistic.

Naturally, this complementarity does not hold in a uniform manner. In the long term, when everything or almost everything may have changed, the 'prospective' approach places almost no reliance on 'classical' forecasting methods since structural changes are the rule. On the other hand, as the forecasting horizon became progressively shorter, 'classical' forecasting methods play an increasingly important role in so far as the existence of structural stability can be assumed not to be violated. Furthermore, trends identified in the past can be extrapolated into the future. The chances of structural changes are considerably less as the forecasting horizon becomes shorter.

The prospective approach is not a substitute for making prophecies about the future. However, by its use of scenarios and by explicitly accepting that the objectives and wishes of the various actors involved do affect the future, it provides the field of forecasting with an alternative approach to studying the future.

BIBLIOGRAPHY

Amin, S. (1971) *L'accumulation à l'Echelle Mondiale*, 2nd edn. Paris: Anthropos.

Berger, G. (1964) *Phénoménologie du Temps et Prospective*. Paris: Presses Universitaires de France.

Berger, G. (1967) *Etapes de la Prospective*. Paris: Presses Universitaires de France.

Cournand, A. and Levy, M. (1973) *Shaping the Future: Gaston Berger and the Concept of Prospective*. New York: Gordon and Breach Science Publishers.

Crozier, M. and Friedberg, E. (1977) *L'Acteur et le Système*. Paris: Le Seuil.

Duperin, J.C. and Godet, M. (1975) 'SMIC 74: a new cross impact method', *Futures,* 7 (4): 302–12.

Godet, M. (1976) 'Scenarios of air transport development to 1990 by SMIC 74 a new cross-impact method', *Technological Forecasting and Social Change*, 9: 279–88.

Godet, M. (1979) *The Crisis in Forecasting and the Emergence of the Prospective Approach*, New York: Pergamon.

Godet, M. (1980) *Demain les Crises: de la Résignation à l'Antifatalité*. Paris: Hachette.

Jouvenel, B. (1964) *L'Art de la Conjecture*. Monaco: Du Rocher.

Lesourne, J. (1979) *Interfutures: Facing the Future, Mastering the Probable and Managing the Unpredictable*. Paris: OECD.

Lesourne, J. (1982) *Les Mille Sentiers de l'Avenir*. Paris: Seghers.

Morgenstern, O. (1972) *Précision et Incertitudes des Données Economiques*. Paris: Dunod.

Saint-Paul, R. and Teniere-Buchot, P. F. (1974) *Innovation et Évaluation Technologique*. Paris: Entreprise Moderne d'Edition.

Godet criticises the bias which tends to lurk behind normal forecasts. His solution is to use scenarios ('La Prospective') to handle the uncertainty of the future. His Table 1 offers a very concise explanation of the differences between scenarios and more conventional means of forecasting.

The technique focuses on the uncertainty itself. On the other hand, it avoids most of the problems by not predicting exactly what will happen! It recognises that there may be many different possible outcomes, and describes all of them. The 'scenario' is, in this context, merely a reporting framework within which all these outcomes may be described.

As can be seen from the article, however, the earliest use of scenarios tended to be the province of academics. Thus, though the concept was first introduced as 'La Prospective' by Berger[2] in 1964, and the word 'scenario' itself was reportedly first used by Herman Kahn[3] in 1967, the theoretical foundations of scenario forecasting were mainly developed in the 1970s, especially by Godet himself (between 1974 and 1979)[4]. By the early 1980s these approaches had developed into a sophisticated forecasting technique which was primarily recommended for integrating the output from other sophisticated qualitative approaches into long-range forecasting, such as those we have already looked at.

[2] G. Berger, *Phénoménologies du Temps et Prospectives* (Presse Universitaires de France, 1964).

[3] H. Kahn, *The Year 2000* (Calman-Levy, 1967).

[4] M. Godet, *Scenarios and Strategic Management* (Butterworth, 1987).

Possibly as a result of these very sophisticated approaches, and of the difficult techniques they employed (which usually demanded the resources of a central planning staff), scenarios earned a reputation for being difficult and costly to use. The MICMAC approach (based on 'cross-impact matrices') which Godet puts at the centre of his method (shown in his Figure 2) is typical of this level of complexity. Even so, the theoretical importance of the use of alternative scenarios, to help address the uncertainty implicit in long-range forecasts, was dramatically underlined by the widespread confusion which followed the Oil Shock of 1973. As a result, many of the larger organisations started to use the technique in one form or another. Indeed, just ten years later, in 1983, Diffenbach[5] reported that 'alternate scenarios' were the third most popular technique for long-range forecasting – used by 68% of the large organisations he surveyed.

6.2 PRACTICAL DEVELOPMENT OF SCENARIOS

The practical development of scenario forecasting to guide strategy, rather than for more limited academic uses, was started by Pierre Wack[6] in 1971 at the Royal Dutch Shell group of companies (hereafter, for simplicity, referred to as 'Shell') – and it, too, was given impetus by the Oil Shock two years later. Shell has, since that time, led the commercial world in the use of scenarios – and in the development of more practical techniques to support scenarios. Indeed, in common with most forms of long-range forecasting, the use of scenarios has (during the depressed trading conditions of much of the last decade) been reduced to only a handful of private-sector organisations. Shell remains almost alone among them in keeping the technique at the forefront of forecasting.

Kees van der Heijden,[7] one of a number of managers from Shell who have subsequently entered the academic world to offer their experience to a wider audience, describes the benefits to be obtained from using scenarios in terms of their value for the *institutional learning process*. He splits them into those for the *individual*:

- *As a Cognitive Device* – as a highly efficient tool for organising data and making data easier to handle
- *As a Perception Device* – increasing the range of what you see, expanding your mental models
- *As a Cognitive Reflection Tool* – helping you think through the ideas.

At the *group* level:

- *As a Ready-Made Language Provider* – assisting strategic conversations
- *As a Conversational Facilitation Vehicle* – offering an organised way of discussing the matters in hand
- *As Vehicle for Mental Model Alignment* – permitting coherent strategic action.

---

[5] J. Diffenbach, 'Corporate environmental analysis in large US corporations', *Long Range Planning*, vol. 16, no. 3, 1983.

[6] P. Wack, 'Scenarios: uncharted waters ahead', *Harvard Business Review*, September–October, 1985.

[7] Kees Van Der Heijden, *Scenarios: The Art of Strategic Conversation* (Wiley, 1997).

Now *quickly* read Article 6.2 by Pierre Wack.[8]

Article 6.2 PIERRE WACK: 'SCENARIOS: SHOOTING THE RAPIDS'

I recently discussed scenario analysis with a well-known futurist. After I had listened to his presentation of a set of six scenarios, he asked me what I thought. 'It was beautifully written, if complex', I replied. When pressed, I admitted that is was 'impenetrable.' I added, 'The managers who hear it won't know what to do with it.' To which the consultant responded, 'That is not really my concern. I simply lay out the possibilities for them. It is up to the managers to know what they should do. I can't possibly tell them.'

This small illustration points up the key problem with scenario planning: the interface of scenarios and decision-makers is ignored or neglected. By interface, I mean the point at which the scenario really touches a chord in the manager's mind – the moment at which it has real meaning for him or her. The fact that those with the responsibility for preparing the scenarios do not feel any responsibility for the interface is the main reason that – despite the logical appeal scenarios should have for managers disenchanted with forecasts – scenario planning has been scarcely developed. Scenarios that merely quantify alternative outcomes of obvious uncertainties never inspire a management team's enthusiasm, even if all the alternatives are plausible. Most executives do not like to face such alternatives. They yearn for some kind of 'definiteness' when dealing with the uncertainty that is the business environment, even if they have had their fingers burned for relying on past forecasts.

The same managers who can easily decide between different courses of action when they are in control often become unstuck when confronted with alternative futures they can't control and don't really understand. The reason is partly historical: many managers developed their skills in the 1950s and 1960s, an era characterised by an unusually high level of economic predictability. Being

competent then meant knowing the right answer; it was considered incompetent or unprofessional to say, 'Things could go this way – or that.'

In truth, scenarios are often popular with middle managers who do not have to make awesome, final decisions. It is really top managers – who have ultimate responsibility for a company's long-term strategy – who find scenarios unhelpful. Most have risen to the top of large organisations based on their good judgement. They are proud of that judgement and trust it; their faith in it is one of their key motivations. The usual scenario analysis confronts them with raw uncertainties on which they cannot exercise their judgement. Because they cannot use what they consider to be their best quality, they often say, 'Why bother with all that scenario stuff? We'll go on as before.' Top management's desire for a framework in which to exercise good judgement is so strong that many executives continue to rely on forecasts, even though they know that forecasts often miss critical turning points in the business environment and even when they have been hurt by poor forecasts before.

What distinguishes Shell's decision scenarios from the first-generation analyses delineated in my earlier article is not primarily technical; it is a different philosophy, having to do with management perceptions and judgement.[1] The technicalities of decision scenarios derive from that philosophy. Almost by definition, scanning the business environment and crystallising the findings in a set of scenarios means dealing with a world outside the corporation: for example, the evolution of demand, supply, prices, technology, competition, business cycle changes, and so forth. But this is only a half-truth and dangerous because there is another half. Because the raw materials of scenarios are made from this stuff of 'outer space,' it is not realised that more is

[8] Reprinted from *Harvard Business Review*, November/December 1985: 139–50. Copyright © 1985 by the President and Fellows of Harvard College.

needed: scenarios must come alive in 'inner space,' the manager's microcosm where choices are played out and judgement exercised.

Scenarios deal with two worlds: the world of facts and the world of perceptions. They explore for facts but they aim at perceptions inside the heads of decision-makers. Their purpose is to gather and transform information of strategic significance into fresh perceptions. This transformation process is not trivial – more often than not it does not happen. When it works it is a creative experience that generates a heartfelt 'Aha!' from your managers and leads to strategic insights beyond the mind's previous reach.

I have found that getting to that management 'Aha!' is the real challenge of scenario analysis. It does not simply leap at you when you've presented all the possible alternatives, no matter how eloquent your expression or how beautifully drawn your charts. It happens when your message reaches the microcosms of decision-makers, obliges them to question their assumptions about how their business world works, and leads them to change and reorganise their inner models of reality.

SETTING OUT

Scenario analysis demands first that managers understand the forces driving their business systems rather than rely on forecasts or alternatives (that is, someone else's understanding and judgement crystallised in a figure that then becomes a substitute for thinking). Using scenarios is as different from relying on forecasts as judo is from boxing: you want to use outside forces to your competitive advantage and make them work for you so that two plus two equals five and even more. You will find little or no power by merely accepting expert information about an outcome like the future price of oil or the future level of demand; power comes with an understanding of the forces behind the outcome. Scenarios must help decision-makers develop their own feel for the nature of the system, the forces at work within it, the uncertainties that underlie the alternative scenarios, and the concepts useful for interpreting key data.

Scenarios structure the future into predetermined and uncertain elements (see Figure 1). The foundation of decision scenarios lies in exploration and expansion of the predetermined elements: events already in the pipeline whose consequences have yet to unfold, interdependencies within the system (surprises often arise from interconnectedness), breaks in trends, or the 'impossible.' Decision scenarios rule out impossible developments; they deny much more than they affirm.

I will now take a risk and describe a ten-year-old scenario analysis. It is a risk because the scenario's subject is the business cycle, and no subject threatens to bore the reader in quite the same way as a business cycle that has passed. Even so, the discussion is important because:

1. We may be near the top of the business cycle, and a recession with serious implications could begin, given the fragility of the world economy. It troubles me that so few companies have analysed the implications for them of economic developments outside the range of surprise-free possibility. Macroeconomists may discuss contingencies but managers do not.

2. The scenario analysis I presented in the first article (in the previous issue of the *Harvard Business Review*) was somewhat atypical. It dealt with an economic disruption of a magnitude we do not often encounter. Moreover, we believed the disruption was a predetermined factor; uncertain were the reactions to it.

The following example deals with more typical cyclical fluctuations. We presented it in May 1975, when the world was nearly at the bottom of the worst recession since World War II.

Analysing the predetermined elements

When the oil shock of 1973–4 made the dreams – and nightmares – described in the scenarios discussed in my first article come true, managers at Shell (like managers everywhere) redirected their attention to the short term, focusing on economic growth, oil demand, inflation, interest rates, and their sensitive relationship with OPEC suppliers. In 1975, we addressed their concerns by developing medium-term scenarios for the rapids. The predetermined elements of these scenarios were:

Predetermined elements

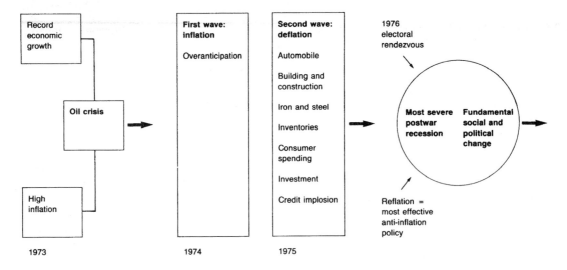

Uncertainties

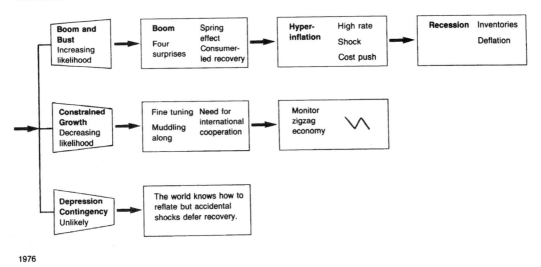

1976

FIGURE 1   Global framework (1975)

The first wave – inflation Like a large rock dropped in a lake, the 1973 oil price increase generated a series of waves, beginning with inflation, which was higher than simple cost-through-the-system arithmetic would indicate (on average, only 3 per cent or 4 per cent). Booming world economies were already out of balance prior to the oil shock and affected by high inflation. Furthermore, the enormous publicity surrounding the oil price increase (coming as it did with production cuts and selective embargoes) caused major economic actors – trade unions, entrepreneurs, and consumers – to overanticipate the actual inflationary impact. Such overreaction added fuel to the fire, accelerating the rate of inflation.

The second wave – deflation From mid-1974, a contraction in demand to well below production capacity followed. The extra cash outflow to

OPEC acted like an external excise tax on consumer demand of some $60 billion each year – or 2.5 per cent of OECD economies. Government anti-inflation policies contributed to pushing demand far below production potential. Economic dominoes fell one by one as:

- The automobile industry, always on the margin of discretionary spending and vulnerable to both the real increase in gasoline prices and the 'oil link' in the consumer's mind, suffered an immediate decline, with extensive multiplier effects through the balance of the economy.
- Building and construction, also a powerful engine of economic activity, fell some six months later as government anti-inflation policies caused a credit crunch.
- The world iron and steel industry remained an island of continuing high activity for nine months after the oil shock. It was propped up by a backlog of orders (from shipyards, for instance) plus some stock building. Large orders from the communist world contributed toward keeping it buoyant longer than other sectors. Eventually, however, the decline in the automobile and construction industries had a domino effect on the iron and steel industry.

Two other actions deepened the recession. First, companies drastically ran down inventories. The imposition of credit controls in the face of shrinking demand and the expectation of a fall in prices guaranteed a drastic drop in inventories. When inventories are reduced by eight days, it is equivalent to forgoing six months of 5 per cent economic growth; inventories in many segments were reduced by more than eight days. Next, consumer spending, long the stable engine of OECD economies, took a nose-dive. For the first time since recovery started in the early 1950s, consumers stopped buying, increased savings, and began to worry about what the future might hold. The resulting recession was the most severe since World War II (see Table 1).

Electoral rendezvous The governments of Japan, Germany, and the United States would each face the electorate in 1976. If the truism applies that people vote with their pocketbooks, then presiding over a recession is an invitation to defeat at the polls. The incentives for incumbent governments to go for growth were thus overwhelming.

Table 1	Decline in industrial production measured from previous cyclical peak		
	USA	Europe	Japan
Recession, first quarter, 1975	–14%	–9%	–19%
Previous post-war recessions	–7%	–2%	–2%

Reflation in the pipeline Not only were politicians anticipating the 1976 elections, but they were also keenly aware that much of the hardship borne in 1975 was unnecessary and self-inflicted – the deflation was too harsh. With excess capacity so widespread, governments could safely reflate and expanding output could reduce unit prices and further curb inflation. Such reflation would largely be self-financing through taxation on increasing income, sales, and profits, and lowered costs for unemployment benefits.

Long-term unemployment was becoming evident as a social problem. Unemployment falls most heavily on the young. Few governments could afford to do nothing about the prospect of a third graduating class moving from the classroom to the welfare rolls.

All these predetermined elements combined to make it virtually certain that governments would attempt to reflate.

REACHING THE RAPIDS

We spent much time developing the predetermined elements and understanding the recent past. To recapitulate, managers will only accept scenarios when their common, predetermined elements enter and unfold in their minds. We call this process 'rooting' because scenarios on their own – that is, as mere description of alternative courses of events – would be effective and alive in the minds of managers as long as a tree without roots. I have seen many scenarios suffer this fate.

That economies would reflate was largely predetermined. What was unknown in the spring of 1975 was the timing and nature of the recovery. To illuminate the forces driving the further development of the system and its critical uncertainties, we designed two scenarios of recovery:

The 'Boom and Bust' scenario foresaw a vigorous recovery that contained the seeds of its own destruction.

The 'Constrained Growth' scenario projected a kind of 'muddling through' recovery that would differ fundamentally from earlier business cycle recoveries.

We also considered the possibility that reflation would not happen; our 'Depression Contingency' scenario seemed so improbable, however, that we did not think it relevant for planning. The three possibilities are arrayed in Figure 1.

Boom and bust: a series of surprises

Boom and Bust described an economic world more characteristic of the 1950s than the 1960s. Cycles of greater amplitude and shorter duration would develop. We believed that the longer the recovery was deferred, the more likely this scenario – as governments turned to panic measures to reflate their economies.

First surprise – rapid recovery Rather than tepid, the recovery would be swift, strong, and forceful, as some economies like that of the United States would grow by 11 per cent or 12 per cent in eighteen months. Such growth would be as if an economy the size of Britain's were to appear all at once on the world map. Such a rebound would

not imply spectacular achievements; it would only reflect the depth of the 1973–5 dent in the economy – a coiled-spring effect.

Second surprise – oil-intensive recovery Reports of OPEC's death, we believed, were premature. Even though news of energy savings might persuade governments that Western conservation measures could negate OPEC's negotiating strength, such a boast could not stand up to analysis. Reduced oil consumption resulted not from a fundamental change in behaviour but mainly from the recession, which had cut both industrial and consumer demand. A boom in 1976 or 1977 would allow most consumers to revert to previous patterns of behaviour and consumption. Economic growth in 1976–7 would have to be fuelled by a rise in energy demand, particularly for oil (see Figure 2).

Third surprise – booming US oil imports The upsurge in US oil imports would easily put to rest talk about 'Project Independence,' President Gerald Ford's import-reduction targets, and alternative energy projects. Our estimates indicated that in such a scenario US imports would rise by 2.5 million barrels per day in 1976 (more than Britain's total imports or Kuwait's current exports), with a further increase of 2 million barrels per day in 1977 (in aggregate, more than Britain's total energy consumption).

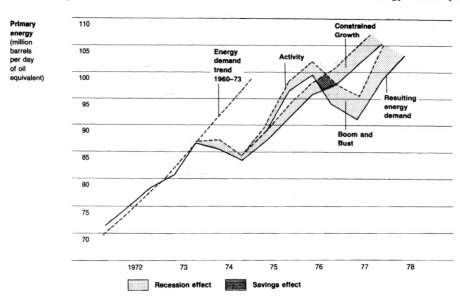

FIGURE 2   World demand for energy

Because we believed that a normal recovery would be equivalent to the sudden creation of a new economic nation, we could now add that the new nation would be almost totally dependent on Middle East oil. Consumer countries would once again be trapped.

Fourth surprise – stagnant alternative energies Countries would find that alternative energy programs consisted largely of empty words and paper tigers. Most nuclear plants operated well below design capacity, and many had been deferred or cancelled. Little had been done in the coal sector. The OECD nations were not meeting their target forecasts for coal production. The world had come far from the crash programs of the dark days of the oil embargo. Alternative energies could do little to relieve consumer countries' continued dependence on Middle East oil.

The bust – a second recession High inflation – approaching hyperinflation in many of the weaker OECD nations – threatened a sustained recovery. Rates that would exceed the highest levels of 1974–5 by a further 5 per cent would become politically and socially intolerable, signalling to governments that the boom was getting out of control. Their reaction would be to reapply deflationary measures, including credit restrictions, higher interest rates, oil import controls, and limits on oil consumption. Just as the recovery would be surprisingly rapid, so the downturn could be sharp. Inventories would play an important role: stock building, starting from the depths of the current recession, would promote growth in production during the upswing. But as liquidity disappeared in the face of strong deflationary measures, stocks would be run down rapidly, making the downturn that much sharper.

How probable was the Boom and Bust scenario? Because it held out dramatic implications for all sectors of the world economy and oil in particular, we found it hard to give equal attention to the other scenario. Even so, in 1975, we still considered it less probable than its alternative, Constrained Growth. While we made no forecasts about the start of a boom, we were willing to assume that the longer the recovery took to get under way, the more likely the Boom and Bust scenario would occur.

Constrained growth: a new economic world

Everything in the Boom and Bust scenario was normal; the 'surprises' were typical of business cycles. The Constrained Growth scenario was built on a more genuine surprise: recovery would be slower and more halting than any upturn of the post-World War II era.

The internal logic of this scenario was that the high-growth trend of the past twenty-five years had come to an end – not only because of the oil shock and the eclipse of the Bretton Woods monetary order, but also because the very success of the post-war economies brought with it limitations on continued vigorous growth. Along with unprecedented economic growth had come unprecedented expectations for higher standards of living and more impressive social welfare programs. High expectations produced a new economic rigidity as governments were locked into a continual round of tax increases to pay for these social programs. Moreover, industrialised countries now were slower to change and adjust to surprises – whether an oil crisis or new competitors like Japan and the industrialising countries of Southeast Asia.

Constrained growth would characterise the first years of this new economic world in which all the engines of growth – consumption, international trade, government spending, and investment – would work with less power.

Investment was emphasised as a change that we called a lasting 'technological recession.' From the end of World War II until the early 1970s, the best new technology in basic industries could, on its own merit, outcompete existing technology. A new steel plant, for example, was more economical than an existing one per ton of capacity; new cement and paper plants, new refineries and tankers, and new power generation plants were regularly more efficient than the previous technology. Beginning in the early 1970s, however, such technological progress could not beat rising costs. It was now cheaper to acquire existing capacity than it was to order new capacity.

For perhaps ten to fifteen years, the unit capital and operating costs of almost all new plants in basic industries would exceed the costs of existing equipment. That would obviously discourage new investment in industries that had been the engine of post-war economic growth and accentuate inflationary pressure. We analysed the other engines of growth: government spending would result in budget deficits and more rigidity; consumer spending would be changed by the maturation in the life-cycle of a large range of consumer durables; and international trade would be characterised by accumulating imbalances and frictions.

The overall conclusion was that the prospects for economic growth would be well below past achievements. This confirmed one of our long-term scenarios introduced in 1974: we would enter – by means of this constrained growth period – a completely new 'world of internal contradictions': a world of low economic growth that would stand in stark contrast to the booming economies of the past twenty-five years.

REACHING SHORE

Let me give one final example of how global scenarios are used to bring focus to particular issues or projects. Scenarios are like cherry trees: their fruit grows neither on the trunk nor on the large boughs but rather on the small branches. The tree needs the trunk and boughs to grow the small branches.

The global scenarios I have described correspond to the tree's trunk; the country scenarios developed by the national Shell operating companies can be likened to boughs. They account for the predetermined and uncertain elements peculiar to their countries. The fruits are picked from the small branches. These are the scenarios that focus on a particular strategic issue, market, or investment.

One such set of focused scenarios has to do with the demand for OPEC oil – as opposed to oil received from other sources. Because OPEC oil is the balancing factor in the world energy system, its fluctuations reflect cyclical economic fluctuations – but amplified several times. A decline in economic activity translates into a larger decline in world oil consumption, which then translates into a much larger decline in OPEC oil

demand. The reasons are: first, energy-intensive industries (like cement and steel) are more than proportionately affected in a recession; second, alternative energy sources are usually cheaper than oil; and third, OPEC oil, unlike domestic oil, has to be paid in foreign exchange.

In a recovery, a small rise in world energy demand would translate into larger rises in oil demand and even larger rises in OPEC oil demand. In the Boom and Bust scenario, for example, a 13 per cent increase in world energy demand in the first two years of a recovery would translate into a 23 per cent increase in world oil demand and a 34 per cent increase in OPEC oil demand. How would this demand match available supply? OPEC's oil production fluctuates in a narrow band between two danger zones (see Figure 3). Technical production capabilities and political willingness to produce determine the upper band, which is dangerous for oil-consuming countries; the threshold of 'OPEC dissatisfaction' is shown in the lower band, which is dangerous for oil-producing countries because the solidarity and discipline of OPEC come under severe stress.

As an illustration, we made two simulations (shown in Figure 3). The demand changes implicit in a normal boom starting in late 1975 would become manifest in the winter of 1976–7, when supply would be tight and prices under severe pressure. A boom starting in late 1976 would be less dangerous.

Looking back at the trip

In the recovery of 1976-8, economies developed mainly along the lines foreseen in the Constrained Growth scenario. We were indeed introduced to the world of internal contradictions. What had been the floor for long-term economic growth expectations before 1973 now became the ceiling. Many Shell managers recognised they were entering an era of slower growth and hedged their business plans accordingly. When the 1980s demanded leanness and restructuring, Shell was ready because it had begun the regimen early. That Shell saw this new world earlier than most could be seen by comparing the various energy forecasts made at that time. Shell consistently projected one of the lowest energy growth paths for the 1980s.

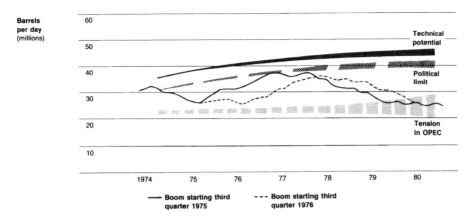

FIGURE 3   OPEC production boundaries

Scenarios serve two main purposes. The first is protective: anticipating and understanding risk. The second is entrepreneurial: discovering strategic options of which you were previously unaware. This latter purpose is in the long run more important. But while the more dramatic and (for Shell) dangerous of the two scenarios – Boom and Bust – did not occur, the exercise proved useful enough to our managers that medium-term scenarios were prepared every year thereafter while in the rapids. As C. W. MacMahon of the Bank of England has succinctly observed: 'No time is as usefully wasted as that spent guarding against disasters that do not in the event occur.'

REFLECTIONS IN TWILIGHT

I have found that scenarios can effectively organise a variety of seemingly unrelated economic, technological, competitive, political, and societal information and translate it into a framework for judgement – in a way that no model could do.

Decision scenarios acknowledge uncertainty and aim at structuring and understanding it – but not by merely criss-crossing variables and producing dozens or hundreds of outcomes. Instead, they create a few alternative and internally consistent pathways into the future. They are not a group of quasi-forecasts, one of which may be right. Decision scenarios describe different worlds, not just different outcomes in the same world. Never more than four (or it becomes unmanageable for

most decision-makers), the ideal number is one plus two; that is, first the surprise-free view (showing explicitly why and where it is fragile) and then two other worlds or different ways of seeing the world that focus on the critical uncertainties.

The point to repeat, is not so much to have one scenario that 'gets it right' as to have a set of scenarios that illuminates the major forces driving the system, their interrelationships, and the critical uncertainties. Users can then sharpen their focus on key environmental questions, aided by new concepts and a richer language system through which they exchange ideas and data.

A design that includes three scenarios describing alternative outcomes along a single dimension is dangerous because many managers cannot resist the temptation to identify the middle scenario as a baseline. A scheme based on two scenarios raises a similar risk if one is easily seen as optimistic and the other pessimistic. Managers then intuitively believe that reality must be somewhere in between. They 'split the difference' to arrive at an answer not very different from a single-line forecast.

Experience shows that decision scenarios focus on critical uncertainties that are often very different from those that seemed obvious to managers at the beginning of the process. Despite this focus on uncertainty, decision scenarios do not paralyse managers. Rather, the deeper understanding of the risks that is gained often makes the decision-maker capable of confronting apparently greater risk.

You can test the value of scenarios by asking two questions:

1 What do they leave out? In five to ten years, managers must not be able to say that the scenario did not warn them of important events that subsequently happened.

2 Do they lead to action? If scenarios do not push managers to do something other than that indicated by past experience, they are nothing more than interesting speculation.

It is impossible to develop a set of decision scenarios without knowledge of managers' deepest concerns – something we did not fully appreciate when we developed our scenarios in the 1970s. We were lucky, however; our managers' concerns turned out to be precisely what we were studying. Later, we developed interview techniques to find out what was on their minds and to illuminate the existing decision framework. Today, the interview is one of the first steps taken when Shell starts a scenario exercise.

The decision scenarios I have described were global, or macroscenarios. To analyse particular aspects of a business, you develop focused scenarios that are custom tailored around a certain strategic issue, market, or investment. But you cannot start with a narrow focus because you will likely miss key things (or dimensions), or else you may cast the scenarios in the wrong way. You must wide-angle first to capture the big picture and then zoom in on the details.

We have found that scenarios are most effective when combined with:

Strategic vision You should have a clear, structured view of what you want your company to be, which precedes your view of what you want your company to do (investing, divesting, penetrating new markets, and so forth).

Option planning In most planning approaches, strategies are put forward on a single line and options – if there are any – are merely straw men. This is even more dangerous than single-line forecasting. Option planning, in which all options are put forward on a neutral mode, is practised at both the business unit and corporate levels.

The purpose of a combined approach is option generation (see Figure 4). If the scenario process does not bring out strategic options previously unconsidered by managers, then it has been sterile.

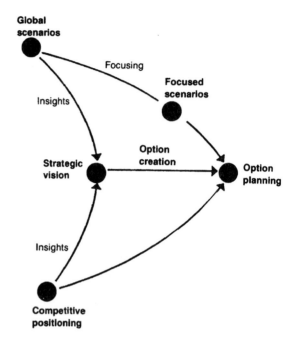

FIGURE 4   Generating management options

The gentle art of reperceiving

Companies differ greatly in their effectiveness and speed in transforming the potential of scientific research into new products and processes. In times of rapid change, their effectiveness and speed in identifying and transforming information of strategic significance into strategic initiatives differ just as much.

Today, however, such a capacity is critical. Unless companies are careful, novel information outside the span of managerial expectations may not penetrate the core of decision-makers' minds, where possible futures are rehearsed and judgement exercised.

Historical examples abound. After concluding the non-aggression pact with Hitler in 1939, Stalin was so convinced the Germans would not attack as early as 1941 – and certainly not without an ultimatum – that he ignored eighty-four warnings to the contrary. According to Barton Whaley, the warnings about Operation Barbarossa included communications from Richard Sorge, a Soviet spy in the German embassy in Tokyo, and Winston Churchill; the withdrawal of German merchant shipping from Soviet ports; and evacuation of German dependants from Moscow.[2]

Or consider the case of Pearl Harbor. 'Noise,' the massive volume of signals, impeded understanding of what was to come. As Roberta Wohlstetter points out, 'To discriminate significant sounds against this backdrop of noise, one has to be listening for something or for one of several things. One needs not only an ear but a *variety of hypotheses* that guide observation'[3] (emphasis added). Indeed, the Japanese commander of the Pearl Harbor attack, Mitsuo Fuchida, surprised at having achieved surprise, asked, 'Had these Americans never heard of Port Arthur?' (the event preceding the Russo-Japanese War of 1904 – and famous in Japan – when the Japanese navy destroyed the Russian Pacific fleet at anchor in Port Arthur in a surprise attack).

Similar business cases are not as well documented. I have observed some: the French steel industry's handling of the 'FOS project' near Marseilles; the tanker market before and after the first oil shock; petrochemical investments in Europe in the 1970s; and a large US automobile manufacturer's misinterpretation and dismissal of Japanese competition during a good part of the 1970s.

In each case, a number of executives – not just one individual – made decisions. Their inappropriate behaviour extended over several months or even years – it was not just a one-time error. Problems resulted from a crisis of perception rather than from poor strategic reasoning. These decision-makers' strategies made sense and indeed were sometimes brilliant – within the context of their limited worldview.

In times of rapid change, a crisis of perception (that is, the inability to see an emerging novel reality by being locked inside obsolete assumptions) often causes strategic failure, particularly in large, well-run companies. Opportunities missed because managers did not recognise them in time are clearly more important than failures, which are visible to all. As Peter

Drucker said, 'The greatest danger in times of turbulence is not the turbulence; it is to act with yesterday's logic.'

Central to decision scenarios – indeed the basis for their success or failure – is the microcosm of the decision-makers: their inner model of reality, their set of assumptions that structure their understanding of the unfolding business environment and the factors critical to success. A manager's inner model never mirrors reality; it is always a construct. It deals with complexity by focusing on what really matters. It is a superior simplification of reality – the more so, the wider a manager's span of responsibility is.

During stable times, the mental model of a successful decision-maker and unfolding reality match. Some adjustment and fine tuning will do. Decision scenarios have little or no leverage.

In times of rapid change and increased complexity, however, the manager's mental model becomes a dangerously mixed bag: rich detail and understanding can coexist with dubious assumptions, selective inattention to alternative ways of interpreting evidence, and illusory projections. In these times, the scenario approach has leverage and can make a difference.

In today's world, a management microcosm shaped by the past and sustained by the usual types of forecast is inherently suspect and inadequate. Yet it is extremely difficult for managers to break out of their worldview while operating within it. When they are committed to a certain way of framing an issue, it is difficult for them to see solutions that lie outside this framework.

By presenting other ways of seeing the world, decision scenarios allow managers to break out of a one-eyed view. Scenarios give managers something very precious: the ability to reperceive reality. In a turbulent business environment, there is more to see than managers normally perceive. Highly relevant information goes unnoticed because, being locked into one way of looking, managers fail to see its significance (Figure 5).

It has been my repeated experience that the perceptions that emerge when the disciplined approach of scenario analysis is practised are richer and often critically different from the previous implicit view. The scenario process of converting information into fresh perceptions has

As any adult knows, a magician cannot produce a rabbit unless it is already in (or very near) his hat. In the same way, surprises in the business environment almost never emerge without warning. To understand the warnings, managers must be able to look at available evidence in alternative ways. Otherwise, they can be badly misled by apparently valid facts if that is all they see, or they do not interpret them in different ways.

After the second oil shock, a 'scenario for the rapids' covering the medium term 1980–5 introduced a notion at odds with prevailing wisdom. Called a 'high savings case,' it alerted management to 'the possibility that consumers themselves would produce a surprise in the form of a much more rapid decrease in energy and oil intensity than that assumed for the reference case.' This would mean a further drop of 6 million barrels per day in the demand for OPEC oil.

At the time, there was little hard evidence to support the case. There is always a lag in the impact on demand of a price rise. Furthermore, there was great uncertainty about the oil market and anxiety about further supplies. The outbreak of the Iran–Iraq war increased anxiety about supplies from the Middle East. Both oil consumers and oil companies tried to increase their stocks of oil; customers' orders were strong; and industry forecasts as well as the 'feel of the market' all pointed towards sustained demand. The mood of the industry leaned towards expansion: 1980–1 saw an enormous increase in drilling activity and feverish competition to secure term contracts for the supply of crude. The problems of the oil industry were obviously on the supply side, not on the demand side.

In March 1981, the new 1981–5 scenarios for the rapids stated that 'last year's conservation surprise can no longer be regarded merely as a contingency.' We also introduced a new scenario, 'Hard Times,' that foresaw an economic recession deeper than most observers expected, an oil conservation surprise (drawn from the remarkable analysis by Aart Beijdorff), and societal change that would significantly affect both economic behavior and oil demand.

Under the Hard Times scenario, the combined effect of these three elements could lead to a totally different – and much lower – level of oil demand (see Figure A) than from the first oil shock – even though the immediate impact on GNP, balance of payment of OECD, and so on was surprisingly similar.

We called the likelihood of there being a real conservation surprise a 'rabbit in the hat.' Moreover, we were increasingly convinced that at least the two ears of our particular 'rabbit' were already visible. First, less than one-sixth of the 1973–4 crude oil price increase had been passed on to final consumers because of the cushioning effect of refining and transport costs and of various taxes in the selling price of the total products barrel. This time, however, more than half of the crude price rise would be felt by final consumers, a change that suggested consumers' reactions would be non-linear.

Second, a radical change in consumers' perceptions seemed likely to reinforce this growing price leverage. Few people had believed in the reality of an oil crisis after 1973–4; now the popular concensus seemed to be that the upward price trend was irreversible. This change in attitude, combined with the normal effect of a large price increase, could reawaken previously dormant price elasticity from the first oil shock.

Finally, we believed that the oil industry and OPEC were being fooled by the demand statistics, which reflected not real demand or actual consumption but deliveries only. Stock building at the consumer level as well as at the oil company level was abnormally high (see Figure B).

It is now clear that much of the oil industry in 1980–1 overestimated future demand. In such a context, a company can make a lot of money selling weeks of unnecessary stocks before prices erode. It may be just a coincidence, but Shell companies' reduction in oil stocks through 1981 was much greater and earlier than that for the commercial stocks of the industry as a whole, even though Shell stocks at the beginning of the year (in terms of days' supply of current demand) were already well below the average.

The Hard Times scenario used a new hypothesis to analyze demand behavior and thereby alerted decision-makers to the possibility of a major discontinuity in future oil demand. We saw more than the conventional consensus view of the industry mainly because we had been looking for alternative ways of seeing our world. A new strategic option emerged that encouraged us to go against the mainstream of the oil industry.

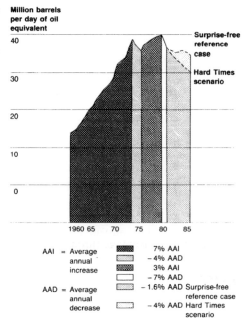

Million barrels per day of oil equivalent

AAI = Average annual increase

AAD = Average annual decrease

- 7% AAI
- – 4% AAD
- 3% AAI
- – 7% AAD
- – 1.6% AAD Surprise-free reference case
- – 4% AAD Hard Times scenario

Figure A   OECD oil consumption

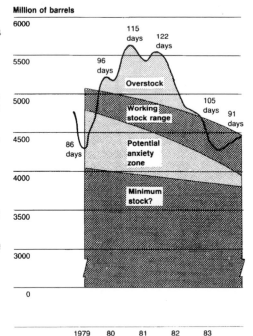

Million of barrels

Figure B   Free world stocks

FIGURE 5   Seeing 'rabbits in the hat'

something of a 'breeder effect': it generates energy, much more energy than has been consumed in time and effort during the process.

A mere high or low around a baseline can never achieve a conceptual reframing. The reperception of reality and the discovery of strategic openings that follow the breaking of the manager's assumptions (many of which are so taken for granted that the manager no longer is aware of them) are, after all, the essence of entrepreneurship. Scenario planning aims to rediscover the original entrepreneurial power of foresight in contexts of change, complexity, and uncertainty. It is precisely in these contexts – not in stable times – that the real opportunities lie to gain competitive advantage through strategy.

NOTES

The illustrations are reprinted with the kind permission of Shell International Petroleum Company. I would like to acknowledge the original contributions of my former colleagues and members of Group Planning. G. A. Wagner, A. Bernard, K. Swart, and J. C. Davidson get special thanks because they were instrumental in launching the concept. My conceptualisation of scenario analysis has benefited greatly from discussion with my former Harvard Business School colleagues, in particular Bruce Scott and David Bell. This chapter would not have been written without Norman Duncan and Peggy Evans. It expresses one or two things I have learned; it does not necessarily represent Shell's current planning views or practices.

1 Pierre Wack, 'Scenarios: uncharted waters ahead', *Harvard Business Review*, September–October 1985: 72.

2 Barton Whaley, *Codeword Barbarossa* (Cambridge, MA: MIT Press, 1973).

3 Roberta Wohlstetter, *Pearl Harbor. Warning and Decision* (Stanford,. CA: Stanford University Press, 1962).

7 CONSTRUCTING SCENARIOS

7.1 ADVANTAGES OF A SIMPLER APPROACH

Despite his attempt at a practical approach, the processes Wack describes still seem too sophisticated for use in most organisations. Mindful that this complexity seems to deter the use of scenarios, and of the resultant scarcity of relevant skills among line managers – who have become the new strategic planners – we have concentrated on making the scenario planning process easier. The resulting 'simple' approach to scenario forecasting, described in this chapter, is designed to make the process more accessible to a wider range of organisations. More importantly, perhaps, it makes the technique suitable for use by line managers across the organisation (perhaps including yourself) as part of their planning processes, without requiring the extended involvement of outside experts or corporate staff specialists.

These simpler processes still retain the ability to handle uncertainty. In our experience, however, their greatest virtue is that using them naturally and painlessly widens managers' outlooks, and helps to extend their planning horizons beyond the short term. Scenarios can alert you to potential long-term threats, while ensuring that you do not overlook major long-term opportunities.

The practical guidelines described are based upon our experience with OUBS students, and especially upon detailed research into the scenarios produced by 250 of these students in 1993.

We have already looked at some other approaches to scenarios, and we will later look at some others. *To avoid confusion, we would stress that the only approach you should initially adopt, if you develop your own scenarios, is that described in the rest of this part.*

The most important message to emerge from our work is that scenarios *CAN* be simple. In our experience, the simpler they are – and the simpler the process used to derive them – the more effective they may be, not least because those using them are able to understand how they work. Even Shell, which is reportedly the world's leading commercial user of scenario forecasting, now uses relatively simple techniques to create its scenarios – techniques that are far removed from the academic sophistication of earlier times.

In fact, even the basic concepts of the process are relatively simple. They comprise three main groups of activities, the first and last of which are common to all long-range planning processes:

- environmental analysis
- scenario forecasting
- strategy.

7.2 ENVIRONMENTAL ANALYSIS BY TEAMS

Scenarios can only be as good as the information upon which they are based. For this reason, the environmental analysis – which can follow any of the paths described in Chapter 2 – must be of as high a quality as possible. Even so – mindful of the limited resources available within most organisations – it will probably not justify an excessive level of sophistication; and, fortunately, our experience again indicates that such sophistication is rarely needed. Thus, in line with our recommendations earlier, our practical advice is simply to cultivate a deep curiosity about the external environment; and to maintain maximum exposure to the widest range of media, as changes often show up in subject areas far from your day-to-day business. You are also recommended to develop an informed viewpoint, which will improve your chances of recognising early signs of change, no matter from what direction they are coming.

We found that almost all our students used general reading as the main source of their analysis, combined with the more specific information from the industry and specialist press they read as a normal part of their work. Indeed, you have probably already assimilated the type of information required for environmental scenarios from your general and specialist reading. Typically, therefore, you need to bring to the process no more than your existing knowledge.

Moreover, there seems to be no special expertise needed to detect shifts. Perhaps the best advice, however, is to analyse the external environment by a team. If nothing else, more of the environment will be analysed – but it also seems to have a deeper effect: to amplify the early signs of change, and to develop resonances as team members interact with each other. On the basis of our work, we generally recommend the use of teams of between six and eight participants; but there may be ten participants if they are used to working together regularly (and this is the number recommended by Shell). We strongly recommend the use of computer conferencing to develop an on-going debate between team members. Although such an approach is not mandatory, we have found that, in general, team-based scenarios are noticeably better – and certainly reflect wider perspectives – than those developed by individuals.

Although it is worthwhile producing scenarios with just the group of people who already work together, and who share the same mindset (and who may be subject to the phenomenon of 'groupthink', which we explored in Chapter 5), it is preferable to involve as diverse a group as possible; and, maybe, use several such groups. Thus, each group should contain people from across the organisation as a whole, so that the widest range of experience can be drawn upon. But it should also contain people with different styles of group-working. In particular, it should include 'dissidents' who will challenge the status quo; Victor Newman[1] describes them graphically as 'lunatics who will rattle the cage'.

---

[1] Victor Newman, Securing Buy-In and Commitment to the Scenario Planning Process, Strategic Planning Conference, 14 May 1997.

It is also a good idea to involve one or two 'reference' outsiders, who can be trusted to introduce a different perspective. Indeed, as practised by some consultancies, GBN (Global Business Network) for instance, the groups are made up entirely of outside experts – chosen for their known contributions to related fields.[2]

Activity 7.1

If you plan to use a team approach to scenarios, you should now set up your team of six to eight active members.

Note: if you choose to undertake your work on an individual basis, you should consider how you will address the possible problems posed by the more limited perspective you will have.

Other approaches are possible. We ourselves typically involve a whole management group (whether it is that of the OUBS or of the other organisations we advise) of around 30 people by splitting it into three separate teams which work in parallel. At the extreme, one of the governments we have advised brought more than 300 managers into the process by running parallel multiple teams.

Activity 7.2

At this stage, whichever approach you adopt, you should start collating the information you hold individually about the subject of your scenarios.

The subsequent analysis needs more academic rigour. The key is the process of educating the team, by total immersion in the facts which define the environment they are studying. When the scenario development finally gets under way, it is not the material available on paper that is productive, it is what is in the team's heads. Indeed, the first stage of scenario forecasting – the choice of assumptions – will be embedded in this earlier process of environmental analysis. It is inevitable that, as the team works together on the analysis, it will start to develop ideas as to what the assumptions might be. The group will probably have spent a considerable time – over the weeks, and perhaps months, that the environmental analysis should take – arguing about what these assumptions mean.

However, if you are following the exercise we have just set, you are taking part in a rather more artificial process, and we recognise that your involvement will be on a more limited scale – probably for no more than one or two weeks. Even so, the general principles hold true. As you formulate the analysis, in conjunction with your fellow team members (through the medium of a

---

[2] Richard O'Brien, Managing the Scope of Scenarios, Strategic Planning Conference, 14 May 1997.

computer conference or in a face-to-face group), you should find that assumptions as to what are the key 'drivers' for change will gradually, but naturally, emerge.

Activity 7.3

You should spend as much time as possible 'analysing' the environment with your fellow team members. As the 'drivers' for change emerge from this process, you should carefully note them down (and the related assumptions upon which they are based).

Individually produced scenarios

We recommend that you undertake scenarios as a group process. The range of viewpoints which such a team contributes is one of the strengths of scenario forecasting.

Even so, it is possible to undertake much the same process – indeed using many of the techniques described in this book – as an individual; and many OUBS students have done just that. As formally described by Kees van der Heijden,[3] the individual should conduct depth interviews with the management team, in order to obtain the basic data: van der Heijden suggests '… it seldom proves necessary to interview more than fifteen or so people.' The resulting statements about the external business environment are then separated from those about internal characteristics of the organisations. The external statements are then clustered (with perhaps 500 elements identified) to produce scenarios by much the same iterative process that a group would use. The internal elements are treated similarly.

7.3 STAGES IN SCENARIO PLANNING

As we have seen, the part of the scenario process which is radically different from most other forms of long-range planning is the central stage, the actual production of the scenarios. At its most basic level, this is relatively simple – requiring just six steps:

1 DECIDE ON THE DRIVERS FOR CHANGE
2 BRING DRIVERS TOGETHER INTO A VIABLE FRAMEWORK
3 PRODUCE INITIAL (SEVEN TO NINE) MINI-SCENARIOS
4 REDUCE TO TWO OR THREE SCENARIOS
5 WRITE THE SCENARIOS
6 IDENTIFY ISSUES ARISING.

[3] Kees Van Der Heijden, *Scenarios: The Art of Strategic Conversation* (Wiley, 1997).

Step 1 – decide on the drivers for change

The first stage is to examine the environmental analysis to determine which are the most important factors that will decide the nature of the future environment. These factors are sometimes called 'variables' (because they will vary over the time period being investigated). We tend to prefer the term 'drivers' (for change), since this term is not laden with quasi-scientific connotations, and reinforces the participant's commitment to search for those forces which will determine the future.

Perhaps the most difficult aspect is freeing the participants from the preconceptions they bring into the process. In particular, in our experience, most participants will want to look no further than the medium term, five to ten years ahead. This may not seem a problem, as a decade is a very long time in many areas of commercial activity; but we have found that a time horizon of anything less than ten years frequently results in participants extrapolating from present trends, rather than considering the alternatives which might face them. When, however, they are asked to consider timescales in excess of ten years, they almost all seem to accept the logic of the scenario planning process, and no longer fall back on extrapolation. It is for this reason that we very specifically ask our students to adopt a timescale well in excess of ten years, indeed in excess of 20 years, for their scenarios.

There is a similar problem with expanding participants' horizons to include the whole of the external environment. Despite all our exhortations, it is our experience that only a fifth of the scenarios produced by students can be truly considered to be externally oriented. The largest category of students take in some of the external environment and mix it with internal factors, but a surprisingly high proportion write what amount to corporate scenarios (which just describe the future of the organisation itself, largely on the basis of internal factors). The good news is that, if you at least address a ten-year horizon (and preferably beyond to 20 years), this tends to make you look further out in terms of the external environment. In addition, the contrasting perspectives which should be held by the various members of a well-chosen team – especially one which contains at least one participant who is willing to challenge the status quo – seem most likely to ensure that the resulting scenarios incorporate the widest range of viewpoints and identify the largest number of significant discontinuities. Once more, this is why we recommend a team approach.

You should deduce from the above that you are likely to obtain the best results if you address the genuinely long term, beyond 20 years, and the wider environment, beyond the boundaries of your own organisation and its immediate customers.

Brainstorming

Brainstorming to discover the less obvious factors is an integral part of practical scenario planning. It may be conducted according to any of a wide range of protocols. Our own experience has ranged from the traditional use of flipcharts to the more adventurous, but equally successful, use of computer conferences by dispersed groups of managers – which we recommend for similarly dispersed OUBS students.

Wall Post-it™ Notes 1

A simple technique we have come to recommend for general use within organisations is based on the now almost universal availability of Post-it™ Notes. It is especially useful at the brainstorming stage but we now use it generally for all scenario planning debates, and it can support any planning process. It requires only a room with a bare wall and copious supplies of Post-it™ Notes!

Even when regular face-to-face meetings are not possible, and computer conferences are used as a substitute – as for most of our OUBS students – it is very helpful for team-building if the first meeting of the scenario group – after the environmental analysis has been completed – is face-to-face, and uses the Wall Post-it™ Notes technique. It also provides a very good introduction for those who are coming to the scenario process for the first time: since the workings are largely self-evident, participants quickly come to understand exactly what is involved.

Ideally, the six to eight people taking part should meet in a conference room, isolated from outside interruptions. At the start of the meeting any topics which have already been identified during the environmental analysis are written (preferably with a thick marker so they can be read from a distance), on separate Post-it™ Notes. These Post-it™ Notes are then, at least in theory, randomly placed on the wall. In practice, we have found that even at this early stage the participants will want to cluster them in groups which seem to make sense. The only requirement – which is why Post-it™ Notes are ideal for this approach – is that there is no bar to taking them off again and moving them to a new cluster.

As in any form of brainstorming, the initial ideas almost invariably stimulate others; demonstrating the value of a team approach. Indeed, everyone should be encouraged to add their own Post-it™ Notes to those on the wall. It should be noted, however, that it differs from the 'rigorous' form of brainstorming described in 'creative thinking' texts, in that it proceeds at a much slower pace, and the ideas are discussed immediately. Ideas may be removed, if they are not relevant, as well as being added. Even so, the process follows many of the same rules as normal brainstorming and typically lasts the same length of time – say, an hour or so at most.

It is important that all the participants feel they 'own' the wall – and are encouraged to move the notes around themselves.

The result is a very powerful form of creative decision-making for groups, which is applicable to a wide range of situations (but is especially powerful in this context).

Although workable scenarios can be produced by teams new to the process, it initially helps if at least one member has had previous experience; and, in particular, has had some experience of the insights which may emerge from the process. In general, it also helps if at least one member is willing to (and indeed motivated to) challenge the basic assumptions held by the organisation. Often the most important insights emerge from such challenges.

Activity 7.4

At this stage, you should 'brainstorm' with the other members of your team to unearth the maximum number of possible drivers for change in the environment you are investigating. You may wish to use the Wall Post-it™ Notes approach, or you may use a computer conference.

If you are doing the work on an individual basis, you might still, at this stage, like to consider discussing the issues involved with your colleagues – in order to widen the perspective you are adopting.

Important and uncertain

This step is also one of selection – since only the most important factors will justify a place in the scenarios. The 80:20 rule here means that, at the end of the process, management's attention must be concentrated on a *limited* number of the most important issues.

In addition, as scenarios are a technique for presenting alternative futures, the factors to be developed must be genuinely variable. They should be capable of significant alternative outcomes. Factors whose outcome is predictable (in other words, inevitable), but important, must be spelled out in the introduction to the scenarios (since they cannot be ignored) or included in *all* of them. The Importance/Uncertainty Matrix, as reported by Kees van der Heijden, is a useful check at this stage.

Thus, only those topics (here topics 5 and 6) in the top-right quadrant (important and uncertain) should be considered as part of the scenario process. Although topics in the bottom right-hand quadrant (here topic 2, and especially topic 1) should not be a part of the scenario process, they should be described as part of an introduction to the final scenarios.

On the other hand, topics in both the left-hand quadrants (here topics 3 and 4) should be ruthlessly *discarded* as merely distractions from the planning process. It should be noted, though, that their importance should be judged in terms of what is important for the organisation not for the individual manager.

This is, in any case, not as easy as it might seem, since organisations too often suffer from myopia; they simply do not recognise the new external forces which will become important.

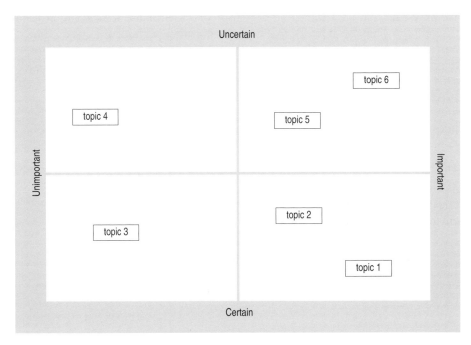

FIGURE 7.1 The Importance/Uncertainty Matrix

Activity 7.5

You should now create such a matrix, plotting on it the 'drivers' you discovered during the 'brainstorming'. You should use this as a technique for focusing on the key (important and uncertain) issues.

On the other hand, you should note that, while this is an elegant approach, it may once more be unnecessary – since only one in ten of our students used it in their scenario work!

At this point it is also worth pointing out that a great virtue of scenarios is that they can accommodate the input from any other form of forecasting. They may use figures, diagrams or words in any combination.

Other ways of identifying drivers for change

You should be aware that some consultancies, such as Idon Associates, go even further by taking out the most uncertain factors at this stage. According to their definition these are 'wild cards' (though others, ourselves included, use this term to mean something rather different). They are returned to the mix only after the final scenarios have been selected.

Idon then go on to use the clusters of uncertain factors, which have emerged, to derive 'dimensions' for the subsequent scenarios.

'Forcing' scenarios

We have said that we believe the best approach to scenario forecasting is also the simplest (initially at least): that of 'brainstorming' without any rules. This best aids the production of divergent scenarios, which bring in all aspects of the future. You should be aware, however, that other approaches to this process – again typically those recommended by a range of consultancies – are based upon creating four-box matrices, derived from the two (or possibly more) dimensions which have emerged during the process of examining the uncertainties. As we saw earlier, something like this can also be derived from Repertory Grid Research.

The outcome (with one dimension stretching from A to B and the other from C to D) will be four scenarios: A+C, C+B, D+B, A+D, as shown in Figure 7.2.

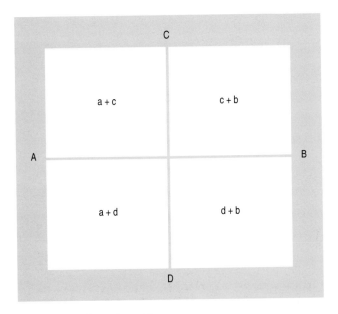

FIGURE 7.2   Scenario matrix

This is just a way of *forcing* a set of titles for the scenarios. What goes into each scenario is then for you to decide, though clearly the title of the scenario will influence your decisions.

Other dimensions may also be used, based upon the concepts emerging from earlier research. Indeed, the process may be iterated (possibly until a consensus emerges), with new four-way boxes (scenarios) derived from the new consensual dimensions being used to rework the picture.

This type of approach can become very sophisticated. It is reported[4] that Battelle Institute assign three levels to each factor before using a cross-impact matrix to resolve these.

At a simpler level, in the mid 1990s British Airways[5] used the two dimensions of 'growth' (a crucial feature of their market) and 'governance' (the regulation/ deregulation which is just as important to their activities around the world) as the basis for their scenarios; though they then focused on just two outcomes – 'Wild Gardens' (with growth as the main focus) and 'New Structures' (where governance/regulation predominated).

A further variation is to look at the outcomes in terms of 'risk' and 'reward' to the organisation, as shown in Figure 7.3. In the event, this looks very much like the well-known Ansoff Matrix (of which more later).

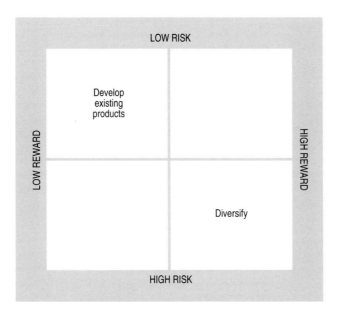

FIGURE 7.3   Scenario matrix based on risk

When you have gained experience of using the basic approach to scenarios, you might like to try one of these 'forcing' approaches, to *add* to your armoury of techniques. The more ways you look at scenarios the better; and these approaches certainly add extra dimensions – especially if your brainstorming is unproductive. They are, though, *convergent* techniques which can hide some aspects of the future – so you should not use them by yourselves! Until you are confident with your new skills, therefore, stick to the basic approach.

---

[4] Idon Associates Ltd, Strategic Planning Conference, 14 May 1997.
[5] Kathy Moyer, Structuring Scenarios, Strategic Planning Conference, 14 May 1997.

Step 2 – bring drivers together into a viable framework

The next step is to link these drivers together to provide a meaningful framework. This is probably the most conceptually difficult step. It is where your 'intuition' – your ability to make sense of complex patterns of 'soft' data, which more rigorous analysis would be unable to handle – plays an important role.

At this stage, therefore, you and your fellow team members should try to arrange the drivers which have emerged from the first stage into groups which seem to make sense to you. Initially, there may be many such small groups. The intention, therefore, should be to gradually merge these (often having to recreate them from new combinations of drivers to make the bigger groups work). The aim of this stage is to make six to eight larger groupings, or 'mini-scenarios'.

Wall Post-it™ Notes 2

This is where, if you are involved in a face-to-face group rather than a computer conference, the Post-it™ Notes are almost essential. They will continue to stick no matter how many times they are moved around (and they may be moved dozens of times over the length of each meeting). While this process is taking place the participants will probably want to add new topics – so more Post-it™ Notes are added to the wall. In the opposite direction, the unimportant topics are removed (possibly to be grouped again as an 'audit trail' on another wall). In particular, though, the topics which are deemed to be 'certain' are also removed from the main area of debate and grouped in a clearly labelled area of the main wall for later inclusion in the final reports.

As the clusters – the 'mini-scenarios' – emerge, the associated Post-it™ Notes may be stuck to each other rather than individually to the wall. This makes it easier to move whole clusters around, and is especially helpful during the final, demanding stage of reducing the number of scenarios to just two or three.

The great benefit of using Post-it™ Notes is that there is no bar to changing your mind. If you want to rearrange the groups – or simply to go back (iterate) to an earlier stage – then you strip them off and put them in their new position. One extra technical device, a Polaroid camera, is a help here. Every so often a series of indexed pictures should be taken of the wall, to record where you are at that point in time. It is advisable to do so before you make any major changes – so that you have a record which enables you to return to where you once were if the new approach turns out to be a blind alley!

If you are computer conferencing, the picture may be more difficult to visualise. If you do not have software (such as that offered by Idon Associates) for sharing 'mind maps' over computer networks, it may be worthwhile tracking the ideas by transferring them to Post-it™ Notes on your own wall at home. If your fellow team members do the same, you can achieve many of the benefits of the equivalent face-to-face approach.

Activity 7.6 _____

Whatever method you choose, you should now group the key (important/ uncertain) drivers into meaningful groups.

The Centre for Defence Analysis (DERA) in the United Kingdom, for instance, discovered 96 core 'trends'[6] (comparable with our own number of 162 drivers). These were then clustered into eight groups which they – confusingly in the context of our own terminology – then chose to call 'drivers'!

Step 3 – produce initial (seven to nine) mini-scenarios

The outcome of the previous step is usually between seven and nine logical groupings of drivers. In our experience this is usually remarkably easy to achieve, even when using the simplest approach to computer conferencing.

Step 4 – reduce to two or three scenarios

The task of reducing the mini-scenarios to just two or three larger scenarios seems to come down to finding two or three 'containers' into which all the topics can be sensibly fitted. This usually requires a considerable amount of debate (whether through a computer conference or face-to-face). The process often produces fundamental insights into what are the really important, perhaps life and death, issues affecting the organisation. During this extended debate – and even before it is summarised in the final reports – the participants come to understand, through their own involvement in the debate, what the most important drivers for change may be, and (perhaps even more importantly) what their fellow team-members think are the most important drivers.

The reason for reducing the groupings to just two or three is practical: the managers who will be asked to use the final scenarios can only cope effectively with a maximum of three versions! Shell started, more than two decades ago, by building half a dozen or more scenarios – but found that their managers selected just one of these on which to concentrate. So their planners progressively reduced the number to two, which is – based on similar experiences – the number we now recommend.

_____

[6] Andrew Sleigh, A Case Study, Strategic Planning Conference, 14 May 1997.

Complementary scenarios

As used by Shell and ourselves, these two scenarios should be complementary – the reason being that this again helps avoid managers 'choosing' just one, 'preferred', scenario and lapsing into single-track forecasting, and so negating the benefits of using 'alternative' scenarios to allow for alternative, uncertain futures. This can be difficult for them to grasp, because managers are used to looking for opposites: a good and a bad scenario, say, or an optimistic one versus a pessimistic one. In the Shell approach, the two scenarios are required to be equally likely, and to cover all the drivers between them. Ideally, they should not be obvious opposites, which might once again bias their acceptance by users, so the choice of 'neutral' titles is important. For example, Shell's two scenarios at the beginning of the 1990s – described below in Article 8.1 – were titled 'Sustainable World' and 'Global Mercantilism'.[7]

In practice, we have found that this requirement, to our surprise, poses few problems for the great majority of participants. Less than a sixth of our students fall into the expected trap of 'good versus bad'.

Activity 7.7

You, and your fellow team members, should now consolidate the groups of drivers to create two complementary scenarios.

Testing

Having grouped the factors into these two scenarios, the next step is to test them, again, for viability. Do they make sense to the participants? If the scenarios do not *intuitively* 'hang together', why not? The usual problem is that one or more of the assumptions turn out to be unrealistic in terms of how the participants see their world. If this is the case then you need to return to the first step – the whole scenario planning process is, above all, an iterative one.

Indeed, when undertaken seriously – as a substantial part of the overall corporate planning process – the iteration may take a number of months. That employed by Northeast Consulting (Boston, USA),[8] for example, can take six months to a year to complete.

Activity 7.8

You should test your two scenarios to ensure that they are viable.

---

[7] A. Kahane, 'Scenarios for energy: sustainable world vs global mercantilism', *Long Range Planning*, vol. 25, no. 4, 1992.

[8] James Herman, How to Run Workshops, Strategic Planning Conference, 14 May 1997.

Step 5 – write the scenarios

The scenarios should then be 'written up' in the most suitable form. The flexibility of this step often confuses planners, for they are used to forecasting processes which have a fixed format. The rule is that, in general, you should produce the scenarios in the form most suitable for use by the managers who are going to base their strategy on them. This is essentially a 'marketing' decision, since it will – as we shall see – be very necessary to 'sell' the final results to the users. On the other hand, although your persuasive powers must be fully exercised, a major consideration may be the form which you, the author, find most comfortable to use.

In the rather artificial situation posed by the exercise you are following, you should simply choose the form you feel happiest with.

Most scenarios will, perhaps, be written in word form (almost as a series of essays about alternative futures), especially as they will almost inevitably be qualitative. Nearly half our students choose to use the normal business report format – hardly surprising as they, and their audience, probably use this format in their day-to-day communications.

Step 6 – identify issues arising

The final stage of the process is to examine these scenarios to determine what are the most critical outcomes: the '*branching points*' relating to the 'issues' which will have the greatest impact (potentially generating 'crises') on the future of the organisation. These are the events or decisions which will determine the long-term survival of the organisation. Although not essential for the scenario process itself, identifying them is the starting point for the production of 'robust strategies' which follows it.

Activity 7.9 _____

Try the 'issues arising' test described above. It is an especially useful test of the viability of your scenarios.

_____

Role playing

An optional, though potentially time-consuming, extra test may be to act out (through role play) what each of the two scenarios means to the key 'actors' involved (say, parts of your own organisation, competitors, government, and so on). It helps to produce a table with the scenarios listed across the top and the key actors down the side, so that what each of these groups feels about each scenario, and what the reaction of each to the outcomes is likely to be, can be recorded. It also helps if a number of managers repeat the process and then enter into a debate about their views, so that a consensus may be achieved.

This is, once more, a useful test of the consistency of the scenarios – if there are any inconsistencies, then it is back to iteration! More importantly, though, it gives a valuable insight into not just what the events in the future might be, but how the key players may respond.

Governments often use this technique by itself, without scenarios, to see how the various actors may react to political developments; this can be an expensive process, since those role-playing the key actors, often at great length, have to be experts. Combining role-playing with scenarios, a much simpler approach, can be even more powerful.

7.4 EVENT STRINGS

So far we have looked at 'drivers' as if they have just one point of occurrence in the future, and their 'impact' on the present is correspondingly simple. This is the basic approach which we recommend you use until you have significant experience of scenario forecasting.

But movement through time towards future events can follow a complex path. A number of intermediary events can take place, and these can be tracked; and they can be predicted in advance. These are 'event strings', the *sequences* of events which lead to the final outcome. An understanding of these event strings can add to your understanding of the final outcomes. There are a number of consultancies – for example Northeast Consulting (Boston, USA)[9] – which focus on production of these event strings as the *main* framework for the production of the scenarios themselves.

There are a number of ways that the event strings (sometimes called 'timelines'), can be plotted. The simplest is to plot them (horizontally) over time, with the various paths developing above and below the central path, as in Figure 7.4.

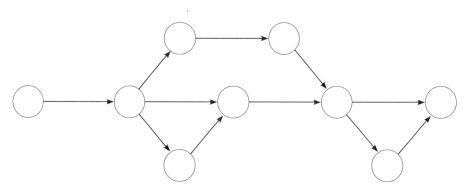

FIGURE 7.4   Event strings

[9] James Herman, How to Run Workshops, Strategic Planning Conference, 14 May 1997.

A more sophisticated approach is exemplified by that used by Northeast Consulting,[10] who develop their scenarios with their client management in six or more one/two-day workshops. In their approach, which they refer to as 'Future Mapping', based initially upon a series of in-depth interviews, they first of all develop a set of alternative *outcomes* (much like the scenarios others finish with), which they refer to as 'end-states', and a related set of *current* positions. The participants in their subsequent workshops are then required to develop the logic (the 'event strings') which link the two; the series of events that will link each current state to the equivalent end-state in the future. Rather confusingly, they then describe these event strings (rather than the end-state) as the 'scenarios'! (Sometimes the most difficult aspect of scenarios is sorting out exactly what the words being used by the expert mean; in many fields we academics and consultants often use exactly the same words – with considerable panache – to mean very different things!)

Having done this, the teams are then asked to combine the end-states and these 'scenarios' (event-strings) into a whole picture.

Yet another approach – which adds yet another perspective – is to use a combinatorial process (like the 'tree structures' and 'morphological analysis' described earlier) to move from the present set of known factors to the sets of multiple futures (which combine the likely possibilities): The Centre for Defence Analysis (DERA) refer to their version of this as a 'Faustian Tree'.[11]

7.5 SYSTEMS DIAGRAMS

The techniques we have looked at so far have been based on *words*. For many situations *graphical* means are preferable. This approach may be especially important in the case of long-range marketing since:

1   verbal descriptions can have difficulty in handling the complexity involved, where 'mental maps' can help you understand the relationships – not least since they typically offer a 'holistic' view

2   similarly, suggested courses of action – revolving around change – may be better communicated to others in this way

3   by using the conventions of systems design, ideas may be clarified

In general, systems *diagrams* are made up of pictures, words and symbols, with an *arrow* being the commonest symbol. The types of diagram can be roughly divided into maps which show *relationships* in space or time, or *logical* diagrams which show how things depend upon each other. Both forms are used in long-range planning, but perhaps the latter offer the most powerful analytical tools.

---

[10] James Herman, How to Run Workshops, Strategic Planning Conference, 14 May 1997.
[11] Andrew Sleigh, A Case Study, Strategic Planning Conference, 14 May 1997.

Input-output diagrams

This is the simplest form, with just one block representing the whole process, and sets of arrows indicating the inputs and outputs. Because it is so simple, the information is expressed in the labels which appear on the arrows and box. An example is shown in Figure 7.5.

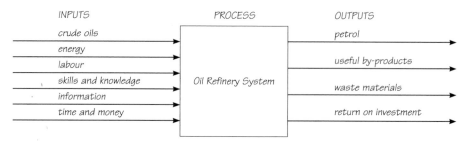

FIGURE 7.5   Input–output diagram

Flow-process diagrams

As shown in Figure 7.6, these extend the technique to show the flow *between* the various processes.

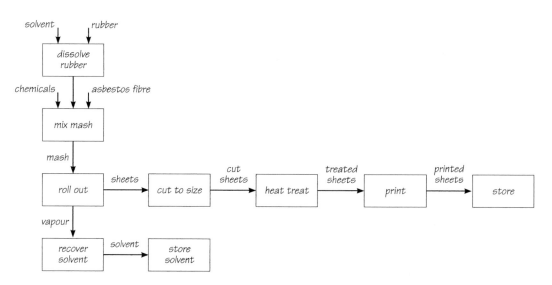

FIGURE 7.6   Flow–process diagram

Activity sequence diagrams

These are frequently used to depict activities – such as those involved in long-range marketing – which are quite independent of technology. An example is shown in Figure 7.7. As each activity may be implemented in many different ways, the bubbles are made soft and rounded rather than well-defined. The arrows may indicate either that one activity follows in time sequence or that there is a logical necessity to carry out one activity before another.

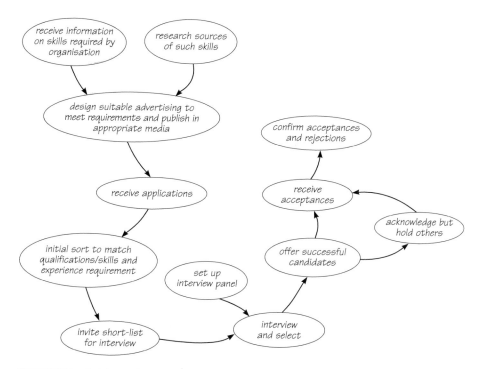

FIGURE 7.7   Activity sequence diagram

Critical Path Network (CPN) or PERT diagrams, for project control, usually fall into this category.

Relationship diagrams

In less well-structured situations, drawing flow diagrams may not be feasible and may fail to reflect the richness of the interactions which are at work. These relationships can be expressed in a diagram which does not presuppose that a line from one 'blob' to another implies any particular type of interaction, but implies only that a relationship of some sort exists. An example is shown in Figure 7.8.

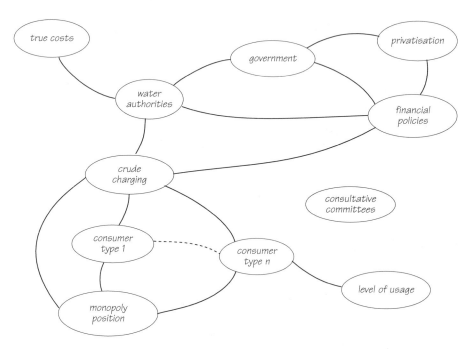

FIGURE 7.8 Relationship diagram

Systems maps

In this case subsets of components which are particularly closely related become 'subsystems'. Moving from a relationship diagram to a systems map involves two or three steps:

1 Removing boxes which contain items which are not components – for instance, 'policy' and 'possibility' in Figure 7.8.
2 Removing the lines which show relationships.
3 Inserting boundaries around groups of related components to indicate systems and/or subsystems. Thus, the systems map developed from the preceding relationship diagram in Figure 7.8 is shown in Figure 7.9.

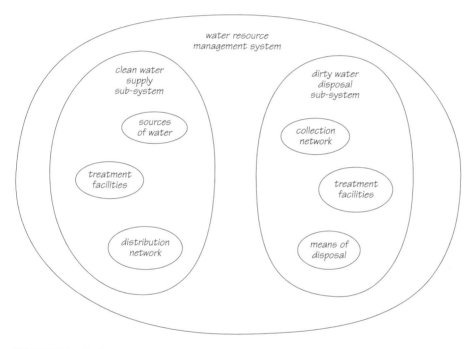

FIGURE 7.9   Systems map

Influence diagrams

These are a hybrid of the last two categories, which go further to seek to define influences which components have on each other, as in Figure 7.10.

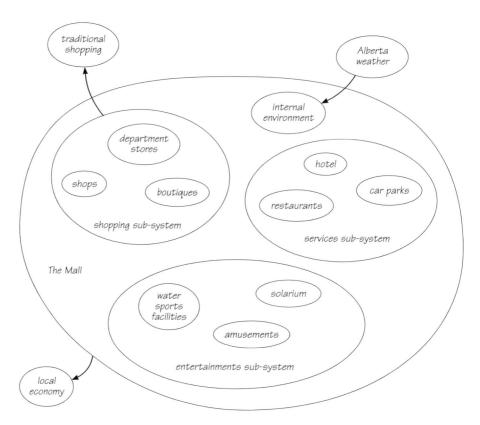

FIGURE 7.10   Influence diagram

Multiple cause diagrams

These are, in the context of long-range marketing, perhaps the most useful development. They are in some ways similar to highly developed influence diagrams but are capable of representing much more complex situations. The form is very simple, words linked with arrows without any labels *on* the arrows. The factor at the tail of the arrow 'causes' or 'leads to' the result at the head; so you should always check that there really is a causal link.

The form of words is very important, and may include events, activities or decisions – but it *must* be an action. An example is shown in Figure 7.11.

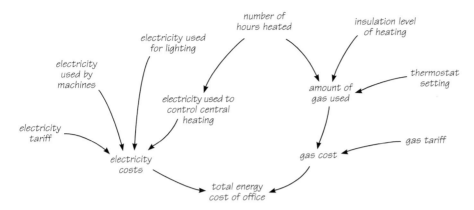

FIGURE 7.11   Multiple cause diagram

This simple example shows how the use of multiple-cause diagrams enables us to get beyond the obvious primary causal factors to the less obvious, but often equally important, secondary factors. If you apply this approach to complex management situations, you will find that you can work back from the final effect or even through layers of causal factors. You should always start with the resultant outcome and work *backwards* through the layers of causal factors.

You have already seen how powerful such visual techniques can be, when you used Post-it™ Notes in your scenario group work. Diagramming is just a more formal approach to this – and can, indeed, be used in combination with them.

Although you should be aware of the alternative and additional techniques described in the last parts of this chapter, we should emphasise that there is no benefit, and significant disadvantage (in terms of unnecessary work and increasing lack of focus), in using more than one or two of these to *complement* the basic approach. The intent is simply to add further perspectives, not to add accuracy.

We recommend that you always start with the basic approach of simple brainstorming – and adopt this as your central framework – whatever else you do.

⁰ Extracted by permission of Pergamon Press Plc from *Long Range Planning*, vol. 22, no. 2, 1989: 37–53.

8 USING SCENARIOS

It is important to note that, however they are produced, the final scenarios may be used in a number of ways.

8.1 ALTERNATIVE USES

Containers for the drivers/event strings

Most basically, scenarios are a logical device, an artificial framework, for presenting the individual drivers (or coherent groups of them) so that these are made easily available for managers' use – as useful ideas in their own right about future developments – without reference to the rest of the scenario. It should be stressed that no important factors should be dropped, or even given lower priority, as a result of producing the scenarios. In this context, which scenario contains which topic (driver), or issue about the future, is irrelevant. Our own, internal (OUBS), scenarios typically contain a dozen or more individual strands, which are subsequently tracked and dealt with separately.

Tests for consistency

At every stage it is necessary to iterate, to check that the contents are viable, and to make any changes necessary to ensure that they are viable. The main test is to see whether the scenarios seem to be internally consistent – if they are not, then you must again loop back to earlier stages to correct the problem. Though it has been mentioned previously, it is important to stress once again that scenario building should be an iterative process. It does not usually just happen in one meeting – though even one attempt is better than none – but should take place over a number of meetings as you gradually refine your ideas.

Positive perspectives

Perhaps the main benefit provided by scenarios, however, comes from the alternative 'flavours' of the future offered by the different perspectives. It is a common experience, when the scenarios finally emerge, for the participants to be startled by the insights they offer as to what the general shape of the future might be. At this stage it is no longer a theoretical exercise, but becomes a genuine framework (or rather a set of alternative frameworks) for dealing with that future. This is probably the main benefit the OUBS has gained from its own use of scenarios. Those in our most recent set, for example, were entitled 'Mass Electronic Education' and 'The Club'. The former encapsulates the events resulting from the expansion, as 'edutainment', of on-going education to wider audiences through the medium of the emerging super-highway, while the latter focuses on a more elitist approach, in which individual education is also a vehicle for social contact between students.

8.2 VALUE OF 'NON-STANDARD' SCENARIOS

The word 'scenario' has now entered into general usage as a term which can be applied to many different approaches. Indeed, at the height of the technique's popularity, Diffenbach[1] found that almost as many of the large organisations he surveyed (55%) used 'single scenarios' as used 'alternative scenarios' (68%). Even within the general area of complementary or alternative scenarios, on which this section focuses, there are a number of variants, and some of them can add to the usefulness of the process in certain situations.

Multiple scenario sets

It is paradoxical, as one main aim of using alternative scenarios is to widen the viewpoints of the participants, that most of the descriptions of the theory behind them seem to imply that – when everything has run its course – there will be just one possible set of (two or three) scenarios, a set which should eventually emerge as the 'true' forecast.

If, however, you run a number of teams in parallel, studying the same areas of the environment and the same timeframe from the same perspective, you may quickly become aware that there is no one obviously 'correct' set. There can be significant differences between the various sets – especially if the profiles of the various teams are different – so much so that sometimes they appear not to be talking about the same future. This can, in the first instance, be worrying, since, despite the variety of alternatives which is inherent in scenario theory, managers still expect the final forecast to be correct! Such worries should be discounted. The greater the number of genuine, significant discontinuities which can be detected – by whatever means – the more robust the subsequent strategies can be made.

Even so, our own experience of running two or three such teams in parallel indicates that, if there are strong forces at work in the external environment, there may be a surprising degree of unanimity on the major features of scenarios. In our most recent work within the OUBS, all three of our teams described one of the two scenarios in much the same terms, and two teams did so for the second scenario. Such a convergence of views is typical of the patterns we have observed in other organisations.

Running teams in parallel in this way is unusual, even for only the first stage of the overall process, since it can demand large amounts of resources.

[1] J. Diffenbach, 'Corporate environmental analysis in large US corporations', *Long Range Planning*, vol. 16, no. 3, 1983.

Apart from our own usage, and of the organisations we have advised, we know of only one 'user' which has done this in practice: a government which used scenarios as part of its three-year planning exercise. They found that it was an excellent way, at least for them, of providing widespread expert input to the final scenarios (they used it to bring together the ideas of more than 300 members of the administration). This provided an indication of the spread of possible scenarios – posing the question 'Why are they so different?' – and it helped get around the problem of incorporating the widest possible environmental analysis.

Activity 8.1

If possible, compare your scenarios, not just with the other members of your team, but with those of other groups which have attempted the same scenarios. How do they differ? Why do you think this is? Is it because of the different profiles of the groups? What does it tell you about the 'accuracy' of your own scenarios?

Hierarchies of scenarios

The government mentioned above went further, in that it used the earlier levels of scenario to provide specific scenarios for the various departments. These scenarios were then, quite naturally, located in a hierarchy which finally linked them to the overall national scenario.

It is possible to reverse this process, to take the overall scenario as the first step, and then break it down into different scenarios, at a lower level, which are more directly related to departmental needs, but are still clearly linked to the overall position. Shell, for example, have individual country scenarios which link to their world-wide ones.

Strategic scenarios

Indeed, Shell's use of scenarios is now so sophisticated that they may even write their consequent strategies in a similar form. Thus, having developed their two environmental scenarios, they undertake much the same corporate planning process as other large multinationals. The difference is that, having decided on the strategies, these may then be written – for use by managers throughout the corporation – in the form of 'strategic scenarios': frameworks which contain alternative strategies for dealing with possible events, in the same way as the original scenarios contained the alternative events themselves. When a manager needs to consult them, he or she has a range of strategies already available, to match to the situation as it has actually developed. This takes alternative scenarios to the logical conclusion of alternative strategies – but requires a very confident (and competent) management. Shell have even gone as far as adopting an 'optimistic' global scenario, and promoting it, in order to send a 'positive' message to the whole organisation. They do, though, emphasise that this needs handling with great care!

As a final note, however, it is worth recording that Shell use a variety of *different* techniques (over a dozen at the last count) to match the different needs of their scenario working groups. For instance, they will use one technique for an inexperienced group of managers dealing with a local problem and quite a different one for the very sophisticated team of planners working on their core global scenarios.

8.3 TOWARDS ROBUST STRATEGIES

Scenarios are, of course, only a means to an end. They identify the long-term forces, and consequent events, which the organisation's long-range planning must address. The final development into corporate strategy (or, more precisely, into the robust strategies which are the focus of the book) will be addressed in later chapters. In the meantime, in order to put scenarios in context, we shall now show how the use of scenarios fits into the strategy process.

The next step is to match the organisation's limited internal resources to the unlimited external challenges which may face it. The special contribution of scenario planning is to allow, and indeed encourage, the development of a robust set of strategies. These will not necessarily result in an optimal outcome in a specific situation, which is the aim of most other forms of corporate planning, but should offer the possibility of achieving the best overall outcome. In particular, they should protect, as far as possible, against all the major threats potentially facing the organisation, and should exploit the most important opportunities open to it.

The use of scenarios, therefore, should ensure that as many as possible of the long-term threats and opportunities facing the organisation are identified and addressed. Shell[2,3,4] has demonstrated a number of times how such an awareness of the alternatives facing it has enabled it, not just to handle changed market conditions, but to capitalise on them. At the beginning of the 1970s, when it first adopted its scenario planning approach, Shell was probably the weakest of the major oil multinationals. Two decades later it has reportedly become the strongest, at least in terms of its market capitalisation. Shell's senior management is convinced that its dedication to scenario planning has made a significant contribution to this dramatic improvement in performance.

[2] P. Wack, 'Scenarios: uncharted waters ahead', *Harvard Business Review*, September–October, 1985.
[3] P. Wack, 'Scenarios: "shooting the rapids"', *Harvard Business Review*, November–December, 1985.
[4] A. Kahane, 'Scenarios for energy: Sustainable World vs. Global Mercantilism', *Long Range Planning*, vol. 25, no. 4, 1992.

Unfortunately, the reality is rather different in most other organisations. Very few organisations these days make any use of scenarios as part of the overall corporate strategy process, perhaps because of their unwarranted reputation for being impossibly sophisticated.

8.4 A PRACTICAL SCENARIO

To help you clarify your understanding of scenarios, Article 8.1 below sets out one of the best sets of practical scenarios we have seen: those produced by Shell at the end of the 1980s.

The first part of the article by Adam Kahane, up to the heading 'Global Mercantilism', describes the assumptions (variables in Shell's terminology) which led to the various factors (drivers in our terminology) being incorporated in the two final scenarios. The scenarios themselves, 'Global Mercantilism' and 'Sustainable World', each contain sections headed 'Implications for energy', which discuss the issues arising from them.

Now *very quickly* read Article 8.1 as an illustration of a most powerful use of scenarios.[5] Its author, Adam Kahane, is head of Socio-Political, Economic and Technological Studies in Group Planning, Shell International Petroleum Co. Ltd.

Article 8.1 ADAM KAHANE: 'SCENARIOS FOR ENERGY: SUSTAINABLE WORLD VS. GLOBAL MERCANTILISM'

Long-term forecasting is not a very successful enterprise. Some of the most important events of the last two years, particularly the political upheavals in Eastern Europe and the Soviet Union, and the Iraqi invasion of Kuwait, caught most observers off guard – even knowledgeable ones. In the oil industry, experts have sometimes been able to suggest, but rarely to predict, the key turning points in crude oil prices. Time after time, events that are considered improbable or even implausible occur.

The future is too important to be ignored, notwithstanding this difficulty. The Shell approach to strategic planning is, instead of forecasts, to use scenarios, a set of 'stories' about alternative possible futures. These stories promote a discussion of possibilities other than the 'most likely' one and encourage the consideration of 'what if' questions. Although scenarios deal with the future, they are essentially a way of structuring the overwhelming, confusing information we have about the present. One of the important uses for this structure is to help us recognise more of what is going on around us, including the early, weak signals of change.

Good scenarios are challenging, plausible and internally consistent. They also illuminate the uncertainties and issues that are critical for the future (in the case of this paper, for the future of the energy industry to the year 2010). Scenarios lead to better decisions if they improve our understanding of the world.

This paper outlines two scenarios prepared in the Group Planning Co-ordination of Shell International Petroleum Company. Two notes are important. First, the author has summarised a

[5] A. Kahane, 'Scenarios for energy: Sustainable World vs. Global Mercantilism', *Long Range Planning*, vol. 25, no. 4, 1992. This article has also been published in the Shell series of Selected Papers.

much larger body of work to which approximately twenty members of Group Planning contributed, under the leadership of Kees van der Heijden. Second, this work was completed in the summer of 1989 and so, naturally, were we to re-formulate the scenarios now, our assessments in many areas would be very different. The value of this paper is therefore less in the content of the scenarios than in the particular approach to thinking about the future.

THE WORLD OF 1990

The only solid basis we have for discussing the future is information about the past and the present. In 1990, the present is a time of promise but also of considerable risk. In these scenarios, we concentrate on three areas of potentially far-reaching change:

- geopolitics
- international economics; and
- the natural environment.

Geopolitical changes

The most spectacular evidence of geopolitical change has been the cascading, 'domino' collapses of communist regimes in Eastern Europe and the Soviet Union. These upheavals have been caused by (and have also revealed) deep economic and environmental problems, and nationalist and ethnic tensions. In the face of these mounting disruptive forces, the authorities are attempting to implement fundamental changes in economic systems and, at the same time, shifts in political power. This is without precedent and will be difficult to achieve.

The other superpower, the United States of America (USA), has also declined in economic importance and power, relative to Western Europe and Japan. Partly because of faster growth in other parts of the world, and partly because of slow productivity growth, low savings and large budget deficits at home, the USA no longer has as dominant an international economic position. This, in turn, has provoked American resentment and isolationism. In spite of this relative decline, however, the USA still has the world's largest economy and can clearly still lead, seen for example in the Gulf crisis.

In Western Europe, fears of 'Euro-sclerosis' have given way to 'Euro-optimism'. The momentum of the European Communities' (EC) 1992 programme has raised the possibility of closer monetary integration, leading ultimately to economic and political union, and has been a powerful policy stimulus to all European countries, including those outside the EC.

However, the recent developments in Eastern Europe and the former USSR, and German reunification, add significant new elements. The emphasis on integration of the current EC members sits uneasily with movements to 'widen' the Communities to include the European Free Trade Area (EFTA) and Eastern European countries.

The very rapid economic growth of East Asia also has geopolitical consequences. Japan and the four Newly Industrialising Countries (NICs) have enjoyed extended periods of growth of above 7% per year (without precedent in this century), and are now widely seen as models of successful development. On the other hand, the success and even dominance of East Asian exports in some product categories has resulted in dislocations in other countries and has provoked friction and protectionist responses.

The international economy

The lengthy expansion of the world economy since 1982 suggests that in some respects there are strategies (or even 'recipes') for economic growth that work and have been learnt. Market-oriented policies have been effective, notably in East Asia, and have won recent 'converts' in Latin America, Eastern Europe and elsewhere. At the same time there are signs of international economic vulnerability. The dramatic increase in international economic interconnection has important advantages, but has also resulted in greater interdependence and scope for disagreement.

The clearest examples of disagreement are over trade and foreign direct investment. There are concerns about unfair or even 'adversarial' trade, accentuated by persistent trade imbalances, and deep disagreements in the Uruguay Round negotiations of the General Agreement on Tariffs and Trade (GATT). There is also friction over foreign direct investment (especially from Japan), and nervousness about international financial vulnerability due to developing country and USA indebtedness and commercial bank over-exposure to highly leveraged borrowers.

One important symptom of, and reaction to, these frictions is the rise in unilateral restrictions and bilateral deals. Examples include protectionist measures, especially 'voluntary export restraints' and other non-tariff barriers, and the USA–Japan Strategic Impediments Initiative. Regional agreements such as the EC Single Market and the widening North American Free Trade Area, initially conceived as liberalising, have the potential to develop into inward-looking trade blocs.

Another symptom of economic difficulties is that average per capita incomes in much of Latin America, Sub-Saharan Africa and Eastern Europe fell over the 1980s. The export and growth prospects of all developing countries are worsened by the constraints on trade, especially of agricultural products, textiles and other manufacturers (Figure 1).

Although concern about environmental degradation is not new, it has recently been heightened. This has been due to a combination of:

- increasingly severe degradation in many areas;
- improved scientific understanding and measurement capability; and
- changed personal values – especially in wealthy countries, as people move up the hierarchy of needs and focus on 'quality of life'.

These changes in perspective have been reflected in new economic models, which point out that sustained economic output depends not only on investment in man-made assets such as machines and buildings, but also in the maintenance of natural assets such as clean air and soil (Figure 2: both the traditional, left-hand loop and the often-ignored right-hand loop are required for 'sustainable development').

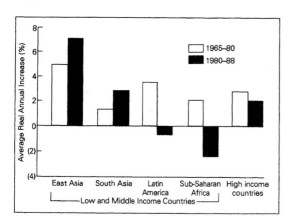

FIGURE 1   Growth in gross domestic product per capita

Environmental concerns

The third important area of change is in perceptions of, and attitudes towards, man's impact on the natural environment. This encompasses a range of concerns, from the local (soil, water, air) and regional (especially acid precipitation, but also river and ocean pollution) to the global (ozone depletion and the enhanced greenhouse effect – so-called global warming).

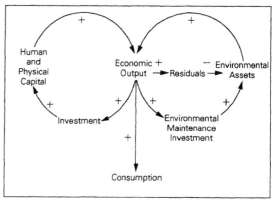

FIGURE 2   The two loops of sustainable economic growth

These scenarios emphasise the approach taken to reduce global warming by reducing the emissions of carbon dioxide. Other environmental concerns may be more immediate and are likely to be tackled first, but the greenhouse effect is important for the energy industry because it raises fundamental questions about the combustion of fossil fuels. In addition, the unprecedented international co-operation required to tackle these sorts of global problems could have important political implications.

The position of developing countries is crucial in global environmental discussions. Developing countries are often the most directly affected by environmental degradation, and will make an increasing contribution to global problems as their populations and economies grow. On the other hand, they have fewer resources available to move towards sustainable development.

Framing scenarios

These three areas of change – geopolitics, economics and environment – are interrelated. The end of the 'Cold War' has opened up many possible avenues for international co-operation, but at the same time has removed the stabilising order provided by the bipolar USA–USSR hegemony. New international mechanisms and alliances for dealing with international political problems have to be found, not only in Europe but also in the Middle East, East Asia and elsewhere.

Similarly, in the international economy the signs of 'overstretch' may point to systemic weaknesses. The consensus in favour of multilateral solutions, previously held together by a dominant USA, is in doubt. Environmental concerns can be divisive, with significant disagreements over the seriousness and urgency of the problems (especially global warming), but may also be an important force for co-operation through the perception of a common threat.

Developments in all three of these areas may therefore lead to fundamental changes in international relations. The role of the nation-state itself is under scrutiny; increasing migration of capital, people, information and pollution makes national borders less relevant, so that the nation-state is too small to be able to deal with many of the large problems (it is also too big to be able to deal with many of the small ones, such as local ethnic or social concerns). Nation-states are continually confronted with the paradoxical need to give up some of their sovereignty to supra-national institutions, in order to deal more effectively with their national problems.

These are all important signs of structural change in a global system 'under stress'. However, the direction of change is not at all clear. These scenarios suggest two possible directions; two alternative interpretations of the present signs of change (Figure 3).

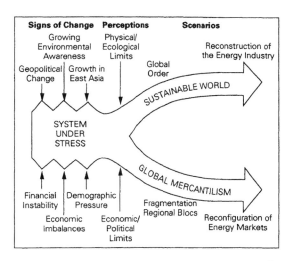

FIGURE 3   Scenario dynamics

In the first scenario, *Global Mercantilism*, the primary challenge (the perceived 'limit') of the 1990s turns out to be the weakness and instability of current international economic and political systems. The structural response is fragmentation and regionalisation. In the second scenario, *Sustainable World*, the primary challenge turns out to be how to deal with common problems, especially ecological problems such as global warming. Here the response is cohesion (and also coercion) and a broadening of international systems.

The starting point, or branching point for these two stories, is a (hypothetical) coincident economic downturn in several major countries. Which challenges will seem most important? Will the response be fragmented or cohesive?

GLOBAL MERCANTILISM

In this scenario, the new post-Cold War international order proves to be too weak to withstand serious political and economic shocks and set-backs. Regional conflicts, such as in the Middle East, are destabilising and difficult for the new order to deal with. The current GATT negotiations fail or, at best, produce a feeble and meaningless agreement. Financial instability is accentuated by deregulation and rising interest rates. Faced with a downturn, politicians focus on national economic difficulties, and there is little international leadership. Continued frustration over trade and investment imbalances leads to increased protectionism. Overall, the response to the downturn is ineffective and confrontational, and it turns into a recession as severe as in the early 1980s.

The series of events is interpreted, in this scenario, as evidence of the weakness (even unworkability) of the current, 'unmanaged' multilateral economic system. Frustration with these international failures leads to a focus on building a new, more managed system based on working with one's neighbours ('starting from here'). The result is increasing emphasis on regional pacts – functional, if variously defined, blocs – particularly the EC (perhaps enlarged to include a few EFTA and Eastern European countries) and North America (perhaps including some Latin American countries). Japan and the NICs find their access to these markets substantially constrained and therefore place more emphasis on Asia–Pacific markets, building up a web of bilateral alliances centred on Japan.

This regionalisation implies the creation of new rules or norms for international economic relations. The emphasis is on bilateral reciprocity between blocs ('I'll let you enter my markets only on the same terms that you let me into yours'). Inter-bloc trade is therefore managed, with a political umbrella erected over economic relations.

The failure of global institutions, and a lessened appreciation of common interests, mean less aid and assistance to poor countries. Countries that are not in a bloc – that is, most of the developing world except East Asia and those natural resource producers that are competitive suppliers – have severe difficulties in this scenario, and the gap between rich and poor countries widens further.

Within the regional blocs, the primary policy objective is to become, and remain, economically efficient and competitive. The 'recipe' that is taken from recent experience is that fierce internal competition is the way to produce world-class, competitive companies, and hence economic efficiency and growth. Although different versions of this recipe are adopted in different parts of the world – emphasising laissez-faire in North America and 'administrative guidance' in Japan – the common themes are liberalisation and deregulation of markets, and privatisation and commercialisation of state owned companies. Governments adopt hands-off, market-oriented policies – within tough money supply and credit rules – and accept the resulting dislocations and volatility; there is little sympathy for industry 'special pleading' (except perhaps for certain industries deemed to be of strategic importance).

Economic policy therefore has a dual character: inter-bloc economic exchanges are politically managed, but intra-bloc exchanges are market oriented. This is like (one interpretation of) the Japanese model, with very competitive domestic markets coexisting with government support for national champions in international markets. The EC 1992 programme turns into a liberalised internal market, protected by a 'wall' to restrict the entry of goods and people. In general, government policy becomes 'neo-mercantilist', with national (or regional) wealth and economic power seen as the proper and ultimate aims of government policy, and pursued on the assumption that global economic arrangements are a 'zero sum game'.

Environmental concerns are not very high on the political agenda. Although local and regional problems are tackled (with careful regard for international competitiveness), there are too many international disagreements for a consensus to be reached on difficult global issues (Figure 4).

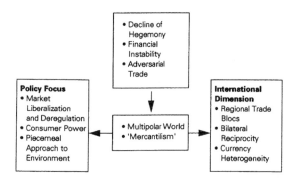

FIGURE 4   The logic of 'Global Mercantilism'

Implications for energy

Both the inter-bloc and intra-bloc aspects of *Global Mercantilism* are reflected in the development of the energy industry. Internationally, crude oil is a key traded commodity, and oil markets are, therefore, strongly influenced by the fundamental changes in the rules of international trade. Emphasis is placed both on regional self-sufficiency – which means that production from countries outside of OPEC (Organisation of Petroleum Exporting Countries) is kept up – and on reciprocal alliances between producers and marketers ('you can have access to my downstream market only if you allow me access to your reserves').

One result is that proportionally less oil falls under OPEC control. Together with volatile economic growth, this makes OPEC management of oil prices very difficult, and a cyclical over-capacity and under-capacity leads to a price 'rollercoaster'. Although temporary over-shoots of very high prices are possible, they are very difficult to maintain.

Within the intra-bloc 'mega-markets', such as the EC, liberalisation means a questioning of the 'special' status of the energy industry, historically justified on the basis of national security, economies of scale and national development. This deregulatory trend is accentuated by the oil price swings which force consumers to emphasise flexibility, fuel-switching and the development of spot markets (increased 'commoditisation'). In all energy sectors, liberalisation means a smaller, or at least less protected role, for state-owned companies. Electric and gas utilities, currently the most regulated sectors, are radically affected by the promotion of common carriage and independent electricity generation.

Liberalisation allows new entrants into downstream markets, including state-owned oil companies (through reciprocal alliances), hypermarkets, independent electricity generators and various intermediaries such as traders, brokers and insurers. The creation of large regional markets and the increase in competition means that protected niches are lost, and there are constant changes in the 'rules of the game'. There is strong pressure to be 'entrepreneurial' and to continuously renew competitive advantage.

SUSTAINABLE WORLD

In this scenario, the international economic frictions that have been in the headlines can be resolved, and attention focuses instead on the resolution of common problems, including environmental ones. There is widespread consensus on recipes for economic stability and growth, and co-operation among the largest economies allows economic shocks to be defused (such as after the October 1987 stock market crash) rather than accentuated. The dangers of a failure in international trade negotiations are recognised, and interdependence (for example in the automobile industry) – especially between the USA and Japan – is seen to be too great for 'divorce' to be a feasible option. Regional conflicts are dealt with effectively by large power alliances. A new security framework is built in Europe around the Conference on Security and Co-operation in Europe (CSCE).

In general, there is a recognition of common interests and the continued development of institutional structures to deal with them (Figure 5).

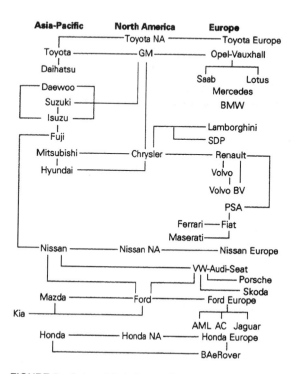

FIGURE 5   Automobile industry alliances

At the same time as this recognition of common economic and political interests among the large powers, international concern grows over all kinds of environmental degradation. There are continued, noticed environmental problems, which are perceived as 'breached limits'. Global warming is believed to be a serious threat. In rich countries, the environment rises to the top of the political agenda and stays there, so that the necessary agreements are reached and action is taken. This perception of limits to acceptable environmental degradation is important, since the difficult and expensive changes required will not be undertaken unless there is a consensus on the seriousness of the problems.

Concern about environmental problems is not limited to rich countries of the OECD (Organisation for Economic Co-operation and Development). Many of the problems are most acute in poor countries, which are heavily dependent on natural resources, especially forestry and agriculture. However, the central political question is how poor countries can be brought 'on board', given the large costs of adjustment. The rich countries lead, providing 'carrots' of aid and technology transfer to encourage sustainable projects, recognising that economic growth is a prerequisite to achieving environmental objectives. At the same time, there are 'sticks' of sanctions and trade barriers against environmental offenders. Coercion is an important aspect of this scenario, with the rich deciding that new global arrangements (on trade, security, environment, etc.) are necessary and, in effect, imposing these priorities and arrangements on the poor.

Two additional political elements are important (Figure 6). There is a three-pronged dynamic interaction between 'leader' and 'laggard' countries, whereby the former pull up the latter:

- politicians compete to be seen as the most 'green'
- technology, developed by the leaders, is less expensive for the laggards, and
- the leaders need to encourage the laggards, if their own efforts on global problems (for example, reduced carbon dioxide emissions) are to be effective.

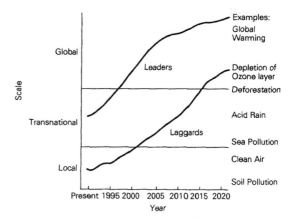

FIGURE 6　National implementation of environmental programmes in 'Sustainable World'

In addition, new cross-national networks of companies, scientists, environmental groups and others accelerate the development of an international consensus.

The mechanisms used to implement environmental objectives are different in different countries ('horses for courses'). Both economic instruments, including taxation, and (re-)regulation play a role. Environmental investments inspire invention and innovation, leading to profitable new economic activities (Figure 7).

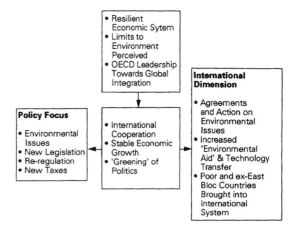

FIGURE 7　The logic of Sustainable World

Implications for energy

The primary effect of *Sustainable World* on the energy industry is greatly increased pressure to reduce the industry's impact on the natural environment. Five aspects are important, ranging from the direct and straightforward (which kind of energy is produced and how) to the indirect and far-reaching (how energy is consumed). These are:

- Tightened regulation of emissions from energy facilities, for example oil wells, refineries and power plants.
- Higher standards for the quality of energy products, such as sulphur in fuel oil.
- Switching to 'cleaner' fuels, for example from coal and oil to natural gas, biomass and perhaps, eventually, nuclear.
- Improvements in the efficiency of energy-using devices, such as light bulbs and automobiles.
- The re-design of whole energy-using systems, such as systems which provide transportation and housing.

The technology already exists to move forward in all of these areas. In many cases, however, economic and other incentives are insufficient for substantial take-up. Furthermore, even when they are adopted, it takes a long time before the effect is significant, because the systems being modified are so large. For example, automobiles with fuel efficiencies much higher than the fleet average are already available, but even with the very rapid introduction assumed in *Sustainable World*, the average fleet efficiency rises slowly. This slow response time is as characteristic of the whole energy system, as of the transport sector (Figure 8). These are the 'big problems, requiring big solutions'.

Both 'market instruments' and 'command and control' regulations are important in implementing these measures. One essential ingredient is greatly increased final energy prices to end-users. It is not obvious, however, how the rents (the difference between final prices and production costs) will be divided between energy companies and producer

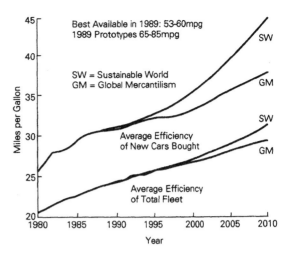

FIGURE 8   Car efficiencies in the OECD

and consumer governments. Although final prices are raised significantly (for example, through a large carbon tax), energy consumption per dollar of Gross Domestic Product (GDP) falls because of improved energy efficiencies, and so the burden of energy costs relative to GDP is not much higher than historic levels. In this sense, the high energy prices are economically manageable.

These measures have radical implications for the energy industry. Growth in total world primary energy supply grows much more slowly, at 1% per annum from 1988 to 2010, instead of 1.6% in *Global Mercantilism* (both exhibit, on average, a 3% per annum growth in real GDP). There is also a substantial shift in the mix of fuels, especially (over this period) from coal to natural gas.

However, even such a scenario – which postulates very severe policy intervention – does not result in reductions in global emissions of carbon dioxide sufficient to meet the 'Toronto target' of a 20% reduction by 2005. Therefore, if the current scientific consensus is correct, some global warming will occur, even in *Sustainable World*; although much less than *Global Mercantilism* (*Figure 9*).

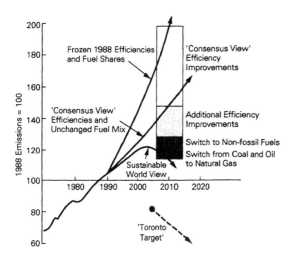

FIGURE 9   Global emissions of carbon dioxide from burning fossil fuels

is cohesive, with enhanced international co-operation (as well as coercion) and new global institutions and mechanisms (Figure 10).

	Global Mercantilism	Sustainable World
Challenge	Hegemonic Decline and Economic Instability	Degradation of the Environment (especially through Global Warming)
Response	Multipolar World and Mercantilism	International Cooperation and Management
Implications for Energy	New Rules for Business and Reconfiguration of Markets	New Values for Fuels and Reconstruction of the Energy Industry

FIGURE 10   Summary of the scenarios

CONCLUSION

These scenarios present two radically different images of the future. In *Global Mercantilism*, the main global challenge is dealing with the decline in the hegemonic position of the two superpowers and instability in international markets. The response is fragmented, with neo-mercantilist economic policies and the establishment of regionally organised – but internally deregulated and competitive – markets. In *Sustainable World*, the central challenge is dealing with common problems, especially global warming; the response

In the first scenario, the energy industry faces new rules and continuous 'reconfiguration' of markets. In the second, it faces sharp increases in the value of clean fuels and processes relative to dirty ones and in the cost of its operations, as well as substantial 'reconstruction' of the industry.

The two scenarios are alternative interpretations of the present. As such, their purpose is to sensitise us to recognise signals of possible changes in the world – which will probably include elements of both scenarios – and to enable us to respond quickly and appropriately. They are less reassuring than conventional forecasts, but more challenging – and therefore more useful.

	Global Mercantilism	Sustainable World
Challenge	Hegemonic decline and economic instability	Degradation of the environment (especially through global warming)
Response	Multipolar world and mercantilism	International co-operation and management
Implications for energy	New rules for business and reconfiguration of markets	New values for fuels and reconstruction of the energy industry

Shell in the 1990s

Five years later, by the mid-1990s, Shell's view was incorporated in two scenarios which were rather different to those described by Pierre Wack and Adam Kahane (though many of the trends described by the latter were still discernible):

JUST DO IT – which focuses on the inevitable consequences (especially for the entrepreneurial individual) of liberalisation (including deregulation) and privatisation, globalisation and the progress of technology. They encapsulated these in TINA (Margaret Thatcher's famous dictum that 'There Is No Alternative').

BIG ME – in this scenario the focus is on the cohesion of the community, with partners who trust each other, and on the long-term vision; which means that government matters.

Even so, the principles involved in Shell's scenario planning remained much the same: only the environment they were describing had changed. These processes are described in the appendix at the end of the chapter. This is a copy of a computer conference we ran, which, led by Graham Galer (then one of Shell's planners, and now with GBN), discussed Shell's use of the various techniques.

As another example, The Centre for Defence Analysis (DERA) describes four separate scenarios which may come about in its particular environment:

Web of Nations – broadly, a loose web of international alignments

Subsidiarity with Independence – where nations group into unions

Fragmentation – national power is diminished by globalisation

Blocs – with powerful economic and cultural groups.

These are then located in three dimensions, against the three axes of 'nature of alliance', 'globalisation' and 'political coherence'.

8.5 'SELLING' SCENARIOS TO MANAGEMENT

We hope that we have been able to show you that scenarios can be both easy to use and very productive. They may, however, still demand a considerable investment of time, often of scarce senior management time, so, if they are to be justified, they must earn their keep. This means that they must be genuinely useful, and used, as the (external) basis for corporate strategy. All those we have met who are actively involved in scenario planning recognise that this is the most difficult part of the whole process. It is no accident that the large corporate planning department at Shell say they spend at least half their time promoting their scenarios. They typically achieve this by running workshops for the local companies, and for other members of management, as the process develops, and make elaborate presentations to them all at the end of the process. It took them a number of years to attain the degree of understanding and trust which their 'users' now have. It is probably no accident that their central planning team see themselves only as *facilitators*, and insist that all planning is actually done by line managers.

Indeed, the whole process of scenario forecasting should be imbued, from the very start, with the objective of positively influencing the strategy of the organisation. There are two requirements for this: the scenarios must be carefully balanced between stretching the imagination of the management and being believable; and there must be significant investment in educating the managers making practical use of scenarios, especially senior management. Marketing the scenarios needs to be every bit as sophisticated as writing them. Introducing the scenario process should be seen as a long-term project. It can take a number of years before senior managers really trust scenarios sufficiently to put their faith in the strategies which are developed from them.

Hence the cultural problems facing those who wish their organisations to take scenarios seriously should not be underestimated. Failure to have an immediate impact on published strategy should not discourage those considering the use of the technique. Our own experience, and that of Shell, was that, while the first scenarios produced are relatively neglected in subsequent planning, participants still do obtain major benefits from the process, even in the short term. The main practical benefit is much less direct than that usually claimed, and indeed is often not even obvious to the participants themselves. It is the enduring change in the viewpoint of all those participating that matters, extending their perspectives to include the wider environment and the longer term. This has been our own experience, not least in terms of the 'surprising' elements which have emerged during the process and been accepted as key determinants of subsequent strategy. In view of the 'short-termism' exhibited by so many managers, this shift in attitude must – by itself – be invaluable. Above all, therefore, scenario planning should be seen as a process of learning.

As a final reminder, we would once more recommend that you always start with simple brainstorming – and adopt this as your central framework – whatever else you do in devising and making use of scenarios.

8.6 APPENDIX: THE SHELL APPROACH TO SCENARIOS

On the first presentation of our MBA elective, *The Challenge of the External Environment*, we ran a computer conference hosted by one of the leading exponents of the technique. As this proved to be very popular and helped many students, we are including below an edited version of Graham Galer's answers to the many questions contributed by students and tutors.

In editing this the sequencing has been changed, so the # numbers show the original number of Graham's message on the conference, and those in brackets show the questions he was answering. Our additions are in italics. Otherwise all the words are exactly as they were on the conference – so this may also give you an idea of how such conferencing works.

Guest CoSy (computer COnferencing SYstem) lecture

by Graham Galer of Shell

Planning in Shell

#1 May I introduce myself – I am Graham Galer, a manager in the Group Planning division of Shell. I have worked for Shell most of my working life (over 30 years now), including assignments in Australia, Italy and the USA. For the last 15 years or so I have specialised in planning.

The Royal Dutch/Shell group of companies ('Shell') is now the largest player in the world oil industry, is second on the Fortune Global 500 list of the world's largest industrial corporations and, for the second year in a row in 1990, earned more profit than any other company or group.

Scenarios

#8(2) Scenario planning is central to Shell's approach. We use them as a means of dealing with uncertainty and for getting the right things on the corporate 'agenda'.

Example of what I mean: we did a lot of scenario work on the future of Europe in 1989/90, at the request of our top management, because we were beginning to think about changes that might be needed in our ways of doing business in Europe, and needed to identify the matters which were really important to us and make sure that everyone involved in Shell made their contribution to the internal debate.

But scenarios are only the beginning. The trick is to find the strategic response to them. We spend at least as much time thinking this through as developing the scenarios in the first place.

#9(2) Everyone can gain from thinking in scenario terms. Imagine the thought process you go through as you leave home on a day of dubious weather and wonder whether or not to take an umbrella with you. You are thinking through scenarios of different kinds of weather and how it would be if you were with, or without, an umbrella! Or suppose you are taking a decision on whether to take on a mortgage commitment in the present uncertain climate or, if you are older, whether to persevere in trying to sell your house or wait for a while.

There's nothing terribly sophisticated about these processes. (The sophistication perhaps comes as your business gets bigger and the decisions more complex.) What's important is the discipline of making yourself think through the different consequences of alternative futures, any of which might come to pass.

Who should produce scenarios?

Line managers *have* to do the planning, including taking responsibility for the scenarios which are used. Letting professional planners (like me) take decisions is an abdication of management, and most likely a recipe for disaster! The planners, if your company is big enough to need and afford them, are there to give staff support. There are simplified methods, and there are also means of helping your managers review scenarios and link them to their business.

We do a lot of this kind of thing, mainly through running 'workshops'. For example, a colleague of mine has just returned from an African country where he ran a 24-hour workshop with the local management team which took them in a fairly structured way through a process of thinking about scenarios of the future in their country and the consequences for their business strategy.

Simple scenarios (1)

#11 Here is a simplified scenario method we sometimes use when working with groups of managers. It is normally used as the basis for a day-long workshop focused on a specific issue. For example, a colleague recently used it to help managers who were thinking about the outlook for the demand for plastics, where market conditions are changing due to the increase in recycling of waste material.

1   Identify the important variables.
    Which aspects of the future (to around the year 2000, say) do you need to know about to formulate strategy? Write these down and sort them according to importance and uncertainty. The scenarios should focus on the variables which are both important and uncertain.

2   Brainstorm for possible stories.
    What *might* happen? Sketch series of events dealing with the important/ uncertain variables.

3   Reduce/refine the scenarios.
    A useful scenario is plausible, recognisable, challenging and internally consistent. Outline scenarios from step 2 should be reduced to between two and four in number using these criteria. It is often helpful to identify 'branching points' where scenarios diverge.

4   Discuss the business issues arising.
    Assess threats and opportunities for the business under each scenario. Then use the scenarios together to consider options – new ones they suggest, and their consequences for existing options. Finally list the strategic issues or questions raised by consideration of the scenarios.

All this is done in workshop mode, working in syndicates some of the time if there are more than eight or so people present and using devices such as Post-it™ Notes to create a pattern of possible events on the conference room wall [or computer conference entries in our case]. It's a crude method, but effective if time and resources are limited.

#49(45) The 'simplified' method is a fairly recent innovation in Shell which we have found very effective in working with managers who are nearer the front line than we (the central planners) are. It gives people a basic framework for thinking (usually in groups, because we use this mainly in workshops) about the future. It's been especially useful in situations where the political outlook is murky – e.g. in some African countries – and the company has to take some rather fundamental decisions.

There's still a place for scenarios of the 'big picture' and for these consistency is quite important, so the degree of rigour has to be higher.

Timespan

#21(16) Our scenarios usually run for about 20 years. This is a function of the subject-matter, since 20 years is the kind of timespan you need to consider in the oil/energy industry.

We have worked with much shorter timespans for shorter-range decisions (e.g. five years) but find it most cost-effective to put our limited resources into the longer periods.

It does depend on circumstances, of course – at a personal level you can go right down to a few hours for some decisions. In the very long run scenarios break down, since they contain the seeds of their own destruction through the emergence of countervailing forces. We occasionally make speculative looks of up to 50 years (e.g. for global warming, what happens when the oil runs out? etc.) but worry much less about scenario logic in these cases.

Contingency plans

#20(15) We only exceptionally make contingency plans against specific scenarios. The 1986 'low oil price' was a case in point and, even then, it was more a case of 'being prepared' than having detailed plans ready to pull out of the drawer.

I don't think we look back much, except once in a while to see if we actually captured the right things. We don't modify scenarios to fit the actual stream of events, but use them as a framework to understand events as they unfold.

I think you should do some scenario planning when you feel uncomfortable about the future, in the sense that you don't understand too well what is happening. This can be in good times or bad – though it's much more difficult to engender discomfort when things are going well. That's part of the art, I suppose!

Alternative scenarios

#29(24) We have been working with two scenarios at Group level for the past few years, and they are not 'good' and 'bad', but different. It can be helpful to have a 'business as usual' or 'surprise-free' scenario, especially when the scenarios are focused on a particular business, and in this case you would probably want to have 'optimistic' and 'pessimistic' scenarios as well.

A few years ago the Shell management deliberately adopted and promoted an optimistic scenario as a means of sending a 'positive' message to the organisation as a whole. This approach needs handling with care, though!

#36(34) We also run our scenarios over the businesses of major competitors, using a simplified model of their portfolios and balance sheets, to get a rough idea of how things will be looking for them over the next few years.

Discontinuities

#49(46) I think the most you can do with discontinuities is to prepare people for the possibility that they might happen. You can also use scenario methods to start thinking about what will happen *after* the discontinuity.

#21(17) The scenarios tend to come in at an earlier stage, when business strategy is being considered; they also provide a basis for the selection of the sensitivities which will be considered.

It's usually practically impossible to tell when something will 'flip', of course. But the scenario approach gives a means of understanding. For example, in 1988 when signs of cracking were beginning to emerge from the USSR (a vital player in the energy business) we prepared (with expert help) four single dynamic scenarios. These didn't predict anything, but helped us understand events as they occurred.

The scenario process

#28(23) As to process, I would involve management from the start. Interview them, find out where the uncertainties are, perhaps identify some differences of opinion, then propose a workshop session where they would sketch their own scenarios, perhaps along the lines of the methods I have previously described.

#12(5) Some of the best debates are with people who feel strongly about one scenario and are prepared to defend it vigorously. Good creative thinking is vital and this doesn't always come through working down lists. However, you need a note of the formal steps to make sure you haven't forgotten anything.

You don't want too many people in the earlier stages of scenario development. The thing is to find people who have something interesting or unusual to say! A group of up to 10 managers usually come up with good material: in our central staff group in Group Planning we have about 10 people working on the scenarios.

#25(19) And good networking inside the company is important. We use e-mail and computer conferencing quite a lot these days to build up networks of people involved in business planning in all parts of the Shell group. These can be used for circulating ideas and flying kites!

#12(4) It helps to be outrageous in the earlier stages of thinking about scenarios, and the whole idea is to help managers themselves 'think the unthinkable'. We had a scenario of low oil prices in the mid-1980s which was seen as absurd by many people but which, once it gained acceptance as at least *possible*, proved very useful when, later, oil prices did fall sharply in 1986.

'Accuracy' has to be judged, I think, in terms of whether the scenarios got the right things on to the management agenda. We've done quite well at this, through (e.g.) timely inclusion in Shell scenarios of fast economic growth in the Far East and the possibility of radical change in Eastern Europe.

#36(33) I don't see why you need more participative management to make the scenario approach succeed. But, if you *do* want management to be more participative, then a scenario process would be a good vehicle for helping to bring it about. Some of our operating companies have used this approach.

Any strategy needs checking with middle management to see if there are going to be implementation problems. But that's just good management!

Other methods

#21(17) We use all the 'traditional' methods too. To get capital authorised in Shell you have to satisfy tough conditions of profitability. There are minimum 'hurdle' rates of return, and multiple sensitivities are run to look at the robustness of proposals. (Managers in our company are very numerate!)

#49(44) We also use 'sensitivity' calculations in Shell too – for example, the earning power of any oil production venture is normally tested against a 'planning value' for the price of oil, plus at the least a downside sensitivity. I think scenario planning is of more value when unknown factors are potentially at work. Quantification is a later step. At the global level unknown *factors* for which we use scenario methods include the outlook for energy taxation and for world trade. At a more local level an investment at a manufacturing site might be at risk from future environmental controls which could restrict the company's freedom to operate.

I believe there is a place in good planning for both scenario thinking and sensitivity analysis.

Simple scenarios (2)

#18 There are many approaches to scenario thinking. Here is a slightly more elaborate version of the earlier (simple) version, in which one goes on to consider 'second generation' scenarios. (This is taken from a Shell computer conference, hence the format. Kees van der Heijden is a colleague of mine.)

[53] Heijden (Kees) 5-Dec-91 12:20AM-PST

Scenario approach

In response to Art's question, here is a one page scenario methodology, inspired by the teachings of Pierre Wack.

Step 1

- Identify interesting developments in the business environment. Extrapolate into the future.
- Plot on a predictability versus importance chart. Predictable are the events which 'are already in the pipeline', unpredictable are developments which can be interpreted in more than one way.
- Everything that falls in the predictable quadrants are the predetermines, and are common to all scenarios.
- Consider what is in the uncertain/important quadrant. Consider what out of that 'would really make a difference'. Pick out the two or three most important.
- Decide on two outcomes of these uncertainties that cover the range of likely outcomes.
- Create a 2 by 2 (or 2 by 2 by 2) matrix giving all possible combinations of these outcomes.
- Rank the four (or eight) combinations in terms of their internal consistency.
- Pick a limited number of the most consistent combinations that cover the territory.
- Work out the resulting scenarios.

The product of this is the so-called first-generation scenarios. If you stop at this point you will find the scenario exercise disappointing. You are urged to move on to the next stage.

Step 2

- Identify the most important actors in each of the first generation scenarios.
- Put yourself in the shoes of one of these actors. Now 'live' through each of the first-generation scenarios from their perspective, and note whether and when/where conditions develop which seem incompatible with the logic of that actor. Consider what action he might take at that point in time.
- Do the same thing for the other actors you have identified, noting down the points of actor inconsistency and therefore discontinuity.
- Redesign the first-generation scenarios to allow for these discontinuities.
- Reiterate until the scenarios become totally feasible from the perspective of all actors in them.

These are the second-generation scenarios. It is only in step 2 that you learn where there might be unexpected discontinuities in the future, and where the exercise becomes really useful for development of strategy.

Contents of scenarios

#12(4) It's essential (at least in the oil business) to include environmental and people values. Reason – these are among the most important and uncertain variables in our business environment! (This may not be the case for all business, of course.)

One of the two 'global' scenarios we are currently working with is called 'Sustainable World' and encompasses many of the forces affecting the ecological sustainability of future economic development in the world. It has proved very useful in the three years or so we have been using it. On the 'people' front – large transnational companies are not the most popular entities around the world and they will only survive if they remain on balance acceptable to the communities they operate in – and this includes being attractive companies to work for. So we need to gather information on values and speculate on ways in which they might evolve in future.

Presenting the results

#25(19) The only way to deal with 'soft' information is through human interaction!

We put considerable effort into presenting our scenarios. For example, a colleague is currently in Japan where he will give a scenario presentation to the management team of Shell Japan (as well as doing some other things while he is there). These presentations are popular and there is not usually much difficulty in getting the access to management that is needed.

We also run workshops. These are either to give a framework for linking the scenarios and business strategy, or sometimes ad hoc on particularly important questions. For instance, a few months ago we ran a workshop for about 10 top Shell managers in which the political and economic outlook for the Islamic republics of the former USSR was reviewed (very important for future oil production in the CIS). To do this, we brought in to the workshop speakers who had expert knowledge of the subject. The role of the planners was to be 'facilitators' and to help workshop participants structure their conclusions in scenario form.

To the extent that soft information is published in book form, I think a good picture, diagram or cartoon is worth 1000 words! Managers are overloaded with information these days, and the corporate provider of information has to keep a careful eye on his competition. A good test of whether a piece of work is worth publishing is – would managers already have read about this in *The Economist* or *Financial Times?*

Quantification

#41(35) How do you 'quantify' your scenarios? This is essential for a company like mine, where we need to know the consequences for energy supply and demand of broad brush economic/political scenarios.

Some elements of the energy scene are scenario-dependent. A good example is the energy-efficiency of vehicles, which will tend to rise in a high-growth scenario, where the vehicle fleet is replaced faster. Some, such as trends in environmental legislation, are less scenario-dependent.

One has to build up a series of links between the framework scenarios and the various components of the energy balance in order to carry out the necessary quantification. The process is iterative, of course, because the energy situation itself (the price of oil, for instance) can affect the general economic situation.

We spend quite a lot of effort on this, incorporating into our scenario work studies made of areas of business which are of particular interest to us – for example, we recently completed a review of the future of transport, which became a scenario 'building block'.

Probability

#42 A topic I think we should mention is the place of probability in scenario planning. Many people try to assign probabilities to scenarios they have developed.

My belief is that probability has little or no place in scenario planning! To give scenarios probabilities is effectively to return to forecasting, since a forecast could be constructed from the weighted average of the scenarios, if they have probabilities attached to them.

Why did scenarios have a bad press in the 1980s?

#9(2) The sort of planning departments which were run down in the 1980s were those, like that of General Electric in the USA, which put in the hands of central planners a lot of influence on the contents of the company's plans.

Shell's Group Planning does not *do* any planning in this sense at all. Our job is to provide systems and processes, propose criteria (of profitability, for example), build up an understanding of the business environment, and to develop planning methodology. We also ask awkward questions! All the planning is actually done (i.e. decisions are made about what the plans should contain) by line managers.

The same is true in our operation units – Shell UK, for example, or Shell Australia or Shell Brazil. The task of the planners in all such units is to *facilitate* the production of good plans by their managers. They strive to avoid living in ivory towers and indeed they would be ignored if they did.

The numbers of people working in planning departments in Shell has probably fallen in recent years. But this is the result of the general trend to reduce 'head office' costs, and to get planning as decentralised and near the front line as possible.

Peter Schwartz (and history)

#22 Here's another thought about scenarios. I was at a conference in the US two weeks ago and heard a talk by Peter Schwartz, a leading exponent. He propounded the interesting idea that we can learn by going back in time and seeing what people then missed. (He began his exposition by a historical account of the mapping of California, which was first thought to be an island, based on erroneous interpretation of the known geography of Baja California.) A brief extract from my notes:

> At 8am the next morning Peter Schwartz gave a keynote presentation on scenario planning, entitled 'Re-perceiving the future through the lens of the past'. This was an excellent talk, which took the years 1960, 1970 and 1980 and showed the conventional wisdom about the future prevalent at those times, how wrong it was and what pointers to the future were in fact available to those prepared to look. For example, IBM in 1980 thought that 275,000 PCs would be sold by 1990: the actual number was 60 million! (Disloyal thought prompted by this session – do Shell's presently evolving global scenarios challenge conventional wisdom to a sufficient degree, or do they just provide a tidy framework for the conventional views emerging from the management interviews?)

#47(38) One reason for the failure of Sinclair's C5 was that he didn't think about the competition. People have other means of gaining mobility which, as it turned out, they preferred to getting asphyxiated and crushed by buses! One does need to be rigorous in scanning the environment, including looking in unlikely directions (you've probably heard the story of how Singapore was lost to the Japanese in WW2 because the defenders were prepared for an attack from the sea, whereas in fact the invaders came along the Malayan peninsula). We try to organise our scanning into economic, political, social, technological and competitive dimensions.

There's no way to be sure you have captured everything – that's the art! But you can systematise up to a point, and keep in touch with insightful people whom you have found to be alert to the signs of change.

You will probably be amazed to hear that oil companies think they have next to no influence over their business environment! Of course we advertise to our customers and lobby government over legislation, but our influence over the things that really matter, such as technical change, economic growth and the price of oil, is very slight indeed. So in our scenario thinking we tend to take the observed environment as given. At the level of individual products, though, I could well see some influence being possible. Have you got some examples in mind?

Further reading

#47(39) There are precious few books about scenario planning that are any good. A recent one which makes a good read is *The Art of the Long View* by Peter Schwartz, an American who used to work for Shell and is now a consultant in California. It was published in the US last year and is, I believe, now available in UK publication. Unlike most management books, especially

American ones, it's refreshingly short! The journal of the US Planning Forum is devoting its first two issues this year to scenario planning, which is getting a good press in the US these days. You will find various articles dotted through the pages of the UK journal *Long Range Planning*. The best articles I know are two published in the *Harvard Business Review* by Pierre Wack, the main pioneer of these ideas in Shell (sorry to keep plugging my friends!).

There are many books and reports describing, not methodology, but actual scenario studies. Some of the books of Herman Kahn are good, as are the new books by Donella Meadows, which updates the Club of Rome report of some years back and, very recently, a four-scenario futures study of the world published by the Dutch government planning office.

Advice from Roy Amara (good forecasting)

#48 As I approach the end of my time with you, I thought I would give you one of the best summaries I have come across of how to think about the future. It comes from Roy Amara, who is President of the Institute for the Future, California.

Amara's comments on the accuracy of his past forecasts provide some good reasons for thinking in terms of scenarios! But his 'do's and don'ts' give some very practical advice on how in general to approach the future.

In a talk I heard him give at a conference in the USA in 1988, Amara started by going back to the forecasts his institute had made in 1978. He found they had made many 'hits', but also quite a few 'misses'. He categorised the latter as follows:

1   Major discontinuities.
   –   Double-digit inflation in the early 1980s.
   –   Persistent trade deficits.
   –   Persistent budget deficits.
2   Energy.
   –   The oil-price collapse in the mid-1980s.
   –   Slow growth of alternative energy sources.
   –   The effectiveness of energy conservation (now no longer a function of prices).
3   Changes in the work environment.
   –   The slow diffusion of information technology.
   –   Mergers and acquisitions.
   –   Massive internal corporate restructuring.
   –   Continuing decline of the labour unions.

The best forecasting, he thought, had been in respect of basic demographics, life-style changes, the labour force, economics and regulatory matters. The worst had concerned politically or internationally driven trends.

Amara then gave his 'do's and don'ts' of forecasting, as follows:

1   Don't be a vacuum-cleaner.

Don't try to include all the material available in your analysis. You cannot represent any complex system by a finite set of variables. You need focus, which means that a forecaster employs filters as well as lenses.

2   Don't substitute error for uncertainty.
Amara thinks that the outlook in the US is for higher inflation, but that the actual level is highly uncertain. He estimates 5–10% during the late 1980s, with double-digit inflation in the early 1990s for a while.

3   At times, lean against the wind.
Seek out inconsistencies in conventional wisdom and look for 'untrends' (by which he meant generally accepted trend projections which are capable of challenge).

4   Hedge forecasts with possible surprises.
Amara suggested a few potential surprises for the early 1990s. These were:

–   Energy prices climb steeply.

–   The US defence budget declines by 3% per year.

–   US manufacturing industry does very well.

–   Large US trade deficits persist.

–   A strong activist government emerges in the US.

5   Look for break points and discontinuities.
Recent such events had been the stock exchange events of October 1987 (where a major problem is that the underlying mechanism is unknown); the oil price collapse (discontinuities in the oil price are easier to foresee on the way down than on the way up); and the breakthrough in superconductivity research.
Most planners and forecasters are 'structural change junkies', always on the lookout for structural change in the systems they monitor. In the last 10 years the major changes of this kind had occurred in oil and communications. Amara expected the 1990s to produce change of similar magnitude in health care and education.

6   Focus on underlying driving forces.
Amara discussed the following phenomena, with the associated driving force in brackets:

–   Corporate restructuring (foreign competition).

–   Diffusion of business PCs (perceiving payback).

–   Growth of small businesses (baby boom bulge).

7   Go from analysis to issues.

8   Don't be fooled by the diffusion curve.
This tends to lead to over-estimation in the short term, and under-estimation in the long term. Analysts using the diffusion curve technique have predicted the emergence of a number of billion-dollar industries which are obviously not going to make it – e.g., videotex and quadraphonic sound.

9   Keep asking 'so what?'
Planning should be integrated with doing through asking 'what if?' questions. Computer simulation is the main mechanism here. Planning should be made less visible, with the planners providing the link between the visionaries and the implementers.

Final summary

#50 Summing up the principles I have found most important:

- Think of yourself or your organisation as working within an environment which you continually scan and, when you have noted something significant happening, monitor.
- Consider using scenarios as a means of exploring the present and future environment when things are going on which you do not understand, or feel uneasy about.
- Look for critical success factors, driving forces and branching points.
- Keep it simple (e.g. not more than three or four scenarios), and make sure everyone is involved in your scenario process who has a stake in the outcome.

SUMMARY OF PART 1

It is worth repeating the strictures about the differences between forecasts and budgets. Forecasts, if they are to be usable, must be unbiased projections of what is likely to happen if no action is taken – or, more precisely, if certain specified assumptions about the future of the market (and the external environment) are fulfilled. Budgets, on the other hand, take into account the wishes of management and directly allow for the organisation's planned actions. Regrettably, too many organisations assume that the two are the same – and are surprised when, all too often, their cherished forecasts are wrong!

In relation to the broader environment, which also tends to be equated with the longer term, environmental analysis is the key activity, and within this, scanning is the most important element. Our overall advice is to cultivate an open and enquiring mind, or – better still – a number of such open and enquiring minds among your team of managers and professionals, supported by the widest possible range of inputs. Perhaps the most important contributor to an open mind is an awareness of the hidden models which affect many seemingly unbiased perspectives. The 'irrational' models, in particular, can very easily distort the picture – without anyone noticing since they are universally accepted (at least until the paradigm, or the custom, changes).

Apart from technological forecasting, most methods of long-range forecasting depend upon expert opinion. This opinion may be an individual or a group – and many of the more sophisticated techniques require team working. The optimal technique will, however, depend upon the circumstances of the particular organisation.

We moved on to explain the value of scenarios as a means of enabling organisations to face up to and prepare for uncertain long-term futures. We emphasised the importance of presenting management with alternative scenarios rather than making a confident single prediction. We looked at a single process of designing scenarios, before illustrating their practical application by Shell.

PART 2

LONG-RANGE MARKETING: ROBUST STRATEGIES

AIMS AND OBJECTIVES

We have now finished our examination of how a variety of *research* tools, especially those relating to *environmental analysis* and *forecasting*, may be used to explore the external forces impinging on organisations. In particular, we have explored in some depth the processes involved in *scenario* writing, as a means of bringing together, in the most meaningful context, a description of forces expected to act on organisations in future, so as to generate an especially powerful form of long-range forecast.

You should, therefore, now be in a position to understand how the external environment is impinging upon your own organisation. You should be able to analyse the various forces involved and, to a degree, predict their future progress (or at least forecast the main alternatives).

Of course, the actions your organisation will take will not just depend upon external factors. They will be constrained by the internal resources which it can bring to bear on them. Indeed (as is shown by the number of courses in MBA programmes which deal with internal issues) managing these *internal* constraints is typically the main role of management.

After studying this part of the book you should be capable of writing a set of *robust strategies* – developed as part of a formal long-range marketing plan, based upon a range of inputs from the *external* environment – which contrast with the short-term corporate strategies which almost inevitably focus on these *internal* constraints.

To achieve this objective, you will need first to understand exactly what *robust* strategies are, and how they differ from traditional *corporate* strategies. In order to develop robust strategies, you will also need to understand the overall planning processes which lead to these – and the main techniques which underpin them; along with the generic robust strategies which may also be deployed and the short-term actions needed to implement them.

The structure of this part is quite simple.

1 **Robust strategies** – after an introductory article, which sets the scene, the first section explains in general what *long-range marketing* is about and more specifically *what robust strategies* are, and *why* they are needed – in *comparison* with the more traditional (shorter-term) corporate strategies. The process of developing these robust strategies then starts by looking at the *key turning points*, the decisions – typically emerging from the scenarios we have already developed – which will shape the future of the organisation.

2 **The long-range-marketing-plan** – the second major section then describes the rest of the overall planning process, step by step, involving the various decisions which will lead to the robust strategies themselves.

3 **Long-range marketing techniques** – supporting the discipline of long-range marketing are a range of specific techniques.

4 **Generic strategies** – there are some generalised strategies which normally result in robust outcomes, even without application of the full planning process. They are described in this section.

5   **Short-term actions** – this section explores the typical range of short-term
    actions which are required to implement robust strategies.

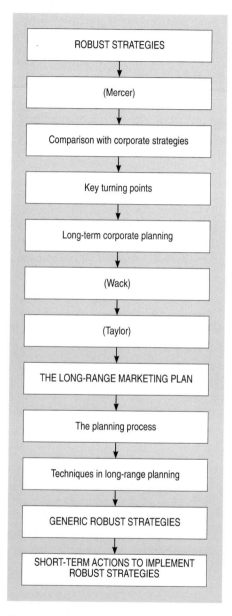

Map of Part 2

9 PURPOSE OF ROBUST STRATEGIES

9.1 ROBUST PLANNING

It is fair to say that producing two or three scenarios is usually the hardest, and certainly the most time consuming, part of the overall long-range planning process. It is arguably also the most important; once you have asked the right *questions* the correct answers usually follow.

This is not, though, the end of the process. There can be no *productive* outcome until an effective set of *robust strategies* has been created, to address the issues which surface in the scenario work. It is the development of these strategies, and the implementation of these, which are the subjects of this part of the book. In view of our focus on the far future of the external environment, we characterise this process as 'long-range marketing'.

To put the whole process in *context*, however, we will start by, once more, briefly looking at a paper we have had published: 'Robust strategies in a day' by David Mercer. This describes the *very simple* process we have developed for use by smaller organisations, and even by departments within larger ones.

We will later return to look at the individual parts of the process in more detail; so you should – at this stage – *skim* the material in order to obtain a flavour of what is involved. Now *quickly* read Article 9.1 below by David Mercer.[1]

Article 9.1 DAVID MERCER: 'ROBUST STRATEGIES IN A DAY'

As a development from previous work on 'simpler scenarios', a format has now been devised which allows the complete scenario planning process, from start of environmental analysis to finished robust strategies, to be run in just one day.

The new process revolves around four main sessions – compressed into a single day:

Development of Global Scenario Drivers for 2025

Development of 'Industry Sector' Drivers for 2010

Development of Alternative Scenarios

Investigation of Key Turning Points and Development of Robust Strategies.

SCENARIOS IN A DAY

Our aim, in simplifying the various scenario planning processes even further, was to widen its use to even less sophisticated organisations. Thus, the new process comprises just four main sessions – compressed into a *single day* – timetabled as follows:

---

[1] Reprinted from *Management Decision*, 35, 3: 219–223.

9.00–9.20	Introduction to Scenarios*
9.20–11.00	Development of Global Scenario Drivers for 2025
11.00–11.15	Coffee
11.15–11.45	Discussion of Results*
11.45–1.15	Development of 'Industry Sector' Drivers for 2010
1.15–2.00	Lunch
2.00–2.30	Discussion of Results*
2.30–3.30	Development of Alternative Scenarios
3.30–3.45	Tea
3.45–4.15	Discussion of Results*
4.15–5.30	Investigation of Key Turning Points and Development of Robust Strategies
5.30–6.00	Discussion of Results – and Agreement on Strategies*

* plenary sessions

PARTICIPANTS AND 'DOMESTIC ARRANGEMENTS'

Our previous papers have described 'single' group sessions; covering six to eight participants from the corporate planning function only. One major change, therefore, is the number and range of participants involved. The new planning process may only last a day but it takes in senior managers from across the whole organisation, ideally including all those who will have to implement strategy. In addition, some organisations also choose to include representatives from their key customers. The result is that something between twenty and thirty senior managers and board members attend the day.

Accordingly, it is necessary to run three to four groups (of six to eight members each) in parallel; to handle the 20–30 managers involved overall. The groups are chosen by the organisation, usually mixing them on the basis of getting managers from the different sides of the business to meet each other – and, as well as fostering building of relationships across the organisation

(an important secondary outcome), this approach also seems to provide the most stimulating format for the groups.

The basic space requirement, thus, is for a large conference room which can accommodate around 30 people seated round a conference table – but with space, behind the chairs, to work in the separate groups. In view of the techniques used, the room should have at least four walls with clear access to eight feet or more of surface which will take Post-it® Notes (most walls do, but not all!). Ideally, this should be supported by four separate seminar rooms. The groups work best, as we will see later, in the main conference room – as they are initially learning the scenario processes, when they need the more immediate support of a trained 'facilitator' – but, later, in seminar rooms as they switch to more traditional 'meeting' mode.

As we would always recommend for such high-level planning meetings, the conference room environment must be isolated from all outside interruptions. A hotel is the usual venue, preferably one which specialises in conference activities.

FIRST SESSION (9.20–11.00 A.M.)

Development of global scenario drivers for 2025

The first stage ('deciding the drivers for change') of our normal scenario forecasting is to examine the results of the prior environmental analysis to determine which are the most important factors that will decide the nature of the future environment within which the organisation operates. In the case of this new approach, there is *no* prior analysis, since most members of the group come fresh to it.

Global scenarios?

One aspect of the process which may seem especially theoretical is the subject of the first session, that of scenarios covering the future of the whole world – for the next 30 years. The very positive rationale for this session – which poses no problems for the participants – is derived from our recent research work [Mercer, 1996]. It allows participants to quickly learn the techniques by exposure to a practical example, where their 'mistakes' do not matter. As such it significantly reduces stress levels. It puts all participants on an equal footing. The 'experts', who might otherwise dominate the overall process, hold no particular expertise here – so hierarchies are avoided. Most important, though, it establishes the widest possible perspective as the context for the rest of the day.

Accordingly, this first session is one key to the success of the new approach.

Group session format

The six to eight people taking part in each group are simply asked to congregate in front of their 'wall' and, at the start of the first scenario session participants are deliberately given a very short briefing – with the bare minimum of information. In essence, apart from introducing the basic principles of using Post-it™ Notes as the vehicle for discussion (and record), little more is said than 'We want you to describe the future of the world in 30 years' time.' In practice this proves quite sufficient for the participants to then engage in free-form debate. Most teams are producing a flow of relevant ideas within five minutes and none take more than ten minutes to become fully involved in the debate.

It is important that the groups are informal, and each person should feel that he or she 'owns' the wall. There should be no chairperson! The only 'official' should be the person who documents the outcomes – on flipcharts or acetates – for the plenary session which follows; and even this role should rotate between members.

Discussion of (first session) results (11.15–11.45 a.m.)

Each group session, throughout the day (except the last), is followed by a 'coffee session' (coffee/lunch/tea) where the informal debate is just as important as that in the formal sessions. These are then followed by a plenary meeting at which the conclusions of the individual groups are reported and debated, so that an overall consensus can emerge.

Depending upon the expertise of the 'facilitator', important (and relevant) global trends which have been missed can also be introduced at this first stage. It should be noted, though, that this is the only stage where the 'facilitator' is allowed to intervene in this way.

SECOND SESSION (11.45 A.M.–1.15 P.M.)

Development of 'industry sector' drivers for 2010

The second session is, in effect, a repeat of the first, except that the question is focused on the *industry sector* within which the organisation operates (not of the whole world) and the timescale is halved, to 15 years. Even so, in order to maintain the wider and long-term perspective, the participants are instructed to start with the relevant drivers which they have discovered in the first session; *deliberately* discarding those which do not *directly* apply to their sector. They are, however, allowed to introduce new drivers – specific to the sector. Indeed, as the day progresses, the groups typically move away from purely global factors towards ones which are specific to their industry.

Once more, this session is followed by a *plenary* – this time after lunch (which allows more time for the most important informal debate) – at which group results are reported and a new consensus developed.

THIRD SESSION (2.30–3.30 P.M.)

Development of alternative scenarios

This is the first session where the scenario process diverges significantly from that which we have previously recommended. In the classical approach the main action is to reduce the seven to nine clusters (or mini-scenarios) detected at the previous stage to the two larger scenarios we now recommend. This is a bottom-up approach which takes considerable amounts of time; it can iterate over a number of weeks. Here, however, we have just one hour, following immediately upon the surfacing of the drivers themselves (and the clusters into which they can be fitted).

Accordingly, a very different approach is necessary; and a top-down framework is used instead.

Thus, the group members are, in the first instance, encouraged to explore the factors they have identified in order to find a *theme* – and in particular a title – for each of the two scenarios. These themes should, as far as possible, encapsulate the main trends which have been unearthed. We have found it best to talk about the '*flavour*' of the future for their industry. They then allocate, again as far as possible, the clusters (or mini-scenarios) to each of these alternative scenarios (themes). The end result is something which looks very like a conventional scenario, and (within the context of being just one of the tools of overall planning) works well as such, but has been arrived at by a much simpler route (and is, accordingly, that much less rich in its connotations).

Our experience is that, during this session (and reflecting the change in style), the groups tend to switch from using Post-it™ Notes to flipcharts.

Discussion of results – third session (3.45–4.15 p.m.)

We have generally found that this plenary session is the most enlightening of the day. It is where, in particular, the hidden assumptions of the participants – and those implicit in the organisation's strategy – are surfaced and challenged. As a result, at times it can seem to be a very fraught session. On the other hand, precisely because it does surface hidden tensions between the various participants, it is often the most productive; though it does sometimes demand a greater degree of intervention by the expert 'facilitator' if it is not to become too negative!

FOURTH SESSION (4.15–5.30 P.M.)

Investigation of key turning points and development of robust strategies

The final stage of the conventional process is to examine these scenarios to determine what are the most critical outcomes: the 'branching points' relating to the '*issues*' which will have the greatest impact (potentially generating '*crises*') on the

future of the organisation. These should once more emerge at the end of an extensive (iterative) process. Here we have barely one-and-a-half hours, at the end of a long day, in which we also have to generate the strategies to address these key turning points! One major advantage, however, is that the 20–30 key decision-makers are present; and they are already converging on much the same pattern of future developments. Under these circumstances, the tight timescale proves not to be a problem – as we feared – but a challenge which rapidly generates the required outcomes; and there is not time for the rancorous differences, which often beset such decision-making, to emerge! In any case, it should be remembered that the aim is to develop robust strategies which complement the main strategy process.

The turning points tend to emerge relatively quickly, since there has usually been debate about them in the previous sessions. Thus, the 'robust strategies' are typically the focus of the session – and this part of the work should be encouraged, since it is important for all involved that the day ends with positive actions (or at least positive – strategic – decisions). In our experience, this session is likely to be conducted much more as a conventional management meeting; albeit one in which there is much better understanding between the participants. Hence, the advantage at this time of the separate seminar rooms; though groups without these find their own private areas, usually in the corner of the hotel bar! Once more, the outcomes are summarised on flipcharts or acetates.

The final plenary session, which follows, is usually much less tense than the previous one. There is typically a significant convergence of views. More important, perhaps, this becomes a very positive session – a fitting climax to the day – as the groups positively agree on robust strategies to address the future dangers.

CONCLUSION

Clearly, the most important – immediate – outcomes are the identification of the alternative futures (and facing up to the uncertainty these imply) and developing the robust strategies to address these (as a complement to the optimal short-term strategies).

As a footnote, the robust strategies which emerge seem to most commonly revolve around the organisation's investment in its marketing position. It is traditionally expected that the really long-term decisions are about the technology, but the indications are that the most robust strategies of all are those which focus on the relationship between the organisation and its customers. In essence, this 'goodwill' provides the breathing space necessary for the organisation to develop its responses to any unexpected challenges it might face.

One especially important outcome of the overall process is, however, the value of the communication process itself. The process of working, under pressure (and without any hierarchical framework), in the close-knit groups very quickly consolidates relationships between participants from different parts of the organisation; and with customers, where these are included. In particular, the underlying tensions are surfaced, and positively addressed. As a result, what often starts as a body of managers which is fearful about what the future might hold usually finishes with a very optimistic one. This is, not least, because the managers' fears have been answered. Accordingly, the overall process turns out to be one which is highly motivational. Indeed, a number of participants have stated that this may be the main benefit; outweighing, even, the benefits of positively addressing the uncertainties lying ahead.

REFERENCES

Mercer, D. (1995) 'Scenarios made easy', *Long Range Planning*, Vol. 28, No. 4, pp. 81–68.

Mercer, D. (1995) 'Simpler scenarios', *Management Decision*, Vol. 33, No. 4, pp. 32–40.

Mercer, D. (1996) 'The foreseeable future', *Management Decision*, Vol. 34, No. 3, pp. 55–61.

9.2 WHAT IS DISTINCTIVE ABOUT ROBUST STRATEGIES?

The question which the approach described in this article begs is how are *robust strategies* different from the marketing or corporate strategy which we – in business schools at least – have been recommending for decades. Surprisingly perhaps, there has been little differentiation made between the short- and long-term processes. Indeed, in general there has been just *one* strategy process, leading to a single (corporate) strategy. Even those who have made extensive use of scenarios have typically seen them as one step towards this final strategy, albeit that their resultant strategy has allowed for some alternative outcomes. Thus, from the mission statement through to the action plans, strategy has been treated as one seamless process.

What our own work has revealed, however, is that – for all but the most sophisticated of organisations – it is advisable to conduct a *separate* investigation of the long-term strategies needed to *exploit* future opportunities at one extreme and to survive major threats at the other. For these *robust strategies* need not necessarily be the same as the conventional (short-term) strategy.

Indeed, the two sets of strategies should have very *different* objectives. Robust (long-term) strategies are, above all, about *survival* in the longer term; ensuring that *all* the potential threats are covered. Corporate (short-term) strategies, on the other hand, are quintessentially about *optimising* current performance. The differences are shown in Table 9.1.

Table 9.1 · Comparison of corporate and robust strategies		
	Corporate strategy	**Robust strategies**
Objective	Optimising performance	Ensuring survival
Characteristics	Short-term	Long-term
	Single-focus	Divergent coverage
Outcome	Effectiveness	Comprehensiveness
	Commitment	Understanding
Beneficiaries	Individuals	Communities

Thus, corporate strategy requires that you find the single *short-term strategy* which will deliver the *optimal (internal) performance* most *effectively*, to which members of the organisation can *commit* themselves. The classical example demands the single objective of producing the highest bottom-line profit for the current year.

Robust strategies, on the other hand, require that *multiple*, and often *divergent*, objectives are met, in order to *exploit* the potential emerging from *changes* in the (*external*) *environment*, and especially to guard against the *whole range* of *threats* which might endanger *survival* in the *longer term*, with the aim of *understanding* what these might be.

In terms of basic characteristics, corporate strategy is usually supposed to follow a rational approach (often deductive, arguing from the general to the particular), where robust strategies are evolutionary in nature (and most often best approached inductively, working from the specific pieces of evidence to some general conclusions).

It should be clear that there could be considerable tension between these two forms of strategy; not least because they have very different objectives aimed at producing very different outcomes to satisfy very different groups of stakeholders!

9.3 DIFFERENT STAKEHOLDERS AND THEIR INTERESTS

To expand upon this last point, in the modern corporation the *individual* shareholders are no longer involved in managing the company themselves. Indeed, their investment in it may be as fleeting as the millisecond, as computers trade the shares on electronic stock-markets around the world. Understandably, therefore, their focus is only on the ephemeral performance of the *share price*. They will not even take an interest in the underlying realities which are tied to the short-term financial results and are – even then only indirectly – reflected in the share price. They bear only a theoretical relationship to the shareholders of the nineteenth century, including the entrepreneurs who are central to the myth of much economic theory. These modern shareholders have no interest in managing the affairs of the corporation – and no power to do so, even if they did take their responsibilities more seriously. The *individual* senior managers of the organisations, on the other hand, *are* interested in managing the company, usually in terms of financial performance, but only for the *short term* results, once more. Their own performance – and even more directly their income – is often tied to the share price. As they are usually but a few years away from claiming their pension, they have every incentive to optimise the current results – on which that pension will be based – and to hell with the long term. Put in this context, it is obvious why these key actors ensure that most corporate strategy focuses on short-term financial performance. To put it crudely, neither group will be around when long-term strategy saves the company!

Even so, it is this tension between the principals (owners/shareholders) and agents (managers) which fuels the debates (in economics) about conflicting objectives.

The various *communities*, though, hold a very different perspective. The employees of the organisation, most of whom are some way from retirement, have a very direct interest in the *long-term survival* of the organisation, for on this depends their own security. Even though many of them will, in fact, change to jobs with other organisations, they still want the safety-net of a future in their current position. The other communities of stakeholders, from suppliers and customers through to the local communities which depend upon the organisation, have similar requirements – demanding long-term survival. In many respects, these other communities have taken over the role of the traditional shareholders; looking to the *long-term* future of the organisation. With the growing involvement of these communities in the management of the organisation, however, it is likely that longer-term viewpoints may prevail – and robust strategies will come into their own! *Stakeholder* theory may, in this way, assume much greater practical importance. As the new 'stockholders', these communities have quite different priorities to these of the historical shareholders. More important, they have *very* different priorities from *modern* shareholders.

9.4 CONVERGENCE OF STRATEGIES

In practice the conflict between robust and corporate strategies is not as acute as it might seem to be. Thus, in our experience – despite the seeming contradictions – the two types of strategy typically converge on much the same approach. This is fortunate, since only a very brave management will propose a *definite* reduction in short-term performance in order to avoid a *possible* threat to longer-term survival. As we will see later, the two typically meet in a range of 'generic' long-term strategies, such as 'building relationships' with stakeholders in general, and with customers in particular.

Even so, even if the two prove to be almost identical, the process of establishing what the robust strategies might be is not just worthwhile but *necessary*. Without undertaking the work it is impossible to see if there are any *hidden* conflicts between the two. It is much better to know about any longer-term problems you may be creating for yourself. With the knowledge that they complement each other, however, you have the additional confidence to positively reinforce your short-term strategies; and, possibly, to make the minor changes in them which will provide an even more secure long-term future.

Generally speaking, therefore, the result of separately identifying robust strategies is not a major revision of corporate strategy. In the relatively few cases where that is needed, the robust strategies clearly become the dominant part of the whole planning process. In general, though, the result is to reprioritise within the existing strategy, with the emphasis subtly shifted to allow for the longer-term in *addition* to the shorter one. The key to this is, in our terminology, *the long-range marketing plan*. This is comparable with the traditional (short-term) marketing plan, and both feed into the final corporate strategy. This plan ensures that the key factors are not merely identified but are understood and incorporated into management's thinking. We will look at this long-range marketing plan later.

Audit 9.1

Examine the possible conflict between your own organisation's (existing) corporate and (potential) robust strategies, in terms of Table 9.1. In particular, you should explore the potential conflict between the short-term demands of the stock markets, and of your senior management, and the longer-term desires of the other stakeholder communities, including the ones to which you belong. This is not intended to be a rigorous exercise – after all you have yet to develop your robust strategies – but is intended to make you think about the differences in the context of your own work.

In this section we will, once more, mainly use 'audits' like this one, applied to your own organisation and its environment, rather than 'activities' based upon theoretical examples. Even so, we will try to provide some feedback by looking at our own organisation, the Open University Business School, in the same context. We experience as much conflict between differing objectives as any other organisation. In the short term our need is to maximise revenue, to cover the rapidly growing costs of meeting the ever more sophisticated needs of our students, mainly by attracting even larger numbers to study our programmes around the world. This problem has been compounded by the cost-cutting in industry, which means that there are less funds available in general for students in the UK. All of this demands an ever-tighter focus on our *current* core business – especially that coming, in terms of increased market share, from new students who will study with us for one programme (such as the MBA).

In the longer term, however, we need to be looking at the factors we have identified in our scenarios, in particular the changing role of business schools in general (and of the MBA in particular). In our case, this demands a long-term investment in the establishment of much closer (and in particular a much more on-going) relationship with our students, to match the needs of the '*life-long club*' – providing ongoing education beyond the traditional qualifications – which was the outcome of one of our scenarios (where the other scenario, computer-based 'edutainment' – for home use by the mass of the population – was only open to massive investment by organisations such as Microsoft or the film studios). This demands we try to meet the longer-term aspirations of our existing students, with highly divergent, individual, modular educational plans to which they can belong through much of their working life.

In theory, as a charitable institution run by its own employees, there should be no tensions between the two types of strategy. In fact, some does remain. The rest of the Open University is under even greater financial pressures than ourselves and, as the OU as a whole is effectively our shareholder, its management tries just as hard to maximise our short-term 'profits' so that these can be used to fund shortfalls elsewhere!

In the next section we will look at how we can start to *develop* robust strategies, by looking in the first instance to existing approaches, and reviewing the pitfalls implicit in some of these.

9.5 TURNING POINTS

In terms of Article 9.1, which you have just read, the first part of the book looked at the first two sessions of that 'day'. We now look at the last two sessions of the day: the identification of the key issues, the turning points, which ultimately leads to the robust strategies needed to address these.

Key issues

The first requirement is to identify what are the *key issues* which the robust strategies should address. This is a process of focusing on the key factors which *must* be addressed, in the context of limited resources.

The main emphasis in this process is, therefore, on prioritisation. Which factors are *crucial* to the future of the organisation, matters of life and death, and which are less important? A lesser consideration will be the likelihood of the 'event' actually occurring; but even a relatively unlikely event must be considered if it could be central to the future development of the organisation.

These two dimensions should remind you of the 'importance/uncertainty' matrix we looked at in Chapter 7. The approach here is, however, quite different. You should roughly chart the various elements against the two dimensions; though, in this case, 'most probable' – rather than 'certain' – should be at the top of a normal (x,y) chart (which is used rather than a four-part matrix). Indeed, the chart will in effect cover only the right half of the original matrix, since the unimportant issues should already have been discarded.

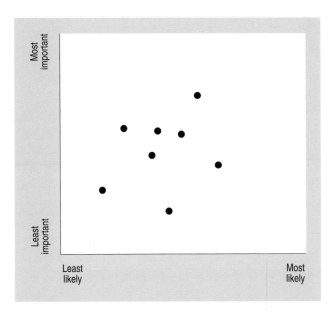

FIGURE 9.1   Importance/uncertainty matrix (modified)

This two-dimensional analysis encapsulates the most critical elements, but to this you can add a third dimension, that of the different impacts on competition, as described by Harold Carter.[2] This takes account of the fact that your competitors might benefit more, or less, from the changes which are likely to take place.

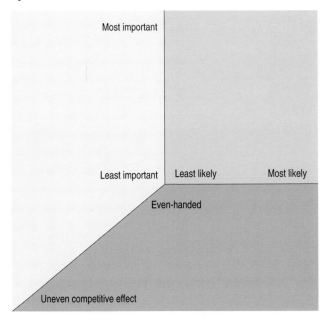

FIGURE 9.2   Matrix with impact on competition

[2] Wakeham Associates.

You should recognise that, as with most aspects of long-term planning, any such chart is largely a matter of personal judgement – and is intended only as an aid to prioritisation – though the processes we set out in this book are intended to ensure that this judgement is as well informed as is possible.

Once again, therefore, producing this plot is probably best undertaken as a group process. Accordingly, many of the group techniques we have explored may be used at this stage. Our practical experience suggests that most groups move, at this stage, from the use of Post-it™ Notes (whose flexibility is no longer needed) to more mundane flip-charts, to communicate and record their decisions.

Audit 9.2

From the scenarios you have now completed, select and plot the key turning points for your own organisation.

A possible chart for the OUBS might be as shown in Figure 9.3.

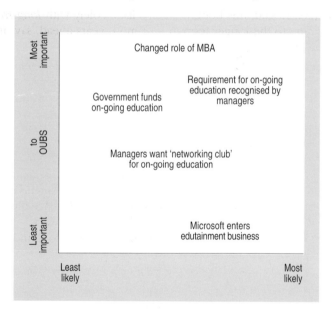

FIGURE 9.3   OUBS key turning points

Whatever the decision-making process chosen, the outcome will be a prioritised set of issues, of turning points, where responses to future changes in the external environment will – one way or another – decide the future fate of the organisation. Of these, the highest priority ones, the life and death decisions, *must* be addressed – and fatal outcomes guarded against – where the others, of decreasing importance, will *preferably* be addressed.

To set the scene for the process which relates to the production of the robust strategies that are needed to address these issues, however, let us first review the *corporate planning process in general.*

10 CORPORATE PLANNING REVISITED

Corporate strategy is a subject you will have come across in a number of previous contexts. The most obvious encounter will have been through those books and courses specifically aimed at this topic, but elements of planning will also have appeared in a variety of guises elsewhere: as, for instance, marketing planning or competitive planning. We will make the basic assumption that you are already comfortable with the processes of management planning.

10.1 STYLES OF LONG-TERM PLANNING

As we have already said, this book concerns itself solely with *long-range planning*: relating to the longer term, ten or more years ahead, say. It will restrict itself to the process of defining the *robust strategies* – which are necessary to protect the long-term survival of the organisation – as opposed to the traditional *optimal strategy* for the shorter term. Even so, let us look at some aspects of the top-level corporate planning process in general. We will start with an example of an approach which by now should be very familiar to you: the completion of a series of scenarios, in this case produced by the Royal Dutch/Shell Group. (You should note, though, that these scenarios cover a shorter, medium-term timescale, which is an interesting departure from their conventional use.) This is reported in one of two articles which appeared in successive issues of the *Harvard Business Review* in 1985, which laid the foundations for the modern, practical use of scenarios. We have already looked at this article – 'Scenarios – shooting the rapids', by Pierre Wack – in Chapter 6, in the context of introducing scenarios. You should return to it and skim through it again now, asking yourself 'How are these scenarios being used by the corporate planners and senior management at Shell in the context of setting their corporate strategy?'

The corporate planners at Shell, originally led by the author of the article, developed what is arguably the most sophisticated use of scenarios anywhere. Their whole planning process still revolves around them. Indeed, as the title they give to these medium-term scenarios – 'decision scenarios' – suggests, to all intents and purposes they are the strategy. Depending upon how future events actually turn out, the scenarios already contain details of the strategic response. By defining scenarios in this way, Shell's management are able to react very rapidly to changes in the environment, thus dealing with one of the major weaknesses – an inability to cope with change in general and with unexpected change in particular – which bedevils many other organisations.

This is, though, a sophisticated use of planning by a sophisticated company which has the luxury of immense resources at its disposal. In any case, even Shell uses a *variety* of planning methods, including more than a dozen *different* approaches to scenarios. More normal, in other organisations, is the use of scenarios as just one part of the overall strategic planning process, providing the 'front-end' or analytical input upon which the corporate strategy itself is then built.

This was the approach adopted by ICI. At this time – the early 1980s – it was in many respects similar to Shell. Like Shell, ICI was a sophisticated user of scenarios, but it concentrated on the other aspects of the corporate planning process.

One especially significant difference from the approach adopted by Shell was that the ICI planners quite deliberately choose *just one of the scenarios* as their 'model' of the future and the sole basis for developing their strategies. This, of course, meant that their scenarios had to be written as viable, self-sufficient alternatives, while the comparable Shell approach, for instance, only requires that the versions be complementary (so that between them they cover all the events which might be expected).

This concentration on a single view of the future (albeit in this case supported by consideration of several other scenarios) is typical of the great majority of approaches to corporate strategy. In this book we have spent a considerable amount of time looking at scenarios, because they offer the best framework for teaching the ideas and techniques covered and, in our opinion, also offer the optimal approach to planning for the long-term future. But you should understand that this approach is rarely used in practice. Organisations like Shell and ICI are in a very small minority which may almost be counted on the fingers of one hand. More generally, because scenarios demand the dedication of significant resources which many organisations cannot (or, more likely, will not) invest, they are replaced by less sophisticated techniques.

Even those other organisations which approach corporate planning on this simpler basis are probably, in turn, still a minority, since most organisations limit themselves to planning for the short term and, occasionally, the medium term. Some of these other corporate planners may still put considerable effort into trying to establish what their future may hold, but this is almost invariably undertaken in terms of a single perspective – a prediction of the one outcome to be expected at each stage.

To put these more traditional approaches into a wider context, now *quickly* read Article 10.1 by Bernard Taylor.[1] This is a classic exposition of strategic planning, from the time when this was at the peak of its popularity. In particular, Taylor describes the role of the large central planning departments which were then in vogue. As such, it both provides a context for and a contrast with the form(s) of planning described in this book.

---

[1] Reprinted by permission of Pergamon Press PLC from *Long Range Planning*, 17(3) 1984: 51–62.

Article 10.1 BERNARD TAYLOR: 'STRATEGIC PLANNING – WHICH STYLE DO YOU NEED?'

Over the past decade [to 1984] the practice of corporate planning has matured and developed in response to pressures from inside and outside the business. What started out as a unique system based on a simple model of problem-solving and decision-making, has evolved into a broad range of philosophies and techniques which are designed to help the executive to build an organisation which is adaptable and responsive in a rapidly changing environment.

Each style of planning has a philosophy, a 'school' of adherents, and a range of techniques which have been tested in practice. And each can provide management with a sensible approach to changing the orientation of a business.

A small- or medium-size firm may adopt only one of these styles – typically a system controlling the allocation of resources, or a framework for generating strategies for new ventures. However, in the large corporation such as General Electric USA, or Shell International, most or all of these approaches will be present. The philosophies and techniques are largely compatible and complementary. The main styles or modes of planning which have emerged in recent years are as follows:

1 Central Control System. The view of planning as a system for acquiring and allocating resources.
2 Framework for Innovation. The idea that planning should provide a framework for the generation of new products and new processes and the entry into new markets and new businesses.
3 Strategic Management. The notion that planning should be concerned not just with formulating strategies but with developing the commitment, the skills and the talents required to implement the strategies.
4 Political Planning. The perspective which sees planning as a process for resolving conflicts between interest groups and organisations inside and outside the business.
5 Futures Research. The concept of planning as exploring and creating the future. Futurists believe that the future cannot be forecast,

therefore decision-makers should consciously assess the uncertainties, then develop and work towards a vision of the future.

Corporate planning has a central role in the management of the modern corporation. It provides a practical approach to changing the way an enterprise is managed. For planning to succeed, however, it needs to be seen not just as a set of techniques, but as part of a coherent programme of change.

This chapter describes five basic approaches to corporate planning. Each represents an important school of thought in management thinking and practice. Each view has a large body of supporters, both academics and practitioners, and each offers a coherent philosophy and a range of practical systems and techniques for implementing them.

In determining their approach to planning, the chief executive and his planning staff need to examine the different methodologies which are available to discover which system best meets their needs. They should then adapt the approach to suit their own organisation. For corporate planning systems do not come ready-made. They have to be tailor-made to fit each enterprise. The decision is important because typically it takes two or three years to introduce a particular planning approach, and if it is to be effective it requires wholehearted commitment from both the board and from operating management.

In any large organisation of course it is likely that several different planning approaches will be present at any one time. And in one part of the business, planning is likely to move through various phases – with the management adopting different planning philosophies at different stages in the development of the firm. Corporate planning, like other managerial activities, is a process which grows and evolves – and sometimes has major setbacks and needs to be re-launched. It is my hope that this chapter will help the reader to assess the state of planning in his own organisation and to suggest areas where the activity may be strengthened or improved. It is rare to find an enterprise where all the available planning approaches are being employed equally effectively.

Table 1 sets out the five main views of planning in broad outline under four headings:

1   The focus – the main objective or purpose.
2   Important ideas – the characteristic view or philosophy of planning.
3   The elements – the key steps or stages in the process.
4   The techniques – some of the techniques which are widely used.

As with any classification system, the categories are not water-tight but they do represent quite distinct traditions in current thinking and practice.'[1]

PLANNING AS A CENTRAL CONTROL SYSTEM

From the beginning, one of the main drives behind the development of corporate planning has been the desire of top management to have a better control over the allocation of capital and other key resources.

The philosophy

The philosophy of planning and control is fundamental to management. Early thinkers on management, like Henri Fayol, described the management process in terms of: 'planning, command, co-ordination and control'. An analogy is often made with an army or another hierarchical organisation, where decisions are taken at the top, instructions are passed down through the enterprise and the leaders get back information which enables them to measure actual results against the plan.

The business enterprise is also frequently compared with a machine which can be regulated by an engineering control system. Automatic control systems such as the domestic thermostat contain certain basic elements: a sensor, a standard of performance, a collator, which compares actual performance with the standard, and an actor, which takes action to make up any deficiency in performance or to change the standard.

Writers and practitioners on planning have seen corporate planning as a comprehensive control system which could be used to regulate the operations of a whole firm – a logical extension of departmental control systems such as stock control, sales control, and production control. They were also attracted by the idea of the business as a total system with an integrated information and control system. It is perhaps natural that accountants should have seen corporate planning as an adjunct to the budgetary control system. There is, however, an important distinction to be drawn between strategic planning and management control – though they are obviously related. Strategic planning includes, for example, choosing company objectives, planning the organisational structure, setting policies for personnel, finance, marketing and research, choosing new product lines, acquiring a new division and deciding on non-routine capital expenditures. Management control is concerned with formulating budgets, determining staff levels, formulating personnel, marketing and research programmes, deciding on routine capital expenditures, measuring, appraising and improving management performance, etc.[2]

The processes

The rise of corporate planning in the 1960s coincided with a period of diversification and international expansion in large companies. In many cases these same firms were divided into product divisions which were designated as profit centres or cost centres. Divisional general managers were appointed and each was instructed to manage his division as if it were an independent business. Unfortunately, some of these executives took the instruction too literally and top management saw their subordinates riding off in all directions. Corporate planning was seized upon as a technique which might enable the main board to re-establish some control over the situation. Traditional budgeting systems proved woefully inadequate to the task of controlling a multidivisional business particularly when the divisional managers usually formed a majority in the main board and sat in judgement on their own capital projects.[3]

Table 1   Strategic planning: five basic approaches

	Central control system	Framework for innovation	Strategic management	Political planning	Futures research
The focus	Allocation and control of resources	Developing new business	Managing organizational change	Mobilizing power and influence	Exploring the future
Important ideas	A rational decision-making and control process	A vehicle for commercializing innovation	A community with common values and culture	Interest groups and organizations competing for resources	A management with a real awareness of future uncertainty
The elements	1 Specific objectives 2 A balanced portfolio of investments 3 Action programmes 4 Monitoring and control	1 Commitment to innovation 2 Funds for new development 3 Strategies for corporate development 4 Organizing project teams and action programmes	1 Organization development 2 Staff development 3 Organization structure 4 Management systems	1 Monitoring and forecasting social and political trends 2 Assessing the impact on the firm 3 Organizing and implementing action programmes	1 Developing alternative futures 2 Assessing social and economic impact 3 Defining key decisions
The techniques	1 SWOT analysis 2 Business portfolio analysis 3 Gap analysis 4 Extrapolative forecasting 5 Extended budgeting	Programmes for: 1 Divestment 2 Diversification 3 Acquisition 4 New product development 5 Market penetration and development	Group work on: 1 Stakeholder analysis 2 SWOT analysis 3 Portfolio analysis etc.	1 Public affairs 2 Civic affairs 3 Employee communication 4 Social issue analysis 5 Country risk analysis 6 Media relations	1 Scenarios 2 Delphi studies 3 Cross-impact analysis 4 Trend analysis 5 Computer simulation 6 Contingency planning

The solution commonly adopted was:

1   To re-structure the board so as to reduce the power of the divisional managers by bringing in heads of functional departments, non-executive directors, and others who could form a board representing the whole corporation rather than specific local interests.

2   Requiring the divisions to put forward Divisional Strategies. This enabled the top management and the central staff groups to debate various options for each product group before divisional plans became embedded in detailed project plans as 'the one true way to go'.

The corporate staff groups (finance, personnel, manufacturing, etc.) and the planners themselves, are involved in the corporate planning process through:

1   preparing the planning guidelines for divisions;
2   reviewing divisional strategies and plans;
3   advising the board or an executive committee in approving the plans; and
4   monitoring divisional performance against the plans.

The problems

The close association between planning and financial control has led to all kinds of problems. In particular there has been a tendency:

1   to confuse strategic planning with extended budgeting;
2   to produce three-year or five-year plans simply by extrapolating or pushing forward the present operations;
3   to prepare company plans by merely consolidating the operational plans of divisions and subsidiaries;
4   to stress the numbers rather than the quality of the thinking.

This still goes on. It is common to find corporate plans which consist of comprehensive and detailed operational plans and budgets – without any discussion of objectives, organisation structure or alternative strategies.

Another problem with the five-year plan and budget is that it can easily degenerate into a sterile but time-consuming routine. Corporate planning has provided many examples of this: highly structured planning systems which required many man-hours to build and maintain – and resulted in plans which were 'wrong to three points of decimals'.

Nevertheless, the resource allocation process is at the core of most planning systems, and the operational plan and budget is the basic planning document. Other 'qualitative' and 'informal' approaches to planning have been developed to compensate for its inflexibility and its narrow scope.

PLANNING AS A FRAMEWORK FOR INNOVATION

One powerful reason, then, for the growth of business planning was the need to establish a central steering mechanism for the direction and co-ordination of large, diverse, multinational operations. An equally strong and opposite motivation was the desire to promote initiative at the local level – in particular to prevent centralisation and bureaucracy from stifling creativity and innovation.

Over time the need for continuous change and innovation has become accepted by many leading businessmen and writers on business as an article of faith. To quote Peter Drucker, the businessman's philosopher:

> In a world buffeted by change, faced daily with new threats to its safety, the only way to conserve is by innovating. The only stability possible is stability in motion.[4]

The implications of this philosophy were spelled out for businessmen, politicians and public health officials by John Gardner, the former US Secretary of Health Education and Welfare in his best-selling book *Self-Renewal*. He wrote:

> A society whose maturing consists simply of acquiring more firmly established ways of doing things is headed for the graveyard – even if it learns to do these things with greater and greater skill. In the ever-renewing society what matures is a system or framework within which continuous innovation, renewal and rebirth can occur.[5]

For a competitive business this process of self-renewal is fundamental to survival. In the short term a management can make profits by mortgaging the future – and many managements are tempted to do this in the present crisis. But in a rapidly changing situation, unless there is continual re-investment in staff training, market development, new products, and up-to-date equipment, companies are likely to find themselves overtaken by their competitors. As the Boston Consulting Group consultants concluded in their enquiry into the failure of the British motorcycle industry:

> The result of the British industry's historic focus on short-term profitability has been low profits and now losses in the long term. The long-term result of the Japanese industry's historic focus on market share and volume, often at the expense of short-term profitability, has been the precise opposite: high and secure profitability.[6]

This process of entrepreneurship has long been acknowledged as a central function of the businessman. It involves:

- identifying a market opportunity,
- developing a product to match it,
- raising the necessary finance and matching the risk to the opportunity,
- mobilising the staff and the other resources necessary to provide the required service,
- producing and distributing the product at a profit.

To quote Donald Schon:

> The firm defines itself as a vehicle for carrying out a special kind of process. It defines itself through its engagement in entrepreneurship, the launching of new ventures, or in commercialising what comes out of development. The principal figure in the firm becomes the manager of the corporate entrepreneurial process; and the question is this: what are the potentials in development for new commercial ventures?[7]

In a one-man business the owner can be his own entrepreneur, but in a large corporation this process has to be formalised and systematised. To quote Peter Drucker again:

> Every one of the great business builders we know of – from the Medici to the founders of the Bank of England down to Thomas Watson in our days – had a definite idea, a clear 'theory of business' which informed his actions and decisions. Indeed a clear simple and penetrating 'theory of the business' rather than 'intuition' characterises the truly successful entrepreneur, the man who not only amasses a large fortune but builds an organisation that can endure and grow long after he is gone.

But the individual entrepreneur does not need to analyse his concepts and to explain his 'theory of business' to others, let alone spell out the details. He is in one person thinker, analyst and executor. Business enterprise, however, requires that entrepreneurship be systematised, spelled out as a discipline and organised as work.[8]

In many corporations strategic planning is regarded as a form of 'organised entrepreneurship'. Patrick Haggerty, the former Chairman of Texas Instruments, described their planning system as a 'framework for innovation'. He said:

> Self-renewal at Texas Instruments begins with deliberate, planned innovation in each of the basic areas of industrial life – creating, making and marketing. With our long range planning system we attempt to manage this innovation so as to provide a continuing stimulus to the company's growth.

The management of corporate development

Most management systems are concerned with operational problems. Operational plans start with the present situation and push it forward in terms of sales quotas, production targets, stock levels, budgets etc. The horizon is typically one year, occasionally two years – or perhaps three to five years for a specific product or facility. Other management systems – performance appraisal, salaries and incentives, promotions and career development – also help to focus managers' ideas on the short-term. A major problem for the large corporation is how to persuade staff to spend some of their time thinking and planning for new products, new markets, new production and administrative processes and maybe entirely new kinds of businesses – joint ventures, mergers and acquisitions, new social and political initiatives.

How, for a start, can top management produce a strategy and a programme for the development of the business? Typically, this involves the formation of *ad hoc* groups which report directly to the Board; project teams, venture groups, a diversification task force, a group to deal with acquisitions or international expansion, etc. In the present recession we have also seen task forces formed to look at closures, divestments, rationalisation and organisational re-structuring.

The challenge is to develop a 'vision of success' for the total enterprise and its parts and then to produce action plans, budgets and timetables to realise the vision.

The techniques which are in common use provide broad frameworks for discussion and analysis. For example:

Gap analysis describes the planning tasks by identifying the gap between the company's objectives and its likely achievement in terms of profits, sales, cash flow, etc. Management is invited to:

(a) set an objective – in quantitative terms – e.g. rate of return on investment or market share;

(b) forecast the 'momentum' line for the present business assuming no major changes;

(c) plan to fill the gap with projects for increased efficiency, expansion and diversification.

SWOT analysis provides a series of check-lists for auditing the company's strengths and weaknesses, and the opportunities and threats in the business environment. The business is assessed against leading competitors in world markets in terms of its technology, market position, financial base, production efficiency, management and organisation. The opportunities and threats are considered in the light of trends in the environment – economic, socio-political, technological and competitive. Then the two analyses are compared to see what are the market opportunities which match the firm's resources, what new resources are required, etc.

Business portfolio analysis – the process of funds allocation (i.e. allocation of both fixed and working capital) is frequently discussed on the basis of a matrix showing the pattern of businesses in the company's 'portfolio'. Many large companies have their own matrix or screen, typically displaying on one scale the prospects for

the industry and on the other the strength of the company's market position. The criteria for the industry's attractiveness might include: growth potential, expected changes in markets and in technology, the strength of competition from existing competitors and possible newcomers, and government and environmental constraints. The analysis of one's own company strengths requires a comparison with leading competitors in terms of market share, production capability, relative costs, technical expertise, patent position, marketing, distribution and service and government support.

PIMS (*Profit Impact of Market Strategy*) – the PIMS database which was set up originally by General Electric, USA, is derived from around a thousand 'businesses' in the USA and Western Europe over a period of up to ten years. The programme collects 300 items of information about each business and attempts to discover which factors have most effect on profitability (return on investment), e.g. market share, product quality, marketing expenditure, capital investment vs. sales, etc. The database is used primarily by holding companies in assessing the performance of divisions and subsidiaries and in making decisions about investment and divestment.

In practice, the majority of managers find the task of strategic planning difficult and they require a good deal of help. This is partly a matter of temperament. Operating managers tend to be chosen for their ability to get things done and it has been well said that 'A man of action, forced into a state of thought, is unhappy until he can get out of it.' It is largely the size and complexity of the task – to try to plan for the long-term development of the total enterprise in all its dimensions. It is also the problem of planning with little *solid information* in a *situation of great uncertainty* where all the elements interact. Inevitably, the manager has to rely on his judgement and imagination much more than he does in operational management.

Faced with these practical difficulties in generating new strategies, leading companies such as General Electric in the USA and Philips in Europe have started to think not just in terms of strategic planning but in terms of strategic management, i.e. changing the whole management system.

226

STRATEGIC MANAGEMENT

This increasingly popular approach takes the view that policy-making is a learning process and strategic planning is the specific activity through which the members of an organisation learn to adapt to radical changes in the external environment.

The philosophy

Consider the changes which are taking place and their impact on human institutions – fluctuations in supply and demand, the advent of new technologies, the appearance of social and political movements, the rise and fall of governments. All these trends are rendering established institutions and traditional ways of thinking and acting obsolete. In a rapidly changing world, organisations must adapt or go under. To quote Donald Schon:

> Our society and all of its institutions are in continuing processes of transformation... we must learn to understand, guide, influence and manage these transformations.
>
> We must invent and develop institutions which are 'learning systems', systems capable of bringing about their own transformations.[9]

This is the theory of natural selection again: the view that organisations must adapt or be replaced by others which are better suited to their environment.

How then can we build institutions which learn to adapt to their environment? Is it possible to develop management's ability to cope with change? Can we help organisations or teams of people to set objectives, to be more aware of the changes taking place around them, and to develop their own plans for the future? Can management learn to do this on a continuing basis?

Those who support the view of planning as part of a process of social change usually reject the theory that planning is a logical search for solutions, a cognitive decision-making process which establishes the area of search and certain performance criteria, collects and analyses data, assesses alternatives and makes an optimal choice.

We are after all dealing not with inert objects but with people who have their own ideas, beliefs and motivations.[10]

In place of this model of planning as rational and sequential, behavioural scientists frequently present it as a trial-and-error process. Managers and administrators are encouraged to adopt an experimental approach. Not looking for comprehensive solutions or great leaps forward but attempting to engineer incremental changes with the top managers and their advisers not moving too far ahead of the group.[11]

The approach

This 'behavioural' view of planning is more human, less comprehensive, more easily related to the organisations which we all know and work in:

1 Planning is seen as a process through which individuals and teams can learn to cope with an unpredictable and rapidly changing environment.

The fact that a forecast or a plan turns out to be wrong is therefore not an indication that the management is incompetent or that planning is not feasible, but rather as confirmation that we are living in an uncertain world and we need to reassess our situation continually. However, we should learn by experience and our involvement in forecasting, strategy-making, planning, programming and budgeting should help us get a better 'feel' for the trends in the environment and should improve the organisation's capacity to respond to them.

2 Planning is seen as one element in a wider programme of organisational change. This may involve many other measures.

    (a) Moves affecting individual managers: retiring or retraining existing managers, recruiting new managers, promoting and developing staff for new roles.

    (b) Changes in organisation structure: these might include, for example:

        i   dividing the company into semi-autonomous units such as product divisions;

        ii   establishing new groupings to co-ordinate policy by geographical regions, by product groups or by strategic business units (i.e. parts of the organisation which have a common business strategy); or

iii   reorganising the board and revising the capital investment procedures to strengthen the role of the board as a policymaking body.

(c)   Changes in management systems:

i   changing the procedures for staff appraisal, promotion and payment, to encourage management to give a higher priority to new company-wide programmes, e.g. social responsibility, new business development or staff development;

ii   the introduction of improved information systems for finance, manpower and production;

iii   the development of planning and control systems to focus management attention on cash flow, productivity, planning for manpower, etc.;

iv   the provision of new procedures for environmental assessment to give managers a better understanding of the external trends which are likely to affect their business.

3   In adopting the organisational learning mode of planning, the planner takes on the role of a 'change agent'. His task is not merely to produce a product, 'the plan', but rather to intervene in 'the process', i.e. to work with management at various levels to help them to define their problems and to produce new programmes directed at changing the orientation of the organisation to fit new circumstances.

Sometimes, the firm is engaged in a slow evolution. Occasionally there is a major crisis. Often the problem is to help a management team to adjust to some kind of radical change or discontinuity:

(a)   the integration and rationalisation of several companies into a larger, divisionalised operation, following a programme of diversification or a series of mergers;

(b)   the closure or sale of a number of businesses, and the slimming down of central staff functions following a reduction in demand or expropriation by government;

(c)   developing the capacity to design, sell and manage total systems or turn-key projects as opposed to selling individual products to developing countries or the communist world; the introduction of a sea-change in technology such as containerisation in shipping or the use of micro-processors and fibre optics in telecommunications.

One of the problems with the 'organisational learning' approach is that these radical changes occur infrequently in the life of an individual firm. It is therefore difficult for a manager to gain experience of closures and divestments, or mergers and acquisitions, within one company, except in a large multidivisional business. In cases of radical change, therefore, it is often necessary for top management to bring in consultants or to recruit managers from outside the company who have acquired the relevant experience in other businesses.

4   However, the strategic planner who adopts a social learning approach does not act merely as a change agent intervening as and when required to carry out an attitude study, diagnose an organisational problem, to improve working relationships between individuals and departments. He is concerned to develop the competence of management teams in various parts of the organisation to take a 'strategic' view of their businesses, to identify the key issues for decisions and to take the action which they regard as necessary for the survival and growth of the enterprise. This usually involves:

i   taking a comprehensive and realistic view of the organisation from various perspectives – the world market, competitors, long-term trends in technology and in society;

ii   assessing in comparative terms the business's overall performance – its levels of costs, productivity, product quality, price, customer service;

iii considering feasible alternative futures for the organisation – making established activities more efficient and more productive, developing new technologies and building new businesses.

PLANNING AS A POLITICAL PROCESS

A fourth approach to planning consists of a kind of realpolitik – a view which says that planning is essentially concerned not with logic, innovation or learning but with *power*. Planning after all is a process which allocates resources. Planning decisions affect people's lives. Planning determines where investments are made and where businesses stop investing; where jobs are created and where employees are made redundant; which new projects go forward and which existing projects are terminated. Dividends, wages and salaries, promotion and advancement, recognition and status – this is what planning is about.

The philosophy

The supporters of this idea share the view that life is a struggle for survival, a continual battle between competing groups.

In the political analyst's eyes, society is made up of organisations and interest groups which are continually competing for support from the public, from politicians and from other decision-makers in public and private organisations. Various groups in society are engaged in a struggle for power. Sometimes the opposing lines are drawn up according to social level in a type of class conflict. On other occasions, or on other issues, they may be arranged by nationality, by religious creed, by race or by sex.

Each political party or pressure group also consists of warring factions all clamouring for the attention of those in power. The business, too, is seen not as a homogeneous unit, a hierarchy led by the board, or a single culture with a common purpose. Instead the firm is conceived as a model or miniature of society itself in which department vies with department, region with region and product division with product division to gain a greater share of the firm's resources and the power which goes with them.

A major danger with this political game is that it can take everyone's eyes off the business of creating wealth. In their own interests and in the interests of society, managers and employees should be mainly concerned with building businesses: introducing new products, increasing productivity and expanding markets at home and abroad. If the political battle inside and outside the firm becomes too intense, then the energies of business leaders and trade union officials can become absorbed in continual in-fighting and negotiation. Too much effort is spent in dividing the cake and too little time is left for the battle to keep ahead of international competition.

The changing political environment

Nevertheless, the businessman has much to learn from politicians, trade unionists and the leaders of political pressure groups when it comes to influencing public opinion and using the media.

Management's authority is continually being challenged by trade unions and groups of workers, by government agencies and by pressure groups acting on behalf of consumers, conservationists, women's liberation and various ethnic minorities. Inside and outside the business the objectives, strategies and plans of management are being questioned. Groups of employees, local politicians and social action groups are rejecting or vetoing the plans of management, demanding the right to be informed or consulted – or to participate in the planning process.

These interest groups are in practice asking: 'Whose objectives?', 'Whose plans?' They oppose the idea of unilateral planning by management and claim the right to employee participation or public participation. Trade unions, committees of shop stewards and action committees working on behalf of local communities are also putting forward their own alternative plans and requesting government assistance in putting their case.

The process of planning in the political arena needs to be studied by management. A number of elements are clear.

1 *Group action.* Planning in the public arena takes place largely between organisations and the groups which are most successful are those which are well organised. In many cases businesses must forget their traditional

229

animosities in working for their common good – to influence government, or to make a case when challenged by social action groups.

2 *Influence and coercion.* In the public arena it is rarely possible for one party to control the activities of another. Each group has to operate by influence and persuasion; and occasionally by threatening sanctions.

3 *Communications.* It becomes essential, therefore, for management to put their case in plain terms to company staff at all levels, to local communities, to particular interest groups, to national governments and to the general public.

4 *Building networks.* Another central activity of the top management team is to deal with the external relations or foreign policy of the firm. This means carrying on a diplomatic campaign. Maintaining liaison within professional and industrial associations, making contacts with political and social interest groups and forming alliances within the industries and in the regions where the business operates.

5 *Liaison with the media.* Continuing contact with the press, radio and television is vital. Demonstrations, protests, marches, petitions – these are the stock-in-trade of the political activist. Industry has to be prepared to put its case like other interest groups through policy statements, manifestos, national conferences, surveys and reports.

6 *Contacts with governments.* Links with government bodies need to be established on a continuing basis, directly in the case of a large firm, indirectly via a trade association for a smaller business. In either case it is essential to know how decisions will be made, who are the decision-makers, and who will influence the decisions. Also it is necessary to identify key social and political issues which are important to the company, to put forward proposals which are constructive and politically feasible – if possible speaking not just for one firm but on behalf of a sector or sub-sector of industry, or a region.

7 *Contact with trade unions.* Employee organisations need to be studied in the same way as government agencies, to determine the political strength of various groups, the

framework of regulations and practices, the arrangements for electing officials, the ambitions and policies of various individuals, etc.

Also it is necessary to establish communications with trade union officials outside the process of wage bargaining, if possible in normal times so that an effective relationship can become established without the pressure of a crisis.

FUTURES RESEARCH

The futures movement grew up in the late 1960s but planning in terms of 'alternative futures' only became fashionable in large companies in the late 1970s. Managers in business and administrators in government are now using scenarios and other futures research techniques to try to cope with what they perceive as discontinuities. The year of the oil crisis, 1974, is seen as a watershed marking the end of an era of relative stability and affluence and the beginning of a period of turbulence and economic stagnation. In this new environment a number of trends – political, social, economic and technological – seem to be gathering momentum and interacting to create a business environment which is highly volatile.

Scenario planning

As management witnessed successive plans being rendered obsolete by unforeseen changes, they began to doubt the value of traditional forecasting and planning techniques based on extrapolation and budgeting and looked for other approaches better suited to a complex and turbulent environment. They were also convinced of the need to expand their planning and forecasting procedures to cover not only economic and market trends but also social and political changes which might be reflected in legislation and in the activities of trade unions and social pressure groups.

The result was a spate of experiments in the use of modern forecasting techniques: Delphi Studies, Cross Impact Analyses, Trend Impact Analyses, etc. Also there was an increase in the use of simple financial models aimed at examining the sensitivity of company plans to changes in assumptions, about prices, levels of sales, costs of raw materials, wages and salaries, interest rates, etc. And companies began to make tentative contingency plans – confidentially and informally to provide for major risks such as a strike, action by a social pressure group, a change of government, a new piece of legislation, the shortage or non-availability of a key raw material or component, or a substantial delay in the construction of a new facility.

However, the most impressive of these changes in planning techniques has been the increasing use of scenarios. In the late 1960s, Herman Kahn and Anthony Wiener defined scenarios as: 'hypothetical sequences of events constructed for the purpose of focusing attention on causal processes and decision points'.[13] As used in business, scenarios usually take the form of 'qualitative descriptions of the situation of a company, an industry, a nation or a region at some specified time in the future'.[14]

Coping with an uncertain environment

Scenario planning has been criticised on the grounds that it is 'a practice without a discipline'; that scenarios lack the exactness of traditional economic forecasting techniques, and there is no proof of their effectiveness. On the other hand, it is the very precision and the bogus authority of conventional approaches to forecasting which has led operating managers and those involved in forecasting to search for other methods which reflect the real uncertainty in the environment. The supporters of scenarios assert that 'it is better to be approximately right than precisely wrong'. To quote Alvin Toffler:

> Linear extrapolation, otherwise known as straight-line thinking is extremely useful and it can tell us many important things. But it works best between revolutionary periods, not in them.[15]

Scenarios are not intended to predict the future. They are designed to help executives deal with a highly uncertain environment: to assist the executive who is used to extrapolative forecasting and budgeting in coping with the unexpected.

Scenarios are not supposed to provide an accurate picture of the future: they are designed to challenge the imagination; to encourage managers to plan, not just for the most likely future but also for other alternative futures which are less likely.

Scenario planning should help managers to be more flexible in various ways.

1   Environmental scanning. It should stimulate managers to scan the business environment for 'weak signals', especially social and political changes, which might foreshadow a crisis.
2   Robust plans. It should encourage executives to produce plans which are 'robust', i.e. which may not be optimal but would keep the business profitable under a wide range of conditions.
3   Contingency planning. It should prompt managers to be prepared for contingencies, e.g. strikes, revolutions or a slump in demand.
4   Awareness of risk. It should make decision-makers more realistic about the risk to their business, social, political, technological and competitive, and persuade them to minimise the risk to the business from overdependence on any one source – a customer group, a technology, a range of products, a national or regional market.
5   Concern with flexibility. Scenario planning also invites businessmen to consider the advantages of building flexibility into their operations, i.e.:

- designing facilities which can be used in different ways;
- training staff for a broad range of tasks;
- consciously carrying 'slack resources' (skilled staff, extra stocks, back-up generators, etc.) in case of a crisis or a new opportunity;
- diversifying one's operations so as to have businesses, suppliers, production facilities, stockholding or computers in more than one country or region.

A possible danger of scenario planning is that managers may become too preoccupied with uncertainty and risk – which is inseparable from business. As a result, they may play safe whilst their less sophisticated competitors are taking new initiatives, accepting or ignoring the risks and capitalising on opportunities for profit and growth.

Planning without information

Futures research is a way of helping managers to think creatively about the future. This is especially important in a business where a technology, a market or the socio-political situation is changing quickly. In such an environment, the management have little useful information. They are planning in a vacuum. Often there is no historical data, the technology could develop in several directions; the market may not exist – the regulatory framework may not yet have been developed. Today, a surprisingly large number of businesses face this type of situation in relation to new technologies; biotechnology, cable television, telecommunications, the next generation of computers, etc. and also in international markets such as Brazil, Mexico, Nigeria, Hong Kong and the Middle East. In these cases the only sensible way of 'planning' seems to be in terms of alternative futures.

THE CONSTRUCTION OF SCENARIOS

The writing of scenarios typically involves using a number of futures research techniques. For example, the approach recommended by the General Electric Company shown in Table 2, includes the use of a Delphi Study, Trend Analysis, Trend Extrapolation, Trend Impact Analysis and Cross Impact Analysis.

A number of the techniques most commonly used in the development of scenarios are listed below.

1   Trend analysis. This involves scanning and analysing publications and other sources of information on a regular basis to plot long-term trends.
2   Computer simulations. This entails building a computer model of an enterprise or an industry and making projections on different assumptions.

3   Decision analysis. Using this technique, the analyst creates a 'road map' of decisions relating to a particular issue or project. At each step he plots the alternatives available to the 'decision-maker', the estimated payoff or loss for each course of action and the probability of success or failure.
The technique is useful to determine the broad dimensions of a decision and as a means of keeping various options open. In analysing real decisions, however, the range of alternatives available is often far too wide for a planner to carry out a comprehensive quantitative analysis.

4   Sensitivity analysis. One of the commonest ways to explore alternative futures is by analysing the sensitivity of a plan to variations in the assumptions. For this purpose it is helpful to have access to a simple computer model. Thus the planner can produce an operating statement, a cash flow analysis or a balance sheet based on different assumptions about investments, sales, costs, prices, interest rates, etc. Many companies require their subsidiaries or divisions to explore the effects of a 10% or 15% increase or decrease in the major assumptions underpinning any major new project.

5   Delphi study. This is a systematic way of carrying out a poll among experts. The experts are asked a series of questions, usually concerning the likelihood of certain events taking place. Then the results are fed back to the panel and they are asked a further set of questions.
Experience to date suggests that the technique is valuable in eliciting the opinion of specialists on a narrow subject such as the probability of a breakthrough in a particular technology which they know well. It seems to be less useful in exploring social and political issues which are much less structured and where there are fewer experts. However, General Electric (USA) have used this technique to explore likely trends in population, employment, education, etc.

6   Impact analysis. This implies setting up a matrix of events which are forced to 'plan' in terms likely to affect other events (Cross Impact Analysis) or exploring the various

impacts that a particular trend may have (Trend Impact Analysis). These techniques involve weighing the likely effects and then assessing which are the most important and the most urgent.

Table 2   Constructing scenarios for an industrial sector (General Electric USA)
1 Prepare background Assess environmental factors – social, regulatory, technological, economic and competitive Develop crude 'systems' model of the industry
2 Select critical indicators Key indicators (trends) Future events affecting key indicators (literature search) Delphi panel to evaluate industry's future
3 Establish past behaviour for each indicator Historical performance Reasons for past behaviour of each trend Delphi questionnaire
4 Verify potential future events Delphi panel Past trends, future events, impact/probability, future trends Assumptions for forecasts, rationale for future trends
5 Forecast each indicator Range of future values for each indicator Results from literature search and Delphi study Trend Impact Analysis and Cross Impact Analysis
6 Write scenarios Guidelines for strategic business units Annual revision

Based on: Rochelle O'Connor, *Planning Under Uncertainty*, Conference Board, New York, p. 8 (1978)

SUMMARY

In the modern business corporation today strategic planning is a widespread and highly diverse activity.

1   Conventional budgeting is being supplemented by a 'funds allocation' procedure based on a systematic evaluation of each business, its general environment, its competitive situation, and its strategy for the future. Also, instead of operating as a simple financial holding company, the top management of multi-industry, multinational businesses are setting out to manage their investments as a 'portfolio of businesses'.

2   It is being recognised that the process of corporate development – improving the competitive performance of existing businesses, generating new products, penetrating new markets, expanding internationally and creating or acquiring new businesses – is a prime task of top management and needs to be fostered and managed with separate budgets, plans, project teams, task forces, etc.

3   Executives who have tried to implement these kinds of changes have found that it is often not enough to set demanding targets, and ask for new strategies. It is a major problem to recruit and train managers who have the capacity to 'think strategically'. Usually a team of managers needs to work together over a period of time. They have to develop a new information system which relates to strategic issues rather than operational problems. Often the organisation structure has to be changed to pull out the separate businesses, or to co-ordinate strategies internationally in world-wide product divisions. The way managers are appraised and rewarded also needs to be adjusted to demonstrate that the development of new strategies and new businesses is just as important as the achievement of this year's targets.

4   The managements of most large business corporations now find themselves in a continual dialogue with governments, international agencies, trade unions, social pressure groups and the media. To handle this socio-political area they now have public affairs' departments and external consultants who monitor social trends, forecast emerging socio-political issues and formulate action programmes to safeguard the interests of the business and to help to contribute to the solution of social problems, such as unemployment and the decline of city centres.

5   In businesses which have to cope with a great deal of uncertainty, e.g. in new and growing technologies, in countries which are politically unstable, or in fluctuating international markets, managers have been forced to 'plan' in terms of alternative futures using simulations, scenarios and contingency plans rather than traditional forecasting based on extrapolation.

Dealing with crises

The strategic planning processes all take time to put into operation. But what about the firm which is in crisis? Often the company which is in a turnaround situation is there because its top management have not been able to think strategically, to anticipate international competition or the appearance of a new technology, and to develop new products or enter new markets in good time.

Their most urgent need is usually to improve the cash flow and buy time by closing loss-making businesses, cutting overheads, reducing staff, selling off assets, etc. But the next step should be to produce a strategy for the future, and to buy or build new businesses. It is interesting to note that in these crisis situations, top managers in such firms as Fisons, the Burton Group, Scandinavian Airlines and Electrolux have discovered that strategic thinking or strategic management is extremely effective without the usual apparatus of five-year planning, portfolio analysis, scenarios, etc.

NOTES

1   For a list of the publications in each of these schools of thought see: B. Taylor, 'New dimensions in corporate planning', *Long Range Planning*, December (1976).

2   Robert N. Anthony, *Planning and Control Systems – A Framework for Analysis*, p. 67, Harvard University, Boston (1965).

3   Joseph Bower, *Managing the Resource Allocation Process*, p. 54, Harvard (1970).

4   Peter F. Drucker, *Landmarks of Tomorrow* (1959).

5   John W. Gardner, *Self-Renewal – The Individual and the Innovative Society*, p. 5, Harper & Row, New York (1963).

6   Boston Consulting Group, *Strategic Alternatives for the British Motorcycle Industry* (2 vols.), Department of Industry, HMSO, London (1975).

7   Donald A. Schon, *Beyond the Stable State*, p. 67, Temple Smith, London (1971).

8   Peter F. Drucker, 'Entrepreneurship in business enterprise', *Journal of Business Policy*, I (1), Autumn (1970).

9   Donald A. Schon, *Beyond the Stable State*, p. 30, Temple Smith, London (1971).

10 Donald N. Michael, *On Learning to Plan and Planning to Learn*, p. 19, Jossey-Bass (1973).

11 J. Friedman, 'The future of comprehensive urban planning: a critique', *Public Administration Review*, 31 (3): 325 (1971).

12 See Rochelle O'Connor, *Planning Under Uncertainty: Multiple Scenarios and Contingency Planning*, Conference Board, New York (1978).

13 Herman Kahn and Anthony Wiener, *The Year 2000*, p. 6, Macmillan, New York (1967).

14 Recent scenarios developed in the UK cover, for example: the British economy, unemployment, supply and demand for energy, banking, the chemical industry, television, the world pharmaceutical industry and the future for Japan.

15 *Choosing Our Environment: Can We Anticipate the Future?*, Senate Committee Report, Washington (1976).

10.2 PITFALLS OF CORPORATE PLANNING

Even in the context of a traditional short-term strategy, many planning techniques pose problems for the unsophisticated user. In the context of long-range planning, they can be positively dangerous. We shall now see what you should avoid if you choose to use some of these much favoured techniques (including those mentioned in Bernard Taylor's article).

Returning to ICI, their emphasis on balancing the 'portfolio' was understandable, at the time, since ICI then owned a diverse range of separate businesses; but it also reflected one of the key preoccupations of corporate planners. You should have encountered the 'Boston Matrix', which deals with this topic.[2] Reinforced by the messages of Theodore Levitt's 'Marketing Myopia' and Igor Ansoff's matrix, this well-publicised technique has probably had the greatest influence on corporate strategy in recent times – to the extent that it may even have distorted the overall pattern of mergers and acquisitions in the 1980s!

Boston matrix

There are important caveats in the use of this and similar techniques, especially in terms of looking at long-term futures

Understanding the theory – the Boston Matrix is primarily designed to illustrate potential cashflow problems in the context of the portfolios of business held by large organisations. Its axes (market growth and relative share) offer a very indirect measure of what is happening – and this needs to be understood. Unfortunately, as used by most practitioners, the message is grossly simplified (usually to Problem Children, Stars, Cash Cows and Dogs) and generalised to an extent that the technique will not support.[3]

A simpler technique, such as the Boston Advantage Matrix (which uses the more obvious 'competitive' dimensions of economies of scale against differentiation), may be easier to grasp – and this is indeed apparently now more favoured by the Boston Consulting Group itself. *The first prerequisite of using any tool is that you fully understand exactly what you are doing*, but this is too often seen as an academic luxury!

Understanding the meaning of 'balance' – with a four quadrant matrix, 'balance' is often seen to mean that there should be equal strengths in each quadrant – sometimes leading to the quite serious proposal that a few 'cash cows' should be abandoned because the organisation does not have enough 'dogs' to balance the matrix! It should be remembered that the best portfolios will always appear visually unbalanced – because they will have most of their 'products' (or, in the corporate strategy context, Strategic Business Units – SBUs) in the 'cash cow' part of the matrix. This is particularly true where

---

[2] A. Morrison and R. Wensley, 'Boxing up or boxed in: a short history of the Boston Consulting Group Share/Growth Matrix, *Journal of Marketing Management*, Vol. 7, 1991.
[3] Scott Armstrong and Roderick J Brodie, 'Effects of portfolio planning methods on decision-making: experimental results', *Journal of Research in Marketing*, Vol. 11, 1994.

market leaders are very difficult to displace and (despite the suggestions of the product life-cycle) stay in the 'cash cow' position for very long periods, often decades. In this context the value lies in demonstrating what backup (in terms of up and coming new products or businesses) there is to insure against future problems.

Comparison – one of the great benefits of these techniques is their ability to plot the comparable positions of competitors, so that their strengths may also be judged.

Time – one of the ways these matrix approaches are simplified is that they are taught in terms of a static picture at one point in time. Yet their main benefit (particularly in terms of analyses of future developments, on which this book focuses) may well be to plot what changes are expected, with both present and future positions plotted. This can give a very useful feel for what these developments may mean in practical terms.

SWOT (strengths, weaknesses, opportunities, threats)

This is another technique which you will have encountered elsewhere. It cannot be ignored, because it is just about the most popular corporate planning technique used by managers.[4]

But, once more, it is often abused due to lack of understanding. It is used in corporate strategy to categorise the factors at work under the four SWOT headings. But the key aspect, which is not always appreciated, is that this categorisation deliberately splits these factors into those generally applying externally (Opportunities and Threats) in the wider environment, and those generally applying internally (Strengths and Weaknesses) in relation to the organisation's own resources.[5]

As such, the technique has its advantages in bringing together the two sides of the strategy we are looking at: external (OT) and internal (SW). It is just a pity that OTSW is not as catchy an acronym as SWOT, since listing the external positions before the internal constraints would provide a more logical framework.

In the context of long-range planning, Kees van der Heijden suggests that a SWOT framework can even be used – in a half-day exercise involving the management team as a whole – to provide the strategic planner (who is here a specialist – typically from a consultancy such as GBN, of which Kees is a partner) with a useful insight into the 'strategic agenda'.[6] In this case the SWOT is highly structured.

[4] D. Mercer, 'Management's commitment to marketing theory compared with actual practice' (Marketing Education Group, 1996).

[5] R. F. Lusch and V. N. Lusch, *Principles of Marketing* (Kent Publishing, 1987).

[6] K. van der Heijden, *Scenarios: The Art of Strategic Conversation* (Wiley, 1996).

Ansoff Matrix

The basis for this widely recommended concept is the idea that, in general, there are four basic product strategies for growth in volume and profit (which is what shareholders conventionally demand). These alternatives were originally, and best, described by Igor Ansoff; and were subsequently developed as the well-known 'Ansoff Matrix', shown in Figure 10.1.[7]

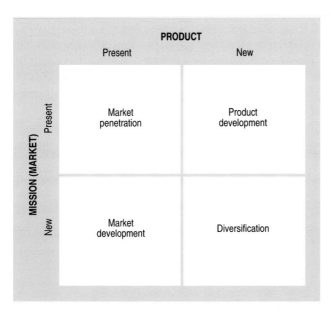

FIGURE 10.1   Ansoff Matrix

Market penetration

Understandably, the most frequently used strategy is to take the existing product (or service) in the existing market and try to obtain improved 'penetration' (or more accurately an increased share) of that market. There are two ways this can be achieved: increasing sales to existing customers, or finding new customers in the same market.

Product (or service) development

This approach, which most closely matches what is thought of as new product development, involves a relatively major modification of the product or service in terms of factors such as quality, style, performance, variety and so on. It will, though, continue to be sold through the same distribution channels to the same markets.

---

[7] I. Ansoff, 'Strategies for diversification', *Harvard Business Review*, September–October 1957.

Market (extension) development

This involves finding new uses for the existing product or service, thereby taking it into entirely new markets.

Diversification

This involves a quantum leap, to a new product and a new market. It consequently involves more risk.

In his original work, which did not use the matrix form, Igor Ansoff stressed: 'The diversification strategy stands apart from the other three. While the latter are usually followed with the same technical, financial, and merchandising resources which are used for the original product line, diversification usually requires new skills, new techniques, and new facilities. As a result it almost invariably leads to physical and organisational changes in the structure of the business which represent a distinct break with past business experience.'

For this reason, amongst others, most marketing activity revolves around penetration; and the Ansoff Matrix, despite its fame, is usually of very limited value[8] – though it does always offer a useful reminder of the options which are open. Its most important lesson, though, is often missed. It is quite simply that risk increases dramatically the further you move away from your home base in the top left-hand corner of the matrix. Market penetration really is a very much safer activity than diversification!

Acquisition strategies

Acquisition strategies (or those for *joint ventures*) are rarely discussed in the context of new product development. Yet there is normally a lower risk attached to buying a going concern (or developing another form of binding commercial relationship with it) than developing your own offering – though the risk may still be very high.

Whatever route you choose you should be aware of, and be prepared to meet, the levels of investment and long timescales involved. Both of these are significantly higher than most product developers are willing to admit to, even to themselves. Thus a survey by Ralph Biggadike of new corporate ventures by 200 members of the Fortune 500 showed that, on average, they suffered *severe* losses through their first four years of operation, and noted that, again on average, they needed eight years before they reached profitability (and it was 12 years before they generated cash flow ratios comparable with the existing businesses)![9]

More importantly, if despite all the odds against it you are determined to go ahead, another important recommendation emerges from Biggadike's research: the way to improve the odds and to build the portfolio is to commit substantial

---

[8] P. Spillard, 'Ansoff revisited: logic, commitment and strategies for change', *The Marketing Digest*, ed. M J. Thomas & N. E. Waite (Heinemann, 1988).

[9] R. Biggadike, 'The risky business of diversification', *Harvard Business Review*, May'June 1979.

resources to each venture and to defer immediate financial performance in favour of market position. This will come as no surprise to those of you who understand the investment nature of most marketing operations. Genuinely new product development is a very expensive process indeed – and takes a very long time to pay off – though the results then may be spectacular.

One further piece of advice emerges from our own research. Always assuming that the owners of the market leaders which you must inevitably challenge are not totally incompetent (though there have been some surprising losses of leadership which must be attributed to gross incompetence on the part of the losing managers), totally new development *must* represent a quantum leap in 'product characteristics' if it is to succeed. Our results for FMCG (Fast Moving Consumer Goods) brands show that almost all genuinely new brand leaders have depended on such dramatic changes – most obviously physical (technological) changes, but just as easily dramatic changes in taste or image.[10]

This chapter has perhaps been somewhat negative. It has focused on what you should not do; the dangers inherent – in the context of long-range marketing – of uncritically using some of the more popular theories. From now on, though, we will be much more positive. The next chapter, for instance, gets down to the core activity – that of developing a practical long-range marketing plan.

[10] D. S. Mercer, 'A two decade test of product life cycle theory', *British Journal of Management*, 1993.

11 THE LONG-RANGE MARKETING PLAN

11.1 SHORT-TERM AND LONG-TERM PLANS

We now move on to examine how you can develop, and ultimately implement, robust strategies.

The climax of many approaches to *traditional* (short-term) marketing is supposed to be the production of the *marketing plan*, which will determine activities for the next year – or at least that is what a number of textbooks (including my own) seem to imply. The reality is rather different. In practice few managers base their day-to-day decisions on the contents of a marketing plan, even though many of them may previously have gone through the motions of producing a plan which was (in theory) intended for just that purpose.

The reasons for this are eminently practical – their actions are, quite understandably, dictated by the reality revealed by subsequent events rather than the historical theory contained in the plan. But there is also a psychological aspect. As Bernard Taylor says: 'Planning is an unnatural process. It is much more fun to do something.' John Preston of Boston College (quoted by Bernard Taylor, but often misquoted by other authors!) went further: 'The nicest thing about not planning is that failure comes as a complete surprise, and is not preceded by a period of worry and depression.'[1]

In the case of long-range marketing, which takes account of robust strategies, the plan really *must* be the basis for long-range decisions; because – without special training and the time to consider the full implications of their actions – most line managers in an organisation quite simply do not have the expertise to understand what are the long-term implications of the decisions which – sometimes by default – they make.

In any case, we should not dismiss even the production of even a conventional (short-term) marketing plan as a total irrelevance. It may not be as central to marketing actions as theorists would like, but its production still results in some important benefits.

1 **Review** – even in the case of the short-term plan, the process forces a full review of *all* the marketing factors, not just those which are currently the focus of attention, albeit that this only happens once a year. This annual review becomes even more important, when, as may will be the case, a similar long-range exercise takes place only once every three years.

---

[1] B. Taylor, 'Corporate planning for the 1990s: the new frontiers', *Long Range Planning*, vol. 19, no. 6, 1986.

2 **Agreement** – it stimulates involvement of a wide range of personnel in the strategic decision-making, and acts as a framework for generating formal agreement amongst them.

3 **Communication** – as we will see, the output, the (long-range) plan itself, can be an especially useful vehicle for communicating the organisation's long-range marketing intentions more widely amongst its staff.

The *traditional* framework of marketing planning is best explained by Malcolm McDonald in his book.[2] The main steps in the process he describes are:

1 Corporate Objectives
2 Marketing Audit
3 SWOT Analysis
4 Assumptions
5 Marketing Objectives and Strategies
6 Estimate Expected Results
7 Identify Alternative Plans and Mixes
8 Programmes
9 Measurement and Review.

The essence of the process is that it moves from the general to the specific; from the overall objectives of the organisation down to the individual action plan for a part of one marketing programme. It is also an iterative process, so that the draft output of each stage is checked to see what impact it has on the earlier stages – which are amended accordingly.

More important, he deliberately separates this three-year strategic marketing plan (sometimes just called the 'strategy') from the one-year operating plan (often what is called the 'marketing plan' itself), which is derived from the strategic plan (but only after this has been approved).

11.2 STEPS IN PREPARING THE LONG-RANGE PLAN

The traditional position has been that the marketing plan – feeding into the corporate plan – should be the *sole* document which encapsulates strategy in this field. Our experience, however, suggests that it is not merely preferable but essential to undertake a separate review of the far future. Otherwise, the overall process tends to be swamped by the shorter-term considerations (and especially problems) which then dominate debates about strategy.

Fortunately, our approach to the long-range plan – and to the documentation of robust strategies which it incorporates – is simpler than that involved in the traditional marketing plan. This is not least because it assumes that most of the work has already been undertaken – you have been carrying it out yourself as you have worked your way through this book. In practice the environmental analysis, and perhaps some of the early stages of scenario planning, would take place across the whole year rather than be concentrated a few weeks.

[2] M. H. B. McDonald, *Marketing Plans* (2nd ed., Heinemann, 1989)

More important, the long-range planning process is confined to a genuine review of what has already emerged from the scenarios, and of what needs to be changed to produce robust strategies which ensure the best long-term future.

As a result, reducing the process to the bare minimum, there are just *five* simple steps to producing a *long-range marketing plan*:

ISOLATE TURNING	**POINTS**
DECIDE	**RO**BUST STRATEGIES
TEST	**A**GAINST 'CORPORATE' STRATEGY
DECIDE STRATEGIC	**C**HANGES
	TRANSLATE TO ACTION

FIGURE 11.1   Steps in preparing a long-range plan

If you need a mnemonic to help you remember these stages, then the bold letters above spell out **PROACT** (*ive*). Being proactive is essential to the best long-range planning.

Isolate turning points

As we have seen, the starting point must be a definitive statement, ideally a formal '*map*' of some kind, of the issues, the turning points, which will decide the long-term future of your organisation – perhaps its very survival. This is arguably the most important step of all, and the one where most organisations fail. If you cannot recognise what factors will determine your fate, then you will not be able to create the most effective robust strategies.

You should condense the outcomes onto just one page (of no more than 500 words, and preferably shown in diagrams). If you feel that there must be some explanatory expansion, put this into an appendix – but be ruthless in limiting yourself to one page in the main body here. This not only makes the document dramatically shorter than most such exercises, and correspondingly easier for the recipients to read (and hence more likely that they will), but it forces you to decide what really are the key issues.

You should also have a separate subsection, but of just half a page – no more than 250 additional words summarising the two scenarios you developed, since these represent the key assumptions about the future. It is essential to spell these out, since most companies do not even realise that they make such assumptions. At the peak of its success, IBM's key product marketing document was simply titled 'Forecast Assumptions' ; and it is arguable that forgetting what the assumptions really were played a major part in IBM's later downfall. The agreement on what are the assumptions is often the key to understanding the marketing plan.

Decide robust strategies

This stage clearly is at the heart of the whole process, and will be covered in more detail in later chapters. Here all we need say is that we have to develop a set of strategies to protect against (or to capitalise on) what has emerged from the previous step, in terms of the key turning points. These strategies should be spelled out – as clearly as possible – on just one page (500 words), with any necessary details consigned to an appendix.

One caveat: formal corporate strategies tend to be documented in terms of profit projections – our managerial culture demands as much – but the unpublished, informal objectives which really drive the actions of most organisations range much wider. It is these wider factors which need to be taken into account here.

Test against 'corporate' strategy

The next step requires a degree of self-confidence! It is to take these (long-term) 'robust' strategies and map them onto the (short-term) 'corporate' strategy which already exists (or is in the process of emerging from the other parts of the strategy process).

Exactly what form this comparison takes will depend upon how you are presenting these strategies. The essence, however, is that each should be compared statement by statement. Ideally this should be in a *single table*, with just two columns, one for each side of the comparison. Again, any additional explanations should be consigned, as end notes, to an appendix. The 'test' itself should be confined to no more than 500 words and, preferably, to no more than half a page.

Audit 11.1

Draw up this table for your own organisation, based on the turning points you identified earlier.

A version for the OUBS is shown below. As we have not yet explained any of the robust strategies which might apply to the OUBS, we have added another column which shows the turning points to which these relate.

Turning points	Robust strategies	Corporate strategy
Weaker market for the MBA	Build presence in wider fields of education	Extend to 'Law'
Requirement for 'on-going' education	Provide suitable courses	Narrowing focus
Managers want a 'club'	Develop new relationships with students	Alumni club as add-on
Government funds on-going education	Lobby government	No action being taken
Microsoft enters edutainment market	No action required	

Decide strategic changes

The previous stage will highlight the divergences, if any, between the two types of strategy – and, hence, the areas where changes may be needed. These should then be addressed, again statement by statement, in terms of the changes which will be made in the overall corporate strategy statement, even if the decision is to do nothing!

The simplest way to record these changes is to add them as a third column to the table from the preceding step.

Audit 11.2

Again, draw up the table for your own organisation.

And, again, we illustrate one possible table for the OUBS.

Robust strategies	Corporate strategy	Strategic changes
Build presence in wider fields of education	Extend to 'Law'	Widen objectives to take in even more disciplines and focus on student needs
Provide suitable courses	Narrowing focus	Progressively widen course coverage and modularise
Develop new relationships with students	Alumni club as add-on	Bring club aspect to centre of strategy
Lobby government	No action being taken	Develop positive strategy to influence government

Translate to action

The final stage of any planning process should always be to do something! It may be that the action is to positively *incorporate* these changes in the overall corporate plan. In this case, a single sentence, stating that this has happened, may be enough; though to reassure yourself, at least, that this has happened, you may want to incorporate a brief statement of what *real* changes have then taken place.

The more thorough alternative is to produce a separate action plan (within the long-range marketing plan) where the shorter-term (more certain) elements of the revised strategy are translated into the necessary actions (and related timescales). Again this should not take more than one page – once more in the form of a table which describes the key activities in terms of the most relevant parameters. Their prioritisation levels and resource requirements should be listed, at least, along with their target outcomes and times. Allowing for updating in this way emphasises the true role of the long-range marketing plan and its relationship to the subsequent monitoring.

Audit 11.3

Once more, create your own version.

The OUBS equivalent might be:

Strategic changes	Strategic actions	Priority	Resources	Action taken
Widen objectives to take in even more disciplines and focus on student needs	Research potential in other disciplines and determine long-term needs of students	2	Limited research funds needed	[ ]
Progressively widen course coverage and modularise	Widen coverage by new courses and modularise existing courses	1	Significant teaching development required	[ ]
Bring club aspect to centre of strategy	Grow role of OUBS alumni and OUSA (the wider OU student body)	2	Limited research and limited additional personnel needed	[ ]
Develop positive strategy to influence government	Involve OU lobbyists	4	Limited funds needed	[ ]

The whole long-range marketing plan (PROACT), and the robust strategies it contains, should be contained in no more than six pages. It should also be, as far as possible, free-form. This may mean that the amount of information on the page may then demand a very small type size is used! The acid test, however, is how short it is. Longer than ten pages (excluding any appendices) may mean that it is not read.

The content of each section should be dictated solely by what is important to the organisation – the philosophy we have been following throughout the book. No doubt you will wish to use many of the ideas contained in the rest of it, not least to test their relevance to your own needs; but only those which are *genuinely* relevant to your needs should be employed – and even then only described (at the length which reflects their specific value) in the appendices. This is a very different approach to that traditionally employed – where the techniques employed at each stage tend to be pre-specified by the 'experts' who have devised the planning process.

We have now looked at one framework for writing the long-range marketing plan. There are other approaches which might be possible. Indeed, the only essential requirement is that you somehow develop a set of robust strategies to compare with your existing corporate strategy; and then reconcile the two.

Whatever your approach, as the next section shows, it is often the process itself which offers the main benefits.

11.3 BENEFITS FROM THE PLANNING PROCESS

Returning to long-range planning, the most valuable aspect is often not the output (the plan) but the *process* leading up to it. Very real benefits can be derived at each of the stages, as we shall now see.

Input

At this stage there may be, if the process is well managed, considerable benefit to be gained from the active involvement of a wide range of staff. This must include all the managers who will be asked to implement the plan, but it should also be extended to the largest possible number of other employees. Involvement in the planning of their own future is highly motivational for all levels of staff and management. Indeed, some organisations have deliberately used our 'Robust strategies in a day' approach to involve managers across all functions in the *overall* planning process; so that they felt they 'owned' it. Exclusion from the process, on the other hand, can lead to frustration and fear.

Barclays (Bank) Technology Services, for instance, used scenario workshops (run by Northeast Consulting, Boston USA) to 'reinforce the teamwork within the organisation' by:[3]

- allowing participants to expand their perspective beyond the confines of their specialisation
- helping build an appreciation of the challenges faced
- fostering better follow-through because the participants understood the reasons for change

Debate

The review process should, again if properly managed, lead to a stimulating challenge to the embedded wisdom. It has to be recognised, though, that the 'logical incrementalism' (the incremental development of strategy, informally and often by default), which you may have come across in other strategy books or courses, is more often replaced by 'illogical incrementalism'. Thus, a decision taken on the spur of the moment – with little thought – subsequently becomes institutionalised as a strategy which is never challenged, regardless of whether it is right or wrong.

'Marketing myopia' is the title of a very influential article by Theodore Levitt.[4] He stated:

> The viewpoint that an industry is a customer-satisfying process, not a goods-producing process, is vital for all businessmen to understand. An industry begins with the customer and his needs, not with a patent, a raw material, or a selling skill. Given the customer's needs, the industry develops backwards, first concerning itself with the physical delivery of customer satisfactions. Then it moves back further to creating the things by which these satisfactions are in

---

[3] Anne Casson, How to Run Effective Workshops, Strategic Planning Conference, 13–14 May 1997.

[4] T. Levitt, 'Marketing myopia', *Harvard Business Review*, July–August 1960.

part achieved. How these materials are created is a matter of indifference to the customer, hence the particular form of manufacturing, processing, or what-have-you cannot be considered as a vital aspect of the marketing.

His reason for this emphasis, supported by considerable anecdotal evidence in the rest of the article, was that most organisations defined their business perspectives (now more often referred to as 'corporate missions') too narrowly, typically based upon the technological processes they employed (but, at best, upon internal factors). His view, which was enthusiastically seized upon by the more adventurous organisations (albeit with some unfortunate results),[5] was that the link with the consumer, the 'customer franchise' , was the most important element.

The corporate vision must, therefore, be defined in terms of the customer's needs and wants. Adopting a wider perspective helped many organisations to better appreciate how they could develop.

Levitt recognised the danger of the possible over-reactions in a later book, where he added the comment:

> Marketing Myopia was not intended as analysis or even prescription; it was intended as manifesto. It did not pretend to take a balanced position.... My scheme, however, tied marketing more closely to the inner orbit of business policy.[6]

Debate should be as wide ranging as possible. Nothing should be exempt from scrutiny, and no idea should be dismissed until fully considered. The range of creativity tools, such as brainstorming, should also be brought into play. It is the one chance, during the year, to think the unthinkable.

Agreement and understanding

Probably the most productive part of the whole process is, though, the opportunity to gain a shared understanding of what the long-range marketing plan means – the fact that it has been 'published' in no way guarantees that it is understood by the recipients.

This internal communication process is best accomplished in an extended meeting away from the pressure of day-to-day business. A two- to three-day meeting – or at least the one day described in our paper at the beginning of this part of the book – is normally the way this is achieved. The fact that this is an extended meeting, in a neutral environment in a suitable hotel, is critical – the discussion in the bar at the end of the day is probably just as important as that in the formal meeting, and the forced concentration over a lengthy period on the issues brings any misunderstandings over their interpretation to the surface. The meeting will inevitably cover far more than is eventually enshrined in the plan itself, and in the process will bring home to the participants (who must include all the key managers responsible for

[5] P. Spillard, 'Ansoff revisited: logic, commitment and strategies for change', *The Marketing Digest*, ed. M J. Thomas and N. E. Waite (Heinemann, 1988).
[6] T. Levitt, *The Marketing Imagination* (Free Press, 1986).

implementation, not just the favoured few) the 'flavour' of (and philosophy behind) what is intended. It is this shared 'flavour' which will inform their actions over the succeeding year – and is the most potent outcome of this part of the process.

But this part of the process should go even further, to obtain agreement from all those involved; and thence to obtain their wholehearted commitment.

Scenarios as a group communication

The development of scenarios is itself an especially useful device for bringing such groups together. It is, of course, usually an integral part of the long-range planning process, but it also proves to be an invaluable device for achieving wider understanding and agreement; as our work on 'Robust strategies in a day' with a variety of organisations has demonstrated.

By this means, 20–30 of the key players within an organisation (and hopefully some key actors from outside) are rapidly exposed not just to the thinking of the organisation as a whole but to that of the various individuals involved. This is a very powerful process for achieving a shared understanding – as well as for organisation-wide motivation.

This approach may be especially important in terms of bringing together not just the different functions/departments but also the range of different management styles:[7]

CREATORS – who introduce the ideas that create instability within the organisation

IMPLEMENTERS – who develop these ideas into workable systems

STABILISERS – who manage the system as a process to reduce variation and improve it.

In terms of their own scenario work with their clients, Northeast Consulting (Boston, USA) look primarily to 'communication' as the most important result of their work,[8] in terms of:

- open and honest debate about the critical challenges facing the organisation
- development of a common language for discussing options and goals
- creation of a framework for assessing on-going progress.

GBN (Global Business Network), on the other hand, who use outside experts for much of the work, emphasise the injection of perspectives from outside the industry and from outside the culture.[9]

[7] Victor Newman and Chaharbaghi, *The Three Innovating Stereotypes* (Cranfield CIM, 1996).

[8] James Herman, How to Run Effective Workshops, Strategic Planning Society Conference, 13–14 May 1997.

[9] Richard O' Brien, Managing the Scope of Scenarios to Ensure They Are Useful, Strategic Planning Society Conference, 13–14 May 1997.

Ringi

This approach is best exemplified by the Japanese corporations. Their decision-making process typically requires that *all* managers involved in implementation of the plan formally sign an agreement to this effect (the documents are called 'ringi' or, more correctly, 'ringi seido'). It is quite normal for as many as 50 managers to sign. The decision-making process is, therefore, much more complex than its Western equivalent – and can take that much longer (though the Japanese have learned to manage it better, so the difference is not that great).[10]

Their gain, though, is in the implementation phase. This is where delays happen in the West. Managers who have not been consulted often pose problems when they are asked to implement the decisions (and may not even be able to implement them). The Japanese managers, in contrast, are already fully committed; and the implementation phase goes much faster. As implementation typically takes far longer than the decision-making, this represents a major gain for the Japanese.

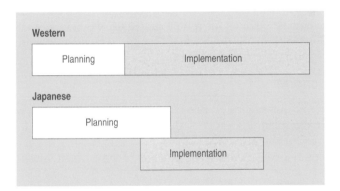

FIGURE 11.2   Western and Japanese planning and implementation

Audit 11.4 _____

If you can persuade some colleagues to participate, it is well worth trying to run a 'robust strategies in a day' seminar – even if it is only with one group of as few as five or six people in your own office. The spread of perspectives should add significantly to the power of the resulting robust strategies.

The value of the process itself, as opposed to any plan which comes out of it, should not be underestimated. Management teams rarely work together as well as they might, and the scenario planning process offers an ideal opportunity for bringing them together to communicate with each other – in the most positive context. Certainly, when I was part of IBM's corporate strategy team in

[10] J. C. Abbeglen and G. Stalk, Jr, *Kaisha, The Japanese Corporation* (Basic Books, 1985).

the United Kingdom, I found that the understanding achieved by a three-day off-site meeting between senior managers typically outweighed the value of the hundreds of pages of plans which were formally agreed at these meetings.

Now, though, we come to the set of techniques which can be deployed in the very open-ended context of long-range marketing.

11.4 TECHNIQUES IN LONG-RANGE PLANNING

We have already looked at some of the techniques which are recommended as parts of the *traditional* strategic planning process. We have also seen that some of these, such as the Boston Matrix, may be too tightly focused – indeed almost prescriptive. On the other hand, the techniques we would recommend for long-range planning are typically unfocused, as we will see later in this section.[11]

First, though, we would suggest that, whatever techniques you consider, it is crucially important that you do not just *blindly* accept anything put in front of you, but critically consider any technique you might be offered – for use in corporate strategy as much as for robust strategies. We have encapsulated our own suggestions in terms of the 'Critic's Charter', which is outlined below.

The critic's charter

Below are set out our suggested rules for choosing what you are going to use in your long-range planning process: the material which is to be input as much as the theory and techniques you employ.

1 Is it directly relevant to the *specific* needs of your organisation? (If not, discard it.)
2 What *other* techniques are claimed to provide the same benefits? (Check for alternatives.)
3 Does it offer the *most* productive approach to meeting your specific needs? (Discard any which are less effective.)
4 How does it *complement* the other approaches you are using to examine other aspects of strategy? (If it clashes with everything else you are doing, again discard it.)
5 What *reliance* can be put upon it, and what evidence is there of its effectiveness? (Discard all techniques with no proven, substantial backing.)
6 Is it 'original' or has it been *distorted* by ornamentation added later? (Discard the offerings of snake-oil merchants.)
7 Does it match with your own experience, and does it make sense? (Discard anything which, after due effort, does not make sense to you.)

---

[11] These techniques have emerged from a variety of sources, but the majority of them can be found, described in more detail, in the book which spells out our views on marketing: *New Marketing Practice* by D. S. Mercer (Penguin, 1997).

8   Then, and only then, use it – but only as a *starting point* for your own further investigations! (Always assume that your own judgement is better than that of any expert, who cannot know the specific situation as well as you do.)

It should be obvious, from the long list above, that the most important feature of the approach is the *rejection* of anything and everything which does not *directly* help you solve your *specific* problem. This may sound trivial, for why should anyone think of offering solutions which are irrelevant or simply do not work? But, in their enthusiasm to help, many experts will rush to do just that! The recognition of the *individuality* of each situation is normally a key requirement for sound long-range marketing practice. *Even if you do not follow all the eight steps, please keep in mind this one simple point!*

This process will almost inevitably result in your discarding most of the techniques on offer – not because they are inherently flawed (though a number are) but because few of them will match the needs of the individual situation. Even so, there is a reasonable chance that, from the wide variety available, there should be at least one idea which can offer some new insight into the problems at hand. What use you then make of it depends entirely upon the specific needs of the moment. The most important advice, however, is given by the last recommendation from the Critic's Charter. It is to use what you have chosen as no more than a *starting point*. Indeed, its main value may be in terms of the new insights it stimulates, which may in turn suggest new solutions. More generally it should offer a productive framework within which answers may more easily be worked out.

You should use any technique only as an *aid* to your own judgement. In long-range marketing you cannot delegate important decisions to outsiders. No matter how expert they are, they cannot have the amount of experience, of the matter in hand, as you do!

Starting with your own judgement

Indeed, no matter how seductive are the arguments of the experts, it is always worthwhile using your own judgement, even if only as a cross-check; for example, against what others say in the group you are working with. In long-range planning, the key to this is keeping your mind open to all possibilities. Accordingly, the next framework we will offer is the 'analytical four-step'. This simply outlines the stages which we believe may best help you to deploy your own unbiased judgement in any given long-range marketing situation.

The analytical four-step

Step Zero – START – with nothing more than a blank sheet of paper.

Step One – SEARCH – without any preconceptions as to the outcome, but using your own knowledge and experience, write down what you think are the key factors (the 'turning points', for instance).

Step Two – SELECT – then progressively discard the least essential until you have reduced the number to six.

Step Three – PRIORITISE – these six factors.

Step Four – SYNTHESISE – identify what relationships and patterns exist, if necessary returning to Step One, to reduce the factors to no more than two 'prime directives' which fully encapsulate these.

This process may be used in a variety of management situations, but is especially suited to handling the complexities and uncertainties to be found in long-range marketing. It is deliberately kept as simple as possible. The hallmark of effective marketing practice is often *simplicity*. If you don't understand exactly what is happening you cannot hope to control it!

The most *powerful* starting point for analysis is, thus, the simplest. It is a *blank sheet of paper*! Without any preconceptions about what to expect, without any artificial frameworks to bias your views, without any tick-lists to limit your horizons, you simply write down the *key factors* about the situation which faces you. This may be the simplest approach, but it is not necessarily the easiest of starting points! Many managers feel threatened by its lack of guidance. Later in this chapter you will find a number of techniques which help you over this first hurdle. In any case, this is a search process, so most of these factors should already have emerged from your previous desk research, or scenario work, or at least will already have been known to you as a result of previous experience.

Then start the selection process. Following much the same process as in the 'Critic's Charter', *delete* all those which will not be absolutely crucial to the long-range strategies or tactics you are planning. It is likely that, even so, few will disappear at this stage – since most will seem essential – so be more ruthless and progressively discard the least essential until you have no more than six factors left (though these may be modified to encompass some aspects of those deleted – as long as this does not dilute their impact). We believe that, to misquote the famous architect Mies van der Rohe, 'less is more'!

Then prioritise these six factors (from one to six, in descending order of importance) and note *why* you have chosen these priorities (since, at a later stage and as conditions change, you may want to change the order of these items).

Finally, try and identify what relationships exist between these factors. Some may be trade-offs (potential against risk, say), some may be complementary (advertising investment and brand image, say). Whatever other aids you use, simply try to see what patterns emerge. At one extreme, this is a process of *synthesis* – trying to combine the components to produce something bigger, and better, than the individual parts. Ideally, you should reduce the six factors to no more than two '*prime directives*' (the concepts or philosophies on which your managers are able to focus, but which still encapsulate the key elements). At the other extreme, the pattern may be one of 'dilemmas', where there are several options which are apparently in conflict with each other. The management of the dilemma, so that apparently conflicting options may need to be simultaneously applied – with synergy rather than friction – is the route to success in these cases. The classic example is that of the Japanese who simply did not accept that raising quality standards would cost more; and who went on to show that in practice it actually *reduced* overall costs.

Depending upon the outcome of this final stage it may then be necessary to return to the first step – to add in the extra factors which this has suggested might be relevant. The whole process is then repeated. In many marketing planning activities, especially those in long-range marketing, *iteration is the key to progressively optimising the final output.*

This, then, is the *analytical four-step* approach to analysis – though, to make it a bit more memorable, there are actually five steps – where *Step Zero* is perhaps the most important of all! In the present context this is referred to as 'zero-level planning'. It is a commitment to approach each new activity afresh – *a blank sheet of paper* – without the prejudices derived from previous exposure to theories.

The factors which you write on that blank sheet of paper, therefore, should only be the key factors which are *directly relevant* to the *individual* situation in hand. The essence of this process, of zero-level planning, is the distillation of exactly what is important to the specific situation – unencumbered by any academic gimmickry (no matter how elegantly it may be packaged!). I repeat that this may be very powerful in its simplicity, but is also quite sophisticated in use; a knowledge of a number of the other ideas described in this book is needed if the manager is to make the most effective use of it.

Having undertaken this exercise in *minimalism*, and having achieved this initial distillation, you can then proceed directly to the rest of the 'Analytical Four-Step', and this is where the rest of the long-range marketing theory should help.

The theory you choose to help at this stage (and especially at Step 4), should of course be tested once more against the eight steps of the Critic's Charter.

I emphasise, however, that this approach, this particular form of analysis, is just one of those which are available. It is, as always, up to you to select (with the aid of the Critic's Charter, say) which one of these is best suited to your specific requirements at the time. If nothing else, this book should convince you that enlightened pragmatism is a virtue and a diversity of approaches a near necessity!

The great virtue of the analytical four-step is that it is totally under your control – *you know exactly where you are.*

Systems diagrams

The techniques described so far in this section have been word-based, but graphical (diagram-based) techniques can be just as useful, and are often even more effective in terms of examining the relationships between the various elements.

We looked at these earlier in the book, so we will not repeat the description again – but please note how effectively they (especially multiple cause diagrams) can also be used at this stage of the planning process – and they can be subjected to exactly the same rules as word-based approaches.

12 DEVISING LONG-RANGE STRATEGIES

So far, we have looked at some general techniques used in long-term planning. Now we will move on to look at some more specific ones. In particular, we will start by looking at those relating to the '*internal*' considerations, typically limited resources, which constrain the robust strategies we might wish to devise.

12.1 ANALYSING CORE COMPETENCES

The first, and most important set of these specific techniques, is used to determine what are the organisation's *core competences*. These are the absolutely essential ingredients of your products/services and/or organization that will be responsible for the sustained success of your organization in the future. It is worth noting that they are just as likely to be intangible or tangible.

The starting point for their determination is zero-level planning, described in Chapter 11, and the subsequent use of the analytical four-step.

The analytical four-step applied to core competences

Once more we will use the simplest possible technique to identify the organisation's core competences.

Step Zero *Start with nothing more than a blank sheet of paper* – try to isolate what makes your product or service unique, what special '*competitive advantages*' does it – and your organisation – have?

Step One *Then, without any preconceptions as to the outcome, write down what you think are the key factors involved* – those which best describe what you have found in step zero, but also including those from other inputs.

Step Two *Then progressively discard the least essential until you have reduced the number to six* – the least essential in this context being defined as those least important to the long-term survival of the product/service or organisation.

Step Three *Prioritise these six* – so that you end up with the absolutely key competence(s) at the top of this list.

Step Four *Identify what relationships and patterns exist, and if necessary return to Step 1* and then start to combine these competences to define, in outline, the core competences on which your product/service package is based. *As new ideas emerge from this process, repeat the whole four-step until you have a well-formed outline.*

The isolation of the core competences represents by far the most productive use of the analytical four-step across the whole of long-range planning. You will need to return to this determination of core competences a number of times, to ensure that they are correct; and then to optimise their positioning in the light of new information. Iteration and incrementalism are central aspects of the strategy process. But – as in most things – *starting* the process from the right place is the best guarantee of finishing in the right position.

Core competences pie

Identifying the core competences as just described can be a daunting task, since you are faced with a blank sheet of paper on which you are required to write only the key competences. It is often easier to take an intermediate step and write down a much bigger list of overall competences (without having to determine how important they are) – and then refine these down to a much smaller list by applying Step 2 of the four-step. Even then it is distinctly possible that you will need some help to get you going, so we have developed the concept of the '*core competences pie*', which distinguishes four separate segments of the organisation's internal and external environment which can be used to stimulate separate approaches to the overall problem.

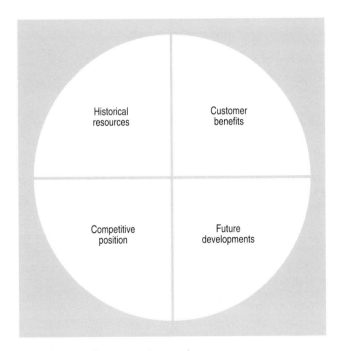

FIGURE 12.1   Core competences pie

Using this intermediate approach, you start by developing your wider list of competences within these initial, broad categories. In the first place this may stimulate your imagination – to unearth competences which, blinkered by the more conventional approaches, you might not have considered. Perhaps more important, it will also show you which competences appear in a *number* of slices; and – since they have wider impact – are more likely to be the crucial ones. The segments we find most useful in this context are set our below.

Historical resources – this slice of the pie represents the traditional, inward-looking view of the organisation which dominates most corporate planning. It reflects what the organisation sees as being most important to itself, typically those competences in which it has most pride, the activities it believes it does better than anyone else – and, in general, what has succeeded in the past is an especially good indication of what will succeed in the future.

Looking at much the same aspect from the opposite direction, Victor Newman suggests that long-range planning should be about *asset risk management* – protecting valuable assets (whatever their form) upon which the organisation depends.[1]

Competitive position – this slice requires you to look more dispassionately at the organisation's position in relation to its 'competitors' (who are defined in the widest possible sense, including government departments in the public sector just as much as commercial competitors in the private sector). Which competences give the organisation a *sustainable* competitive advantage over those competitors? The key word here is sustainable. In this context *short-term* advantage means little – to be a genuine core competence it has to be sustainable over the *long term.*

Customer benefits – shifting your viewpoint, and remembering you are producing a long-range *marketing* plan, you also need to consider those competences which you (the supplier) think offer most to (or are most wanted by) the *customer.*

Future developments – for the majority of organisations this is the aspect most often neglected, since most managers tend to look *backward* rather than forward. Put in a nutshell it simply asks which competences will become important in the future; in five or ten years time, say. This often turns out to be the most powerful contributor of all, because our experience is that managers find it easiest to widen their vision if the timescale they are talking about is (in their terms) very long: this freedom acts as a potent stimulant for their, and your, imagination. This is, after all, the main lesson of this book!

It should be noted that the whole point of the Core Competences Pie lies in *integrating* the slices; the reverse of what might be expected – but we hope this will make it that much more memorable!

Even so, I must issue a stern warning about its use. Remember that the ultimate aim is to *condense* the number of those core competences and to *prioritise* them. There is no virtue, and much vice, in lengthening the lists in each slice; and considerable danger in trying to balance them with those in the other slices. If you simply cannot think of anything to put under 'Future Developments', say, then leave it *blank*!

---

[1] V. Newman, Securing Buy-In and Commitment to the Scenario Planning Process, Strategic Planning Society Conference, 13–14 May 1997.

The immediate outcome of all this work is listing (and, hopefully, understanding) what is central to the current work of, and the future of, the organisation; its core competences. We shall see next how this knowledge is used.

The 80:20 rule

One of the most important keys to success, in almost all walks of life, is to *concentrate* resources where they may be most productively deployed. Resources, even in the richest of organisations, are never boundless; and are rarely sufficient to meet all the demands which might be placed upon them. Resources have, therefore, to be allocated – even rationed – between groups of competing activities. In practice this often appears, at least to outsiders, to be a remarkably random process.

As you are probably aware, the 80:20 rule (often called the Pareto rule) is the most general and powerful rule of all. It simply states that, across a wide range of situations, 20% of the contributors (customers, say) will account for 80% of the performance (sales volumes, for instance).

It is even more powerful in the context of long-range planning, where the philosophy of 'Support Success Forget Failure' (SSFF) holds much the same lesson. It asks that you abandon the tendency of managements to throw good money after bad, by trying to rescue projects which can never succeed, and in the process ignoring the opportunities offered by those that are a success. 'Discard Peripherals' works from the other extreme, and is even more ruthless. It demands that you do not just ignore the weaker elements of your operations, which some define as anything which is not central to the core competences, but that you actually discard them. But 'Boost Core Competences' is the most positive statement of all. It says that resources should be reallocated to those activities which have the most beneficial impact on the development of, or application of, the core competences.

It is the *boosting of the core competences* which is the most positive act. Core competences are sometimes described – by Michael Porter,[2] for example – as 'focus' on what the organisation does best, but to me the term 'core competences' (albeit now already associated with the ornamentation and gimmickry which seems to be added to any useful idea) best encapsulates what is needed. It is not just resources which need to be concentrated; the *attention* of management in general, and yourself in particular, must be focused on those core competences.

That having been said, deciding just what *are* these core competences is a long process, which demands constant review – as new lessons are learned. If you are using the Analytical Four-Step as a device to aid this analysis then this is Step 3, where you have ruthlessly to cut back to no more than six competences (though these may be portmanteau categories) and prioritise them.

---

[2] M. Porter, *Competitive Strategy* (Free Press, 1980).

These core competences are, then, a *distillation* of what gives your organisation its distinctive character; or, to be more precise, that which positively distinguishes it from other organisations in the same field (in the commercial field this is now often referred to as 'competitive advantage'). This must, though, be looked at in the context of the longer term – thus, it must also represent substantial competitive advantage.

12.2 EMERGENT STRATEGIES

Returning to strategy itself, and taking a pragmatic rather than a theoretical viewpoint, a considerable amount of strategy *emerges* as a result of unpredictable changes in the environment rather than from rational control by management. This emergent strategy means that managers are forced to follow courses of action which they had not planned.

This is most clearly illustrated by one of the various versions of Henry Minzberg's famous diagram.[3]

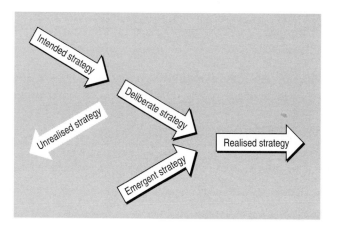

FIGURE 12.2   Minzberg's analysis of strategy

This diagram very clearly shows how the *intended* strategy, decided upon traditionally or incrementally, is overtaken by events in two main ways. One, which will probably be recognised by the organization, is that of *unrealised* strategy, where it proves impossible to implement the chosen strategy in practice.

Less obvious is the *emergent* strategy which is decided by events in the external environment; and, thus, forced upon the organisation. Johnson and Scholes refer to this process as 'natural selection', which nicely encapsulates both its potentially random nature and its powerful impact.[4] This strategy may

[3] H. Minzberg and J. H. Waters, 'Of strategies deliberate and emergent', *Strategic Management Journal*, Vol. 6, 1988.

[4] G. Johnson and Kevan Scholes, *Exploring Corporate Strategy* (3rd ed., Prentice Hall, 1993).

not necessarily be recognized, in its totality, by the organisation – since many of its implications may be hidden. As markets become more complex, however, such emergent strategies are becoming more common.

Many organisations see both these processes in terms of failure – they have been forced, usually by unpredictable events, to abandon their own strategy. There is, accordingly, a tendency for this unwelcome fact to be ignored until it is so obvious it cannot be avoided. This is a major error. Such deviations must be recognized (probably through one or other form of environmental analysis coupled with personal networking) as soon as possible – so that the organisation can react in good time. Henry Minzberg summarises the problem succinctly as strategic planning's 'obsession with the illusion of control'.[5]

A much more powerful approach is, though, to be *proactive* – to seize upon these deviations as the basis for future developments. What needs to be recognised is that emergent strategies are the most *powerful* strategies of all. They must, by definition, be directly derived from the needs of the market. Indeed, where even successful deliberate strategies may not ideally match market needs, but may achieve their targets by sheer force (especially where conviction marketing lies behind them), *emergent strategies* are likely to be 'naturally' vigorous ones even without such force being applied.

Managing emergent strategies

There are two main approaches to capitalising on such emergent strategies. The first of these, favoured in the West, is the *umbrella strategy*, using Henry Minzberg's term.[6]

This is a form of very positive delegation, in that the overall strategies, the umbrella, are very general in nature – and allow the lower-level managers, who are closest to the external environment, the freedom to react to changes.

A much more direct, and hence even more powerful, approach is that favoured by Japanese corporations. They *integrate* emergent strategies with their own. The Tao famously counsels 'It is well to persist like water', which Pascale and Athos succinctly translate as '*Let things flow: let events take their course*'.[7] Indeed it is arguable that, in terms of marketing, to a large extent the leading Japanese corporations use emergent strategies instead of their own deliberate strategies. This is evidenced as much by an attitude of mind as by any other feature. They deliberately go out to look for symptoms of such emergent trends which can be detected in the performance of their own products. More than that, though, they often deliberately launch a *range* of products rather than a single one, to see which is most successful. It is almost as if they deliberately seek out the emergent strategies by offering the best environment for them to develop – the very reverse of the Western approach which seeks to avoid them! The Japanese then go on to build on these emergent strategies

[5] H. Minzberg, 'The pitfalls of strategic planning', *California Management Review*, Fall 1993.
[6] H. Minzberg and J. H. Waters, 'Of strategies deliberate and emergent', *Strategic Management Journal*, vol 6, 1988.
[7] R. T. Pascale and Anthony G. Athos, *The Art of Japanese Management* (Simon & Schuster, 1981).

with a number of very effective tools. Most of these are designed to overcome the major problem which accompanies emergent strategies, that these came on the scene much later than deliberate ones (and are likely to be visible to all the competitors at the same time), so that *time* is the essence. Thus, time management techniques (including parallel development along with flexible manufacturing and JIT) which have been developed by the Japanese offer them a significant competitive advantage in handling such emergent strategies.

Paradigm shift

This is the ultimate emergent strategy. In this case the emergent effects are so powerful that they force a complete *shift in perspective* by the organisation. It is forced to rethink its complete strategic position from this new viewpoint. It is most obvious in the field of science (and indeed the term 'paradigm shift' was coined by Thomas Kuhn to describe the dramatic changes which take place in science when a new set of theories, the new paradigm, supersedes the old set).[8] The important implication of this theory is that a paradigm shift is a discontinuous process (rather like catastrophe theory). There is no gentle move from one viewpoint to the other taking place over a lengthy period. Instead there is a nearly instantaneous, almost violent, shift from one to the other.

Paradigm blinkers

The reason for the suddenness of the shift is the investment (in terms of management commitment) in the *previous* paradigm. Because it is too 'painful' to abandon their cherished viewpoint, until events finally force this upon them, managers may adopt a number of devices to deny or minimise the existence of the changes; including *blindness, misinterpretation, opposition*. Those 'paradigm blinkers' are organisation-wide and go far beyond the groupthink[9] we looked at earlier.

(a) **Blindness** – most basic of all, they simply will not see the changes, or will persuade themselves that they do not apply to their own position (thus the British motorcycle industry convinced itself that the Japanese were only making small bikes, which was a different market and no threat to themselves!).

(b) **Misinterpretation** – or the signals may be forced to fit the existing paradigm.

(c) **Opposition** – but, if the signals are too obvious to ignore, then the management may fight the imminent shift in paradigm by a number of means. These may include calling on the basic philosophies of the organisation (the new paradigm is a 'heresy'), developing highly political defences within the organisation against them and/or partially assimilating those elements which can be accepted by the existing paradigm.

---

[8] T. Kuhn, *The Structure of Scientific Revolutions* (University of Chicago Press, 1970).

[9] Irving L. Janis, 'Groupthink', *Psychology Today* (US), November 1971.

The above tools may represent stages which take place before the new paradigm overpowers the old. Assuming its overthrow is inevitable these delays in recognition may be very damaging, and are often fatal. Even if the new paradigm is eventually accepted, there is likely to be, as shown in Figure 12.3, a period of *'paradigm dissonance'* when the organisation is demoralized and its confidence sapped.

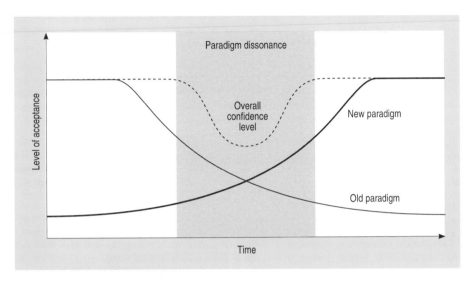

FIGURE 12.3   Paradigm shift

Unfreezing an organisation which is caught in such a trap is not an easy task. It may involve political moves to encourage dissent, particularly by more junior managers, but it often requires a very strong lead from the CEO – and often the appointment of an outsider (and a charismatic one) to provide this new lead.

12.3 GAP ANALYSIS

One traditional marketing approach to the future is to examine what *gaps* exist in the current business.

Figure 12.4 represents a very crude approach to gap analysis – but one which has a degree of immediacy for many companies. The bottom line shows what the profits are forecast to be, for the organisation as a whole. The upper line shows where the organisation, and in particular its shareholders, want to be; almost inevitably that will require an ascending line, implying growth in profit! The shaded area, between these lines, represents what is often also called the *'planning gap'*; and this shows what is needed from new activities in general and 'new products' in particular.

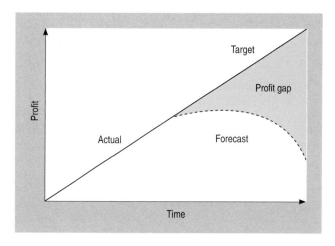

FIGURE 12.4   The profit gap

In 'gap analysis' this gap is seen to come from four main causes:[10]

USAGE GAP
DISTRIBUTION GAP
'PRODUCT' GAP
COMPETITIVE GAP.

The relationship between these is best illustrated by the bar chart in Figure 12.5.

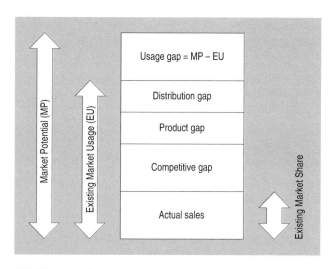

FIGURE 12.5   Usage gap

[10] D. Mercer, *Marketing* (2nd edn, Blackwell, 1996).

Usage gap

This is the gap between the total potential for the market and the actual current usage by all the consumers in the market.

Market Potential – the most difficult estimate to make is probably that of the total potential available to the whole market, including all segments covered by all competitive brands. It is often reached by determining the maximum potential individual usage, and extrapolating this by the maximum number of potential consumers. This is inevitably a judgement rather than a scientific extrapolation.

Existing (Market) Usage – the existing usage by consumers makes up the total current market, from which market shares are, for example, calculated. It is usually derived from market research, most accurately from panel research such as that undertaken by A. C. Nielsen but also from *ad hoc* work. Sometimes it may be available from figures collected by government departments or industry bodies.

The usage gap is thus:

USAGE GAP = MARKET POTENTIAL – EXISTING USAGE

This is an important calculation to make. Many, if not most, marketers accept the existing market size, suitably projected over the timescales of their forecasts, as the boundary for their expansion plans. Although this is often the most realistic assumption, it may sometimes impose an unnecessary limitation on their horizons.

This 'usage gap' is most important for the brand leaders. If any of these have a significant share of the whole market, say in excess of 30%, it may become worthwhile for them to invest in expanding the total market.

All other 'gaps' relate to the difference between the organisation's existing sales (its market share) and the total sales of the market as a whole. This difference is the share held by competitors. These 'gaps' will, therefore, relate to competitive activity.

Distribution gap

The second level of 'gap' is posed by the limits on the distribution of the product or service. If it is limited to certain geographical regions (as some draught beers still are) it cannot expect to make sales in other regions. At the other end of the spectrum, the multinationals may take this to the extremes of globalisation, where no part of the Earth can avoid exposure to their products. Equally, if the product is limited to certain outlets, as some categories of widely advertised drugs are limited by law to pharmacies, then other outlets will not be able to sell them. More likely, perhaps, is that by not being the market leader a brand will find its overall percentage of distribution limited. The remedy for this is simply to maximise distribution! Unfortunately, that is not quite as easy as it sounds, except for the obvious market leaders.

Product (or service) gap

This could also be described as the segment or positioning gap. It represents that part of the market from which the individual organisation is excluded because of product or service characteristics. This may have come about because the market has been segmented, and the organisation does not have offerings in some segments, or it may be because the positioning of its offering effectively excludes it from certain groups of potential consumers, because there are competitive offerings much better placed in relation to these groups. This segmentation may well be the result of deliberate policy. Segmentation and positioning are very powerful marketing techniques; but the trade-off, to be set against the improved focus, is that some parts of the market may effectively be put beyond reach. Often the gap has arisen by default: the organisation has not thought about its positioning, and has simply let its offerings 'drift' to where they now are.

This is probably the main 'gap' where the organisation can have a productive input; and hence our own emphasis in the next chapter on the importance of correct *positioning*.

Competitive gap

What is left represents the gap resulting from your competitive performance. This is the share of business achieved amongst similar products, sold in the same market segment, and with similar distribution patterns; or, at least in any comparison, after such effects have been discounted.

It represents the effects of factors such as price and promotion, in terms of both their absolute level and the effectiveness of their messages. It is what marketing is popularly supposed to be about. But the product or service itself will still be the prime focus of marketing activity.

Gap analysis should be used as a tool to help you examine as thoroughly and objectively as possible your current marketing position and the strategies which you could follow to improve it. It offers a starting point for developing fresh product/market strategies and alerts you to the need for developing new and improved products.

Market gap analysis

In the type of analysis described above, gaps in the *product range* are looked for. Another perspective (essentially taking the 'product gap' to its logical conclusion) is to look for gaps in the *market* (in a variation on 'product positioning') which the company could profitably address, regardless of where its current products stand. This is called market gap analysis.

Many marketers would, however, question the practical worth of either sort of (theoretical) gap analysis. As with most management techniques it has too often been oversold by its supporters. Instead these practising managers would adopt a more pragmatic approach to development. They would, for instance, immediately start to 'proactively' pursue a search for a competitive advantage!

Finding the gaps – the customer bonus

In this context, the best R & D of all is to let the *customer* or consumer tell you how the existing product or service should be developed.

This approach is most obvious in those industrial markets where some customers naturally undertake a substantial share of application development; that is, the work on the uses to which the product or service is put. Sound development strategy in these cases may simply be based upon observing what these customers are doing, and selecting the best solution(s) which emerge – and then translating them to the wider customer set. In the process the required changes to the product or service itself may also emerge, being inherent in the demands posed by these new applications.

The same principle can as successfully be applied to consumer products; after all, that is what much of marketing research aims to achieve. As practised by the Japanese, it can be approached more and directly (and hence be much better understood) by the manager. Thus, the Japanese take enormous pains to find out what changes their customers want. Often they launch multiple versions of the product or service, the ultimate test of consumer taste being those which sell best. They are fortunate in having a public educated to try the many new products brought to market.

12.4 CREATIVE IMITATION

The greatest innovation threat usually comes from known competitors. It is important, therefore, to monitor their developments very closely, and to respond in kind immediately. Theodore Levitt refers to this as 'innovative imitation'.[11] Any major new change they introduce must be taken seriously, and immediately evaluated to see if it is a genuine threat to the (position of) the brand. At the same time, where time is the essence of such competition, contingency plans must be prepared and development work on a response begun.

The main point to remember is that a brand/market leader with a strong position rarely loses that position to even a serious threat – just so long as it delivers an effective counter (usually by imitation) fast enough.

[11] T. Levitt, *The Marketing Imagination* (Free Press, 1983).

'Creative imitation', as Peter Drucker calls it, can offer wider benefits.[12] Many ideas can be productively transferred from other fields of human activity.

Creative scanning

The most important technique for finding major new product developments is scanning the horizon – preferably a decade or more ahead (since such major developments take time as well as money). It is true to say that the origins of major innovations can usually be seen a number of years (or even decades) ahead. The scientific breakthroughs which lead to new technologies normally follow this rule, but so also do the changes in lifestyles which lead to new consumer demands.

Leapfrog

A more sophisticated version of creative imitation is to put a very high level of resources into developing the next 'generation' of product 'after' your rival's innovation – and launching this before your competitor, thus leapfrogging it. The Japanese have managed to turn this almost into an art-form, by their mastery of time management in product development. Such practices, which stress time as much as flexibility (JIT, for example), are not production techniques in the Western sense, but are an outcome of many years of training their workforce. Despite those 'experts' who would promise to instantaneously provide you with these secrets, you would be wise to assume that they take decades (as they did at Toyota), rather than a matter of days, to become effective.

Product development of this type is facilitated by siting the developers in the plant. This may reduce the productivity, at the early stages, by a notch or two, but it vastly improves the implementation stage – where (as we have seen earlier) the Japanese gain nearly all their advantage.

In the area of product development the Japanese use another technique – *parallel development.* Western organisations complete one stage of development before they start the next, because they believe, quite correctly, that otherwise development effort may be wasted (as each stage sets unexpected requirements for the next). The Japanese recognise this inefficiency, but believe that the benefit gained, which is a much faster overall development process (with overlap of stages still giving faster times, despite some of the work having to be redone), far outweighs the extra costs – since it gives them market leadership. Note, however, that more recently some Japanese corporations (Toyota among them) have been reducing the amount of parallel work, because it had become too expensive.

[12] P. F. Drucker, *Innovation and Entrepreneurship* (Heinemann, 1985).

Existing market leaders may take this process a stage further, by having *two* development teams working in parallel. While one is implementing the last stages of the next generation, the other is working on the earlier stages of the next generation but one. This is illustrated in Figure 12.6.

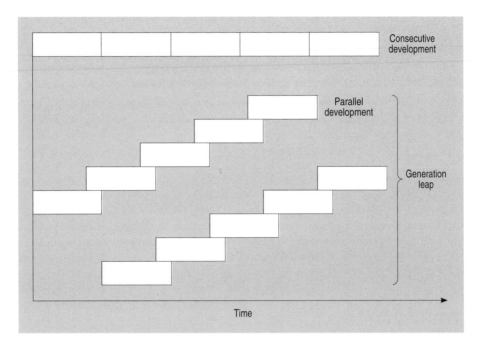

FIGURE 12.6   Parallel development teams

Victor Newman, coming at the problem from another direction (that of CIM at Cranfield) looks at the 'life-cycle' of technological learning, which, he says, typically now lasts around 40 years.[13] The learning moves from Data (which is given) to Information (when the patterns become meaningful) to Knowledge (when opportunities are first created) to the widespread use of the Technology itself (after the applications are first created). This 'Dikt' learning model may look much the same as the traditional definition of the steps from data to knowledge, but here it is applied over much longer timescales – and it allows a more creative viewpoint when examining technologies already in the pipeline.

We can conclude our look at these more specific approaches, which aim to manage the process of long-range planning, by observing that they take on many of the features of riding a tiger! Thus, at one extreme, they adopt the totally open-ended approaches inherent in emergent strategies and, at the other, they use the structured approaches of gap analysis. Perhaps the most productive, though, is that of constantly scanning the horizon; as a precursor to 'creative imitation'.

[13] V. Newman, Securing Buy-In and Commitment to the Scenario Planning Process, Strategic Planning Society Conference, 13–14 May 1997.

13 'GENERIC' ROBUST STRATEGIES

The approaches we have focused on up to this point have revolved around determining the *specific* robust strategies which will offer the best long-term future for an organisation, making the most of opportunities and avoiding the worst threats to its survival. Clearly, such '*tailored*' solutions must be the best, where they are available.

Nevertheless, our work has shown that there are some traditional 'investments', typically in intangibles, which can go some way to underwriting the long-term survival of most organisations regardless of what the future holds. This section describes some of these '*generic*' robust strategies. It should be noted that these are quite different from Michael Porter's generic strategies, which relate to (shorter-term) corporate strategies.[1]

In general, the main investments in this category relate to relationships built up with the main groups of *stakeholders*. The benefit of such investment is to create the *goodwill* which allows an organisation the breathing space for it to regroup – for instance, carrying through a programme of creative imitation – in the face of changes which would otherwise be cataclysmic. Of course, the organisation has to have sufficient speed of reaction to overcome the problems before the goodwill runs out, but the goodwill itself is what allows the possibility of recovery.

It is important to note that the following 'strategies' are introduced not in this book – as they usually are – because of their *short-term* efficacy, but because, if well implemented, they will usually underpin *long-term* survival. Remember this whilst you are exploring them in this chapter.

13.1 THE CUSTOMER FRANCHISE

The most obvious such relationship is with the *customer*. A close relationship with him or her, much as with a friend, will help you weather future difficulties.

One of the most positive ways of consolidating the consumer as the most important focus of the organisation is to look on this relationship[2] as a *prime* asset of the business; one that has been built up by a series of marketing *investments* over the years. As with any other asset, this investment can be expected to bring returns over subsequent years. On the other hand, like any other asset, it has to be protected and husbanded.

---

[1] M. Porter, *Competitive Advantage* (Free Press, 1985).

[2] Christian Gronroos, 'From marketing mix to relationship marketing', *Management Decision*, Vol. 32, No. 2, 1994.

This 'asset' is often referred to as the *'customer franchise'*.[3]

At one extreme it may come from an individual relationship developed face to face by the sales professional. At the other it is the cumulative image, held by the consumer, resulting from long exposure to all aspects of the product or service, and especially to a number of advertising and promotional campaigns.

In some markets the customer franchise may be so strong as to be exclusive, in effect giving the supplier a monopoly; even if consumers regularly switch brands, for variety, they may still retain an image of your brand which may tip the balance in their next purchase decision. This image may still have a value upon which the advertiser can build, even if the current purchasing decision goes against it.

The customer franchise is based on an accumulation of impacts over time. Unfortunately, too many marketers – particularly those in creative departments within advertising agencies – signally fail to recognise the importance, and long-term nature, of this *investment*. They treat each new campaign as if it could be taken in isolation, ignoring how it meshes with previous messages to the consumer. The evidence is that the consumer does not view such advertising and promotion in isolation, but instead incorporates it into their existing image – to good or bad effect, depending upon how well the new campaign complements the old.

The consumer franchise is, to all practical intents, the mirror image of the *brand*. The brand is how the producer sees the (internal) investment. The customer franchise is the outcome of that internal investment – the counterbalancing entry with the customers.

The special characteristics of this investment are shown in Figure 13.1.[4]

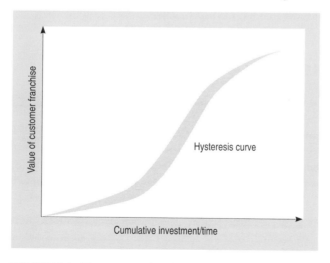

FIGURE 13.1   The customer franchise curve

[3] D. Mercer, *New Marketing Practice*, Penguin, 1997.
[4] D. Mercer, *New Marketing Practice*, Penguin, 1997.

This curve shows how the value of the customer franchise – which is notional – grows slowly at first and then rapidly before it finally saturates (albeit probably after a number of years). It is *indicative* of what happens rather than an exact measure, since it is very difficult to put an exact figure to this value. The most important aspect is that the curve shows '*hysteresis*' – the lagging of an effect behind its cause. After investment is stopped (note that the bottom axis is the cumulative investment over time), the fall in value is at first slow (sales may not show any significant impact), but then drops very rapidly indeed, faster than it rose over the same time intervals. When reinvestment occurs, however, it has to be raised to the higher curve again. The result is that there is a significant gap between the curves. That gap represents the *cost of failing to sustain the investment*. In the short term there is very little penalty, but in the longer term extended periods of no investment prove to be very costly indeed.

Another aspect, of course, is that of defence against a sudden threat to survival. If the threat hits you when you are at the bottom of this cycle, in your weakest position, your chances of recovery are that much reduced. You must aim *always* to be close to your greatest strength, no matter how strong the temptation to milk the position.

In view of my earlier strictures about theory, incorporated in the Critic's Charter, I should emphasise that you should not be fooled by graphical 'accuracy' into thinking that this curve has been measured. It has not as yet and, if it ever were, it would be very difficult indeed to put anything other than notional figures to the customer franchise values at each stage. It is simply intended as a *model* to help you understand the sort of forces at work; it does nicely illustrate the main features of the long investment process, and then the very real costs of failing to maintain that investment – which all too many organisations have experienced in practice.

13.2 THE POWER OF THE BRAND

The power of the brand, which is – as we have seen – the mirror image of the customer franchise, is especially seen in the case of brand leaders. In FMCG markets, for instance, the brand leader often holds 40% or more of the overall market. This level is usually highly profitable: in addition to the value of sales generated, the strong position in the market normally allows the setting of a higher price (and hence significantly higher profit), and economies of scale are possible (not least in terms of promotional and distribution costs).

The profitability that a brand leader commands usually offers, therefore, ample justification – especially over the longer term (where such brands can easily maintain leadership for decades) – for the high levels of investment which are needed to achieve this position. The Japanese corporations, who are willing to make such long-term investments in markets, have been especially well rewarded for their efforts.

More important perhaps, in the context of generic strategies, this is also by far the most powerful position from which to defend against future challenges. If you own the brand leader you have the benefit of 'market inertia', which will allow you some breathing space, the crucial *time* to implement necessary changes, and you still have the cashflow to *fund* the changes you will need to make.

The Rule of 1:2:3

The most stable competitive markets are typically dominated by two or three brands, between them accounting for around 70% of total sales.[5] For maximum stability the ratio of share between these should be the brand leader holding twice the share of the second and three times the share of the third – hence the 1:2:3 rule. In this situation, the brand leader usually has 40% of the overall market, and is correspondingly profitable, justifying the high investment policies needed to achieve this position.[6]

In practice, the exact ratios vary from market to market, and even the average may vary somewhat – depending upon what parcel of products is examined. The Boston Consulting Group agree that the brand leader should hold twice the share of the second brand, but suggest that it should hold four times that of the third brand (giving a rule of 1:2:4!).[7] But the general principle of the Rule of 1:2:3 seems to hold.

You can see that the theory behind branding is particularly important in terms of longer-term survival.

Branding policies

Branding has traditionally been seen as the almost exclusive territory of consumer goods companies, but it has much wider application. *All* organisations, whether they sell to consumers or industrial users, whether they offer products or services, whether they are profit-making or non-profit, have at least one brand, which is usually the name of the organisation. This may come as a surprise, or even as a shock, to those organisations whose focus in life is the product or service they produce, and who think brands are only for goods which appear on supermarket shelves. Nothing could be further from the truth.

There are, though, a number of possible approaches:

Company name – often, especially in the industrial sector, it is just the company's name which is promoted.

Family branding – in this case a very strong brand name (or company name) is made the vehicle for a range of products.

[5] D Mercer, 'A two decade test of product life cycle theory', *British Journal of Management*, Vol. 4, 1993.
[6] D Mercer, 'Death of the product life cycle', *ADMAP,* September 1993.
[7] B. D. Henderson, 'The Rule of Three and Four', The Boston Consulting Group, 1985.

Individual branding – each brand has a separate name, and may even compete against other brands from the same company.

In terms of these existing products, brands may be developed in two ways:

Brand extension – the existing strong brand name can be used as a vehicle for new or modified products. This now appears to be the most prevalent form of development,[8] which is understandable since it maximises the use of the investment in the brand name.[9] Some, including Procter and Gamble (recognised world leaders in the field of branding), now argue that this process has gone too far, diluting the strength of core brands.

Multibrands – alternatively, in a market that is fragmented amongst a number of brands, a supplier can choose to deliberately launch totally new brands in apparent competition with its own existing strong brand(s).[10]

Perhaps the most important fact, and one which is sadly neglected in most organisations, is that the brand is the most important and valuable *investment* that most organisations own. It contains all the value which has been added to the organisation by its investments in service to the customer over the years: image, reputation, loyalty, trust etc. These are assets which are worth far more than the stocks and equipment which feature on most balance sheets. On the few occasions when a brand valuation actually has been added to a balance sheet it has dwarfed everything else.

Yet most organisations still treat their brand(s) as if they were worthless. They gratuitously damage them by constant changes in strategy, by confusing switches in image, by employees offering poor service, etc. If anyone in their organisation vandalised any piece of capital equipment in such a manner they would be instantly disciplined! The most important aspect of the brand, as stated above, is that it must be recognised as the organisation's most important *investment*.

This has two major implications. The first is that, as with any investment, this implies long timescales. The investment in a brand will typically take a number of years to pay dividends. The second is, also like any other investment, the development and use of the investment should be carefully planned; and, most important, it should be zealously safeguarded from damage. Paradoxically, the worst damage is usually inflicted by its owners; by neglect, by cavalier changes in direction (often brought about by marketing departments which want to do something, *anything*, new!), by focusing on short-term solutions, etc.

It is worth repeating: the brand(s) is the organisation's most important investment – and should be viewed as such; if you appreciate its true value it will serve you well.

[8] D. Mercer, 'A two decade test of product life cycle theory', *British Journal of Management*, Vol. 4, 1993.

[9] Byron M. Sharp, 'Managing brand extension', *Journal of Consumer Marketing*, Vol. 10, No. 3, 1993.

[10] C. J. Roberts & G. M. McDonald, 'Alternative naming strategies: family versus individual brand names', *Management Decision*, Vol. 2, No. 6, 1989.

Audit 13.1

What is your (organisation's) customer franchise? How do you measure up against the curve showing hysteresis? Can you claim any of the benefits of the Rule of 1:2:3 – a monopoly for instance? What form does your branding policy take? How are you developing this?

Our own answers might be:

What is your (organisation's) customer franchise? – The OUBS is fortunate in being able to build on the remarkably strong OU franchise, adding its own powerful links to its management students.

How do you measure up against the curve showing hysteresis? – Fortunately, our investment in the brand has been consistent, and accordingly efficient.

Can you claim any of the benefits of the Rule of 1:2:3, a monopoly for instance? – We are, again, very fortunate in being able to use the OU brand, which is not just the brand leader in mass higher education but has possibly the most valuable brand of any in the UK (with more than 95% spontaneous awareness and an image which is arguably the most positive of any brand). On the other hand, the market, which also includes part-time education, is so cut-throat (with many institutions, whose accounting systems are even worse than ours, unintentionally subsidising students) that we are not really able to obtain any monopoly benefits.

What form does your branding policy take? – In general, we are in the business of company branding, with the OU as the company name. The position is complicated, however, by the additional differentiation of the Open University Business School, as a family brand within this. The importance of the links between these was, indeed, indicated by our relatively recent decision to move from just 'Open Business School' to emphasise the OU brand element. It is further complicated by the MBA programme as a sub-element – though this is not so emphasised, since it might add to any confusion. It does, however, indicate that our underlying policy is that of brand extension; which also is our answer to – 'How are you developing this?'

13.3 SEGMENTATION

The problem with using the brand leadership position to help ensure survival is that this is an option open to only a few organisations – those owning such a brand leader in a major market. It is often possible, however, to break the larger markets into smaller segments. These larger markets frequently contain groups of customers with quite different detailed needs and wants; and each of these represents a different '*segment*', with different characteristics in terms of consumers. This process is called 'segmentation' (or sometimes '*target marketing*',[11] because the supplier carefully targets a specific group of customers).

The value of discovering such separate segments, each with rather different characteristics, is that they allow producers to offer products which address the needs of just one segment, and hence are not in direct competition with the *overall* market leaders.

You should note that 'segmentation' in one sense is a *strategy* used by vendors to concentrate, and thus optimise, the use of their resources within an overall market. In another sense, though, it is also that group of *techniques* which are used by these vendors for segmenting the market.

Audit 13.2

What segment(s) does your organisation operate in?

You may find this difficult to answer, since very few organisations understand how important a decision this is. It is not sufficient to put down the 'product categories'. You must decide who are the groups of customers that you serve.

In OUBS we consciously decided (after considerable debate) that, as by far the biggest supplier to the UK market, we would **not** segment the MBA market until the level of competition forced this upon us. That time has not yet arrived, but it is arguable that our 'market' is itself a segment of the overall management education market (and beyond that for the whole of higher education and even for training in general). This means that our UK students tend, on average, to be middle managers in their mid-thirties and mid-family! Indeed, we often sympathise with them as being mid-everything, and this colours their approach to education; they cannot afford the luxury – in terms of time rather than money – of walking away from their career (or their family) for a year. Clearly, the picture is more complex than this – not least there are significant differences between a segment which revolves around local part-time education rather than distance learning. Outside the UK the picture is, of course, different; some of our programmes have included local 'part-time' education (albeit for governments!).

Possible approaches to segmentation

There are several main strategies which may be adopted.

(a) **Single segment** – the simplest response is to concentrate on one segment, and position the product firmly within that segment. This is often the case where limited funds are available. The increasing variety demanded, combined with the new flexible manufacturing methods, has now

[11] Philip Kotler, *Marketing Management* (7th. edn, Prentice Hall, 1991).

extended this to 'customised marketing';[12] so that even some 'mass marketers' can now offer (at least to a degree) individually customised products.

(b) **Multiple segments** – a more complex response is to address several major segments with one brand, or to launch several brands each targeted against different segments.

(c) **Cross-segment** – some, probably most, suppliers resolutely ignore segments and pattern their marketing on other factors.

(d) **Full coverage** (or 'mass marketing') – limited to those organisations (such as ourselves) which can afford the strategy, the intent is to address the whole market.

(f) **Niches** – a specialised, and indeed extreme, version of segmentation is that of creating 'niches', practised especially by some organisations in the retail sector. In this form the 'niche' (the segment) chosen is barely viable for one 'supplier'. The organisation then sets out to capture this segment (and possibly to expand it), confident in the knowledge that no competitor will subsequently be able to follow profitably.

(g) **Countersegmentation** – there is an argument that segmentation may have been taken too far in some areas. The response could, accordingly, be to consolidate several segments.

Segmentation is a time- and resource-consuming process, but the benefits to be derived more than outweigh this. Tony Lunn reports, for example, that 'In all cases marketing men volunteered the information that the benefits more than justified the time and expenditure involved. In some cases the findings were held to have contributed to substantial gains in market share, in others to arresting decline in share in the light of fierce competition'.[13] The latter aspect may be what is important in the current context.

Positioning is a separate technique – albeit one that works most effectively in conjunction with segmentation. The process can also be associated with 'product differentiation', in this case the practical 'positioning' of products or services so that they are recognisably different from their competitors, as measured in terms of their positions on the 'map' of competitive brand positions – against the dimensions which matter to the consumer – and, positively gain a competitive advantage as a result.

There can be some confusion between 'segmentation' and 'positioning', and – as we have seen – the two processes often overlap. The key difference is that segmentation applies to the market, to the customers who are clustered into the 'natural' segments which occur in that market. Positioning relates to the product or service; and to what the supplier can do with these products to best 'position' them against these segments.

[12] Thomas Robertson, 'New developments in marketing: a European perspective', *European Management Journal*, Vol. 12, No. 4, 1994.
[13] A. Lunn, 'Segmenting and constructing markets' in *Consumer Market Research Handbook*, ed. R. Worcester and J. Downham (3rd edn, McGraw-Hill, 1986).

A further complication is that 'positioning' can sometimes be divorced from 'segmentation', in that the supplier can choose dimensions on which to position the brand that are not derived from research – but are of his or her own choosing. Indeed, such positioning can be applied (to differentiate a brand, for instance) even when segmentation is not found to be viable!

Audit 13.3

What, if any, is your organisation's segmentation policy?

As you will have realised, OUBS aims for full coverage (within the distance-taught markets in which it operates); but within this, perhaps (depending upon your definitions), it adopts a differentiated approach – covering the MBA and Certificate/Diploma markets separately (and the corporate programmes separately from individuals).

13.4 PRODUCT (OR SERVICE) POSITIONING

Positioning, we believe, is the single most important activity in the whole of marketing (in both the short- and long-term). Carried out effectively by design, or poorly by default, it determines every other element of marketing; and, ultimately, the chances of long-term survival.

It uses many of the sophisticated techniques applied to segmentation, but in its simple essence it only requires that you decide 'where' you want your product or service to be against the critical dimensions (or variables) which are applied by its market/customers. Most graphically, literally, and easiest to use are 'maps' which show the position(s) against these dimensions. Figure 13.2 shows a positioning map.

If the positioning research is carried out regularly, over time, the map can also show how these positions are changing, especially in terms of the insidious threats (even to survival) developing over the longer term. Tracking changes in position is a very powerful tool of marketing.

Because of its importance, we will repeat the statement from the beginning of this section. Positioning, we believe, *is the single most important activity in the whole of marketing. Carried out effectively by design, or poorly by default, it determines every other element of marketing.*

Audit 13.4

Draw the position your organisation has adopted, against the four main factors governing the market (segment) in which it operates. This will require you to draw two product space diagrams (each showing two factors, and the clusters of customers and competitors). It is unlikely that you will be able to plot these definitively, but even a rough sketch will usually add to your knowledge!

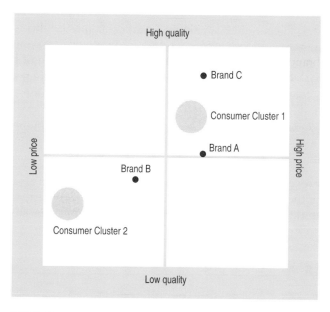

FIGURE 13.2   Positioning map

Advertising investment

In turning your positioning objectives into reality, especially in terms of genuinely robust strategies, what you achieve with your promotional (advertising) messages will be determined by how well they relate to the task of moving from the *existing* positioning to the planned repositioning (or of maintaining the existing one). This is not a simple task, as is indicated by the investment processes illustrated in Figure 13.3.

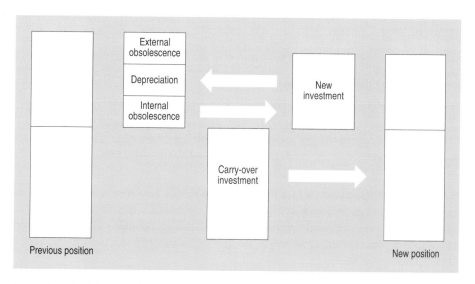

FIGURE 13.3   Advertising investment

The most obvious feature is that of the general decline which the investment in brand position experiences over time. In Figure 13.3 this arises from two main components. One, referred to as '*depreciation*', simply represents the attrition which the brand suffers as customers' attention is distracted by all the other stimuli which continuously inundate them. It also reflects the drift away from optimal positioning, over time as tastes change. The second, '*external obsolescence*', reflects the attrition caused by the activities of competitors. Their promotion will reshape the market, so that your own brand's positioning again drifts away from the optimum.

The chart shows one further element, '*internal obsolescence*'. This is a polite description for the self-inflicted wounds, often caused by overly-anxious creative departments, where the brand positioning is actively moved away from the optimum position by new advertising!

Audit 13.5

Once more, it is very unlikely that you will have detailed data needed to make any of these calculations. Even so, try the process with some rule of thumb figures. You may be surprised, and disturbed, by what you find. Very few organisations understand, let alone allow for, this sort of investment!

13.5 CUSTOMER BEHAVIOUR

Investment in opinion leaders

In the context of *investment* in relationships with customers, it is often argued that, especially in the case of a new product, the effect of any promotion may occur in two stages. The promotion itself (usually advertising) persuades the more adventurous opinion *leaders* in the population to try the product or service. These opinion leaders then carry the message to those who are less exposed to it; and in the mass markets this often means to those who may be less exposed to the mass media.

This is not the same as the *trickle-down theory*, much favoured in certain parts of the social sciences, which assumes that patterns of consumption are led by the upper classes and then 'trickle down' to the lower classes. It is important to note that 'opinion leaders' influence members of their own class – 'horizontally', in terms of class groupings.

It is clear that the impact of any investment in media advertising may be much more complex than many practitioners allow for. Much advertising theory concentrates upon the 'direct' receipt of these 'indirect' communications; it assumes that the consumer receives the message directly from the media, and only from the media.

In practice, the message may well be received by word of mouth from a contact (who may have seen the advertising – or may, in turn, have received it from someone else). Equally, even if the consumer had previously seen the advertising, word of mouth comments may reinforce (or undermine) what this has achieved directly. So we shall now revisit the traditional models of buying behaviour, to see how they may perform in the context of long-range marketing.

Models of purchase behaviour

This brings us to a review of what we know about customer behaviour. To know literally everything about your customers would require such vast volumes of information that you would never be able to make practical use of it – or even find the few facts relevant to any specific situation. In the more traditional forms of marketing the search is narrowed down to those facts which are of most direct use, by using models (theories) which map just the *purchase* process. This approach focuses on the aspect of the customer's life which is of particular interest to the marketer. There are a range of alternative models, such as that often quoted in management textbooks by Howard and Sheth.[14] We believe the most generally useful is the AIUAPR model, widely used by marketers and which most directly links to the steps in the marketing/ promotional process. The components of the model are illustrated in Figure 13.4, and explained below.

Awareness – before anything else can happen the potential customers must become aware that the product or service exists. Thus, the first task must be to gain the attention of the target audience. All the different models are agreed on this first step. If the audience never hears the message they will not act on it, no matter how powerful it is.

Interest – it is not sufficient just to grab their attention. The message must *interest* them and persuade them that the product or service is relevant to their needs. The content of the message(s) must therefore be meaningful and clearly relevant to that target audience's needs, and this is where *marketing research* can come into its own.

Understanding – once an interest is established, the prospective customer must be able to *appreciate* how well the offering may meet his or her needs, again as revealed by the marketing research. This may be no mean achievement where the copywriter has just fifty words, or ten seconds, to convey everything there is to say about it.

Attitudes – the message must go even further: to persuade the reader to adopt a sufficiently positive attitude towards the product or service that he or she will purchase it, albeit as a trial. There is no adequate way of describing how this may be achieved. It is simply down to the *magic of the copywriter's art,* based on the strength of the product or service itself.

---

[14] J. A. Howard and J. N. Sheth, *The Theory of Buyer Behaviour* (Wiley, 1969).

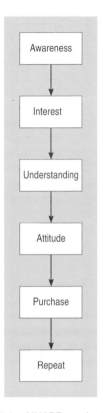

FIGURE 13.4   AIUAPR purchasing model

Purchase – all the above stages might happen in a few minutes while the reader is considering the advertisement, in the comfort of his or her favourite armchair. The final *buying decision*, on the other hand, may take place some time later, perhaps weeks later, when the prospective buyer actually tries to find a shop which stocks the product.

Repeat purchase – in most cases this first purchase is best viewed as just a trial. Only if the experience is a success for the customer will it be turned into repeat purchases. These repeats, not the single purchase which is the focus of most models, are where the vendors' focus should be, for these are where the profits are generated. The earlier stages are merely a very necessary *prerequisite* for this!

This is a very simple model, and as such does apply quite generally, in the shorter term. Its lessons are that you cannot obtain repeat purchasing without going through the stages of building awareness and then obtaining trial use, which has to be successful. It is a pattern which applies to all *repeat purchase* products and services, industrial goods just as much as baked beans.

Unfortunately, especially in terms of long-range marketing, this simple theory is rarely taken any further – to look at the series of transactions which such repeat purchasing implies. The consumer's growing experience over a number of such transactions is often the determining factor in the later – and *future* –

purchases. All the succeeding transactions are, thus, *interdependent* – and the overall decision-making process may accordingly be much more complex than most models allow for. Investment in this longer-term aspect is usually ignored.

Enhanced AIUAPR

Accordingly, in the much longer timescales over which long-range marketing operates, we will need to complicate matters! But, fortunately, the additional complexity has a logic to it. In the single dimension which the original model inhabits there is, from 'top' to 'bottom', a growing involvement of the customer with the product or service. The 'enhanced AIUAPR model',[15] illustrated in Figure 13.5, takes this and adds a further dimension which makes explicit on one side the attempts by the *vendor* to influence this process – which were implicit in the original model. It shows, however, the way in which the vendor's involvement changes from the most impactful *advertising* at the start of the process to the highest quality support at the end – a progression which is not fully described in less complex models, but which is now characteristic of the mature markets in which most organisations operate.

On the other side, though, it also shows the involvement of the *customer* with his or her peers whose influence is not even hinted at in the original version.

Despite our interest in the longer term, the starting point is earlier than in the original model.

Susceptibility – even before you can build awareness, the consumer's mind has to have been opened up to the concept behind the product or service. This acceptance of a new need may have emerged from the workings of the *opinion leaders* in the consumer's peer group. On the other hand, this is also the stage where the new supplier has to accept some form of market (or segment) building role; often making use of public relations as much as advertising. For the 'sitting tenant', this is especially good news. He or she has a breathing space while the new supplier is forced to build this 'susceptibility', and can use that time to develop their own response(s) which will be introduced later to safeguard their brand.

It should be noted, however, that the seemingly distinct steps often, indeed usually, overlap. Thus, some sections of the population – the opinion leaders say – could be well into the repeat purchasing stage while other sections are only just beginning to perceive the need. Accordingly, promotion and advertising often will have to meet the requirements of a number of stages at the same time – a complex demand which is one reason why very successful advertising campaigns are so rare!

Awareness – you have already seen how this works in the original model; though the role of high impact advertising (or prospecting in industrial markets) was there implicit rather than being a formal part of the model. The main difference is that research shows that the stimulus is likely to come from an *opinion leader* in the peer group. These offer a hidden, and potentially very

---

[15] D. Mercer, *New Marketing Practice*, Penguin, 1997.

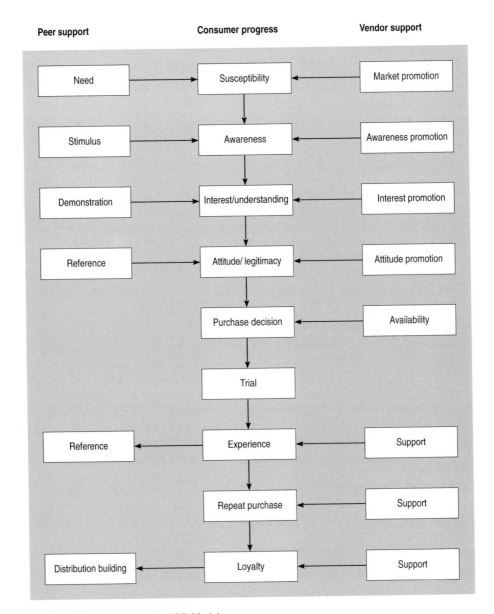

FIGURE 13.5   Enhanced AIUAPR Model

powerful, 'sales force' on behalf of the product or service, albeit that they in turn have necessarily been recruited by advertising (or by public relations activities – often a neglected medium, which is especially important in reaching this group).

Interest/understanding – these two are coupled together, since it is difficult to conceive of one happening without the other being at least in part also involved; though they may offer very different challenges to the advertiser. Again, however, it is members of the peer group, already users, who may be most likely to be able to proffer the '*demonstration*' of the product (or the results of the service) to the prospective consumer. This is, of course, a stage in which the existing brand leader – if it responds effectively and promptly – may still hold an almost unassailable position.

Attitude/legitimacy – although one further stage is added, that of 'legitimacy' (persuading the prospective purchaser that, backed by his or her favourable attitudes, a purchase may be justified), this is merged with the attitude-building process. Both depend on the 'reference' support from members of the peer group who are already loyal users as much as on traditional advertising. Again, the brand leader is in a very strong position.

Purchase decision – this should be, by this stage of the process, almost automatic; and, for once, the consumer is probably alone in making this particular decision. A key element, also featured in the original model but often (wrongly) taken for granted, is that the product or service must be easily *available* for the consumer to achieve that purchase.

Experience – one stage ignored by the original model is that which happens when the consumer tries the product or service for the first time. This may, or may not, be a favourable experience; but whichever end of the spectrum it lies it still represents a major discontinuity in the model. At this point the nature of the accompanying processes changes. In the case of the vendor's promotional activities the emphasis switches abruptly from recruitment to support (perhaps still involving advertising, but mainly by conventional support services). This is perhaps best illustrated by the switch from new account selling before to account management afterwards, in face-to-face selling. At the same time the consumer switches from being a recipient of advice to one who can, from experience, give it to his or her peer group. This is hopefully of a positive nature, since a bad experience is typically reported to many more peers than a good one!

In the context of long-range marketing, this has two key implications. The first is that the existing brand leader must be rapidly made at least as attractive as its new challengers. Less obvious, but probably more important, it should not have previously developed any history of disappointing its customers with failures. Customers are generally remarkably loyal, but if you fail them – in whatever way – they become vulnerable to predation by your competitors.

Repeat purchase – in this development of the original model this becomes almost a technicality.

Loyalty – more important – much more important, as we have seen, in the context of the genuinely robust strategies demanded by long-range marketing – is the final step, that of creating a loyal user based upon successive positive experiences and backed by sound customer support. These loyal users become, in turn, the 'references' for new users (or even the 'opinion leaders' who feature so strongly in this enhanced model).

The three pillars of the purchasing process

Having made the model necessarily complex – to explain the underlying processes – we will now offer a much more practical, condensed version of this, as shown in Figure 13.6.

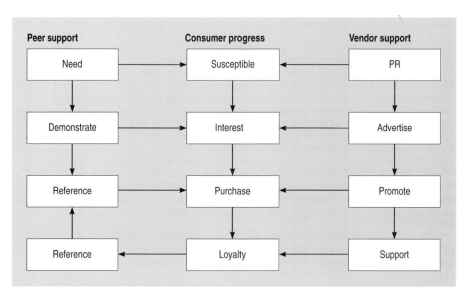

FIGURE 13.6   The three pillars of the purchasing process

This embodies, in a simpler form, most of the essentials of the process. Thus, the central pillar (the consumer's progress) highlights the tentative nature of the first stages, as the consumer moves from 'susceptibility' to the actual 'purchase'; and then the no less important subsequent stages as confidence builds into the *loyalty* we are seeking.

The break point, at the time of the first (trial) purchase, is reflected in the vendor's pillar by the switch from promotion to support (though this aspect is rarely emphasised in theory). It is even more obvious in the 'peer' pillar in the switch from 'taker' (of advice) before first purchase to 'giver' (as a loyal referee) after purchase.

Audit 13.6

Compare your organisation's current view of its relationships with its customers with that which would emerge if you used the 'three pillars'. Again, this will be bound to be approximate, but – again – it should be enlightening.

The peer pyramid

Whilst the three pillars model is especially useful in providing a framework which most effectively shows the new consumer's progress over time, it does not really do full justice to the richness of the interaction of the individual consumer with the whole community – not just the direct peer group – and the 'inertia' which this may lead to. Added to this is the wealth of (personal and community) experience built up over time, which multiplies the problems of access by the marketer – and often slows down the rate of structural change so that it occurs over the decades measured by the sociologist rather than the months in the marketer's plan. Our research shows that the great majority (more than 80%) of marketers recognise the importance of long-term relationships with customers. The model which best demonstrates this complementary aspect is that of the '*peer pyramid*', illustrated in Figure 13.7.[16]

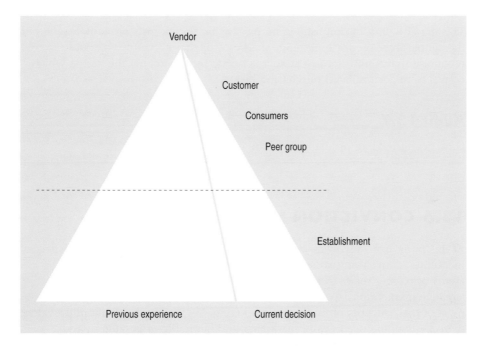

FIGURE 13.7   The peer pyramid

The pyramid represents the *customer* as being at the apex of a layered set of influences. Not least amongst these are the *consumers*: the family for consumer goods and services, and the users in an organisation. Their views are frequently decisive – perhaps, over the longer term, even more so than those of the direct buyer. But beyond them, and beyond the *peer group* which was so influential in the 'pillars' model, are the whole range of *establishment* forces, which regulate what may happen, as do a range of government bodies, or which control the processes of communication, as do the various media. It is

[16] D. Mercer, *New Marketing Practice*, Penguin, 1997.

these longer-term 'structures' in society which marketers fail to see (though, as already suggested, sociologists do track the slow movements of these over decades). This conservatism will, if correctly managed, also allow a brand leader some breathing space to regroup.

The drag of history

The vertical/diagonal split in the diagram is important. The large part to the left represents the great body of past experience that the customers, along with all those involved in the various layers of the pyramid, have already built up by the time they come to the current decision. The *current* portion on the right may indeed be at the forefront of the customer's mind – but need not necessarily outweigh that body of *previous* experience (despite the fervent hopes of the vendor – and the lack of reference to such past experience by most marketing theory). Again, all of this is – if correctly handled – of immense advantage to a defending brand leader.

This may be unduly simplistic in terms of what sociologists are looking for, but the simple message for long-range marketers is that all vendors should recognise that significant investment is needed to overcome the inertia which comes from accumulated purchasing history.

Audit 13.7 _____

How does the 'drag of history' operate on your organisation?

13.6 CONVICTION MARKETING

At this point may we divert into an important – but little recognised – aspect of marketing: conviction marketing, sometimes called *commitment marketing*; Henry Minzberg refers to it as 'ideological strategy' and Philip Kotler as 'creative marketing'.[17,18] Whatever its name, it is, in many respects, alien to most of the concepts of traditional marketing. Yet it is probably more prevalent than the genuine use of *pure* marketing and, arguably, it is often more successful. It is especially important – as both a source of great strength and weakness – in long-range marketing.

It has a long and chequered history. The propaganda machines developed by the Nazis offered some of the most potent, and widely deplored, demonstrations of its power (and this represents one possible reason why discussion of this style of marketing is even now generally avoided). The religious 'marketing machines' had been even more effective in earlier

---

[17] H. Minzberg and J. H. Waters, 'Of strategies deliberate and emergent', *Strategic Management Journal*, Vol. 6, 1988.

[18] P. Kotler, 'Reconceptualising marketing: an interview with Philip Kotler', *European Management Journal*, Vol. 12, No. 4, 1994.

generations (and can even now be very powerful, as is evidenced by the case of Islamic fundamentalism). In the commercial sector, though, its use has sometimes been just as powerful – and very productive! Indeed, the majority of the few truly global brands have embodied it to some degree: IBM, with its philosophy of 'Customer Service'; McDonald's, with QSC & V; Coca Cola, with its embodiment of the American teenage dream; Marlboro, and the wide open spaces of the frontier!

The power-house of 'conviction marketing' is the *idea* (the 'conviction' to which the organisation has made its 'commitment') to which – the organisation *believes* – the consumers are also committed (despite any evidence to the contrary!) or need (for their own good!). Despite the focus on the consumer, and frequent reference to the importance of that consumer, the real organisational commitment is to the overarching idea (or set of ideas, often a 'lifestyle'). The essence of, and the strength of, such 'conviction marketing' is the power it gives to the marketing organisation – to 'evangelise', where religious as well as political parallels are often more relevant than those of conventional marketing theory.

Conviction marketing's focus is *one-sided*. There is little or no attempt to use market research to find out what the consumers need or want, though research is sometimes used to justify the organisation's existing prejudices – and is frequently used, to great effect, to optimise the presentation of its chosen message.

This power of conviction marketing derives from a number of factors, as shown in Figure 13.8.[19]

The concept being marketed must be *distinctive*. Successful conviction marketing is not the province of the marketer who is dedicated to pallid incrementalism. It has to be readily identifiable, as Coca Cola was – in terms of the very powerful image of the bottle, if not necessarily the product contained. Beyond that, however, it has to be based on an *identity, a brand personality*. The beneficiaries of conviction marketing are typically not products where technical features are predominant. Coca Cola and Marlboro are a matter of personal taste, but it is the images associated with them, their brand persona, which add the necessary richness to the relatively mundane. Even in the case of IBM it was the marketing and support (rather than the very complex technology) which was its outstanding feature. Richness and depth seem necessary (at least in the most successful examples), to give an almost human identity. In any case, a long-established brand leader will, almost by default, have developed a rich persona.

Despite the richness of the concept it has to be instantly communicable, which demands that it be *clear*, and preferably *simple*. It has to be conveyed by simple messages, such as the shape of the bottle (or now the graphics on the can) of Coca Cola, or the cowboy and Marlboro. Where the product is complex, and none could be more complex than that of IBM, it has to be

---

[19] Michael R. Czinkota, Massaki Kotabe and David Mercer, *Marketing Management* (Blackwell Inc., 1997).

enshrined in an associated philosophy, 'Customer Service' (which used to be personified by the field personnel in the now rather outdated, but then very necessary, dark suits and white shirts). It is frequently associated with a distinctive form of quality; McDonald's' 'Hamburger University', for example. In the case of long-established brands, this communication is perhaps less important – where the long-term effects of previous communications will have reserved its place in people's consciousness.

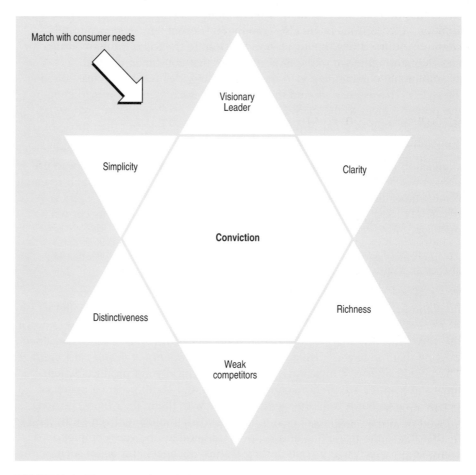

FIGURE 13.8   The powers of conviction marketing

Conviction marketing is, above all, dependent upon the consumers' belief in what its communicators say. Being somewhat unrelated to basic needs, the '*vision*' of the 'product' (of its identity) has to be conveyed to the target audience. They, in turn, have to enter into a '*belief*' in the 'product' before they can fully appreciate it. This means that the message being communicated has to be believed; and that in turn means that the communicators themselves need to believed. In some cases the 'communicators' can be those of conventional marketing; the Marlboro cowboy in the advertising, or the bright clean image of McDonald's' outlets. But behind them there is often a human face. In IBM it was the sales force, immensely capable and imbued with (many would argue indoctrinated in) the IBM culture; and which of their customers could resist such evangelists? But, above all, it usually requires a strong (and almost obsessively dedicated) human personality at the centre, to make the vision work; the Watsons at IBM and Ray Kroc at McDonald's developed very rich cultures which were aimed more at their own employees (the 'communicators' the public see) rather than at their markets.

There is one element of conviction marketing which is beyond the control of the organisation itself, and that is what its *competitors* choose to do. Almost by definition, a 'conviction marketed' brand will develop a new segment of the market. Its unique identity will, at least for a time, give it a monopoly there. Eventually, though, competitors will recognise the success of the brand; and will want some of the action.

Separation by conviction

Fortunately, it is usually the case that competitors can be mesmerised into accepting the dominance of the leading brand. It is a peculiarity of conviction marketing that the almost hypnotic effect of the message also seems to infect competitors. They usually attempt, with only marginal success, to copy the original. Inevitably, the copies turn out to be pale imitations: Burger King could not match the evangelical dedication to standards of McDonald's; Pepsi, for many decades, had to follow Coca Cola. The competitors usually have to wait, therefore, for the leader to make a mistake, or for the market to change; Pepsi was eventually rewarded when the market did change, and Coca Cola made a very public mistake with its change in recipe! Compaq similarly capitalised on both the changes in the PC market and IBM's uncharacteristically unsure handling of its own responses. The earlier comment about the danger of *failing* customers is especially important here. It is only during such a period of failure, when customers are vulnerable, that a conviction brand leader can be under real threat.

Although *customer needs* are at the heart of conventional marketing, they are only an 'enabling' factor in conviction marketing. If the 'vision' is too far removed from the consumer's view of reality, it will not be accepted. Even so, Clive Sinclair's C5 electric/pedal-power car (eventually, derisively, called the 'electric clog') was initially accepted with praise by the media, based on his own charismatic image and obvious commitment to it; and it took nearly three months for commentators to admit that the idea was in reality laughable. The resultant shock to believability, on the other hand, probably brought down the remainder of his business empire (which was unconnected to the C5, and more soundly based)! There have been other spectacular mismatches to reality: IBM's PC Junior, Ford's Edsel. These are, however, the recorded exceptions; for most mismatches fail at the 'new product' stage – and disappear along with the 90% of such new products which do not achieve acceptance.

Conviction marketed products can be broadly divided into two groups:

PRODUCT BASED <> VALUE BASED

The former are products, or services – frequently in the high technology field – whose creator has a blinding faith in what product or service features are needed. Steve Jobs, at Apple, believed in the special technology of his products (even after IBM set new standards – and John Sculley had to be recruited from Pepsi, to inject more conventional marketing expertise); Alan Sugar believed in his personal ability to put together low-priced electronics packages. The problem with conviction marketed products in this category is that they can be very rapidly overtaken by changes in the market; typically, new technology supersedes them (as the Commodore Pet, one of the original PCs, was displaced from the business market by Apple, which in turn was superseded – as brand leader – by IBM), or tastes change (as Woolworth found out when its traditional place on the High Street was undermined).

Conviction value

As already indicated, the strongest 'conviction marketed' brands are those in very general markets where the distinctiveness comes from the image – from the intangible values associated with the brand. This is perhaps the most positive approach of all, in terms of (generic) robust strategies which invest in the relationship with the customer.

These brands are usually much more capable of change, since the identity is not usually locked into 'physical' features. The customers (and the organisation's own employees) can easily accommodate the new features needed to accommodate developments in technology and taste. IBM's 'Customer Service' carried it through decades of revolutionary change, and Disneyland is constantly absorbing new rides – but still keeping them immaculately clean! Even McDonald's, which should perhaps be one of the most product-based of retailers, is in reality based on conviction marketing of values: QSC & V (Quality, Service, Cleanliness & Value). It has managed to change what it serves (adding a breakfast menu – and lines based on chicken and fish, as well as pizza) and how it serves (increasing the size of its 'sit down' sections – so that it has become a restaurant rather than just a take-away outlet).

The challenge for all of us committed to the wisdom of the 'outside-in' viewpoint, and especially for less charismatic marketers, is to understand to what extent the success of 'conviction marketing' undermines *traditional* marketing theory. This is a question mark which implicitly hung over much of marketing theory through the 1980s; and, in particular, drove practitioners and academics alike to look for alternative approaches – such as competitive advantage. The reality is that *most* products and services (at least in terms of numbers of lines, if not of value of sales) are managed without reference to the principles of marketing; and have been throughout history. The difference is that 'conviction marketers' have very successfully extended this common 'inside-out' approach by adopting some of the tools of marketing. Indeed, the conviction marketers probably make greater use of marketing tools (albeit to somewhat perverted ends) than do many of those who would pay lip-service to traditional marketing. Philip Morris, which owns the Marlboro cigarette brand, also owns the Miller Brewing Company of Milwaukee. In applying the same sort of charismatic (and 'macho') image to 'Miller High Life' they used extensive market research to fine tune the positioning. More important, the company continued to be aware of the demands of its market-place, and subsequently launched the highly successful 'Miller-Lite' (low calorie beer) as a 'less filling' beer which fitted this image.

At the end of the day, the basic justification for *conventional marketing*, in the absence of the blinding (and hopefully viable) vision of the conviction marketer, is simply that it is generally the most successful approach to product or service management in the shorter term. Giving the customer what he or she wants rarely fails! It does, though, mean that they must take the development of robust strategies, for the longer term, that much more seriously.

As already stated, what often makes the task easier for conviction marketers is that their competitors seem even more mesmerised than their customers. Many organisations are '*dedicated followers*'; they always look to their competitors to take the lead. Their adherence to this creed goes beyond that required of 'followers', the subsidiary brands in a market which are simply not in any position to set the pace. It goes beyond the IBM approach of '*constructive following*', where that organisation (in its days of market dominance) deliberately let other, smaller, organisations explore (and take the risks inherent in) new developments – only to recapture the initiative (by deploying the vast resources at its command) when the markets prove viable. This strategy usually proves successful (if potentially risking loss of leadership, as IBM eventually found out when it lost its lead in the PC market to Compaq).

'Dedicated followers', though, assume that the market leader *always* knows best. So that even IBM's mistakes were ascribed to covert machinations, which must have some ultimate value, and these too were copied! 'Dedicated followers' represent a terminal case of myopia. They are organisations which, in effect, sub-contract their policy making to their competitors; something you would hardly want to do if you take long-range marketing seriously! As such, they deserve to, and usually do, pay the ultimate price. In terms of long-range marketing, this is yet another advantage which the leaders can claim – and the followers must overcome.

Looking to the *dangers*, though, the main problem facing conviction marketers is that the necessary strength of their commitment may blind them to the realities facing them and their customers. It is difficult enough for any marketer to adopt the unbiased perspective essential to understanding the customer's needs and wants. It may be impossible for a conviction marketer, whose 'vision' may be so powerful that it precludes any doubts about the 'product'. The *Concorde* airliner development team were convinced of the market for their 'baby'; and their market research supported that view – it was only the market which disagreed. Even IBM can fall foul of this problem, as it did with its personal computers; when its immensely strong corporate 'vision' got in the way of any meaningful recognition of the scale of the problem posed by its wayward dealers.

Audit 13.8

A simple question, but often a very enlightening one: is your organisation dominated by conviction marketing (either with the agenda set by yourselves or by the market leader)?

Catastrophe theory

This is derived from science and technology; but it is very applicable to long-range marketing in general, and to conviction marketing in particular.[20] In a very simplified form (for it is the idea, not the detail, which is important) it states that some systems can be 'over-stressed', so that they will support loads beyond the point at which other systems would obviously start to deteriorate. When they pass the point of no return, however, their performance degrades and they fail *suddenly and catastrophically*. This contrasts with most other systems where the fail point may be reached much more quickly, but the subsequent degradation in performance is much more gradual and, hence, predictable and controllable (allowing, perhaps, for the possibility of recovery).

Catastrophe theory is conventionally shown as a three-dimensional surface, but it is easier to see the main features in a two-dimensional illustration, as in Figure 13.9.

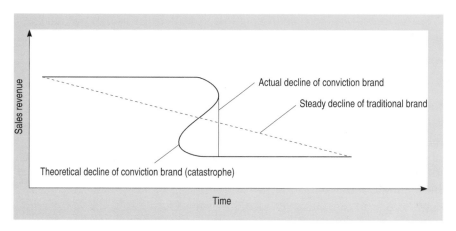

FIGURE 13.9   Impact of catastrophe

This is an example specific to marketing, but it is the most typical one in this field. Above, the thinner line illustrates the traditional decline, say of a brand. Following (unspecified) changed circumstances, the position (typically relative brand share of the brand leader) declines gently until it reaches its new, lower equilibrium. This gentle change allows the brand owner to adjust the business to these new circumstances; and may even allow the brand to be restored to its

[20] W. E. Halal and R. A. Lasken, 'Management applications of catastrophe theory', *Business Horizons*, December 1980.

original leadership. The value of 'generic' robust strategies is based upon the assumption that any pattern of decline will be gentle, so that there will be *time* to recover. But the thicker line shows the path followed by the conviction-marketed brand; or by a brand which has, by default, assumed some of the same characteristics as a result of a long history of successfully meeting customer needs. This line is maintained at the higher level far beyond the point where a traditional brand would have been well into decline – allowing a greater recovery of funds (and possibly even allowing it to override a short-lived challenge). When the line does begin to dip, however, it does so very steeply indeed (and in theory doubles back on itself – though, as this is physically not possible, the 'actual' line follows the vertical dotted path). The problem this poses for the brand owner is the suddenness of the change. There is no time for adjustments to be made, and certainly none to allow any recovery plan to work – and the business as a whole may be destroyed by the shock.

This phenomenon is characteristic of conviction marketing. The conviction marketer often goes further than the steady state shown above, and persuades the customer (and the competitors) to defy the laws of 'marketing gravity' and slowly pushes them uphill! Often this is a process of *incrementalism*; making many, gradual changes – which are not individually noticed by the customers. This results in them achieving market positions, often of dominance, which are apparently unassailable – since their competitors cannot match this miraculous performance. IBM in some respects achieved this feat before the introduction of the PC brought about the start of its own catastrophe phase. 'Salami slicing' (gradual reduction) of quality is a way of doing this which may, in the short (and even medium) term, produce high profits: but contains the seeds of its own catastrophic demise.

The problem is that, once past the point of no return (which is frequently triggered by an apparently trivial change in circumstances), the position can be destroyed, by simply being forced, almost overnight, to obey the normal rules of the game (plummeting, as in Figure 13.9, to the bottom line).

This phenomenon has been most notable in the financial futures markets (the October 1987 crash, for instance), or in political circles (even Communism in Eastern Europe suffered this fate in 1989). In a less dramatic manner it might also be seen at work in those national industries (such as the UK motorcycle industry) virtually destroyed by Japanese competition; or the coal industry which we looked at earlier.

Needless to say, in the context of robust strategies, it is one feature which you must anticipate!

There are a number of sound management strategies, already in existence, which can usually have robust outcomes in the longer term as well as producing optimal performance in the shorter term. The most powerful of these are, perhaps, those which invest in the relationships with customers; established via the customer franchise and encapsulated in branding (and the related investment in advertising), at one extreme, and in face-to-face relationships at the other. Both of these demand new models of customer behaviour (such as the 'three pillars') which fully allow for the (investment) developments over time. Almost by default, however, conviction marketing may be the most prevalent form – which is uniquely powerful, up to the point where a catastrophic failure destroys it.

Now, though, let us move, from the longer-term to the shorter- to examine what we can productively do now!

14 SHORT-TERM ACTIONS ON LONG-TERM ISSUES

So far we have looked, in some detail, at the processes involved in long-range *planning*, and at the long-range investments which can underpin them. There are, however, a number of theories and techniques which operate in the *shorter term* but which also have significant impact on longer-term outcomes. Most of these, which we will examine in the next section, are best thought of as routinely applied processes which '*steer*' the organisation towards that long-term future. In many respects the best analogy is that of travelling on an airliner, where long-range planning sets the flight plan needed to take you to your ultimate destination. During the flight, however, the auto-pilot (the short-term processes) intervenes regularly to bring the aircraft back on to the correct heading.

To set the context, we will start with one traditional set of processes which can give very dubious results!

14.1 LESSONS OF THE PRODUCT LIFE-CYCLE

The classical concept which is used to represent the longest-term position of an organisation's offerings is the product life-cycle. It should be noted, though, that 'long-term' in this context is rarely more than three years ahead! Indeed, every product or service must, almost by definition, have such a life cycle. It is launched, it grows, then it dies. As such, it offers a useful 'model' to keep at the back of your mind.

The most important aspect of product life-cycles is *that to all practical intents and purposes – in terms of marketing planning – they often do not exist!* In most markets the majority of the dominant brands have held their position for at least two decades.[1] The dominant product life-cycle, that of the brand leaders which almost monopolise many markets, is therefore one of *continuity!*[2]

In the most respected criticism of the product life-cycle, Dhalla and Yuspeh state:

> ... clearly, the PLC [product life cycle] is a dependent variable which is determined by market actions; it is not an independent variable to which companies should adapt their marketing programs. Marketing management itself can alter the shape and duration of a brand's life cycle.[3]

---

[1] D. Mercer, 'A two decade test of product life cycle theory', *British Journal of Management*, Vol. 4, 1993.

[2] D. Mercer, 'Intimations of immortality: death of the product life cycle', *ADMAP*, September, 1993. As a result, the whole of product life-cycle theory is so fatally flawed as to be useless for most marketers – especially in the short term, but even in the longer term!

[3] K. N. Dhalla and S. Yuspeh, 'Forget the product life cycle concept', *Harvard Business Review*, January–February 1976.

Thus, the life cycle may be useful as a description, but not as a predictor; and usually should be firmly under the control of the marketer! The important point is that in many, if not most, markets the product or brand life cycle is significantly longer than the planning cycle of the organisations involved. It thus offers little of *practical* value for most marketers. Even if the product life-cycle exists for them, their plans will be based just upon that piece of the curve where they currently reside (most probably in the 'mature' stage); and their view of that part of it will almost certainly be 'linear', and will not encompass the whole range from growth to decline.

We mention the product life-cycle only to warn you that we think that it has little value in practice. Indeed, we believe that its use may be positively *dangerous* for many organisations, since it tempts managers of successful, mature brands to prematurely anticipate their move into decline. But it is probably the most widely known, and taught and respected, piece of marketing theory! It is imperative, therefore, that you appreciate the problems that its use, in any form, might pose.

How, then, might you manage change?

We believe that handling the less dramatic changes which *regularly* occur in stable markets, which is the type of market in which most organisations operate, demands a very different solution. The technique which has been developed for this, for the regular 'steering' adjustments which need to be made to help the brand on its path towards its long-term goals, is called the 'competitive saw' (so-called because of its appearance when expressed diagrammatically, as in Figure 14.1).[4]

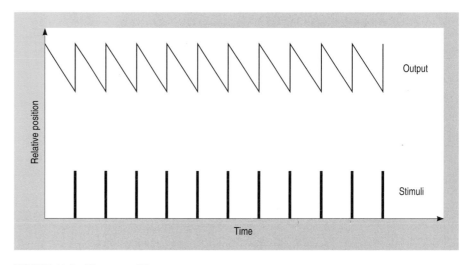

FIGURE 14.1   The competitive saw

---

[4] D. Mercer, 'Intimations of immortality: death of the product life cycle', *ADMAP,* September, 1993.

14.2 THE COMPETITIVE SAW

The principles involved are very simple, as is indicated in Figure 14.1. The first is quite simply that every 'stimulus' (every investment, be it an advertising or promotional campaign or a new feature added to the 'product') results, after a short delay, in a rapid improvement in the product or service's position, returning the brand to the path needed to achieve long-term goals just as much as optimising short-term performance. This advantage is then diluted as competitors invest in their own activities, and the performance level (the competitive advantage or sales) slowly drops until the next stimulus is applied. The measurements in the saw diagram are generally of market share rather than sales levels, both to focus on the competitive situation and to minimise variations due to seasonality, etc.

This is a very simplified model of what actually happens, though something approaching it can be observed in practice (which is not the case with the product life-cycle) and it offers the benefits explained below.

Intimations of mortality. It very effectively replaces the one important function of the product life-cycle, that of reminding managers that there will be no future if they do not look after their brands, and continue to invest in them. It does this more directly, and without the drawbacks of the other model. Where a constant reminder is needed, that long-term survival is by no means automatic, this is an important role.

Timescaling. On much the same theme, it is an ever-present reminder that you cannot neglect your brands, or stop investing in them for too long. We have already seen the problems this may cause, not least in rendering a brand vulnerable to attack.

Linkage of inputs and outputs. It encourages, and provides a framework for, managers to actively plan what inputs are needed, when and what the outputs will be – and what the efficiency of conversion of inputs to outputs is – so that the best possible 'steering' may be achieved.

Surfacing of investment. It makes very clear the need for, and the results of, long-term investment policies on brands. This is even more clear in the 'stepped saw', in Figure 14.2.

This looks at the effect of *major* inputs, such as new products or significantly increased promotional spending. These may have the effect of raising the average level of the 'saw teeth', though, as shown above, later neglect (or a comparably strong competitive response) can just as easily result in a step down to a lower average level, as seen in Figure 14.3.

As Figure 14.3 shows, there are two elements to performance. One is the *average* level, averaged over a number of short-term stimulus/response cycles. This is strategically most important since it shows longer-term trends (a slowly decreasing average might be hidden by the variations in the saw).

The other is the short-run pattern, the individual stimulus/response cycles of the saw itself, which determines the tactical approach.

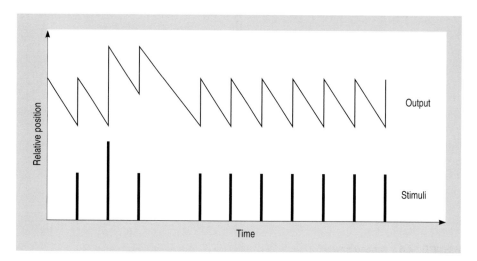

FIGURE 14.2   The stepped saw

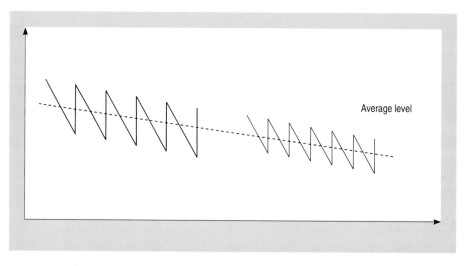

FIGURE 14.3   Average performance in the saw

The saw should not lull you into expecting regularity. Different stimuli will have different impacts, and will be more or less efficient, so the saw can be a jagged one, as in Figure 14.4.

As the saw is primarily an illustration of the impact of short-term investments, the main criterion will be which of the stimuli available will result in the most efficient investment pattern (e.g. whether advertising or new features will have the greatest impact for the same amount of money), though a mix of stimuli will usually produce the highest efficiency overall.

The three main lessons of the competitive saw are the importance of relative performance, the time-related nature of this, and the investments which underlie performance.

FIGURE 14.4   Jagged saw

14.3 ADVERTISING INVESTMENT

We have already looked at this in the longer term, but it can be seen to have a shorter-term component. Traditionally advertising and promotion have been treated as current costs, with an immediate but short-term effect. Although this view probably is justified in terms of most forms of *sales promotion,* it seriously distorts some important aspects of *advertising* and *PR.* A more useful view in this context is that almost any *advertising should be treated as a fixed asset.*[5]

Adopting such a long-term perspective has a number of important implications. The first of these revolves around the patterns of performance which might be expected. The basic pattern is not that of the short-run supply and demand curve, but that of the *longer-term competitive saw.*

Following the principle of the fixed asset, the sawtooth maintenance pattern can be overlaid on a gradually declining trend in performance, notionally equivalent to *depreciation* in financial accounting. Thus, over time there may be a slow drift away from the ideal position – as the customers' needs and wants change and/or competitors' positioning improves. Your own response to this may take two forms. The first, and perhaps the most effective, is *dynamic repositioning* – change in relative positions should be regularly tracked and the brand's position readjusted (steered) to take account of this. The emphasis here is on the dynamic approach to (current) change – in contrast to traditional marketing theory revolving around static historic positions – and the pattern of stimulus and response, which the competitive saw highlights, is the best approach to this.

[5] D. Mercer, *New Marketing Practice*, Penguin, 1997.

If such dynamic repositioning is not possible, perhaps because the necessary product changes come in discrete steps, then *periodic readjustments* may be needed. This is where the concept of *advertising depreciation* allows the build-up of reserves to cover the significant costs of major repositioning exercises.

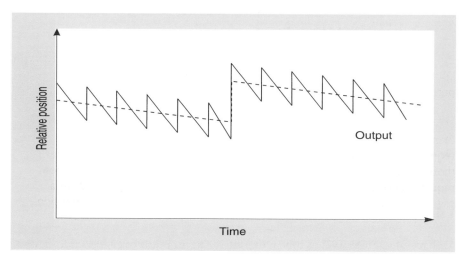

FIGURE 14.5   Relative position and output

This long-term asset investment aspect of brand performance is largely ignored by traditional marketing theory.

The above pattern of responses assumes, however, a complementary repositioning process – which builds upon existing strengths. This process cannot, though, be held to be true of a new product launch, where the logistic curve may be most effectively used to represent the relatively slow build-up of brand position which results from even quite high levels of investment – for the key aspect is the *level* of investment needed. It has two main dimensions.

One is the amount of (financial) investment needed. To buy your way into a market is a very expensive process indeed. The main practical feature, though, is the level of risk. Most managements believe, quite incorrectly, that risk is reduced if the levels of investment are minimised; the reverse is true. Once you accept the basic level of risk *the more money you invest in a major change, the more you reduce the risk.*[6] If you want to make a major impact on a market (one that will, for instance, put you into the most profitable Rule of 1:2:3 slots) you must recognise that the level of investment needed will be correspondingly high; in major markets, probably beyond the reach of all but the largest Japanese corporations (and hence the significance of segmentation).

[6] R. Biggadike, 'The risky business of diversification', *Harvard Business Review*, May–June 1979.

The second dimension is time. Any new penetration of a market takes far longer than is expected. Rather than the one to two years that optimists expect, and the three to four years that pessimists allow for, the reality of new launches is a mean of *eight* years to break-even.[7]

14.4 POSITION DRIFT

If we look at the *product or service* itself, rather than the promotional messages applied to it, in most markets customer requirements change over time, perhaps due to social or fashion factors or – more likely – to technological changes in the market. These changes may be relatively slow for long-established brands or very rapid for some fashion products. It is imperative, therefore, that you develop your existing products in line with these changing requirements. This is just as true for long-established brands as new ones, though – because the changes are slow – there is a danger that these new requirements are overlooked. If you do not develop existing brands in a regular, and rigorous, manner you may find yourself the victim of 'Position Drift'; and, once more, vulnerable.

You will remember that *positioning* was a key element in our approach to long-term strategies. A further example of a position map is shown in Figure 14.6.

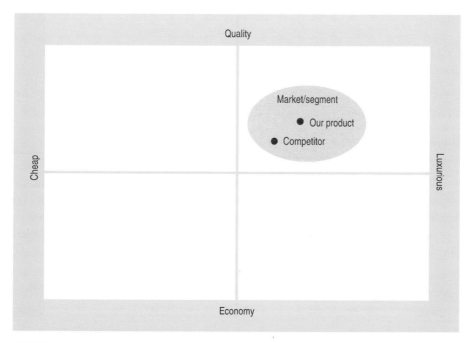

FIGURE 14.6   Position map

[7] R. Biggadike, 'The risky business of diversification', *Harvard Business Review*, May–June 1979.

You will also remember that you should use this map to position your brand as close to the ideal as is possible for the segment(s) you wish to address (and hopefully dominate). The problem is that this shows only a static picture. Over time 'position drift' can significantly change the picture. This may come about for three main reasons: consumer drift, competitor drift and ego drift.

1   **Consumer drift** – as consumer tastes change, the segment (cluster) which contains them will shift its position. Its centre of gravity will move – and its size may change as consumers switch to other, perhaps newer, segments. This is shown in Figure 14.7.

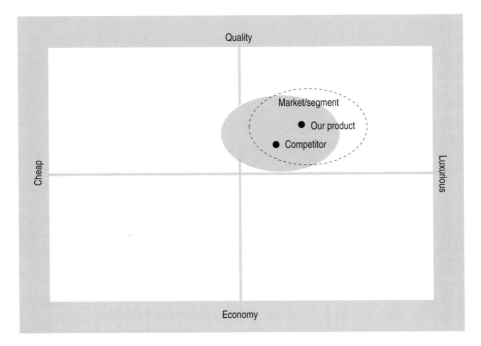

FIGURE 14.7   Consumer drift

The position of your brand *relative* to the ideal position within this cluster will reflect this drift.

2   **Competitor drift** – *your competitors may shift their positions*, so that your own relative position (your competitive advantage) may become less than optimal, as shown in Figure 14.8.

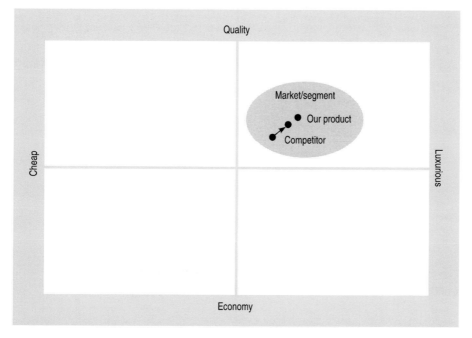

FIGURE 14.8   Competitor drift

This may pose a particular problem if you are trying to target several segments with just one brand, since any move to respond to a competitive threat in one segment may leave the rest of the segments exposed.

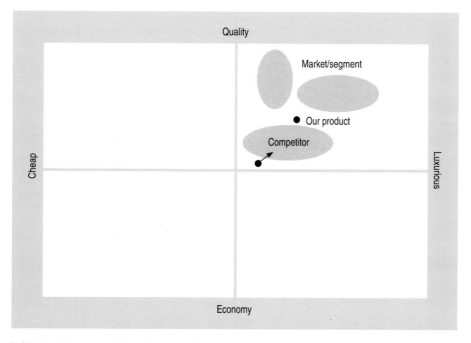

FIGURE 14.9   Competitor drift and multi-market product

3 **Ego drift** – perhaps the most prevalent drift of all occurs where 'brand managers' (or their advertising agencies) gratuitously reposition their own brand in a less optimal location, as shown in Figure 14.10. This is usually justified on the basis that consumers are bored with the existing messages, and an exciting new approach is needed. The real reason often is that members of the management team, frequently persuaded by an agency creative team itching to make their own distinctive mark, are themselves bored.

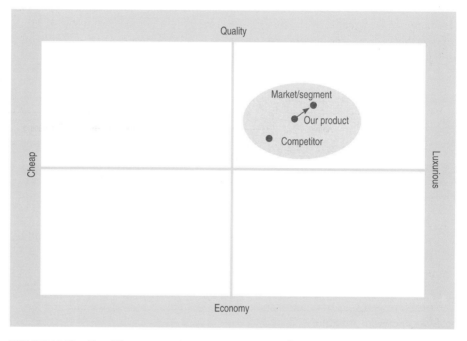

FIGURE 14.10   Ego drift

The biggest problem caused by drift, of any of these types, is that it usually occurs so slowly that it is not noticed by the brand manager. In the timescales that he or she works to, the changes are imperceptible. It is for this reason that brand positioning maps must be updated regularly, and the changes plotted as accurately as possible, so that the trajectory of any drift may be determined, and corrected. Consequent upon the outcome of these revisions to the maps, it is likely that most product/service packages will need to be redeveloped, from time to time, to compensate for this drift.

Audit 14.1

As we have indicated, it is very unlikely that you will be able to plot these relationships. On the other hand, you can look at the patterns of stimuli, your inputs to the process, to see how you might be performing.

14.5 RELATIONSHIPS WITH CUSTOMERS

We have spent some considerable time looking at the investment in the *brand*, most obviously typified by what happens in consumer markets. In most organisations, especially those operating in industrial markets, the investment in *relationships* is made *personally* by the '*sales personnel*'. This title covers a wide range of staff who might not all think of themselves as being in this category: from telephone operators – who are the first point of contact – through to service personnel (who often have the most frequent contact, and set the standards the customer or client sees).

The range of contacts is, thus, much more extensive than is often allowed for. Even at the very simplest level, the picture will probably include those shown in Figure 14.11.

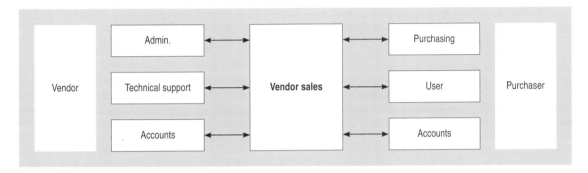

FIGURE 14.11   Vendor/purchaser contacts

The problem is, of course, that funnelling all communications through the sales professional is impossible.

In this context the professional salesperson, who is traditionally the main point of contact, is likely to have to *manage* the range of relationships involved in a 'complex sale'. This is the sale where a number of individuals are involved even in the original buying decision, and the sales campaign extends over a number of calls. Miller, Heiman and Tuleja comment:

> In a complex sale, you have short-term and long-term objectives. In the short term, you must close as many individual deals as you possibly can, and as quickly as possible. In the long term, you want to maintain healthy relations with the customers signing the deals, so they'll be willing to make further purchases in the months and years to come. It would be great if these two objectives always coincided, but you know that they don't.[8]

In many ways this environment is very different from that of the single call sale, which is the staple diet provided by many (if not most) sales trainers.

[8] R. B. Miller, S. E. Heiman and T. Tuleja, *Strategic Selling* (William Morrow, 1985).

Perhaps the most distinctive characteristic of the complex sale is the multiplicity of 'buyers' involved. It is no longer just sufficient to persuade one buyer. Instead the sales professionals have to convince a whole range of individuals, all with different (often contradictory) requirements! The first problem this poses is that of identifying who are the various buyers, which will not be an easy task. It is no longer a matter of looking for the door helpfully labelled 'buyer'. The 'buyers' involved in the complex sale can range down from the Chief Executive to word-processor operators.

The convention is to split these 'buyers' into 'decision-makers' and 'influencers',[9] with the implication that the small group of decision-makers should be the prime target, though influencers should not be neglected. This is a useful distinction: it correctly focuses the sales professional's attention on the key decision-makers, and forces him or her to contact these, whereas too many sales personnel remain bogged down amongst the 'influencers'.

Selling has traditionally been seen as a *confrontational* activity, with the salesperson 'hierarchically' subservient to the buyer: the former is trying to persuade the latter to buy something not wanted or needed. It is seen as a 'zero-sum game', where each of the participants can gain only at the expense of the other. This is at odds with the trust which is so important in building *relationships* with customers of all types. Thus, in recent years, it has been argued that the most productive relationship in such sales deals is based on an approach in which it is expected that both sides will 'win' (i.e. gain from the deal, albeit in different ways), so that they start out with the intention of producing a mutually beneficial arrangement. Miller, Heiman and Tuleja encapsulated this relationship in the concept of 'Win-Win'.[10]

An increasing number of organisations have, indeed, come to see the relationship as one of *interdependence*, where the two sides adopt a 'peer to peer' relationship. The sales role here is sometimes described as '*relationship management*'.[11] As this type of relationship requires a higher level of personal support, from a more skilled sales professional (a 'relationship manager'), it will typically be limited to the five or ten most important customers (or 'accounts').

Account management

Probably the most important activity in developing relationships with these key accounts is a sound plan: the *account plan*. Unlike the overall sales plan, which will deal with groups of customers, each account plan (or 'key account plan') deals quite specifically with a *single* customer; and will plan the activities, and in particular the relationships, of *all* the many individuals involved in servicing the account.

---

[9] F. E. Webster and Y. Wind, *Organisational Buying Behaviour* (Prentice Hall, 1972).

[10] R. B. Miller, S. E. Heiman and T. Tuleja, *Strategic Selling* (William Morrow, 1985).

[11] T. Levitt, 'After the sale is over', *Harvard Business Review*, September–October 1983.

For each of these key accounts a unique plan should be developed, which matches (at least in its scope) the overall marketing plan. It should detail the specific objectives, which will be individually related to the customer's needs and wants. It should detail the activities which are planned to meet these objectives, and to build the 'relationship'.

If such a plan is produced internally within the selling organisation it will be a productive exercise. If it is produced in co-operation with the customer, so that the resulting plan becomes a *shared* plan, it may make a major contribution to the development of that business relationship. It then becomes a genuine peer-to-peer relationship, which will underwrite the vendor's position over the longer term.

Audit 14.2

Obtain a copy of one of your organisation's account plans, or sit down with one of its account managers (if there are any, and if there aren't this fact alone may in any case answer your questions), and see how the real needs of customer relationship management are matched by the plan or by the manager's activities.

Laws of service

One important aspect of developing long-term relationships with customers is their perception of the 'service' they receive. David Maister formulated two 'Laws of Service', the first being expressed as: 'Satisfaction equals perception minus expectation'. If you expect a certain level of service and perceive the service received to be higher, you will be a satisfied customer. If you perceive this same level where you had expected a higher one, you will be disappointed and therefore a dissatisfied customer.'[12] This is illustrated in Figure 14.14.

[12] D. H. Maister, 'The psychology of waiting lines', *Managing Services: Marketing, Operations and Human Resources* (Prentice-Hall, 1988).

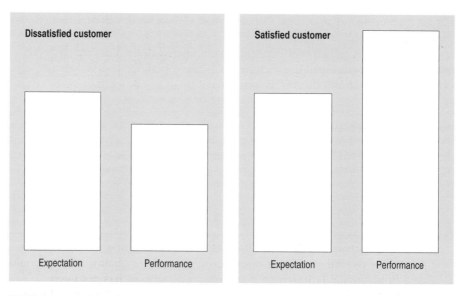

FIGURE 14.14   Satisfaction and dissatisfaction

The important point is that both what is perceived and what is expected are psychological phenomena – and it is the *relative* level of service – related to expectations – which is important, not the absolute one. This is illustrated in Figure 14.15 where one customer is satisfied and the other is not, with identical levels of performance.

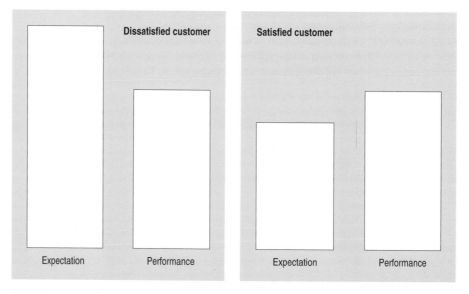

FIGURE 14.15   Effect of expectation on satisfaction

David Maister went further, to posit a *second law of service*: it is hard to play 'catch-up ball'. This means that the earliest stages of a service encounter are crucial in creating perceptions, so that a problem earlier on can sour the whole process. If, on the other hand, first impressions are favourable, this can create a 'halo effect' which will colour later experiences.

Customer complaints

It may seem inappropriate to consider short-term customer complaints in the context of long-range marketing. Indeed, complaints are not merely seen as a very short-term issue, they are often treated as a *nuisance* by many organisations, Yet the way complaints are handled demonstrates just how short-term 'steering' can build long-term success or failure:

1   Although there will always be a small proportion of 'frivolous complaints', a complaint usually *highlights* something which has gone wrong with a part of the overall marketing operation. Usually high quality, which should be a fundamental requirement for most organisations, has not been achieved. Whatever the reason, the sensible marketer will want to know exactly what has gone wrong, so that remedial actions may be taken. The danger, otherwise, is that a *failure* undermines the brand's position, and leaves it vulnerable. The importance of this cannot be overstated – especially to those marketing personnel who delegate handling complaints to lesser (and worse trained) mortals!

2   The way a complaint is handled is often seen by customers, and their many contacts, as an *acid test* of the true quality of support, and of the supplier's relationship with them. What is more, it is also a powerful reminder to the organisation's own staff of just how important is quality.

3   Not least, customers who complain are usually *loyal customers* (those who are not loyal tend just to switch to another supplier), and will continue to be loyal (and valuable) customers – so long as their complaint is handled well. If you fail, and lose even these loyal customers, you might as well write off the long-term future of the organisation!

The first requirement, therefore, is that complaints should be positively *encouraged* (that is not the same as saying that causes of complaints should be encouraged!). Not only should you put nothing in the way of any customer who wants to complain; you should positively encourage such complaints, since the problem lies with the many more customers who do not complain (and instead change to another supplier) rather than with the few who abuse the complaints system.

The second requirement is that all complaints should be *carefully handled* by painstakingly controlled and monitored procedures.[13] Complaints must be handled well, and must be seen to be well handled – by the complainant, and by the organisation's own staff.

---

[13] C. G. A. Godley, 'Marketing control', in *The Principles and Practice of Management*, ed. E. F. L. Brech, (Longman, 1975).

The third, and most important requirement, is that the complaint should then be fully *investigated, and the cause remedied.* Complaints are only symptoms. The disease needs to be cured! There may be an understandable temptation to overlook complaints until they reach a 'significant level' – but holding off until the complaints reach this 'pain level' usually means that they have already become damaging to the organisation's image, and have made it vulnerable. It is far better to assume that 'one complaint is too many'!

The reality in most organisations is very different. The number of complaints is minimised, not by remedying the reasons for them but by evading the complainants! The assumption is usually made that complainants are trouble-makers, and have to be handled in a confrontational manner! In fact, most dissatisfied customers do not complain (a US survey[14] showed that 97% didn't!), but they do tell their friends (the same survey showed that 13% complained to more than 20 other people!).

Satisfaction surveys

It is essential – once again for the longer term as much as the shorter term – that an organisation monitors the *satisfaction* level of its customers. This may be, all else failing, measured by market research. Preferably, though, it should be at the level of the individuals or groups. Any organisation should be highly motivated to make certain its customers are satisfied. If they are not, the brand once more becomes vulnerable. Yet, in practice, remarkably few do so!

IBM, at the peak of its success, every year conducted a survey of all its direct customers. The results were analysed to produce overall satisfaction indices – and senior management viewed any deterioration with alarm – and were also provided to field management so that they could rectify any individual problem situations, where the customer was dissatisfied with any aspect of the IBM service and the IBM representative did not realise this (presumably in 96% of the occasions if the US survey quoted above held true in this case!).

There are a number of advantages to conducting satisfaction surveys, particularly where individual problems highlighted can be subsequently dealt with:[15]

1   Like complaints, *they indicate where problems – which make the brand vulnerable – lie*
2   If they cover all customers, they allow the 96% of non-complainers to communicate their feelings, *and vent their anger,* so that their long-term relationship does not suffer
3   They positively show, even to the satisfied customers, that their supplier is *interested in the customer* and their complaints, which is at least half-way to satisfying those complainants
4   They help persuade the supplier's staff to take *customer* service more seriously.

---

[14] K. Albrecht and R. Zemke, *Service America* (Dow-Jones Irwin, 1985).

[15] D. Mercer, *Marketing* (2nd edn, Blackwell, 1996).

The importance of very high standards of customer service is evidenced by two examples. The marketing philosophy of McDonald's, the world's largest food service organisation, is encapsulated in its motto 'QSC & V' (Quality, Service, Cleanliness & Value). The standards, enforced somewhat quixotically (but memorably) on its franchisees and managers at the Hamburger University in Elk Grove Village (Illinois), require that the customer receive a 'good-tasting' hamburger in no more than five minutes, from a friendly host or hostess, in a spotlessly clean restaurant. The second example, Disneyland, also insists on spotless cleanliness, and on the customer being 'The Guest'. It is salutary to observe how few of the competitors in either of these fields manage the simple task of keeping their premises clean, let alone being able to think of their customers as 'guests'; while the terms used in the fairground trade (with which Disney competes, albeit at a very different level) usually see the customer as some form of victim ('pigeon', 'mark', 'punter' etc.) to be fleeced before the fair moves on!

Audit 14.3

How well does your organisation handle customer complaints? How does it monitor customer satisfaction?. These are simple, but usually very revealing, questions.

14.6 RELATIONSHIPS WITH COMPETITORS

Returning to relationships, we would suggest that a much more radical approach to *competitors* might prove profitable, in the context of long-range marketing.

Collaborators and cartels

It seems to be a requirement that managers swear an oath of 'death to the enemy': few will publicly admit to anything less. We have christened this the 'warrior' approach: it wins battles in war, but produces few profits. In any case, according to our research, the opposite would appear to be true in practice. Indeed, in group discussions – when the participants realised that the majority of those present collaborated – they admitted that they did the same; and we eventually had a majority (in these small groups) who even said that the organisations in their industry operated almost as an informal cartel! These alternative relationships are illustrated in Figure 14.16.

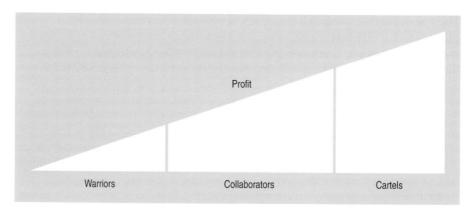

FIGURE 14.16   Relationships with competitors

Warriors – these brave individuals, with their militaristic approach, win the war – though not necessarily the peace – and all too often pay a high price for their achievements: the industry has been destroyed in the course of their battles.

Collaborators – work together to stabilise their industry. In Michael Porter's terms they are the 'good' competitors.[16] They do not engage in destructive rivalry, and avoid price battles.

Cartels – these go one step further, to work positively work together to develop the future of the industry, with mechanisms for collaborating on joint projects.

Positive collaboration

It is our experience that more co-operative relations with competitors, jointly building a profitable future for the shared 'industry', offer the best guarantee of a long-term future. By managing the industry to keep the shared environment stable, the organisations are that much less vulnerable to unpredictable developments. We encapsulate our suggestions in three paired rules.[17]

Rule one, part one – **positively** outperform your competitors, by as large a margin on as many fronts as possible. Collaboration does not in any way mean that you stop competing. Collaboration is not the same as surrender, and competitors respect the organisation which is simply better than the rest.

Rule one, part two – **never indulge in negative attacks**, on any front. Do not, even temporarily, pursue campaigns which competitors might see as destructive (price wars, dirty advertising or whatever).

[16] M. E. Porter, *Competitive Strategy* (Free Press, 1980).

[17] D. Mercer, *New Marketing Practice* (Penguin, 1997).

Rule two, part one – **understand your competitors**. You would need to understand your competitors in order to beat them, but here I suggest that you understand them in order to recognise *why* they take the actions they do – and hence not to read into those actions hostile intent where there is none.

Rule two, part two – **be straightforward and trustworthy**. If your competitors understand you, and trust you, they will tolerate even actions they don't like. When trust breaks down, however, beware; some of the most destructive industry wars have come about because of misunderstandings.

Rule three, part one – **talk industry not organisation**. The one thing you have in common with your competitors, and the thing you both want to promote, is the industry you share. Always emphasise your commitment to maintaining and developing that industry.

Rule three, part two – **jaw-jaw not war-war**. Above all, talk to your competitors whenever you can. When you meet them, at industry conferences or socially, say, go out of your way to be positively friendly towards them; and to discuss positively the future of your shared industry.

Additional rules for cartels

Eventually, you may be able to go even further:

Rule one – **join, or set up, an industry forum**, so that you have positive ground on which to discuss your shared objectives and, if necessary, to debate those which divide you.

Rule two – **run industry campaigns**, which may be good for the industry in themselves, but more importantly force all the collaborators to think positively.

Rule three – **think collectively**, so that you can – within the constraints imposed by law – jointly act in the common interest of the industry, even while competing strenuously within it.

These positive approaches are the most productive of all, if your competitors will support them; and the indications are that, in the great majority of cases, they will. They are so clearly in everyone's best interests that only a fool would think otherwise. Unfortunately there are still some fools around! If they are merely foolish, and not dangerously insane, one of the best strategies for teaching them the lessons of good (competitor) manners is 'tit for tat'.

Tit for tat

'This context is a very simple approach.[18] If your competitor makes an aggressive move you respond with one, but as soon as the other's aggressive move ceases so should yours. This has the virtue that the competitor is not rewarded for 'bad' behaviour (since you immediately undermine any gain that might have been made); and is rewarded for 'good' behaviour (by your immediate removal of your matching action).

[18] R. Axelrod, *The Evolution of Co-operation* (Penguin, 1990).

Most important of all, it very clearly shows what are your rules of engagement: you are a 'good' competitor, but will not tolerate bad behaviour.

Audit 14.4

What is your organisation's relationship with its competitors? If it operates in the same way as most other organisations it will be tacitly co-operating with them. What would be the impact if this process was managed more effectively?

14.7 INNER MARKETING: RELATIONSHIPS WITH STAFF

Finally, we move onto another generic investment in relationships, arguably the most important of all: investment *in the organisation's own personnel*.

Most marketing is, by definition, primarily concerned with the world outside the organisation. But, if it is to optimise the use of resources, it also has at times to be concerned with what lies *inside* the organisational perimeter. This is *inner marketing*.

Increasingly, indeed, the most valuable resource of any organisation (and particularly those in the service sector) is its people, and the skills they possess. In tapping this internal resource, so that the organisation can face up to its external environment, it turns out that many of the traditional tools of marketing can be used to great effect in the very important areas of internal communication and motivation; of harnessing and focusing this resource to meet the objectives of the marketing plan.

Recently, such campaigns have tended to focus on *Total Quality Management* (TQM), on the principle that the overall quality that the customer perceives comes from every part of the organisation – from support and administration staff just as much as from the workers (or the robots) on the production lines. 'Inner marketing' is in many ways the ultimate extension of TQM, in that for every employee it defines 'quality' exclusively in terms of the marketing context, i.e. of what is important to the customer.

In a similar vein, many organisations in the service sector, and not a few in the manufacturing sector, have '*customer service programmes*'. These use many of the promotional devices of marketing – advertising, incentives, seminars etc. – to persuade employees (particularly those in contact with customers) to adopt the correct attitude to those customers. Such campaigns have received a mixed response. The problem has often been that the management implementing them are themselves unconvinced of the message; and it is unrealistic, under these circumstances, to expect the employees to react more favourably. Probably the most frequent failing is that such campaigns are run as very short-term programmes, as flavour of the month; which everyone knows they can ignore, since the next month will be bound to bring a newer flavour.

Where this has been the case, inner marketing can have a powerful effect. It says quite simply that employees should be 'marketed' to in exactly the same way as customers. Implicit in this concept (which should not be confused with the internal market) is that all the aspects of marketing as a whole should be incorporated; in particular, that a 'dialogue' takes place – 'inner marketing' is as much about finding out what the employees want as persuading them to do what the organisation wants!

Stages of inner marketing

It is useful to follow a progression through 4 Cs, as shown in Figure 14.17.[19]

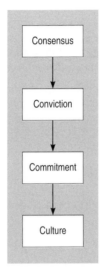

FIGURE 14.17   Stages of inner marketing

The first requirement is some form of *marketing research* – exactly as with any other marketing programme, but here conducted on the organisation's own employees. This research should be used to determine where they stand, for example, in relation to their perceptions of the customer (Is the customer seen as friend or foe?) and of the customer service programmes which are likely to be the main focus of the research (Does anyone do anything more than pay lip-service to them? Why?). Moreover, as with any piece of sound research, it should also attempt to find out where employees might wish to stand in the future, exploring their attitudes and motivations (Do they really want to offer a good service? If not, why not? How can they be persuaded to change their views?). The outcome is most productively described as *consensus*, since this best incorporates the attitude of mind which should lie behind it – the search

[19] D. Mercer, *Marketing* (2nd edn, Blackwell, 1996).

should be positively designed to find the outcomes, especially in terms of values, to which all the participants (most importantly members of staff at all levels, but also managers and customers) will be able to *commit* themselves.

Internal opinion surveys

Internal research may, in any case, have great benefits. Such 'opinion surveys' are remarkably effective devices for obtaining information on the 'inner market'. If applied regularly to all staff, they are also good motivators and contributors to a positive culture.

One of IBM's most powerful tools, in developing its justly famed relationship with its staff, was the 'Opinion Survey'. Every two years, every employee in IBM took part in an anonymous survey of how they felt about IBM and what it was doing; as well as how they felt about their immediate management – which was, since the results were published, a powerful device for ensuring that managers took note of their subordinates' opinions! The results were very publicly acted upon, to the benefit of the 'inner market' – not least because the employees (unlike those in most other organisations) recognised that IBM was listening to them. Unfortunately, few other managers use them. Only with this basic information on employee attitudes (however derived) can the 'inner marketer' start to devise the programmes necessary to create the new attitudes, the conviction in the goals handed down, which will deliver the requisite service to external customers.

The actions needed to achieve the end result follow the well trod path of any marketing campaign, although they are alien to much of human resource management. Even in the marketing context, it should be recognised that it may take far longer to achieve the desired results than in a traditional consumer marketing campaign, for often the requirement is to make fundamental shifts in attitude.

At the most basic level, the staff will need to understand what is expected of them, both by their own management and by their customers. It is remarkable how many 'improvements' in customer service are advertised to the customers but never explained to the employees who are to deliver them; let alone agreed with those employees. Beyond this, the essence of any marketing campaign, as with any military one, is that all the actions happen at the right time, and in the manner planned. The inner marketing campaign is essential (whether it is formally or informally implemented) to ensure this happens. How many times have you heard of, or even experienced, offers advertised by retailers which their branch staff deny exist!

Managed suggestions

One especially powerful approach lies at the heart of so-called Japanese techniques; and, indeed, at the heart of Toyota's success. This was developed by the American Philip Crosby, but adopted by Japanese rather than US corporations, as the eleventh step of his famous fourteen-step 'zero-defects' programme. In the original, as developed for the Pershing missile programme in the US, it was titled 'Error Cause Removal (ECR)'. This eminently forgettable

title may be why it has been neglected by the West! Toyota, however, retitled it
– confusingly for the outside world – as their 'Suggestions Scheme'. Like the
Western version, the idea is that any employee puts a suggestion into the
nearest suggestion box as soon as he or she recognises a problem which needs
solving; and they are then rewarded for this observation (in the case of Toyota,
the company receives more than two million suggestions each year, and
implements more than 90% of them). The crucial difference from the Western
equivalent is that the employee is only required to identify the *problem*, and
need not suggest a solution (which is the main thrust of Western schemes,
where it is the *solution* which justifies the payment). At Toyota the problem is
then passed to the relevant management, and it is *their* task to find a solution.
To clearly distinguish between the two, I call this process '*managed
suggestions*'.

Managed suggestions is, for many organisations, simultaneously the simplest
and the most powerful technique in inner marketing. Employees are merely
required to submit their 'suggestions' (their identification) of problems as soon
as they recognise them, and *management* are then required to solve them.

This may sound a trivial process, but it is usually *identification* of the problem
(the correct question to ask) which is the most difficult part of problem
solving. The Crosby approach directly addresses this difficulty, and ensures that
the problem is captured immediately it is identified. This technique, originally
proposed for use in quality improvement, can be used in a wide range of
situations (ranging from JIT to customer complaints). It is, at the same time,
one of the simplest techniques (in principle it could be implemented in any
company in a matter of days), and one of the most powerful.

The one inherent limitation is that it can be too successful too soon. It can
pose impossible demands on managers who are unprepared to deal with the
problems thus unearthed. How many managers could respond effectively to
each worker under their control generating dozens of 'suggestions' a year? That
the benefit only comes after the manager has identified the solution is bad
enough, as is the demoralisation of the managers faced with a massive backlog
of suggestions, but the demoralisation of the workers whose suggestions are
not being dealt with is even worse. Thus, in practice, this simple technique can
only be used by an organisation which has already implemented many of the
other techniques (typically those problem-solving techniques used by the
Japanese corporations) – and whose managers are *already* conditioned to meet
its demands. Crosby deliberately waits until later in his overall programme,
typically until more than a year after the start, to introduce this step. Thus, in
order to cope with the demands imposed by a managed suggestions scheme,
the management must have already been trained in many of the 'Japanese'
problem-solving techniques.

Leadership

The most difficult problem of all is the process of changing *attitudes*; of
developing the necessary conviction. Staff who have been bound by the rigid
rules of a bureaucracy, for example, will not suddenly become receptive to the

concept that the 'customer is always right' just because a memo from head office states that this will be the case in future! The most important input from management at this stage is *leadership*. If senior management are believed and seen to be highly committed to goals (and especially to values) which take account of the consensus views, then the majority of staff are likely to be convinced by the validity of those goals. Thus the first stage in effectively implementing the plans needed to reach the organisation's long-range marketing goals is to match these external goals to a realistic appreciation of what the inner market can (and is willing to) deliver. This is an essential step, but one which is taken by very few organisations!

But the process does not stop there. The most important – but least appreciated – aspect of 'inner marketing' is that it is a process of managing change, and the marketing department needs to adopt the role (consciously or not) of 'change agent'. This process should lead to a positive commitment by the staff to meeting the goals of the organisation in general and of customer service in particular. The process of bringing customer and staff expectations into alignment is illustrated in Figure 14.18.[20]

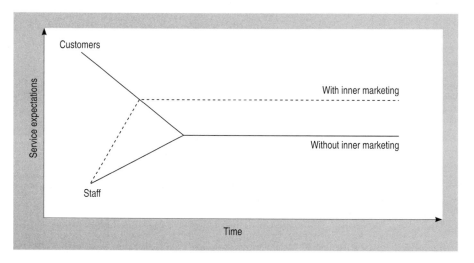

FIGURE 14.18   The inner marketing bonus

The important fact to note here is that the process also includes the *lowering* of customers' expectations, as experience brings home the truth of what they may realistically expect. In many situations, it is the customers' expectations which are steadily adjusted downwards (without *any* improvement of staff positions) until their view accords with the lower levels on offer. The dotted line shows what might be achieved with the application of inner marketing to positively improve the response rate of staff. The end result is that the final level of perception is significantly higher, potentially offering a major competitive advantage.

---

[20] D. Mercer, *New Marketing Practice* (Penguin, 1997).

The techniques here may often be closer to those of education – and, indeed, may revolve around significant amounts of retraining. The service offered to customers, for instance, is in many cases only as good as the skills available to provide it; and those skills may, and usually do, need developing.

Audit 14.5 _____

This is a very difficult, indeed potentially controversial, topic to investigate. Even so, in this context, what is your view of your organisation's management of its own staff? How could this be improved, and what effect would this have?

Culture

In the ultimate extension of 'inner marketing', especially in the context of long-range marketing, Peters and Waterman stress that the resulting '*culture*' of an organisation can be a very important contributor to its success.[21] An organisation's culture is, generally speaking, the common values that its employees share – whether developed positively by management, as suggested here, or by default. Such culture can be even more important in determining what customer service is provided. Peters and Waterman conceptualise this cultural element as '*shared values*', as we do, but they do not spell out, as we do, the very lengthy steps needed to achieve it.

The culture of the company is often what conditions customer service. IBM – as their supreme example – maintained a philosophy of customer service throughout the whole company (applying to all employees) as its only marketing objective for more than half a century; with spectacularly successful results (and an equally spectacular disaster when it abandoned it). Both McDonald's and Disney have similarly strong cultures, which are reflected not least in their spotlessly clean premises, but also in their bottom-line profits. The problem of addressing the 'cultural dimension', even though this is an essential element in any marketing operation, is that of *time*. Changes in the culture of an existing organisation may take years; indeed, if existing cultures are strong and the changes required are major, the process may take decades. Both IBM and the Japanese corporations, who probably have the strongest cultures of all, needed as much as fifteen years to fully develop all aspects of the new and rich cultures they were introducing. Culture is not, therefore, a topic to be taken lightly, though minor changes (particularly those which 'complement' the existing culture, and characterise the earlier conviction and commitment stages) may be accepted more rapidly (but, even then, not in days!).

An extended consideration of organisational culture is not appropriate in this book, but such cultures do provide a fitting context within which to end our review of robust strategies:

---

[21] T. J. Peters and R. H. Waterman, *In Search of Excellence* (Harper & Row, 1982).

Generic robust strategies – a suitable culture encapsulates the value of the investment in relationships with stakeholders, on two fronts. Firstly, and most obviously, it optimises relationships with your own staff. Then, secondly, it persuades those staff to optimise their relationships with your customers.

Flexibility – a suitable culture also predisposes your staff both to recognise the changes which are occurring in the external environment before these assume fatal proportions, and then it ensures that they are open to the resulting measures which need to be made to their world.

SUMMARY OF PART 2

The key to short-term implementation of robust strategies is the concept of 'steering'. This may be in terms of managing the (advertising) investment in a brand (and ensuring that position drift is countered) or in maintaining the investment in face-to-face relationships at the heart of the complex sale. In both cases, monitoring customer satisfaction (and positively dealing with complaints) may be crucial. Inner marketing, to ensure that staff live up to management's aspirations, may well be the route to this – ultimately encapsulated in the organisational culture.

In this second part of the book we looked first at the purpose of robust strategies in securing the long-term future of the organisation, and at their relationship to traditional shorter-term corporate strategies. We then examined the steps in the long-term planning process which leads to the production of such strategies. We saw how to devise strategies specific to a particular organisational situation, before surveying 'generic' (or ready-made) strategies likely to be useful to a wide range of organisations. Finally, we considered elements of marketing strategies which, though themselves short term, can contribute to the success of long-term plans.

All that is needed to underwrite survival is to recognise the correct robust strategies in sufficient time to allow the requisite changes to be rapidly put in place by a sufficiently flexible organisation. That may sound simple and is – as you have seen – far simpler than many allow for. Yet it is the outcome of a powerful set of processes which will only succeed if you understand them and – most important of all – fully *commit* yourself to them.

INDEX

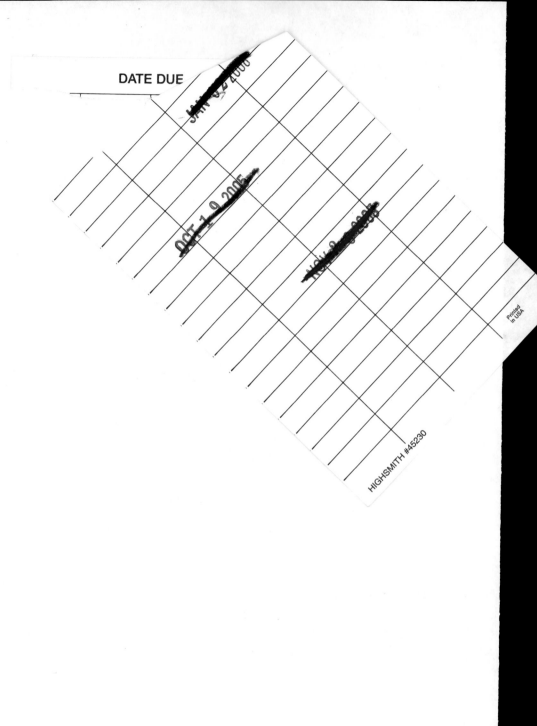

DATE DUE

JAN 2 4 2000

OCT 1 9 2005

NOV

HIGHSMITH #45230

Printed in USA